Current Insights in Obsessive Compulsive Disorder

This book is the proceedings of the First International Congress on Obsessive Compulsive Disorder held in Capri in March 1993 and is supported by an unrestricted educational grant from Solvay Duphar and the Upjohn Company.

Current Insights in Obsessive Compulsive Disorder

Edited by

Eric Hollander
Mount Sinai School of Medicine, New York, USA

Joseph Zohar
Division of Psychiatry, The Chaim Sheba Medical Center, Tel Hashomer, Israel

Donatella Marazziti
Institute of Psychiatry, University of Pisa, Italy

and

Berend Olivier
CNS Research, Solvay Duphar BV, The Netherlands

JOHN WILEY & SONS

Chichester · New York · Brisbane · Toronto · Singapore

Other Wiley Editorial Offices

John Wiley & Sons, Inc., 605 Third Avenue,
New York, NY 10158-0012, USA

Jacaranda Wiley Ltd, 33 Park Road, Milton,
Queensland 4064, Australia

John Wiley & Sons (Canada) Ltd, 22 Worcester Road,
Rexdale, Ontario M9W 1L1, Canada

John Wiley & Sons (SEA) Pte Ltd, 37 Jalan Pemimpin #05-04,
Block B, Union Industrial Building, Singapore 2057

British Library Cataloguing in Publication Data

A catalogue record for this book is available from the British Library

ISBN 0 471 95142 0

Typeset in 10/12pt Palatino by Keytec Typesetting Ltd, Bridport, Dorset
Printed and bound in Great Britain by Bookcraft (Bath) Ltd, Midsomer Norton, Avon

CONTENTS

CONTRIBUTORS

Jules Angst
Psychiatric University Hospital Zurich, Research Department, PO Box 68, 8029 Zurich, Switzerland

Lee Baer
Department of Clinical Neuroscience, Building R3, Karolinska Hospital, S-171 76 Stockholm, Sweden

Chawki Benkelfat
Neurobiological Psychiatry Unit, Department of Psychiatry, McGill University, 1033 Ave des Pins ouest, Suite 135, Montreal QC, H3A 1A1, Canada

Giovanni B Cassano
Institute of Psychiatry, University of Pisa, Via Roma 67, 56100 Pisa, Italy

Lisa Cohen
Mount Sinai School of Medicine, Queen's Hospital Center, 82/68 164th St., N. Building, Room 523, Jamaica, NY 11432, USA

Concetta M DeCaria
Mount Sinai School of Medicine, Queen's Hospital Center, 82/68 164th St., N. Building, Room 523, Jamaica, NY 11432, USA

Orna Dolberg
Division of Psychiatry, The Chaim Sheba Medical Center, Tel Hashomer, 52621, Israel

Gunnar Edman
Department of Psychiatry, Building R3, Karolinska Hospital, S-171 76 Stockholm, Sweden

Jane L Eisen
Department of Psychiatry and Human Behavior, Brown University, Providence, RI 02906, USA

Martine F Flament
Chargée de Recherche, INSERM U 202, Hôpital La Salpêtrière, 47 Blvd de l'Hôpital, 75013, Paris, France

Edna B Foa
Center for the Treatment and Study of Anxiety, Medical College of Pennsylvania/EPPI, 3200 Henry Avenue, Philadelphia, PA 19129, USA

David Greenberg
Jerusalem Mental Health Center, Herzog Hospital, PO Box 35300, Jerusalem, 91351, Israel

Talma Hendler
Division of Psychiatry, The Chaim Sheba Medical Center, Tel Hashomer, 52621, Israel

Rudolf Hoehn-Saric
The Hopkins Medical Institutions, Department of Psychiatry and Behavioral Sciences, The Henry Phipps Psychiatric Services, 600 North Wolfe Street/Meyer 144, Baltimore, MD 21287-7144, USA

Eric Hollander
Mount Sinai School of Medicine, Queen's Hospital Center, 82/68 164th St., N. Building, Room 523, Jamaica, NY 11432, USA

Thomas R Insel
NIH, Animal Center, Laboratory of Neurophysiology, Building 110, Room 100, Elmer School Road, Poolesville, MD 20837, USA

Ruth Gross-Isseroff
Division of Psychiatry, The Chaim Sheba Medical Center, Tel Hashomer, 52621, Israel

Michael A Jenike
Department of Psychiatry, OCD Unit, 9th Floor, Massachusetts General Hospital–East, 149 Thirteenth Street, Charlestown, MA 02129, USA

Seth Kindler
Division of Psychiatry, The Chaim Sheba Medical Center, Tel Hashomer, 52621, Israel

Moshe Kotler
Division of Psychiatry, The Chaim Sheba Medical Center, Tel Hashomer, 52621, Israel

Michael Kozak
Center for the Treatment and Study of Anxiety, Medical College of Pennsylvania/EPPI, 3200 Henry Avenue, Philadelphia, PA 19129, USA

Donatella Marazziti
Institute of Psychiatry, University of Pisa, Via Roma 67, 56100 Pisa, Italy

Per Mindus
Department of Psychiatry, Building R3, Karolinska Hospital, S-171 76 Stockholm, Sweden

Stuart A Montgomery
St Mary's Hospital Medical School, Academic Department of Psychiatry, St Mary's Hospital, Praed Street, London W2 1NY, UK

Jan Mos
Department of CNS-Psychopharmacology, Solvay Duphar BV, PO Box 900, 1380 DA Weesp, The Netherlands

Hakan Nyman
Department of Psychiatry, Building R3, Karolinska Hospital, S-171 76 Stockholm, Sweden

Berend Olivier
CNS Research, Solvay Duphar BV, PO Box 900, 1380 DA Weesp, The Netherlands

Carlos N Pato
Department of Psychiatry and Human Behavior, Brown University, Providence, RI 02906, USA

Michele Tortora Pato
Department of Psychiatry and Human Behavior, Brown University, Providence, RI 02906, USA

Roger K Pitman
VA Research Service, 228 Maple Street, Manchester, NH 03103, USA

Steven A Rasmussen
Brown University School of Medicine, Butler Hospital, 345 Blackstone Boulevard, Providence, RI 02906, USA

Scott L Rauch
Department of Psychiatry, Harvard Medical School and Massachusetts General Hospital, Building 149 – 13th Street – Floor 9, Charlestown, MA 02129, USA

Yehuda Sasson
Division of Psychiatry, The Chaim Sheba Medical Center, Tel Hashomer, 52621, Israel

Daphne Simeon
Mount Sinai School of Medicine, Queen's Hospital Center, 82/68 164th St., N. Building, Room 523, Jamaica, NY 11432, USA

Dan J Stein
Mount Sinai School of Medicine, Queen's Hospital Center, 82/68 164th St., N. Building, Room 523, Jamaica, NY 11432, USA

Eliezer Witztum
Jerusalem Mental Health Center, Herzog Hospital, PO Box 35300, Jerusalem, 91351, Israel

Joseph Zohar
Division of Psychiatry, The Chaim Sheba Medical Center, Tel Hashomer, 52621, Israel

FOREWORD

The island of Capri is little more than a rugged, rocky outcropping off the Italian Napoli coast. Within its 10 square kilometers, Capri offers magnificent vistas, ancient Roman ruins, and the legendary Blue Grotto—a cave cut into the rock by the sapphire blue Mediterranean. In Greek mythology, this island may have been the home of the seductive maidens, the Sirens, who enchanted Odysseus. According to Homer's epic, Odysseus was tied to the mast while his crew, their ears plugged with wax, rowed past the island. The Sirens sang out to charm their visitor (1):

> Sea rovers here take joy
> Voyaging onward,
> As from our song of Troy
> Greybeard and rower-boy
> Goeth more learned
>
> All feats on that great field
> In the long warfare,
> Dark days the bright gods willed,
> Wounds you bore there,
>
> Argos' old soldiery
> On Troy breach teeming,
> Charmed out of time we see.
> No life on earth can be
> Hid from our dreaming.

Homer could scarcely have imagined that in March 1993, Capri would also be the site of the first International Congress on Obsessive Compulsive Disorder. This meeting convened 100 investigators from more than a dozen countries for 3 days of presentations about obsessive compulsive disorder. The participants—all of whom arrived by boat but none of whom had ears plugged with wax—represented almost as many scientific disciplines as nationalities, with psychoanalysts, behavior therapists, pharmacologists, epidemiologists, neuropsychologists and many others trading insights about this curious illness. The diversity of this group, along with the clarity that comes with brisk walks in the sea air of a Mediterranean island, provided a unique opportunity to learn about recent developments in the study of obsessive compulsive disorder. This volume attempts to distill much of what transpired at this Congress by summarizing the conclusions from each of the major sessions of the meeting.

It was clear to the participants that we have recently been through a revolution in our thinking about this illness. In the span of a decade, the research image of obsessive compulsive disorder has changed from a little-known, poorly understood "neurosis" to one of the most exciting frontiers in psychiatry. During this decade, we have witnessed the advent of specific behavioral and pharmacological antiobsessional treatments and the emergence of neuroimaging studies demonstrating altered activity in a specific neural circuit. The definition of obsessive compulsive disorder has been refined and reliable tools for assessing the symptoms of this disorder have been developed. We now have an ontogenetic picture of this disorder and we have epidemiological data on prevalence and co-morbidity. This disorder, which was so recently a research "orphan", is becoming one of the most intensively studied illnesses in the psychiatric family.

But fundamental questions about obsessive compulsive disorder remain. It was these questions that formed the basis for most of the discussions in Capri. What are the boundaries of obsessive compulsive disorder? What about patients with tics, with psychotic ideas, with morbid jealousy or monosymptomatic delusions? Is obsessive compulsive disorder one disorder or several, with different pathophysiological mechanisms but possibly shared responses to treatment? Behavioral and pharmacological treatments are effective, but are they effective in the same people? In the same way? Do they share a therapeutic mechanism? How long must a patient remain in drug treatment? What are the implications of comorbid conditions? A cortical–basal ganglia–thalamic loop has been implicated in blood flow and metabolic studies of obsessive compulsive disorder patients, but is this circuit directly involved patho-physiologically or does it become activated to compensate for a deficit elsewhere in the brain?

It is a truism in psychiatry that for most disorders we understand more about the treatment than the cause. For obsessive compulsive disorder, we now have several effective treatments. Questions remain, but for the vast majority of patients there is reason to be optimistic. The cause of this disorder remains more mysterious. Although there is considerable excite-ment about the power of molecular genetics, the role of serotonin, and the new tools of cerebral imaging, the Sirens of Capri who purported to know all the ills that the gods laid upon the Argives and the Trojans were not entirely forthcoming on this particular disorder. They did, however, deliver on their promise that all "goeth more learned". This volume, with its clues about the etiology and pathophysiology of obsessive compulsive disorder, shares the excitement and information of the Capri Congress. Now the task is to determine which of the many clues provided will prove most important for the second International Congress on Obsessive Compulsive Disorder.

Thomas R Insel, MD
NIMH
Poolesville, MD
30 November 1993

Reference

1. Homer. The Odyssey [transl Fitzgerald R]. Doubleday, Garden City, NJ, 1963, p 215.

Part I
CLINICAL CONCERNS

1 OBSESSIVE COMPULSIVE DISORDER IN WESTERN HISTORY

Roger K Pitman

VA Medical Center, Manchester, NH and Harvard Medical School, Boston, MA, USA

Over the centuries, a variety of terms have been used to designate the fascinating, multifaceted disorder that is the topic of the chapters awaiting the reader of this book. What we now confidently call obsessive compulsive disorder (OCD) has variously been termed, among other things, demonic possession, religious melancholy, scrupulosity, *folie du doute*, psychasthenia, and compulsion neurosis. One wonders what this condition will be called in the 21st century; it is very likely to be something other than OCD. Yet despite its varying appellations, the phenomenology of this disorder has been remarkably stable. Case descriptions we would have no trouble recognizing as OCD regularly appear in the ecclesiastical literature, starting as early as the 15th century.

An early description of what we would today view as a compulsive symptom appeared in 1486 in the *Malleus Maleficarum*, the infamous 15th century compendium on psychopathology and witchcraft (1 p. 1506):

> A certain Bohemian . . . brought his only son, a secular priest, to Rome to be delivered because he was possessed . . . When he passed any church, and genuflected in honour of the Glorious Virgin, the devil made him thrust his tongue far out of this mouth . . . when [he] tr[ied] to engage in prayer, [the devil] attack[ed him] more violently.

This medieval boy's unfortunate affliction illustrates a phenomenon that

---

Current Insights in Obsessive Compulsive Disorder. Edited by E. Hollander, J. Zohar, D. Marazzati and B. Olivier
Published by John Wiley & Sons 1994. This chapter was written by an official of the US Government during the course of official duties and is therefore in the public domain. No copyright is available.

was referred to by Pierre Janet more than 400 years later as "association by contrast", in which the patient is driven to do the opposite of what he seemingly wants to do. Taken as an example of copropraxia, this 15th century symptom provides an early clue to the overlap between compulsive and tic disorders, a subject of current interest.

The phenomenon of association by contrast was again noted 200 years later in 1692 by Bishop John Moore (2 pp. 252–253):

> ... [they have] naughty, and sometimes Blasphemous Thoughts [which] start in their Minds, while they are exercised in the Worship of God [despite] all their endeavors to stifle and suppress them ... the more they struggle with them, the more they encrease ...

In 1658, Flecknoe perfectly captured what Janet later termed "mania of deliberation" (3 p. 116):

> He hovers in his choice, like an empty Ballance with no waight of Judgement to incline him to either scale ... every thing he thinks on, is matter of deliberation ... and he does nothing readily, but what he thinks not on ... when he begins to deliberate, never makes an end ... some dull demon cryes, *do not, do not* still, when hee's on the point of doing anything ... He plays at *shall I, shall I?* so long, till opportunity be past ... and then repents at leasure.

An early scholar of the disorder that interests us here was Jeremy Taylor, Bishop of Down and Connor. Referring in 1660 to the derivation of the word "scruple" from the Latin "small, sharp stone", Taylor captured the inherent conflict that plagues obsessional patients (4 pp. 163–164):

> A scruple is a great trouble of minde proceeding from a little motive, and a great indisposition, by which the conscience though sufficiently determined by proper arguments, dares not proceed to action, or if it doe, it cannot rest ... Scruple is a little stone in the foot, if you set it upon the ground it hurts you, if you hold it up you cannot goe forward; it is a trouble where the trouble is over, a doubt when doubts are resolved ...

Taylor also documented a case of what we now call arithmomania (4 pp. 164–165):

> William of Oseney ... read two or three Books of Religion and devotion very often ... [he] had read over those books three hours every day. In a short time he had read over the books three times more ... [He] began to think ... that now he was to spend six hours every day in reading those books, because he had now read them over six times. He presently considered that ... he must be tied to twelve hours every day.

Taylor's observation that "Some people dare not eat for fear of gluttony

..." presaged current observations regarding the relationship between OCD and anorexia.

The sometimes currently encountered, pathological obsession with having AIDS has its own historical counterpart. In 1724, the Englishman Daniel Turner, Member of the Barber-Surgeon's Company, described (5 p. 316) the case of:

> A Tradesman in good Business, of a thoughtful Temper, or inclining to Melancholy, having in his younger Days, been too familiar with a Wench living in the same House as a Servant, grew soon after very pensive, as fancying he had got the Foul Disease . . . He sat down and fell into Tears, wringing his Hands, and telling me he was ruin'd . . . I now plainly perceiv'd it was all Delusion.

Interestingly, Turner was the first recipient of an honorary M.D. degree from a colonial American university, viz. Yale. Indeed, some still regard his recognition of syphilophobia as the high water mark of that University's contribution to psychiatry.

In addition to clinical observation, history offers theoretical approaches to OCD. In 1749, David Hartley expounded the "Doctrine of Vibrations" (6 pp. 379, 381):

> The Doctrine of Vibrations [and the Doctrine of] Association . . . contain the Laws of the Bodily and Mental Powers respectively [and] must be related to each other, since the Body and Mind are . . . Vibrations should infer Association as their Effect, and Association point to Vibrations as its Cause . . . The perpetual Recurrency of particular Ideas and Terms makes the Vibrations belonging thereto become more than ordinarily vivid, converts feeble Associations into strong ones . . . at the same time . . . [diminishes] . . . other Ideas and Terms, that are kept out of View . . . The same perpetual Recurrency of Vibrations affect[s] one and the same Part of the Brain, in nearly one and the same manner . . .

How fortunate are today's investigators to be able to fulfill Hartley's vision by measuring the "vibrations" of the obsessing human brain by means of neuroimaging techniques.

The relationship between obsessions and compulsions and depression was recognized by Samuel Johnson, himself an obsessional and ticquer, who wrote in 1759 (7 p. 418):

> No disease of the imagination . . . is so difficult to cure, as that which is complicated with the dread of guilt: fancy and conscience then act interchangably upon us . . . the superstitious are often melancholy, and the melancholy almost always superstitious.

Modern clinical and scientific inquiry into OCD may be regarded as having begun around the turn of the current century. The German neurologist Carl Westphal (1878) argued for an independent existence of the condition outside affective disorder (8 p. 735):

> By compulsive ideas I understand those that in an otherwise intact intelligence, and without being caused by an emotional or affect-like state, against the will of the person concerned come into the foreground of the consciousness. They cannot be dispelled, they hinder and frustrate the normal course of ideas, although the afflicted always recognizes them as abnormal and alien ... most of the time, [they are] absurd, and ha[ve] no demonstrable connection with previous ideas, but rather [seem] even to the patient himself incomprehensible and appearing out of thin air.

Westphal believed that the most common etiology of compulsive ideas lay in a hereditary predisposition to neurosis, but he observed that in isolated cases they could occur in connection with epilepsy. Westphal described the case of a 14-year-old girl with compulsive thoughts who displayed twitching movements, vocalizations, coughing tics, and motor explosiveness alternating with immobility. We would now recognize in this case signs and symptoms of Tourette's disorder or syndrome (TS), which has recognized comorbidity with OCD (see later). Westphal commented that "essentially a mental process was involved in all these ... spasm-like acts". In passing, Westphal mentioned that the referring diagnosis had been St. Vitus' dance, "excusable ... after a superficial examination". Westphal did not pursue the possibility that a neurological condition such as St. Vitus' dance (also known as Sydenham's chorea) might underlie both a compulsive mental process and motor pathology.

A few years later in France, Georges Gilles de la Tourette (9) described the neurological syndrome of multiple tics, vocalizations, and coprolalia which was to bear his name. Although he himself described obsessional qualities in the coprolalia of one patient, a dissociation of motor from mental symptoms appeared early in the TS literature and persisted until only recently, when the comorbidity of TS and OCD became clearly recognized.

The connection between obsessions and compulsions and tics was not lost on the French neurologists Meige and Feindel, who wrote in 1902 (10 pp. 82–83):

> The frequency with which obsessions, or at least a proclivity for them, and tics are associated, cannot be a simple coincidence ... if we compare the psychical stigmata of obsessional patients ... with the mental equipment of the sufferer from tic, we cannot but notice intimate analogies between the two ... the obsession is irresistible, as is the tic ... As one thinks, so does one tic.

These authors' emphasis, with their contemporaries, on the constitutional, hereditary basis of tics and OCD symptoms is supported in part by modern research.

Further early contributions to a neurological understanding of OCD came from observations of compulsive thoughts and behaviors in victims of the 1915–26 encephalitis pandemic, especially those accompanying oculogyric crises [reviewed by Green and Pitman (11)]. Schilder (12) specified the OCD symptoms that are more specific to neurological cases, including repetition, counting, and a special relationship to symmetry.

Janet's vast and monumental contribution, *Les Obsessions et la Psych-asthénie* (13, 14) reviewed and critiqued in greater detail elsewhere (15), still serves as the definitive descriptive and psychopathological work on OCD. Janet considered that obsessions and compulsions constituted the most advanced manifestation of a condition he termed "psychasthenia". Janet noted that although obsessions and compulsions, when present, constitute its most dramatic manifestation, psychasthenic disorder also entails symptoms closely, but not quite properly, related to obsessions and compulsions, viz. the "forced agitations". These include "manias" (e.g. of symmetry, repetition, and checking), rumination, tics, phobias, and anxiety. Underlying obsessions, compulsions, and forced agitations is the psychasthenic mental state, characterized by feelings of incompleteness, psychological imperfection, and depersonalization. Janet also emphasized the importance of what we now might call the "negative" symptoms of OCD, especially the failure of "presentification", i.e. the inability to relate to and function in the present. Janet wrote in 1903 (14 p. 302):

> Psychasthenics experience their mental activity as incomplete, and indeed it seems to be. The problem consists of finding out what is this psychological imperfection that perpetually torments them. Much of their symptomatology may be designated as loss of reality function, which includes loss of the capacity to appreciate the reality of an act to be performed and loss of the feeling, but not the perception of external reality. These patients' reason, attention, and appreciation of situations are perfectly preserved when applied to fantasy or to the past or future; they fail when applied to present reality.

Although Janet considered most psychasthenic cases to be of constitutional origin, he recognized acquired, including traumatically induced, cases. In his "psychasthenic synthesis", Janet included under the psychasthenic umbrella a number of what we would diagnose as separate DSM-III-R mental disorders. However, Janet's synthesis receives current support from the recognition of OCD's comorbidity and related disorders.

In an open letter to Janet written in 1933, whom he admired, Ivan Pavlov wrote (16 p. 303):

> I am a physiologist . . . You are a neurologist, psychiatrist and psychologist . . . It seems we should give proper consideration to our reciprocal work and co-operate in our research, for, after all, we are investigating the activity of one and the same organ (concerning which there can hardly be any doubt now).

Pavlov believed, probably along with most readers of this book, in the ultimate explanatory superiority of physiology over psychology, because the latter derives from the former. In the same year, he suggested that the psychological manifestations of OCD could be explained by a physiological phenomenon observable in his experimental dogs (17 p. 314):

> I find it possible to assume that in stereotypy, iteration, and perseveration as symptoms, as well as in the essence of the compulsive neurosis and paranoia, the basic pathophysiological phenomenon is the same, namely what came to the fore in our experiments and what we have designated by the term "pathological inertness" [of the excitatory process] in the motor area of the cortex . . . [and] other cortical cells connected with our other sensations, feelings, and ideas.

Sigmund Freud's ideas about psychopathology, including obsessive compulsive symptoms, have been so widely promulgated during this century as to make it unnecessary to present them in any detail here. Freud believed that obsessional neurosis resulted from a preponderant sadistic–anal–erotic sexual organization, which in the individual patient could arise from fixation at the anal level during development, or more commonly from regression to it as a consequence of frustration of functioning at the higher genital level (18). The most frequent reason for genital-level frustration, Freud suggested, is intrapsychic, especially Oedipal, conflict.

The credibility of psychoanalysis has suffered in recent years due to an overambitious claim to status as a general psychology, an antiquated metapsychology, and an implausible, dogmatic insistence on the exclusively childhood libidinal origin of neurosis. Nevertheless, Freud's 1909 "Rat Man" (19) still stands as the leading OCD case history, illustrating as it does the complex associative processes entering into the formation of an obsession, as well as the role of intrapsychic conflict (19 p. 376):

> The [obsessional neurotic patient's] doubt corresponds to the patient's internal perception of his own indecision, which, in consequence of the inhibition of his love by his hatred, takes possession of him in the race of every intended action. The doubt is in reality a doubt of his own love— which ought to be the most certain thing in his whole mind; and it becomes diffused over everything else, and is especially apt to become displaced on to what is most insignificant and trivial. A man who doubts his own love may, or rather *must*, doubt every lesser thing.

The theme of the existential battle between good and evil within the OCD sufferer appears throughout the disorder's history, from the Bohemian priest's doubt of his love for the Virgin to the Rat Man's doubt of his love for his father and lady. Perhaps more than anything else, this theme conveys the uniquely human experience that is OCD, an experience that animal models, synaptic chemistry, and PET scans, despite their impressive scientific utility, can never fully capture.

References

1. Kramer H, Sprenger J. Malleus Maleficarum. Pushkin Press, London, 1951. [Quoted in Kaplan HI, Freedman AM, Sadock BJ: Comprehensive Textbook of Psychiatry/III, vol 2, Williams & Wilkins, Baltimore, 1980.]
2. Moore J. Of Religious Melancholy. London, 1692. [Quoted in Hunter R, Macalpine I: Three Hundred Years of Psychiatry 1535–1860: A History Presented in Selected English Texts, Carlisle, Hartsdale, New York, 1982.]
3. Flecknoe R. Enigmaticall Characters. London, 1658. [Quoted in Hunter R, Macalpine I: Three Hundred Years of Psychiatry 1535–1860: A History Presented in Selected English Texts, Carlisle, Hartsdale, New York, 1982.]
4. Taylor J. Ductor Dubitantium, or The Rule of Conscience, vol 1. Royston, London, 1660. [Quoted in Hunter R, Macalpine I: Three Hundred Years of Psychiatry 1535–1860: A History Presented in Selected English Texts, Carlisle, Hartsdale, New York, 1982.]
5. Turner D. Syphilis: A Practical Dissertation on the Venereal Disease, vol 1, 2nd edn. Bonwicke et al., London, 1724. [Quoted in Hunter R, Macalpine I: Three Hundred Years of Psychiatry 1535–1860: A History Presented in Selected English Texts, Carlisle, Hartsdale, New York, 1982.]
6. Hartley D. Observations on Man, His Frame, His Duty, and His Expectations, Part 1. Leake & Frederick, London, 1749. [Quoted in Hunter R, Macalpine I: Three Hundred Years of Psychiatry 1535–1860: A History Presented in Selected English Texts, Carlisle, Hartsdale, New York, 1982.]
7. Johnson S. The Prince of Abissinia, vol 2. Dodsley & Johnston, London, 1759. [Quoted in Hunter R, Macalpine I: Three Hundred Years of Psychiatry 1535–1860: A History Presented in Selected English Texts, Carlisle, Hartsdale, New York, 1982.]
8. Westphal C. Über Zwangsvorstellungen. Arch Psychiatr Nervenkr 1878; 8: 734–750. [Quotation from unpublished National Institutes of Health Library Translation.]
9. Gilles de la Tourette G. Étude sur une affection nerveuse caracterisée par de l'incoordination motrice accompagnée de echolalie et de coprolalie. Arch Neurol 1885; 9: 19–42, 158–200.
10. Meige H, Feindel E. Tics and Their Treatment [Transl Wilson SAK]. William Wood, New York, 1907.
11. Green RC, Pitman RK. Tourette syndrome and obsessive–compulsive disorder: Clinical relationships. In: Obsessive–Compulsive Disorder: Theory and Management, 2nd edn (eds Jenike MA, Baer L, Minichiello WE). Year Book Medical Publishers, Chicago, 1990, pp 61–75.
12. Schilder P. The organic background of obsessions and compulsions. Am J Psychiatry 1938; 94: 1397–1416.
13. Janet P. Les Obsessions et la Psychasthénie, vol 1. Alcan, Paris, 1903.

14. Pitman RK. Janet's *Obsessions and Psychasthenia*: A synopsis. Psychiatr Q 1984;
    56: 291–314.
15. Pitman RK. Pierre Janet on obsessive–compulsive disorder (1903): Review
    and commentary. Arch Gen Psychiatry 1987; 44: 226–232.
16. Pavlov IP. Feelings of possession and the ultraparadoxical phase: Open letter
    to Prof. Pierre Janet. In: Psychopathology and Psychiatry. Foreign Languages
    Publishing House, Moscow, 1960, pp 303–308.
17. Pavlov IP. Attempt at a physiological interpretation of compulsive neurosis
    and paranoia. In: Psychopathology and Psychiatry. Foreign Languages Pub-
    lishing House, Moscow, 1960, pp 309–324.
18. Freud S. The predisposition to obsessional neurosis [1913]. In: Collected
    Papers, vol 2. Hogarth Press, London, 1924, pp 122–132.
19. Freud S. Notes upon a case of obsessional neurosis [1909]. In: Collected
    Papers, vol 3. Hogarth Press, London, 1925, pp 293–383.

2 CULTURAL ASPECTS OF OBSESSIVE COMPULSIVE DISORDER

David Greenberg and Eliezer Witztum

Jerusalem Mental Health Center, Herzog Hospital, Jerusalem, Israel

Introduction

The study of the interaction between culture and psychopathology may further understanding of the factors affecting nosological entities, and the validity of the entities themselves (1). Is there a core feature, such as distress, which presents in some cultures as depression and in others as hysteria or neurasthenia, or are psychiatric disorders discrete entities that will be present in all cultures? Three issues in psychiatric anthropology will be examined with reference to obsessive compulsive disorder (OCD):

1. Does the prevalence of OCD vary between cultures? What is the significance of such findings?
2. Is the form of OCD influenced by culture?
3. Is the content of OCD influenced by culture?

Does the prevalence of OCD vary between cultures? What is the significance of such findings?

The writings of early psychoanalysts on the link between toilet training and the development of the obsessive compulsive character influenced the attitudes of early psychiatric anthropologists. Weston LaBarre wrote in 1946: "The Chinese are as free from compulsiveness about time and performance as they are unobsessive in all the other spheres of life" (2). He concluded that OCD is uncommon in China, but more common in the

Current Insights in Obsessive Compulsive Disorder. Edited by E. Hollander, J. Zohar, D. Marazzati and B. Olivier
© 1994 John Wiley & Sons Ltd

West, where toilet training was more rigid. These speculations are refuted by the Taiwan Psychiatric Epidemiological Project, including 11 000 subjects in Taipei city and local towns and villages, finding a lifetime prevalence rate of OCD between 0.3 and 0.9% (3).

At the other extreme, Berkeley-Hill (4) described what he termed "the anal–erotic factor in the religion, philosophy and character of the Hindus", and Chackraborty (5) described a normative Indian ritual based on a fear of contamination and a desire to remain clean, known as *Suchi-bai*. Both authors noted the central role of washing and purity in Indian life and considered some normative states to include many sufferers from OCD. Over the last three decades, three studies have described large samples of OCD in India (6–8). None have suggested that the preoccupation of Indian religious life with cleanliness and purity is associated with a higher prevalence of OCD. A recent epidemiological study of 2360 residents of Bangalore, India found 12 with current OCD (9). The lifetime prevalence of 0.59% in Bangalore is similar to that in Taiwan (3), demonstrating that two societies, considered to be at the opposite poles of obsessionality in their everyday lives, do not differ in the prevalence of OCD.

The few epidemiological studies in different countries reveal certain variations. In the Epidemiological Catchment Area survey of 18 500 residents of five cities in the USA (10), there was a lifetime prevalence rate of OCD of 1.9–3.3%. Using the same design in Puerto Rico, Canino et al (11) found a lifetime prevalence rate of 3.2% for OCD in a sample of 1800. An earlier study of 221 members of two Ugandan villages, by Orley and Wing (12), found obsessions in 2% of the women and 2.8% of the men. A study of 562 consecutive 16–17 year olds in Israel found a point prevalence rate of 3.6% for OCD using a structured interview based on DSM-III-R criteria (13).

Obsessive compulsive disorder emerges as a common disorder in all of the above studies, with, however, a 10-fold variation—between 0.3% [Taipei city (3)] and 3% [USA, (10)]. Furthermore, one finding merits careful attention. The Taiwan study (3) found that while disorders such as schizophrenia and paranoid disorders were equally prevalent in city, town, and village, the lifetime prevalence of OCD was 0.3% in the city, 0.54% in the towns, and 0.94% in the villages. The authors were not surprised: city life demands accuracy and punctuality, while village life is traditional, rural, and family oriented. These explanations are reminiscent of the speculations of LaBarre (2), and are refuted by the findings in Puerto Rico (11) and Africa (12), where a prevalence rate of about 3% was noted in nonurban societies.

In conclusion, it appears that wherever careful surveys are carried out, OCD is found in at least 0.3% of the adult population. The variation (up to 10-fold) in prevalence rates between different countries, and between urban and village populations, suggests that further research could provide important information on factors influencing the prevalence and possibly the development of OCD.

Is the form of OCD influenced by the surrounding culture?

Khanna et al (8) described OCD as having form and content. Form is the structure of the phenomena, such as fears, thoughts, doubts, urges, convictions, images, repeating, rituals, checking, and avoiding. Washing is not included as an independent form, but is included under "content", as a version of repeating compulsions. Are OCD rituals (defined by Khanna as behaviors performed in a set, precise manner, often felt to have a symbolic significance) more likely in a society with more rituals, or does a stable society provide a normative framework for such inclinations? If a culture emphasizes exactness, does this encourage pathological expression, or alternatively institutionalize and thereby normalize checking and repeating?

Historical accounts provide a view of the interplay between culture, in this case religious ritual, and the form of OCD. Roman Catholicism has two sacraments that must be repeated frequently, one of which, confession, featured repeatedly in both historical and recent accounts of OCD. Ignatius of Loyola, father of the Jesuit order, and Martin Luther, who was a devout Catholic monk before founding Protestant Christianity, both spent many hours ruminating over their transgressions, and recounting them in detail in confession (14). Three decades ago, Weisner and Riffel (15) reported 23 Roman Catholic referrals to a Child Guidance Center, who were "continually consulting the priest . . . they felt past sins were either not properly confessed or not properly understood by the priest . . . Many found it difficult going to Communion because of their inability to resolve their doubt about sin on their soul". Similar cases were described by Vergote, a Catholic philosopher and psychoanalyst, as the "religious neurosis of culpability" (16). Of 10 cases of religious OCD, described by Fallon et al, five were Catholic: three confessed repeatedly, and two had blasphemous thoughts (17).

Protestant Christianity places less emphasis on ritual and greater value on prayer. Consistent with this prime role of prayer, Enoch and Trethowan (18) found an early definition of "a compulsion to blaspheme or swear aloud in church . . . referred to as the 'devil in the tongue'", while John Moore, Bishop of Norwich, preached before Queen Mary II at Whitehall in 1691 on the subject of *Religious Melancholy*, telling of good moral worshippers who are assailed by "naughty and sometimes blasphemous thoughts" which "start in their minds, while they are exercised in the worship of God" despite "all their efforts to stifle and suppress them" (19). Similarly, in his treatise "The anatomy of melancholy" written in 1621, Robert Burton described someone who "If he was in a silent auditorium as at a sermon, he was afraid he shall speak aloud at unawares, something indecent, unfit to be said" (20). Obsessive urges of blasphemy or of illness and harm coming to other people are described among Protestants at prayer.

Historical accounts and recent case reports of OCD, then, give the impression that there is a close link between normative religious ritual and the form of OCD, in that Catholics, influenced by the ritual of confession, tend to compulsive behaviors of repeating, rituals, and checking related to the confession of sins, while Protestants with OCD, less encumbered by rituals, contend with blasphemous urges at prayer time. Both feel guilty about their sins.

Accounts of OCD around the world will now be reviewed to demonstrate the distribution of the forms of OCD in different cultures. Two studies from the UK, a primarily Protestant country, found religious concerns in two out of 41 cases of OCD (21), and none in a sample of 45 (22), possibly a reflection on the lack of centrality of religion in life in the UK. Over 50% of both samples had cleaning rituals and avoidance, and about 40% checking. Studies in the USA have not tended to differentiate forms of obsessions into Khanna's typology of fears, thoughts, doubts, urges, convictions, and images. Swedo et al (23) described 70 cases of child and adolescent OCD and found washing in 85%, repeating in 51% and checking in 46%, while Riddle et al (24), in a sample of 21, found washing in 67%, repeating in 76%, putting in order in 62%, and checking in 57%.

Thomsen (25) used Khanna's typology in a survey of 61 child and adolescent cases of OCD in Denmark. Fears, doubts, and urges were the commonest obsessions. Rituals, usually concerning cleanliness, were the commonest compulsions. A study by Honjo et al of 61 cases in Nagoya, Japan, found washing ("related to dirt phobia") in 38%, checking in 23%, ritualistic behavior in 15%, and, interestingly, spitting in 13% and over-concern with discipline in 12% (26). A study carried out by Wakabayashi in the same clinic 20 years earlier, of 25 children with OCD, found only 16% with dirt phobia (27), and Honjo et al suggested that this reflects changing societal values.

The US and UK studies reported above noted washing and repeating compulsions in over 50% of any sample, so that the earlier Japanese finding of 16% concerned with cleanliness, the recent Japanese finding of 38%, and the Western findings possibly imply the impact of societal attitudes and practices on the forms of OCD. These apparent differences, their significance limited by the small sample sizes, can be analysed only if these and other factors are understood in each society. Similarly, the role of spitting and discipline in Japanese society in contrast to other societies and their unique presentation in OCD merit attention.

In India, Akhtar found obsessive doubts in 75% of his sample of 82 cases of OCD (28). Thoughts and fears were present in 34 and 26%, respectively. Khanna and Channabasavanna's study of 410 cases found fears, thoughts, and doubts to be the most common obsessions (29). In a separate study of compulsions among 270 cases of OCD at the same clinic, repeating constituted 59% of the compulsions, rituals 21%, checking 15%, and avoiding 4% (30).

In Saudi Arabia, Mahgoub and Abdel-Hafeiz found repeating in 51%, washing in 37% and checking in 31% of their sample of 32 cases of OCD in a Moslem population (31).

There have been few reports providing details of psychopathology in Africa. A recent report (32) of five cases in Benin is therefore particularly interesting. The five were the only cases of OCD among 351 patients at a neuropsychiatric outpatient clinic. In only one case was cleanliness the main concern. In another, besides an urge to smile inappropriately and concerns over religious convictions, the patient "refused to eat at the university restaurant because the forks were not always well cleaned. When he ate a piece of cake without carefully washing his hands, he would not eat the part which had been in contact with his hands; such a behavior", note the authors, "*particularly in the African context*, always amazed his fellows" (our italics). Unfortunately, the authors do not go on to explain the cultural context of the amazement of the patient's student colleagues, to enable cross-cultural comparisons. Overall, they were impressed with the similarity between their own sample and the world literature. More samples from Black Africa, noting variables such as city or village dwellers, and cultural groups, are awaited.

Overall, the data on forms of OCD are sparse, and the items noted vary between researchers, so that the results presented above are not easily compared with each other. Furthermore, while Khanna (33) has demonstrated the reliability of his classification into form and content, the validity of the forms of obsessions and their significance remain to be demonstrated.

Is the content of OCD influenced by culture?

Anthropologists and the most biologically oriented psychiatrists tend to agree that environment influences the content of psychiatric disorder. In schizophrenia, Kroll and Bachrach (34) compared the religious symptoms of 23 psychotics with the symptoms of visionaries of the Middle Ages. Eight of the psychotics described possession experiences, such as angels speaking through one's voice, or the Holy Spirit taking over one's thoughts. This symptomatology would not have been considered pathological in the Middle Ages, when mental illness presented differently:

babbling, howling, biting, tearing oneself to pieces. Time and place alter the content of psychopathology.

What are the findings in OCD? Using the main topics of OCD listed by Lewis (35), a picture across cultures emerges, as shown in Table 2.1. Conclusions should be cautious, as not all studies used the same categories; the categories were not carefully defined, and in most cases the samples were small. Nevertheless, the similarities around the world are notable. Dirt and contamination are the commonest topic in all but the Moslem countries. Religion is more common in the Moslem and Jewish populations, and, as Saul Bellow tells us in *Herzog* (36), Western man fears death.

It appears that religious topics are more common and cleanliness less common in OCD in Moslem countries. Detailed examination of the symptoms and their cultural context, however, leads to alternative conclusions. The main symptoms among 90 cases of OCD in Egypt were noted by Okasha (37) to be an exaggeration of the normative ritual of *Al Woodo* in which the five orifices of the body are cleaned three times after the toilet or after intercourse and before five-times daily prayer. Furthermore, Pfeifer (38) has described a normative condition in Islamic communities known as *Waswas* in which preprayer washings continue because the person does not feel clean enough, the opening words and movements of the prayers are repeated because the person does not feel that his concentration is adequate, and at the close of the prayer he fears he has left words out and must start afresh. The term *Waswas* is taken from a verse in the Koran, referring to the mind being preoccupied with evil thoughts or doubts preventing religious practice. These behaviors are subsumed under the rubric of "religious topics", yet they abound with issues of contamination and cleanliness, so the Saudi study may have viewed a topic as religious even though it also concerned (religious) cleanliness.

The religious context of symptoms and the content of religious symptoms of OCD will be discussed in more detail in the ensuing analysis of the religious symptoms of OCD that we reported from Jerusalem in Table 2.1. All 34 patients were Jewish, yet they were far from being one cultural entity. Fifty percent of the population of the catchment area were ultra-orthodox Jews, and the normative beliefs and practices of this group will be presented in order to understand the symptoms they develop in OCD.

The ultra-orthodox Jewish population in Israel is in many ways a culture distinct from the surrounding culture (39). Its members guide their lives according to a text known as the Code of Jewish Law (in Hebrew, *Shulkhan Arukh*). Their clothing is distinctive, they avoid social contact with the surrounding culture, they have minimal secular education, and often they do not work but instead spend every day of their

Table 2.1 Content of obsessive compulsive disorder in different countries (% of sample)

	Denmark (25)	UK (21)	USA (23)	UK (22)	Japan (26)	India (28)	India (29)	Saudi Arabia (31)	Egypt (36)	Israel
Sample size	61	41	70	45	61	82	410	32	90	34
Dirt/contamination	34	56	48	38	39	46	32	12	60	50
Religion	8	5	13			11	4.7	50+	60	41
Sex	6.5	12	8	9	5	10	21	6	48	6
Aggression	5	32		7		29	9	9	41	17
Death	21		24		13		11	12		
Illness	18				13		14	3	49	3
Harm	18	12	4	16	12		11	3		3
Past	2	49					13			
Daily acts	6.5			11		27	27			
Inanimate				11	7	22	9	19		21
Other		58		8			15		37	

lives in the study of Talmud. The features of this population that make it valuable for a study of the effects of culture on OCD are the avoidance of contact with secular society and values, the primacy of religious values and rituals, the judgement of failure to comply with normative demands as wrong or sinful, and the penetration of ultra-orthodox religious ritual into the smallest details of daily life.

Of the 34 referrals, 15 were not ultra-orthodox and 19 were ultra-orthodox. Of the 19 ultra-orthodox cases of OCD, six had obsessive compulsive (OC) symptoms only of a nonreligious nature, eight had both religious and nonreligious symptoms, while five had only religious symptoms. Restated, 13 out of 19 ultra-orthodox cases of OCD had religious symptoms and 14 had nonreligious symptoms. Considering the exclusion of secular values from daily life and study, it is surprising that there were so many nonreligious symptoms.

Of the 13 cases with religious symptoms, prayer was the topic in seven cases, dietary laws in two cases, menstrual laws in two cases, and cleanliness before prayer in five cases. There were no other religious topics in this sample, although we have encountered single cases elsewhere of a compulsion for a ceremony to counteract dreams and for a ceremony to annul vows. The compulsive behaviors noted in these 13 cases of religious symptoms were cleaning (seven cases), repeating (six cases), checking (1 case) and slowness (two cases).

Of interest, and in keeping with the accounts of normative religious behavior in Islam (*Al Woodo* and *Waswas*) and Hinduism (*Suchi-bai*), the Jewish laws are in each case very stringent in their demands. Nevertheless, most ultra-orthodox Jews will care about precise performance, but will not repeat, and these repetitions will not be at the expense of other observances. The areas of ritual behavior that were the focus of OC symptomatology in our patients are not central to Jewish ritual practice. They are, however, typical of obsessive compulsive disorder. If the religious context of the symptoms of our patients is ignored, all 13 cases of religious symptoms can be reclassified as concerning dirt and contamination (eight cases), orderliness (six), aggression, including blasphemy (two), and sex (one). It is as if the patients with OCD go through a directory of ultra-orthodox religious practices and "get stuck" only at the rituals typical of OCD. This is similar to the finding of Leonard et al that children who go on to develop OCD do not have more pronounced performance of childhood rituals, except in the behaviors of their future symptoms (40).

The overall impression is that OC symptomatology does not appear in all areas of religious ritual life, but "selects" areas typical of OCD in other less ritualized cultures. If the religious setting is ignored, the obsessive concerns of dirt, orderliness, aggression, and sex, and the compulsive behaviors of washing, repeating, checking, and slowness are typical of OCD.

Conclusions

Obsessive compulsive disorder has been found in all cultures that have been the subject of epidemiological study. Up to 10-fold variations have been noted in the prevalence rate between cultures, although most of these studies have not noted ethnic, religious, and urban/rural variations within their samples. The content of OCD does vary according to culture, although the variation may be more apparent than real. These observations will be verified only if future samples permit examination of the presentation of cultural subgroups within samples. Only then will it be possible to approach definitive answers to the above questions and gain greater understanding of the factors influencing the prevalence, form, and content of OCD.

Acknowledgment

Our thanks to Jamilla Ayalan for her advice on Islamic practices.

References

1. Kleinman A. Rethinking Psychiatry. Free Press, New York, 1988, pp 34–52.
2. LaBarre W. Some observations on character structure in the Orient, II. The Chinese. Psychiatry 1946; 9: 378–380.
3. Hwu HG, Yeh EK, Chang LY. Prevalence of psychiatric disorders in Taiwan defined by the Chinese Diagnostic Interview Schedule. Acta Psychiatr Scand 1989; 79: 136–147.
4. Berkeley-Hill O. The anal-erotic factor in the religion, philosophy and character of the Hindus. Int J Psychoanal 1921; 2: 306–329.
5. Chackraborty A. Ritual, a culture specific neurosis, and obsessional states in Bengali culture. Ind J Psychiatry 1975; 17: 211–216, 273–283.
6. Akhtar S, Wig NN, Varma VK, Pershad D, Verma SK. Socio-cultural and clinical determinants of symptomatology in obsessional neurosis. Int J Soc Psychiatry 1978; 24: 157–162.
7. Dutta Ray S. Obsessional states observed in New Delhi. Br J Psychiatry 1964; 110: 181–182.
8. Khanna S, Kaliaperumal VG, Channabasavanna SM. Clusters of obsessive compulsive phenomena in obsessive compulsive disorder. Br J Psychiatry 1990; 156: 51–54.
9. Khanna S, Gururaj G, Sriram TG. Epidemiology of obsessive compulsive disorder in India. Presented at First International Obsessive Compulsive Disorder Congress, Capri, 12–13 Mar 1993.
10. Karno M, Golding JM, Sorenson SB, Burnam MA. The epidemiology of obsessive compulsive disorder in five US communities. Arch Gen Psychiatry 1988; 45: 1094–1099.
11. Canino GJ, Bird HR, Shrout PE et al. The prevalence of specific psychiatric disorders in Puerto Rico. Arch Gen Psychiatry 1987; 44: 727–735.
12. Orley J, Wing JK. Psychiatric disorders in two African villages. Arch Gen Psychiatry 1979; 36: 513–520.

13. Zohar AH, Ratzoni G, Pauls DL et al. An epidemiological study of obsessive–compulsive disorder and related disorders in Israeli adolescents. J Am Acad Child Adolesc Psychiatry 1992; 31: 1057–1061.
14. Greenberg D, Witztum E, Pisante J. Scrupulosity: Religious attitudes and clinical presentations. Br J Med Psychol 1987; 60: 29–37.
15. Weisner WM, Riffel PA. Scrupulosity: Religion and obsessive–compulsive behavior in children. Am J Psychiatry 1960; 117: 314–318.
16. Vergote A (1988). Guilt and Desire: Religious Attitudes and Their Pathological Derivatives. Yale University, New Haven, pp 48–71.
17. Fallon BA, Liebowitz MR, Hollander E et al. The pharmacotherapy of moral or religious scrupulosity. J Clin Psychiatry 1990; 51: 517–521.
18. Enoch MD, Trethowan WH. Uncommon Psychiatric Syndromes, 2nd edn. Wright, Bristol, 1979.
19. Moore J. Of Religious melancholy. In: Three Hundred Years of Psychiatry 1535–1860 (eds Hunter D, Macalpine I). Cambridge University, Cambridge, 1963, pp 252–253.
20. Burton R. The Anatomy of Melancholy [1621]. Vintage, New York, 1977.
21. Dowson JH. The phenomenology of severe obsessive–compulsive neurosis. Br J Psychiatry 1977; 131: 75–78.
22. Stern RS, Cobb JP. Phenomenology of obsessive–compulsive neurosis. Br J Psychiatry 1978; 132: 233–239.
23. Swedo SE, Rapoport JL, Leonard H, Lenane M, Cheslow D. Obsessive–compulsive disorder in children and adolescents: Clinical phenomenology of 70 consecutive cases. Arch Gen Psychiatry 1989; 46: 335–341.
24. Riddle MA, Scahill L, King R et al. Obsessive compulsive disorder in children and adolescents: Phenomenology and family history. J Am Acad Child Adolesc Psychiatry 1990; 29: 766–772.
25. Thomsen PH. Obsessive–compulsive symptoms in children and adolescents: A phenomenological analysis of 61 Danish cases. Psychopathology 1991; 24: 12–18.
26. Honjo S, Hirano C, Murase S et al. Obsessive–compulsive symptoms in childhood and adolescence. Acta Psychiatr Scand 1989; 80: 83–91.
27. Wakabayashi S. A study of the obsessions and compulsions of tics in children. Jpn J Child Psychiatry 1967; 8: 196–206 [in Japanese].
28. Akhtar S, Wig NN, Varma VK, Pershad D, Verma SK. A phenomenological analysis of symptoms in obsessive-compulsive neurosis. Br J Psychiatry 1975; 227: 342–348.
29. Khanna S, Channabasavanna SM. Phenomenology of obsessions in obsessive–compulsive neurosis. Psychopathology 1988; 21: 12–18.
30. Khanna S, Channabasavanna SM. Towards a classification of compulsions in obsessive compulsive neurosis. Psychopathology 1987; 20: 23–28.
31. Mahgoub OM, Abdel-Hafeiz HB. Pattern of obsessive–compulsive disorder in Eastern Saudi Arabia. Br J Psychiatry 1991; 158: 840–842.
32. Bertschy G, Ahyi RG. Obsessive–compulsive disorders in Benin: Five case reports. Psychopathology 1991; 24: 398–401.
33. Khanna S, Rajendra PN, Karur BV, Channabasavanna SM. Inter-rater reliability of a classification of obsessions and compulsions. Psychopathology 1987; 20: 29–33.
34. Kroll J, Bachrach B. Medieval visions and contemporary hallucinations. Psychol Med 1982; 12: 709–721.
35. Lewis A. Problems of obsessional illness. Proc R Soc Med 1935; 29: 13–24.
36. Bellow S. Herzog. Penguin, Harmondsworth, 1964.
37. Okasha A, Saad A, Khalil AH, Seif El Dawla A, Yehia N. Phenomenology of

obsessive compulsive disorder (OCD). A transcultural study. Submitted for publication.

38. Pfeifer WM. Culture-bound syndromes. In: Culture and Psychopathology (ed Al-Issa I). University Park, Baltimore, Maryland, 1982.

39. Helmreich WB. The World of the Yeshiva: An Intimate Portrait of Orthodox Jewry. Yale University, New Haven, 1992, pp 52–93.

40. Leonard HL, Goldberger EL, Rapoport JL, Cheslow DL, Swedo SE. Childhood rituals: Normal development of obsessive–compulsive symptoms? J Am Acad Child Adolesc Psychiatry 1990; 29: 17–23.

3 RECENT FINDINGS IN CHILDHOOD ONSET OBSESSIVE COMPULSIVE DISORDER

Martine F Flament

Hôpital La Salpêtrière, Paris, France

Introduction

Childhood obsessive compulsive disorder (OCD) has emerged from text-book descriptions of the early psychopathological development of an adult neurosis to being seen as a major disturbance of childhood, as well as a challenging model for research on mind–brain relationships and the intricate roles of biology and development. Recent epidemiological and phenomenological studies have shown that in children, adolescents, and adults, OCD is a common disorder with a chronic course and significant morbidity. The current prevalence rate ($\pm$ SD) of OCD in adolescence has been estimated to be 1.0% ($\pm$ 0.5%), and its lifetime prevalence rate 1.9% ($\pm$ 0.7%) (1); these figures are close to those reported for the adult general population (see Chapter 8).

The isomorphism between childhood and adult presentations of OCD has been documented in different cultures (2–4). In children, rituals are frequently the presenting complaint. As in adults, obsessions deal primarily with contamination, danger to self or others, symmetry, and moral issues. Contrary to classic teaching, early in the disorder compulsive rituals without obsessions are common. In most pediatric OCD samples, males outnumber females by 2:1, males tending to have an earlier age of onset and more severe symptoms.

New research has greatly expanded our knowledge of childhood OCD,

Current Insights in Obsessive Compulsive Disorder. Edited by E. Hollander, J. Zohar, D. Marazzati and B. Olivier
© 1994 John Wiley & Sons Ltd

its phenomenology, comorbidity, long-term course, and treatment. It has also brought an increased neurobiological perspective to the disorder.

This chapter will review findings from recent work on childhood OCD. It will not deal with the specific behavioral treatments which apply to children as well as to adults with the disorder, because no research in this area has focused specifically on younger subjects. In addition, we refer the reader to Chapter 14 for a discussion of the very promising neuroanatomical and neurophysiological findings from recent brain imaging studies, many of which have been done with childhood onset obsessive compulsive (OC) patients.

Assessment of OC symptoms in children

The Yale–Brown Obsessive Compulsive Scale (Y-BOCS) has been widely used for assessing the severity of symptoms in adults with OCD. Considerable data exist to support its reliability, validity, and sensitivity to change (5, 6).

Goodman and collaborators in consultation with Rapoport and others, modified the Y-BOCS so that it could be used to assess OC symptoms in children and adolescents aged 6–17 years (CY-BOCS). Several modifications were made: the wording of various items was modified, the instructions were expanded, and two items (1b and 6b) were added to provide an alternative method for assessing time occupied by obsessions or compulsions. A major difference from the Y-BOCS is that, in the CY-BOCS, both the child and parent(s) are interviewed, and all information combined to estimate the score for each item. The CY-BOCS, which also include six "associated features items" (items 11–16) and two "global assessment items" (items 17–18) is available on request from W. Goodman or M. Riddle.

The reliability and validity of the CY-BOCS were assessed by MA Riddle et al (personal communication). Seven girls and 12 boys, aged 8–17 years, who met DSM-III-R criteria for OCD were interviewed, in the company of a parent (for at least part of the interview), by one rater, and the videotaped interviews were scored by three additional independent raters. Three self-report measures were obtained from the children: the Leyton Obsessional Inventory–Child Version (LOI-CV) (7, 8), the Children's Manifest Anxiety Scale–Revised (CMAS-R) (9), and the Children's Depression Inventory (CDI) (10).

The intraclass correlation coefficients (ICCs) indicated excellent reliability for obsessions (0.90) and the total score (0.80), and acceptable reliability for compulsions (0.59). For single-item scores, the κ coefficients ranged widely, generally higher for obsessions (mean $\pm$ SD = 0.75 $\pm$ 0.10) than for compulsions (mean $\pm$ SD = 0.40 $\pm$ 0.20). Cronbach's α coefficients for the four raters ranged from 0.82 to 0.90, indicating a high level of internal consistency in this scale.

There was good convergent validity between CY-BOCS and LOI-CV total scores ($r = 0.77$, $p = 0.001$). Mean scores on the CDI and the CMAS-R were in the subclinical range, suggesting a good discriminant validity, although there was some overlap between the CY-BOCS and the CDI ($r = 0.49$, $p = 0.06$) and more between the CY-BOCS and the CMAS-R ($r = 0.73$, $p = 0.004$).

Overall, the CY-BOCS can be considered to be of sufficient psychometric quality to be used in clinical practice or research, although at the present time, scores generated for individual items, particularly for compulsions, are not sufficiently reliable.

Longitudinal studies

ARE CHILDHOOD ANXIETY DISORDERS PRECURSORS OF ADULT OCD? THE COLUMBIA STUDY

Children with OCD who come for clinical treatment frequently present with an array of anxiety symptoms seemingly unrelated to one another and to the OC symptoms. The most common comorbid disorders in children and adolescents with OCD consist of depressive disorders and anxiety disorders: in a systematic descriptive study at the NIMH, 40% of a group of 70 OC subjects had concurrent anxiety disorders (2). It is difficult to ascertain the specific evolution of the respective disorders. Does OCD lead to secondary anxiety disorders? Do severe childhood anxiety disorders represent risk factors for the eventual development of OCD?

A prospective longitudinal study by R Klein et al addresses the issue of the risk of developing OCD in adulthood for children and adolescents with severe separation anxiety disorder.

The longitudinal course of 6- to 15-year-old (mean age, 11 years) patients referred because of persistent school phobia, and diagnosed as having separation anxiety, was examined in a controlled, blind, prospective study. In childhood, one boy had rituals without functional interference but none of the children met criteria for OCD.

Fifteen years later, 54 subjects (70% of the original cohort) were reevaluated by means of a systematic clinical interview for lifetime diagnoses (Conduct Hyperactivity Anxiety Psychiatric Schedule, R Klein et al, personal communication). Specific enquiry was made regarding OCD symptoms (OC traits, OC features, subclinical OCD). Probands were matched for race, gender and social class with controls identified through random phoning in the cases' communities. The reliability of retrospective psychiatric diagnoses is documented by the finding that, based on blind assessments, 76% of probands but only 4% of controls received a childhood diagnosis of separation anxiety disorder.

At follow up, probands were 29 men and 25 women, aged between 23

Table 3.1 DSM-III-R adult anxiety disorders for children who had separation anxiety disorder (R Klein, personal communication)

Lifetime diagnosis	Probands (%) ($n = 54$)	Controls (%) ($n = 60$)	p^*
Panic disorder	7	0	0.025
Social phobia	11	3	NS†
Simple phobia	2	5	NS
Generalized anxiety disorder	0	2	NS
Obsessive compulsive disorder	0	0	NS

*One-tailed tests.
†NS, Not significant.

and 33 years (mean ± SD = 27.3 ± 2.7 years); controls were 27 men and 33 women, aged 23–34 years (mean ± SD = 28.3 ± 2.8 years).

Table 3.1 shows that early anxiety disorders carry long-term morbidity for adult anxiety disorders: 7% of the probands had panic disorder, 11% social phobia, and 2% simple phobia. In contrast to significant elevations of panic disorder in probands compared with controls, no single case of OCD occurred in either group.

Therefore, in spite of the frequent co-occurrence of separation anxiety disorder in children with OCD, the results of this prospective study do not support the likelihood that childhood separation anxiety disorder in itself is a risk factor for the development of OCD later in life.

NIMH PROSPECTIVE LONGITUDINAL STUDIES OF CHILDREN AND ADOLESCENTS WITH OCD

In the first prospective longitudinal study of children and adolescents with OCD, Flament et al (11) reported the outcome for 25 of 27 patients (93%) admitted between 1977 and 1983 to the NIMH Child Psychiatry Branch for a 5-week treatment trial with clomipramine (12). At first evaluation patients, aged 10–18 years, were matched for sex, age, and IQ with normal controls from the local community. Following the initial drug trial, few patients received continued treatment (clomipramine or other treatments).

Patients and controls were re-evaluated at 2–7 years' follow up (mean follow-up period ± SD, 4.4 ± 1.7 years) with an assessment battery including, for lifetime diagnoses, the Diagnostic Interview for Children and Adolescents (DICA) (13) or the NIMH Diagnostic Interview Schedule (DIS) (14), according to age. The patients (mean age ± SD, 18.8 ± 2.6 years) had marked psychosocial impairment and most had continuing psychopathology: 17 patients (68%) still met criteria for OCD, and comorbidity was common, as 13 (52%) of the group had another Axis I psychiatric disorder, most commonly an anxiety and/or depressive disorder. No baseline criteria were predictive of outcome.

The second study by Leonard et al (15) concerned children and adolescents who participated in the NIMH clomipramine treatment studies (12, 16) between 1984 and 1988. The objective of this study was to assess the outcome of patients who had access to continuing psychopharmacological treatments, to determine whether there had been any long-term gains and whether there were any predictors of outcome.

Probands were 18 girls and 36 boys aged, at initial evaluation, between 7 and 19 years (mean ± SD, 14.0 ± 3.0 years); the age at onset of OCD ranged from 2 to 16 years (mean ± SD, 9.9 ± 3.3 years). After discharge from the NIMH, 96% of the patients received additional pharmacological treatment (clomipramine for 90%, fluoxetine for 48%, fluvoxamine for 4%), 33% behavioral therapy, 54% individual therapy, and 20% family therapy. At the time of follow up, 70% were still taking psychoactive medication.

During the follow-up period, several interim contacts with most of the subjects showed that many patients met DSM-III-R criteria for OCD at some times but not at others, illustrating the waxing and waning pattern of the disorder.

All subjects were assessed 2–7 years after first referral (mean ± SD, 3.4 ± 1.0 years), 89% by direct clinical interviews and the remaining 11% by telephone interviews of the patient or other informant(s). Patients were 10–24 years old (mean ± SD, 17.4 ± 3.0 years). Twenty-three (43%) still had a DSM-III-R diagnosis of OCD, 10 (18%) had subclinical OCD, 15 (28%) had "obsessive–compulsive features", and only six (11%) were free of any obsessions or compulsions. Of those six, three were still under medication, therefore only three (6% of the sample) could be considered in true remission. Although OC symptoms continued, the group as a whole was significantly improved from endpoint of initial clomipramine treatment on measures of OCD, anxiety, depression, and global functioning, indicating significant gains over those on short-term treatment; only 10 subjects (19%) were rated as unchanged or worse.

Comorbidity was extremely high: at follow up, only two subjects (4%) had no current psychiatric diagnosis. The most common lifetime diagnoses were tic disorder (59%), major depression (56%), overanxious disorder (54%), and oppositional disorder (30%). Three patients (6%) had developed a psychotic disorder subsequent to baseline evaluation; this disorder resolved in two of the patients (one of whom had a brief reactive psychosis while receiving medication), but the third patient had comorbid schizoaffective disorder and severe OCD at follow up.

A worse OCD outcome score at follow up was predicted in a stepwise multiple regression by (a) a more severe OCD symptom score after 5 weeks of clomipramine therapy (NIMH OCD severity scale), (b) a lifetime history of a tic disorder, and (c) presence of parental Axis I psychiatric diagnosis ($R^2 = 0.31$, $p < 0.01$).

DANISH 6- TO 22-YEAR FOLLOW-UP STUDY OF CHILDHOOD OCD

A Danish study by Thomsen et al examined the clinical course of childhood OCD in 47 subjects (28 males and 19 females) re-evaluated 6–22 years (mean = 15.6 years) after initial referral (17, 18). These subjects were 85% of all patients admitted for treatment of OCD between 1970 and 1986 in the Children's Psychiatric Hospital in Aarhus (Denmark); they were compared with a control group of 49 age- and sex-matched control patients with former admissions for other nonpsychotic disorders during the same period (17 with "emotional disorder", 14 conduct disorder, six oppositional disorder, five attention-deficit hyperactivity disorder, two anorexia nervosa, five other diagnoses). For OCD probands, the mean age at admission in childhood was 11.8 (SD = 2.4) years for boys and 12.4 (SD = 2.3) years for girls.

At follow up, subjects were interviewed directly (except four cases and six controls, who had only a telephone interview) with the Y-BOCS, the General Assessment Scale (GAS) (19) and the Structured Clinical Interview for DSM-III-R Personality Disorders (SCID-II) (20). On the latter, the overall agreement between two raters for presence or absence of at least one personality disorder was 88%, and there was a 76% agreement for specific personality disorders.

The mean age of patients at follow up was 27.4 (SD = 5.0) years (range 18–36 years). Thirty-four childhood OCD patients (72%) had at least one Axis I diagnosis at follow up, 22 (47%) with OCD. In the control group, rates of psychiatric diagnoses at follow up ranged from 17% to 40% according to initial diagnostic group, except for the two anorexic patients, who both still had an eating disorder; one child with "emotional disorder" had developed OCD at follow up.

General functioning was impaired in both groups: the mean score on the GAS was 66.6 (SD = 16.2) for OCD probands and 72.0 (SD = 12.9) for controls (not significant). In the OCD group, more males ($n = 9$; 32%) than females ($n = 1$; 5%) belonged to the poorest outcome group (GAS < 50). Education and employment were comparable in the two groups, but OCD patients were more socially isolated: more still lived with their parents (30% vs 4% of the controls) and fewer had partners (32% vs 59%, respectively).

Regarding OCD in adulthood, the OCD probands could be divided into four groups of approximately equal size: one group had no longer OCD ($n = 13$; 28%), one group had OCD on a subclinical level ($n = 12$; 25%), one group had a phasic course of OCD ($n = 10$; 21%), and the last group had a chronic and often very disabling OCD ($n = 12$; 25%). More girls than boys had a phasic course, but the overall status was similar for the two sexes. Neither symptomatology at discharge in childhood/adolescence nor age at onset of the disorder predicted long-term outcome. For OCD probands, comorbid diagnoses during the interim period and/or at follow up included major depression ($n = 8$), anorexia nervosa (four girls, two with bulimia), Tourette's syndrome (one male), and other tic disorders ($n = 6$); at follow up, two males were diagnosed with Asperger's syndrome and one male as schizophrenic.

At follow up, 68% of the OCD probands, like 61% of the psychiatric controls, had at least one personality disorder (see Table 3.2). Among OCD probands, the most common personality disorder was avoidant personality disorder (23%), significantly more frequent than in controls (8%), whereas obsessive compulsive personality disorder (OCPD) was not found more often in the OCD group (17% vs 10% of controls); however, in the OCD group, seven of the eight subjects with OCDP had continued OCD at follow up. Generally, most personality disorders (20 out of 38) were found in the group of patients with chronic OCD at follow up, and fewest (only three) in the group without OCD or subclinical OCD. No

Table 3.2 Personality disorders in adulthood for childhood obsessive compulsive disorder (OCD) probands and psychiatric controls [data from Thomsen and Mikkelsen (17)]

| Disorder | Childhood OCD probands ($n = 47$) | | | Psychiatric controls ($n = 49$) |
	No adult OCD n (%)	Adult OCD n (%)	Total n(%)	n (%)
Avoidant*	6 (13)	5 (11)	11 (23)	4 (8)
Dependent	2 (4)	6 (13)	8 (17)	7 (14)
OCPD†	1 (2)	7 (15)	8 (17)	5 (10)
Passive-aggressive	1 (2)	0 (0)	1 (2)	2 (4)
Self-defeating	0 (0)	3 (6)	3 (6)	1 (2)
Paranoid*	0 (0)	0 (0)	0 (0)	4 (8)‡
Schizotypal	0 (0)	2 (4)	2 (4)‡	1 (2)‡
Schizoid	0 (0)	0 (0)	0 (0)	0 (0)
Histrionic	0 (0)	2 (4)	2 (4)§	4 (8)§
Narcissistic	0 (0)	0 (0)	0 (0)	0 (0)
Borderline	0 (0)	3 (6)	3 (6)	3 (6)
Antisocial	1 (2)	1 (2)	2 (4)‡	3 (6)‡

*OCD Probands significantly different from controls (Fischer's exact test, $p < 0.05$).
†OCPD, Obsessive compulsive personality disorder.
‡All boys.
§All girls.

significant predictive factors from childhood were found for presence of OCDP or any personality disorder at follow up.

Pharmacological treatment

Although most classes of psychopharmacological agents have been tried for the treatment of OCD, only drugs with a potent effect on serotonin reuptake inhibition have shown efficacy. This has been documented in a number of rigorously designed studies with adult patients. Fewer controlled studies have demonstrated similar results for children and adolescents with OCD. We will summarize the results of the initial studies using the tricyclic antidepressant clomipramine, and report in more details recent trials with the newer specific serotonergic reuptake inhibitors (SSRI).

CLOMIPRAMINE

Clomipramine hydrochloride has been the first known antiobsessional agent. Its efficacy for children and adolescents with OCD has been demonstrated in three controlled studies. The first one by Flament et al (12) at the NIMH concerned 19 children (mean ± SD age, 14.5 ± 2.3 years) with severe, primary OCD, who completed a 10-week double-blind crossover trial with clomipramine (mean ± SD dose, 141 ± 30 mg/day) and placebo. At week 3 and week 5 of treatment, clomipramine was significantly superior to placebo for improvement of both observed and self-reported obsessions and compulsions; this was independant of the presence of depressive symptoms at baseline. Improvement of obsessive compulsive symptoms was closely correlated with pretreatment platelet serotonin concentration ($R = 78$, $p < 001$) as well as with decrease of this measure during clomipramine administration (21).

A subsequent study by Leonard et al (16) at the NIMH further documented the specificity of the antiobsessional effect of clomipramine. 47 OC children and adolescents received clomipramine (mean ± SD dose, 150 ± 53 mg/day) and desipramine (mean ± SD dose, 153 ± 55 mg/day) in a double-blind crossover trial. Clomipramine was clearly superior to desipramine in significantly reducing obsessive compulsive symptoms. As in the previous study, age of onset, duration or severity of illness, type of symptoms, and plasma concentrations did not predict clinical response to clomipramine. 64% of patients who received clomipramine as their first active treatment showed at least some sign of relapse during desipramine treatment.

De Veaugh-Geiss et al (22) reported on 60 children and adolescents with OCD included in an 8-week, multicenter, double-blind, parallel groups trial of clomipramine (75–200 mg/day) versus placebo. At the end of eight weeks, clomipramine-treated patients showed a mean reduction in CY-BOCS score of 37% compared to 8% in the placebo group ($p < 05$). At the terminal visit, 53% of patients receiving active drug rated themselves as very much improved or much improved versus 8% receiving placebo. Side effects were typical of tricyclic antidepressants. In a subsequent one year open label treatment for 47 patients, clomipramine continued to be effective and well tolerated.

FLUOXETINE

Fluoxetine, a novel SSRI with a bicyclic structure, which has demonstrated efficacy and safety in treating adults with major depressive disorder and OCD, was investigated by Riddle et al (23) in a double-blind, placebo-controlled, fixed-dose (20 mg/day), crossover study of 14 children and adolescents with OCD.

The subjects were six boys and eight girls aged 8.6 to 15.6 years (mean ± SD = 11.8 ± 2.3 years). The study design was an initial 8-week period on the first randomly assigned agent, followed by a 12-week period on the second agent (the second agent was given for longer because of the long half-life of fluoxetine and norfluoxetine).

One subject did not enter the study because of noncompliance, five discontinued because of nonresponse or exacerbation on placebo, one due to lack of response under both conditions, and one due to suicidal ideas while under fluoxetine. Because only six subjects completed the full 20-week study, a parallel analysis of the first 8 weeks was performed. After 8 weeks of treatment, OC symptom severity for the seven subjects receiving fluoxetine had decreased significantly [on CY-BOCS: total score = -44%, $p = 0.003$; obsessions score = -54%, $p = 0.009$; compulsions score = -33%, $p = 0.005$; on clinical global improvement (CGI)-OCD: score = -0.33%, $p = 0.0004$]. On all measures, improvement was evident by week 4. There was a small decrease on the anxiety score (CMAS-R score = -10%, $p = 0.02$), but the depression score (CDI), which was low at baseline, was not significantly reduced. For the six subjects receiving placebo, decreases in OC symptom severity were smaller (CY-BOCS total score = -27%, CGI-OCD score = -12%) and not significant. Comparison of change scores from baseline across groups showed an advantage to fluoxetine only on the CGI-OCD score ($t = -3.09$, $p = 0.01$).

The most commonly reported side effects on fluoxetine were insomnia (55%), fatigue (55%), motoric activation (27%), and nausea (27%). Two of three subjects who had chronic motor tics at baseline had exacerbation of tic symptoms under active treatment. The only major adverse event, which resulted in the subject discontinuing the study, was the development of suicidal ideation in a 13-year-old boy with a comorbid diagnosis of major depressive disorder after 3 weeks of treatment; the suicidal thoughts resolved after treatment discontinuation.

Mean plasma levels at the end of the treatment period were 150 (SD = 57) ng/ml for fluoxetine and 172 (SD = 58) ng/ml for norfluoxetine. Plasma concentrations of fluoxetine, but not norfluoxetine, correlated positively with fluoxetine dose, expressed as mg/kg ($r = 0.70$, $p = 0.02$), and with total change scores on both CY-BOCS ($r = 0.62$, $p = 0.04$) and CGI-OCD ($r = 0.65$, $p = 0.03$).

The degree of symptomatic improvement on fluoxetine is comparable with that observed in similar trials of clomipramine [22–47% across the four measures in the Flament et al study (12), 19–29% in the Leonard et al study (16) and 34–37% in the DeVeaugh-Geiss et al study (22)].

The findings suggest that fluoxetine is generally safe and effective for short-term treatment of childhood OCD. Obviously the major limitations of this study are the small number of subjects and the fixed dosage of 20 mg/day, which might be too high for some children. Clearly, larger numbers of children and adolescents with OCD need to be studied to generalize about efficacy as well as safety results and assess their relationship with dosage and plasma levels.

FLUVOXAMINE

Fluvoxamine, a newly developed monocyclic SSRI, has been recently marketed in over 30 countries worldwide. In an initial 8-week open-label trial by Apter et al (24) in Israel, fluvoxamine was administered to 20 adolescent inpatients, 10 boys and 10 girls aged 13 to 19 years, treated for OCD ($n = 14$) or major depressive disorder (MDD; $n = 6$). Of the OCD patients, 11 had a comorbid DSM-III-R diagnosis: four Tourette's syndrome (TS), three anorexia nervosa (AN), and four schizophrenia.

All patients received standard inpatient treatment. One to three weeks following admission, fluvoxamine was administered at doses increased by 50 mg weekly (maximum 300 mg/day), until therapeutic effect was obtained or severe side effects emerged. The patients with TS or schizophrenia also received haloperidol (0.5–15.0 mg daily).

As a group, the OCD patients showed a significant decrease in the severity of their OC symptoms as reflected in their CY-BOCS scores ($t = 9.35$, $p = 0.0001$). Patients with comorbid TS or schizophrenia responded well to therapy, while only one of those with AN showed improvement. The six patients with MDD showed a significant decrease in depressive symptoms measured on the Beck Depression Inventory ($t = 9.46$, $p = 0.0002$).

Treatment was not exempt from adverse effects. It had to be discontinued in one OC patient who developed hypomania, one underweight anorectic who manifested confusion, delirium and hallucinations, and three patients with dermatitis. All these conditions were reversible. The most common side effects were transient activating side effects: hyperactivity (20%), anxiety (20%), insomnia (20%), excitement (15%), and nausea (15%).

This preliminary evidence of response of diverse adolescent disorders to fluvoxamine should be confirmed in controlled studies with more stringent diagnosis and treatment conditions.

DESIPRAMINE

The selective efficacy of serotonin reuptake-blocking agents is also supported by Leonard's desipramine substitution study during long-term clomipramine maintenance treatment of a group of 26 children and adolescents with severe primary OCD (25). After at least 3 months of continued clomipramine treatment, half of the patients had desipramine blindly substituted for the following 2 months; all subjects received clomipramine again for the last 3 study months. Eight (89%) out of nine of the substituted and only two out of 11 of the nonsubstituted group subjects relapsed during the 2-month comparison period. All eight patients who relapsed with desipramine regained their clinical response within 1 month of clomipramine reinstallment.

The study shows that long-term clomipramine treatment may be required for many clomipramine-responsive child and adolescent patients with OCD. The duration of clomipramine treatment was unrelated to degree of relapse. Even patients receiving maintenance clomipramine treatment throughout the 8 months of the study had some continued OC symptoms, which varied in severity over time.

The OCD spectrum

The greater focus on the complex perseverative motor pattern in the early years of the disorder has led Rapoport et al to the consideration of a broad group of behaviors in relation to OCD (26). Other repetitive unwanted behaviors of childhood onset, such as trichotillomania (TT) or onychophagia, may fall into an OCD spectrum crossing current diagnostic categories.

The first evidence supporting this hypothesis came from psychopharmacological data. In a double-blind crossover comparison of clomipramine and desipramine treatment of 13 women with severe TT, Swedo et al (27) have shown that, like OCD, TT was responsive to 5 weeks of treatment with clomipramine (mean dose $\pm$ SD, 181 $\pm$ 56 mg/day) but not desipramine. A group of 14 subjects with childhood onset severe chronic onychophagia has been treated using the same study design (28). With similar doses and blood concentrations, of the two tricyclics, clomipramine was slightly but significantly superior to desipramine in ameliorating nail-biting symptoms.

A more cogent argument for an OCD spectrum would come from evidence of genetic relatedness. At the NIMH, Lenane et al (29) found that 10% of 65 first-degree relatives of 16 trichotillomanic children had a diagnosis of OCD. In a recent study at Yale by King et al (30), among 15 patients referred for TT (13 girls and two boys, aged 9–17 years), only one girl received a concurrent diagnosis of OCD; a total of 10 of the 30 parents had a lifetime history of TS (two fathers), tics, OCD (two fathers), OC features, TT, onychophagia, or face picking.

A further link with OCD might come from neuropsychological studies, which indicate that the same relatively selective spatioperceptual deficit found in OCD patients is also present in trichotillomanics (31).

Rapoport has proposed that OCD and related disorders (trichotillomania, onychophagia) may be viewed ethologically as part of a larger spectrum of biologically determined and inappropriately released pathological "grooming" behaviors (26). Two naturally occurring conditions in animals, compulsive feather picking in birds (32) and acral lick dermatitis in dogs (33), have both been shown to improve with clomipramine, suggesting that a similar central mechanism mediating grooming behaviors may be involved across species.

OCD and basal ganglia pathology

An increased incidence of motor tics, as well as choreiform movements, has been observed in children and adolescents with OCD (34), suggesting basal ganglia pathology in association with early onset OCD.

Furthermore, OCD has been reported in association with a number of basal ganglia disorders, many of which occur in childhood. This has been summarized by Rapoport et al (35) and is shown in Table 3.3. Under particular scrutiny have been Tourette's syndrome and Sydenham's chorea.

TICS AND TOURETTE'S SYNDROME

One-third to one-half of adult (40, 41) and child (42) patients with TS also have OCD. Pauls et al (36) reported that the rate of OCD among 45 first-degree relatives of 13 probands with TS without OCD was 26%.

In the follow-up study described above, Leonard et al (39) have obtained information on the personal and family history of TS and other tic disorders for the 54 OCD probands, using the TS/tic section—modified from the Yale Schedule for Tourette and Other Behavioral Syndromes (40). At baseline, a diagnosis of TS was an exclusionary criterion, but a chronic vocal or motor tic disorder was not.

Table 3.3 Regional effects of basal ganglia disease and association with obsessive compulsive disorder (OCD) [extracted from Rapoport JL, Swedo SE, Leonard HJ; J Clin Psychiatry 1992; 53(4, suppl): 11–16. Copyright 1992, Physicians Postgraduate Press.]

Disease	Cause	Basal ganglia area most affected	Most prominent signs	Association with OCD*
Sydenham's chorea	Autoimmune cross reaction in *streptococcus* A/B	Caudate and putamen	Chorea	+++
Huntington's chorea	Genetic	Caudate and putamen	Chorea	+
Wilson's disease	Genetic	Putamen and caudate	Tremor and rigidity	?
Vascular disease	Vascular	Putamen	Dystonia	+
Parkinson's disease				
Idiopathic	Unknown	Substantia nigra	Akinetic rigidity	–
Postencephalitic	Infection	Substantia nigra	Akinetic rigidity	++
Segawa's dystonia	Genetic	Unknown	Dystonia	++
Tourette's disorder	Genetic	Unknown	Motor-vocal tics	+++

*?, Unknown; –, none; +, suspected; ++, probable; +++, well documented.

At follow up, 32 subjects (59%) had lifetime histories of tics. Eight of these (15%), all males, met the criteria for TS (six had developed the disorder, and two, it could be argued in retrospect, might have met the criteria at baseline); all still had a current (albeit mild) OCD, and all but one had a lifetime history of tics at baseline.

Using a stepwise discriminant analysis, the variables best able to distinguish the patients with a lifetime history of tics from those without were, in order of significance, a higher anxiety score (NIMH Global Anxiety Scale) at baseline, a greater baseline ratio of cerebrospinal fluid 5-hydroxyindoleacetic acid (5-HIAA) to homovanillic acid (HVA), and a younger age at onset of OCD. Besides all being males, the patients with TS differed from those with chronic/transient tics and those without any tic diagnosis only in their earlier age at onset of OCD (mean ± SD, 6.5 ± 3.5 years, vs 10.4 ± 2.9 and 11.3 ± 3.1, respectively).

Of the 171 first-degree relatives, 1.8% had TS, 14% had a tic disorder, and 17% OCD (age-corrected prevalence rates). Male relatives were found to have a greater risk of both tics and OCD ($p < 0.03$).

These seemingly high rates of TS and, more generally, tic disorders in patients with OCD and their first-degree relatives, far greater than the reported range of prevalence for these disorders in the general population, support the hypothesis that some cases of OCD and TS may be etiologically related.

SYDENHAM'S CHOREA

A first retrospective comparison of obsessionality in 23 Sydenham's chorea patients and 24 rheumatic fever patients without chorea showed significantly increased OC symptoms (on the LOI-CV) in the choreic patients, with three such patients meeting diagnostic criteria for OCD (41).

In a second study, 11 children (eight girls and three boys, aged 4–12 years) with Sydenham's chorea of recent onset (1–12 months) were examined by Swedo et al at the NIMH (42). Antibodies directed against human caudate tissue (antineural antibodies) were present in the serum of 10 of the 11 children (compared to only nine out of 18 healthy control subjects). Follow-up interviews with patients and parents (DICA and DICA-P; several standard OC severity ratings) were conducted regularly until 18 months after the onset of chorea.

All children exhibited psychological dysfunction concomitant with the choreic disorder, of abrupt onset or worsening. Nine of the 11 children experienced an acute onset of OC symptomatology. None had had previous obsessionality, but during their illness, four children met DSM-III-R criteria for OCD. The OC symptoms started shortly before the onset of the movement disorder, peaked as the chorea did, and waned over time, usually disappearing before the cessation of the choreic movements. The mean total duration of chorea symptoms was 7 months. Eighteen months after onset, the patients were doing well; none of the subjects met criteria for OCD, nor did they continue to have obsessional thoughts or compulsive rituals.

In Sydenham's chorea, recent magnetic resonance imaging and positron emission tomography examinations have provided further support for involvement of both cortical and striatal regions (43, 44). These results support other findings suggesting that OCD might be associated with dysfunction of basal ganglia–limbic–frontal lobe tracts.

Conclusions

One might infer from the results of the longitudinal studies that multiple treatment interventions can improve long-term prognosis of childhood onset OCD and reduce impairment from the condition. However, with treatments available to date, the disorder still appears to be chronic and unremitting; most pediatric OCD patients can expect long-term improvement but not complete remission. Ongoing treatment may be required for this population.

Clinical presentation of OCD, comorbidity, response to behavioral treatment, and pharmacotherapy are similar across ages. However, the strong family influence, male predominance, presence of tics or other neurological abnormalities, and possible impact on personality development might represent specific features of childhood onset OCD and may provide etiological clues to the disorder.

The obsessive compulsive symptoms associated with basal ganglia disorders, as well as with specific basal ganglia lesions in individuals, the response to psychosurgery, the efficacy of serotonergic drugs in OCD and related disorders, and recent brain imaging studies, all support the hypothesis of a basal ganglia dysfunction in OCD. However, many questions remain unanswered. The current consensus developing towards a neuroanatomical model of the pathophysiological characteristics of OCD, may be considered as one of the various neurobiological and psychological variables that contribute to what remains an intriguing syndrome.

References

1. Flament MF, Whitaker A, Rapoport JL et al. Obsessive compulsive disorder in adolescence: An epidemiological study. J Am Acad Child Adolesc Psychiatry 1988; 27: 764–771.

2. Swedo SE, Rapoport JL, Leonard H, Lenane M, Cheslow D. Obsessive–compulsive disorder in children and adolescents. Clinical phenomenology of 70 consecutive cases. Arch Gen Psychiatry 1989; 46: 335–340.

3. Honjo S, Hirano C, Murase S et al. Obsessive–compulsive symptoms in childhood and adolescence. Acta Psychiatr Scand 1989; 80: 83–91.

4. Khanna S, Srinath S. Childhood obsessive compulsive disorder. I. Psychopathology. Psychopathology 1989; 32: 47–54.

5. Goodman WK, Price LH, Rasmussen SA et al. The Yale–Brown Obsessive Compulsive Scale: I. Development, use and reliability. Arch Gen Psychiatry 1989; 46: 1006–1011.

6. Goodman WK, Price LH, Rasmussen SA et al. The Yale–Brown Obsessive Compulsive Scale: II. Validity. Arch Gen Psychiatry 1989; 46: 1012–1016.

7. Berg CZ, Rapoport JL, Flament MF. The Leyton Obsessional Inventory—Child Version. J Am Acad Child Psychiatry 1986; 25: 84–91.

8. Berg CZ, Whitaker A, Davies M, Flament MF, Rapoport JL. The survey form of the Leyton Obsessional Inventory—Child Version: Norms from an epidemiological study. J Am Acad Child Adolesc Psychiatry 1988; 27: 758–763.

9. Reynolds CR, Richmond B. Revised Children's Manifest Anxiety Scale (RCMAS) Manual (1987). Western Psychological Services, Los Angeles, 1987.

10. Kovacs M. The Children Depression Inventory (CDI). Psychopharmacol 1985; 21: 995–998.

11. Flament MF, Koby E, Rapoport JL et al. Childhood obsessive–compulsive disorder: A prospective follow-up study. J Child Psychol Psychiatry 1990; 31: 363–380.

12. Flament MF, Rapoport JL, Berg CJ et al. Clomipramine treatment of childhood obsessive–compulsive disorder. A double-blind controlled study. Arch Gen Psychiatry 1985; 42: 977–983.

13. Herjanic B, Campbell JW. Differentiating psychiatrically disturbed children on the basis of a structured interview. J Abnorm Child Psychol 1977; 5: 125–137.

14. Robins L, Helzer J, Croughan J, Ratcliff K. National Institute of Mental Health Diagnostic Interview Schedule: Its history, characteristics and validity. Arch Gen Psychiatry 1981; 38: 381–391.

15. Leonard HL, Swedo SE, Lenane MC et al. A 2- to 7-year follow-up study of 54 obsessive–compulsive children and adolescents. Arch Gen Psychiatry 1993; 50: 429–439.

16. Leonard HL, Swedo SE, Rapoport JL et al. Treatment of obsessive–compulsive disorder with clomipramine and desipramine in children and adolescents. Arch Gen Psychiatry 1989; 46: 1088–1092.

17. Thomsen PH, Mikkelsen HU. Development of personality disorders in children and adolescents with obsessive–compulsive disorder. A 6- to 22-year follow-up study. Acta Psychiatr Scand 1993; 87: 456–462.

18. Thomsen PH. Obsessive–compulsive disorder in Danish children and adolescents. A follow-up study. Eur Child Adolesc Psychiatry [in press].

19. Endicott J, Spitzer RL, Fleiss JL, Cohen J. The Global Assessment Scale. A procedure for measuring overall severity of psychiatric disturbance. Arch Gen Psychiatry 1976; 33: 766–771.

20. Spitzer RL, Williams JBW, Gibbon M, First M. Structured Clinical Interview for DSM-III-R Personality Disorders (SCID-II). Biometrics Research, New York State Psychiatric Institute, New York, 1987.

21. Flament MF, Rapoport JL, Murphy DL, Lake CR, Berg CJ. Biochemical changes during clomipramine treatment of childhood obsessive compulsive disorder. Arch Gen Psychiatry 1987; 44: 219–225.

22. DeVeaugh-Geiss J, Moroz G, Biederman J et al. Clomipramine hydrochloride in childhood and adolescent obsessive–compulsive disorder: A multicenter trial. J Am Acad Child Adolesc Psychiatry 1992; 31: 45–49.
23. Riddle MA, Scahill L, King RA et al. Double-blind, crossover trial of fluoxetine and placebo in children and adolescents with obsessive–compulsive disorder. J Am Acad Child Adolesc Psychiatry 1992; 31: 1062–1069.
24. Apter A, Ratzoni G, King RA, Weizman A, Iancu I, Binder M, Riddle MA. Fluvoxamine open-label treatment of adolescent inpatients with obsessive-compulsive disorder or depression. J Am Acad Child Adolesc Psychiatry 1994; 33: 342–348.
25. Leonard HL, Swedo SE, Lenane MC et al. A double-blind desipramine substitution during long-term clomipramine treatment in children and adolescents with obsessive–compulsive disorder. Arch Gen Psychiatry 1991; 48: 922–927.
26. Rapoport JL. Recent advances in obsessive compulsive disorder. Neuropsychopharmacology 1991; 5: 1–10.
27. Swedo SE, Leonard HL, Rapoport JL, Lenane MC, Goldberger EL, Cheslow DL. A double-blind comparison of clomipramine and desipramine in the treatment of trichotillomania (hair pulling). N Engl J Med 1989; 497–501.
28. Leonard HL, Lenane MC, Swedo SE et al. A double-blind comparison of clomipramine and desipramine treatment of severe onychophagia (nail biting). Arch Gen Psychiatry 1991; 48: 821–827.
29. Lenane M, Swedo SE, Rapoport JL. Rates of obsessive compulsive disorder for first-degree relatives of patients with trichotillomania: A research note. J Child Psychol Psychiatry 1992; 33: 925–933.
30. King RA, Scahill L, Vitulano LA, Schwab-Stone M, Tercyak KP, Riddle MA. Childhood trichotillomania: Clinical phenomenology, comorbidity, and family genetics. J Am Acad Child Adolesc Psychiatry (in press).
31. Rettew D, Cheslow D, Rapoport JL, Leonard H, Lenane M. Neuropsychological test performance in trichotillomania: A further link with obsessive-compulsive disorder. J Anxiety Disorders 1991; 5: 225–235.
32. Grindlinger HM, Ramsay E. Compulsive feather picking in birds. Arch Gen Psychiatry 1991; 48: 857.
33. Rapoport JL, Ryland DH, Kriete M. Drug treatment of canine acral lick: An animal model of obsessive–compulsive disorder. Arch Gen Psychiatry 1992; 49: 517–521.
34. Denckla MB. The neurological examination. In: Obsessive Disorder in Children and Adolescents (ed Rapoport JL). American Psychiatric Press, Washington DC, 1989, pp 107–118.
35. Rapoport JL, Swedo SE, Leonard HL. Childhood obsessive compulsive disorder. J Clin Psychiatry 1992; 53 (4, suppl): 11–16.
36. Pauls DL, Towbin KE, Leckman JF, Zahner GEP, Cohen DJ. Gilles de la Tourette's syndrome and obsessive–compulsive disorder. Evidence supporting a genetic relationship. Arch Gen Psychiatry 1986; 43: 1180–1182.
37. Pitman RK, Green RC, Jenike MA, Mesulam MM. Clinical comparison of Tourette's disorder and obsessive–compulsive disorder. Am J Psychiatry 1987; 144: 1166–1171.
38. Grad LR, Pelcovitz D, Olson M, Matthews M, Grad GJ. Obsessive–compulsive symptomatology in children with Tourette's syndrome. J Am Acad Child Adolesc Psychiatry 1987; 26: 69–73.
39. Leonard HL, Lenane MC, Swedo SE, Rettew DC, Gershon ES, Rapoport JL. Tics and Tourette's disorder. A 2- to 7-year follow-up study of 54 obsessive-compulsive children. Am J Psychiatry 1992; 149: 1244–1251.

40. Pauls DL, Hurst CR. Schedule for Tourette and Other Behavioral Syndromes. Child Study Center, Yale University School of Medicine, New Haven, 1981.

41. Swedo SE, Rapoport JL, Cheslow DL, Leonard HL, Ayoub EM, Hosier DM, Wald ER. High prevalence of obsessive–compulsive symptoms in patients with Sydenham's chorea. Am J Psychiatry 1989; 146: 246–249.

42. Swedo SE, Leonard H, Shapiro MB, Casey BJ, Mannheim GB, Lenane M, Rettew DC. Sydenham's chorea: Physical and psychological symptoms of Saint Vitus dance. Pediatrics 1993; 91: 706–713.

43. Kienzle GD, Breger RK, Chun RWM, Zupanc ML, Sackett JF. Sydenham chorea: MR manifestations in two cases. Am J Neurol Res 1991; 21: 73–76.

44. Goldman S, Amron D, Szliwowski HB et al. Asymmetrical striatal glucose metabolism in a case of Sydenham's chorea with lateralized symptoms. Neurology 1992; 42 (suppl 3): 320 [abstr 611P].

4 PERSONALITY DISORDERS AND OBSESSIVE COMPULSIVE DISORDER

Dan J Stein, Eric Hollander and Concetta M DeCaria
Mount Sinai School of Medicine, NY, USA

Introduction

The DSM-III added a second axis for diagnosis of personality disorders, partly in order to ensure that these disorders were not overlooked in the face of the usually more florid Axis I disorders. Indeed, since the publication of the DSM-III manuals, an increasing amount of research has been devoted to the comorbidity of Axis I and Axis II disorders. While much of this research has focused on mood disorders (1), there has also been increasing attention to comorbidity of the anxiety disorders (2), including obsessive compulsive disorder (OCD) (3).

This research is important for a number of reasons. In particular, better understanding of Axis II disorders in OCD may shed light on the heterogeneity of this complex disorder. Obsessive compulsive disorder presents with different kinds of clinical symptoms, neurobiological investigation reveals diverse neurochemical and neuroanatomical features, and treatment responses are varied. Perhaps an understanding of comorbid personality features can help explain some of this variation.

Before going on to review research on the comorbidity of OCD and personality disorders, it is relevant to review some conceptual and methodological issues [which we have also raised elsewhere (2)].

Relationship of Axis I and II disorders

The relationship between Axis I and Axis II disorders has been conceptualized in a number of different ways. First, Axis II disorders may

Current Insights in Obsessive Compulsive Disorder. Edited by E. Hollander, J. Zohar, D. Marazzati and B. Olivier
© 1994 John Wiley & Sons Ltd

predispose to the development of Axis I disorders, either by increasing vulnerability or by modifying symptomatology. This view is consistent with much early psychoanalytical thinking, which focused on how character traits predispose toward the development of symptoms. Thus, several psychodynamically oriented theorists have viewed obsessive compulsive character as a factor in the development of obsessive compulsive symptoms (4).

A diametrically opposed view can perhaps be traced back to the work of early descriptive psychiatrists, including Kraepelin. In this view, Axis II disorders follow Axis I disorders, constituting either subclinical forms of Axis I disorders or their sequelae. Thus, for example, the International Classification of Diseases, 10th revision (ICD-10) has a category of enduring personality change secondary to chronic disorders. Similarly, certain personality disorder traits have been hypothesized to result from the experience of having OCD (5, 6).

Both these models can be termed "linear", in so far as they emphasize a sequential relationship between Axis I and Axis II disorders, with the one leading to the other. In opposition, a third position emphasizes that neither Axis I nor Axis II disorder is primary to the other. Thus the disorders may have a common etiology, or they may have independent etiologies but nevertheless interact in significant ways.

This third position is supported by recent work demonstrating that both Axis I and Axis II disorders have multifactorial (biological and psychological) underpinnings (7). However, when both Axis I and Axis II result from similar factors, then the very division of the two axes comes into question, and a notion of comorbidity as the co-occurrence of two or more discrete disorders may no longer be suitable. Widiger (8), for example, has suggested that chronic depressive syndromes cannot be separated from longstanding depressive personality on the basis of operational criteria. Similarly, OCD often has a chronic course, so that the feasibility of distinguishing between chronic OCD symptoms and particular personality traits may be questioned.

A number of different methods may be employed to explore empirically these putative relationships between Axis I and Axis II disorders. These methods include study of (a) the prevalence of comorbidity, (b) the course, and (c) the treatment outcome of comorbid disorders. We discuss certain limitations of these approaches in the next section.

Methodological issues

Several authors have pointed out that, in clinical practice, DSM-III diagnoses of personality disorder have relatively low reliability (9, 10). On the other hand, the diagnostic criteria provided by the DSM manuals have clearly encouraged empirical research on personality disorders, and the use of structured interviews to assess personality disorders has led to improved inter-rater reliability. Nevertheless, different structured interviews of personality disorder do not necessarily yield similar results (11, 12). Furthermore, consideration of sources of information other than the patient also has an impact on the results of structured interviews.

Assessment of the prevalence of comorbidity between Axis I and Axis II disorders is even more difficult because, in the presence of an Axis I disorder, there may be distortion of the assessment of Axis II pathology. For example, a current depressive or anxiety syndrome may influence the report of premorbid personality traits, and may overlap phenomenologically with certain personality disorder traits (13, 14).

In addition, DSM criteria for personality disorder have been criticized for lacking a rigorous conceptual and empirical foundation. In studying the relationship between OCD and personality disorder, for example, it may be important to focus not only on categorical personality disorders, but also on dimensional traits.

Another consideration is that the observed relationship between Axis I and II disorders may be highly influenced by sample selection. Patients presenting for inpatient and outpatient treatment of the same Axis I disorder, for example, may have entirely different personality disorder profiles. Similarly, different base rates of OCD in specialty versus general outpatient clinics may affect the degree of overlap observed between OCD and personality disorders.

Longitudinal studies may offer greater hope of unravelling the relationship between Axis I and Axis II disorders. However, the diagnosis of personality disorders in children, and in particular the differential diagnosis of Axis I and Axis II disorders in children, is problematic. Furthermore, the stability of personality disorder traits between childhood and adulthood is a subject of controversy.

Finally, studies of treatment outcome of comorbid Axis I and Axis II disorders often have an intrinsic ambiguity. Poor outcome may be interpreted as a specific effect of personality disorder on Axis I symptoms, as a general effect of personality disorder on coping ability, or as indicative of a more severe Axis I disorder. Conversely, finding that pharmacotherapy leads to resolution of both Axis I and Axis II symptoms may suggest that the underlying Axis II disorder is also responsive to medication, or that a complicated Axis I disorder has resolved.

With these methodological limitations in mind, we now go on to review empirical studies of the relationship between OCD and personality disorders.

Prevalence of comorbidity

Black (15) reviewed several early studies of obsessional neurosis. He reported that, on average, 71% of patients had moderate to marked premorbid obsessional traits. The highest proportion reported was 84%

(16). These studies did not, however, include operational definitions of OCD or obsessive compulsive personality disorder (OCP).

The DSM-III provided clear criteria to distinguish from OCP. Insel (17) reported that, on the basis of clinical history, only seven of 20 OCD patients had clear premorbid obsessive compulsive traits. Rasmussen and Tsuang (18), on the other hand, using a broad semistructured interview with DSM-III Axis II checklists, found that 66% of 44 OCD patients had a personality disorder; 55% of the sample met criteria for OCP. These studies suffer, however, from the lack of standardized personality assessments.

Joffee et al (19), using the self-report Millon Clinical Multiaxial Inventory (MCMI), found that 83% of 23 OCD patients had a personality disorder. Passive–aggressive (61%), avoidant (56%), dependent (56%), and borderline (39%) personality disorders were most common. Only one patient (4%) met criteria for OCP. On comparison with a group of depressed patients, there were no significant differences in personality profile.

Black et al (20) administered the self-report Personality Diagnostic Questionnaire (PDQ) to 21 OCD patients and 42 normal controls. Thirty-three (33%) of OCD patients and 12% of controls had at least one personality disorder. In the OCD patients dependent, histrionic, and borderline personality disorder (all at 24%) were frequent, but no patients had OCP. The OCD patients were significantly more likely than normal controls to have cluster B personality diagnoses or traits, especially borderline personality disorder (five out of 21). Mean PDQ scores for dramatic cluster and anxious cluster traits were higher for patients than for controls.

Mavissakalian et al (21), also using the PDQ, found that 53% of 43 OCD patients received at least one PD diagnosis. The most frequent diagnoses were avoidant (30%), histrionic (26%), dependent (19%), and schizotypal (16%). Only one patient (2%) met criteria for OCP. Patients with a greater number of personality traits were significantly more symptomatic. In regression analyses, the most important correlate of personality disorder was dysphoric mood. Mavissakalian et al (22) also compared PDQ in 51 OCD patients and 187 panic disorder patients. Personality disorder profiles were similar between the two diagnostic groups, although the OCD group had more pronounced cluster C personality traits. The authors concluded that the link between OCD and personality disorder is nonspecific.

While the above studies used standardized assessments of personality, these were self-reported. Pfhol et al (22), using the Structured Interview for DSM-III Personality Disorders (SIDP), found that OCD patients had higher rates of cluster A and cluster C personality disorders (especially passive-aggressive and dependent personality disorder) than did control groups of depressed patients, panic disorder patients, and normal controls. In addition, 19% of 37 OCD patients had borderline personality disorder. The authors argued that differences in distribution of individual personality diagnoses among patients with various Axis I disorders suggest that the criteria for personality disorder measure more than nonspecific psychosocial impairment.

Baer et al (23), also using the SIDP, found that 52% of 96 OCD patients had personality disorder, with mixed, dependent, and histrionic personality disorders most frequently diagnosed. Only 6% of patients had OCP, and five of these had had early-onset OCD. In addition, comparison of the OCD sample with a previous sample of patients with mixed nonpsychotic psychiatric disorders showed no significant differences. However, administration of the SIDP-R, which generates DSM-III-R diagnoses, yielded a higher incidence of OCP (25%). The presence of mixed personality disorder correlated with longer duration of OCD. The authors concluded that there was little evidence to suggest that DSM-III OCP is an invariable premorbid factor in OCD patients. DSM-III-R OCP may be closer to the traditional psychodynamic concept of obsessional personality (24), and was more commonly seen with OCD. Furthermore, the correlation of mixed personality disorder and duration of OCD may reflect behavioral changes secondary to OCD. In a more recent report of 55 OCD patients, Baer et al (25) found that severity of OCD correlated with the presence of a cluster A personality disorder diagnosis, as well as with the total number of personality disorders.

Horesh et al (26) assessed 45 OCD patients using the Structured Clinical Interview for the Diagnosis of Axis II Disorders (SCID-II). Diagnoses were validated by interview with a family member. Seventy-five percent of patients had at least one personality disorder: OCP (17%), histrionic (15%), paranoid (14%), and schizotypal (12%) personality disorders were most common. They also found that 66% of checkers had no personality disorder, whereas patients with mixed symptoms all had personality disorders, especially cluster A personality disorders. The authors therefore suggested that there may be an interaction between type of symptomatology and personality disorder.

While the various studies that used structured diagnostic interviews suffer from the methodological limitation of assessing personality disorder in the presence of an untreated Axis I disorder, they agree on a number of findings. A substantial number of OCD patients meet criteria for at least one comorbid personality disorder. Whether the profile of comorbid personality disorder differs from that seen in other Axis I disorders remains controversial. Nevertheless, the comorbid personality disorder in OCD is most often not OCP. Personality disorders commonly found in OCD include, however, cluster A (e.g. schizotypal), cluster B (e.g. borderline), and cluster C (e.g. passive-aggressive) disorders.

Personality traits

Pfohl et al (27) administered the Tridimensional Personality Questionnaire (TPQ) to OCD patients. This self-report scale has three dimensions—harm-avoidance, novelty-seeking, and reward-dependence—which are thought to reflect serotonergic, dopaminergic, and noradrenergic function, respectively. The OCD patients were found to have high harm-avoidance compared to normal controls. However, there was no association between harm-avoidance and platelet-imipramine binding.

Stein et al (28) administered the TPQ to patients with OCD and related disorders (trichotillomania, Tourette's syndrome) as well as to borderline personality disorder patients. There were no significant differences in scores between groups. The OCD patients, however, had significantly lower scores than other groups on an impulsiveness scale, and borderline patients had significantly higher scores on a venturesomeness scale. Nevertheless, the groups did not differ on measures of aggression. This finding is consistent with a series of studies indicating that a subgroup of OCD patients have increased impulsive-aggression (29).

Rasmussen and Eisen (30) have attempted to define subtypes of OCD that relate phenomenological heterogeneity to Axis I and II comorbidity. They proposed that patients with increased harm avoidance have co-existing anxiety disorders, childhood histories of behavioral inhibition, and dependent and avoidant personality traits. In contrast, patients with the core feature of incompleteness may have comorbid tics, and tend to have compulsive personality traits as children. A third group of OCD patients are characterized by pathological doubt, and may have different degrees of harm avoidance and incompleteness.

The characterization of specific subgroups of OCD patients on the basis of both clinical features and underlying neurobiology clearly remains a task for the future. Inability to determine goal completion and exaggeration of goal discrepancy are, for example, theoretically possible psychological dysfunctions in OCD for which there is some evidence of neurobiological base (31). Rasmussen and Eisen (30) provide an interesting schema to guide empirical work in this area.

Psychometric studies

Slade (32) reviewed early psychometric studies of obsessive compulsive patients and concluded that there was good evidence in favor of a distinction between OCD and OCP. In a more recent review, Pollack (33) came to a similar conclusion. He noted, for example, that obsessive compulsive traits relate inversely with neuroticism, whereas obsessive compulsive symptoms correlate positively with neuroticism.

Family studies

Insel et al (34) reviewed seven studies that included a cumulative total of more than 500 OCD patients. Obsessive compulsive traits were found in 3.3–37.0% of parents of OCD patients. Rasmussen and Tsuang (18) found that 11% of parents were judged by OCD patients as having significant obsessive compulsive traits. However, many of these studies did not include comparison with control groups.

Clark and Bolton (35) found that parents of adolescents with OCD had significantly higher scores on the trait scale of the Leyton Obsessional Inventory (LOI) than normal adults, but did not differ from parents of adolescents with other anxiety disorders. Thus, while some of these data are consistent with a link between OCP and OCD, such a link has not been firmly established.

Treatment studies

A retrospective analysis of 43 OCD patients demonstrated that those with comorbid schizotypal personality disorder (33%) were comparatively unresponsive to both pharmacotherapy (36) and behavioral therapy (37). Similarly, Hermesh et al (38) reported that in 39 OCD patients, all of those with borderline personality (20%) failed to respond to either pharmacotherapy or behavior therapy, primarily because of poor compliance. Pfohl et al (6) noted that in 22 OCD patients who received the SIDP prior to treatment with clomipramine, 11 responders had significantly fewer total Axis II criteria than did the 11 nonresponders.

Mavissakalian et al (39) compared 27 patients on the self-rated PDQ before and after 12 weeks of clomipramine treatment. Treatment was accompanied by improvement on several personality variables. Improvement in personality functioning was significantly greater in responders than nonresponders. The authors concluded that severity of OCD can in fact confound assessment of Axis II disorders. However, they noted that personality profile remained essentially the same after treatment. In addition, Mavissakalian et al (39) did not find that personality disorder was predictive of treatment response.

Ricciardi et al (40) reported on assessment of personality disorder with the SIDP-R in 17 OCD patients with personality disorder before and after treatment. Nine of 10 responders no longer met criteria for personality disorder, while five of seven nonresponders continued to meet criteria for personality disorder. This group also reported (25) on 55 OCD patients who received the SIDP prior to entry into a clomipramine study. They found no difference in treatment outcome between patients with no personality disorder and those with at least one personality disorder. The presence of schizotypal, borderline, and avoidant personality disorder, along with total number of personality disorders did, however, predict poor treatment outcome.

The phenomenon of comorbid personality disorders in OCD as predictors of poor treatment outcome has therefore been found in several studies. As discussed earlier, this finding is often ambiguous, suggesting either a specific effect of the Axis II disorder, or increased severity of the OCD. The specificity of the personality disorders that do affect treatment outcome (schizotypal, borderline) suggests that the first explanation may be correct. However, correlation of the severity of OCD with presence of such personality disorders suggests that the second explanation may be correct. A more complex model, that entails an overlap in the biological bases for OCD and these personality disorders may ultimately be useful, but presently requires further empirical investigation.

Discussion

Given limitations in the reliability and validity of assessment of Axis II disorders in the presence of Axis I disorders, research on their comorbidity seems theoretically difficult. This theoretical difficulty is given some empirical confirmation by the recent finding that personality disorder is no longer found in OCD treatment responders, but remains in OCD treatment nonresponders (40). On the other hand, comorbidity research may provide a useful focus on the heterogeneity of OCD.

A number of tentative conclusions may be drawn from this review. Most patients with OCD have at least one personality disorder. Whether the profile of comorbid personality disorder differs from that seen in other Axis I disorders is an issue that deserves further research. Nevertheless, the comorbid personality disorder in OCD is most often not OCP, and evidence for a clear relationship between OCD and OCP also fails to emerge from psychometric and family studies. Personality disorders commonly found in OCD do, however, include cluster A (e.g. schizotypal), cluster B (e.g. borderline), and cluster C (e.g. passive-aggressive) disorders. Furthermore, the presence of certain of these personality disorders in OCD appears to predict poor response to treatment.

Until recently, the predominant view of the relationship between obsessive compulsive symptoms and traits has been that of psychoanalytical theory. In this view, an obsessive compulsive personality structure predisposes to obsessive compulsive symptoms (4). However, as noted above, there is little evidence from empirical work on OCD patients for a link with OCP. In addition, OCP has been reported in association with a variety of Axis I disorders (41–43). Nevertheless, the lack of association between OCD and OCP may not hold for all patient samples; Oldham and Skodol (43) report an association between OCD and OCP in patients who present for treatment of personality disorders.

Some evidence is perhaps consistent with the hypothesis that the presence of OCD itself leads to certain personality disorder traits. These may be relatively nonspecific (23), or may involve OCP (5) or dependent personality traits (6). Such traits may improve with OCD treatment (40). Future longitudinal studies may lead to more substantial evidence for this sequence.

Finally, it may be useful to conceptualise some personality disorders and OCD as having overlapping neurobiological bases. It is possible to speculate, for example, that OCD with comorbid cluster A personality disorder involves dopaminergic as well as serotonergic pathways. Further empirical work is, however, necessary in order to develop such models, and to determine more clearly the clinical and neurobiological heterogeneity of OCD.

References

1. Docherty JP, Fiester SJ, Shea T. Syndrome diagnosis and personality disorder. Annu Rev Psychiatry; 1986; 5; 315–355.
2. Stein DJ, Hollander E, Skodol AE. Anxiety disorders and personality disorders: A review. J Pers Disord 1993; 7: 87–104.
3. Baer L, Jenike MA. Personality disorders in obsessive compulsive disorder. Psychiatr Clin North Am 1992; 15: 803–812.
4. Salzman L. Obsessional Personality. Science House, New York, 1968.
5. Swedo SE, Rapoport JL, Leonard H et al. Obsessive–compulsive disorder in children and adolescents: clinical phenomenology of 70 consecutive cases. Arch Gen Psychiatry 1989; 46: 335–341.
6. Pfohl B, Black DW, Noyes R, Coryell WH, Barrash J. Axis I and axis II comorbidity findings: implications for validity in Personality Disorders. In: New Perspectives on Diagnostic Validity (ed Oldham JM). Washington, DC, American Psychiatric Press, 1991, pp 147–161.
7. Gunderson JG, Pollack WS. Conceptual risk of the axis I-II division. In: Biological Response Styles: Clinical Implications (eds Klar H, Siever LJ). American Psychiatric Press, Washington DC, 1985.
8. Widiger TA. The categorical distinction between personality and affective disorders. J Pers Disord 1989; 3: 77–91.
9. Spitzer RL, Forman JBW, Nee J. DSM-III field trails, I: initial interrater diagnostic reliability. Am J Psychiatry 1979; 136: 815–817.
10. Mellsop G, Varghese F, Joshua S et al. The reliability of axis II of DSM-III. Am J Psychiatry 1982; 139: 1360–1361.
11. O'Boyd M, Self D. A comparison of two interviews for DSM-III-R personality disorders. Psychiatry Res 1990; 32: 85–92.
12. Skodol AE, Oldham JM, Rosnick L et al. Diagnosis of DSM-III-R personality disorders: A comparison of two structured interviews. Int J Methods Psychiatry Res 1991; 1: 13–26.
13. Hirschfeld RMA, Klerman GL, Clayton PJ et al. Assessing personality: Effects of the depressive state on trait measurements. Am J Psychiatry 1983; 140: 695–699.

14. Reich J, Noyes R Jr, Coryell W, O'Gorman TW. The effect of state anxiety on personality measurement. Am J Psychiatry 1986; 143: 760–763.
15. Black A. The natural history of obsessional neurosis in: Obsessional States (ed Beech HR). Methuen, London, 1974, pp 19–54.
16. Ingram IM. The obsessional personality and obsessional illness. Am J Psychiatry 1961; 117: 1016–1019.
17. Insel TR. Obsessive–compulsive disorder—five clinical questions and a suggested approach. Comp Psychiatry 1982; 23: 241–251.
18. Rasmussen SA, Tsuang MT. Clinical characteristics and family history in DSM-III obsessive-compulsive disorder. Am J Psychiatry 1986; 143: 317–322.
19. Joffee RT, Swinson RP, Regan JJ. Personality features of obsessive–compulsive disorder. Am J Psychiatry 1988; 145: 1127–1129.
20. Black DW, Yates WR, Noyes R, Pfohl B, Kelley M. DSM-III personality disorder in obsessive-compulsive study volunteers: A controlled study. J Pers Disord 1989; 3: 58–62.
21. Mavissakalian M, Hamann MS, Jones B. Correlates of DSM-III personality disorder in obsessive–compulsive disorder. Comp Psychiatry 1990; 31: 481–489.
22. Mavissakalian M, Hamann MS, Jones B. A comparison of DSM-III personality disorders in panic/agoraphobia and obsessive–compulsive disorder. Comp Psychiatry 1990; 31: 238–244.
23. Baer L, Jenike MA, Ricciardi JN, Holland AD, Seymour RJ, Minichiello WE, Buttolph ML. Standardized assessment of personality disorders in obsessive-compulsive disorder. Arch Gen Psychiatry 1990; 47: 826–830.
24. Goldstein WN. Obsessive–compulsive behavior, DSM-III and a psychodynamic classification of psychopathology. Am J Psychother 1985; 39: 346–359.
25. Baer L, Jenike MA, Black DW, Treece C, Rosenfeld R, Greist J. Effects of axis II diagnoses on treatment outcome with clomipramine in 55 patients with obsessive-compulsive disorder. Arch Gen Psychiatry 1992; 49: 862–866.
26. Horesh N, Kimchi N, Kindler S, Sason Y, Zohar J. Personality traits of OCD patients. Presented at the First International Obsessive–Compulsive Disorder Congress, Capri, Italy, Mar 1993.
27. Pfohl B, Black D, Noyes R et al. A test of the tridimensional personality theory: association with diagnosis and platelet imipramine binding in obsessive–compulsive disorder. Biol Psychiatry 1990; 28: 41–46.
28. Stein DJ, Hollander E, Islam MN et al. Impulsive and compulsive symptoms in the obsessive–compulsive spectrum disorders. Presented at the First International Obsessive–Compulsive Disorder Congress, Capri, Italy, Mar 1993.
29. Stein DJ, Hollander E. Impulsive–aggression and obsessive–compulsive disorder. Psychiatr Ann 1993; 23: 1–7.
30. Rasmussen SA, Eisen J. Heterogeneity and comorbidity in OCD: Relationship to core psychopathology. Presented at the First International Obsessive–Compulsive Disorder Congress, Capri, Italy, Mar 1993.
31. Stein DJ, Hollander E. Cognitive science and obsessive–compulsive disorder. In: Cognitive Science and Clinical Disorders (ed Stein DJ, Young JE). Academic Press, San Diego, Florida, pp 235–247.
32. Slade PD. Psychometric studies of obsessional illness and obsessional personality. In: Obsessional States (ed Beech HR). Methuen, London, 1974, pp 95–109.
33. Pollack JM. Obsessive–compulsive personality: A review. Psychol Bull 1979; 86: 225–241.

34. Insel TR, Hoover C, Murphy DL. Parents of patients with obsessive-compulsive disorder. Psychol Med 1983; 13: 807–811.
35. Clark DA, Bolton D. Obsessive–compulsive adolescents and their parents: A psychometric study. J. Child Psychol Psychiatry, 1985; 26: 267–276.
36. Jenike MA, Baer L, Minichiello WE, Schwartz CE, Carey RJ. Concomitant obsessive–compulsive disorder and schizotypal personality disorder. Am J Psychiatry 1986; 143: 530–532.
37. Minichiello WE, Baer L, Jenike MA. Schizotypal personality disorder: a poor prognostic indicator for behavior therapy in the treatment of obsessive-compulsive disorder. J Anxiety Disord 1987; 1: 273–276.
38. Hermesh H, Shahar A, Munitz H. Obsessive–compulsive disorder and borderline personality disorder. Am J Psychiatry 1987; 144: 120–121.
39. Mavissakalian M, Hamann MS, Jones B. DSM-III personality disorders in obsessive–compulsive disorder: changes with treatment. Comp Psychiatry 1990; 31: 432–437.
40. Ricciardi JN, Baer L, Jenike MA, Fischer SC, Sholtz D, Buttoph ML. Changes in DSM-III-R axis II diagnoses following treatment of obsessive–compulsive disorder. Am J Psychiatry 1992; 149: 829–831.
41. Pollack J. Relationship of obsessive–compulsive personality to obsessive-compulsive disorder: a review of the literature. J Psychol 1987; 12: 137–148.
42. Mauri M, Armani A, Cecconi D, Sarno N, Zambotto S. Obsessive–compulsive personality disorder and obsessive–compulsive disorder: A complex relationship. Presented at the First International Obsessive–Compulsive Disorder Congress, Capri, Italy, Mar 1993.
43. Oldham JM, Skodol AE. OCD/OCPD comorbidity. Presented at the First International Obsessive–Compulsive Disorder Congress, Capri, Italy, Mar 1993.

5 OBSESSIVE COMPULSIVE RELATED DISORDERS

Daphne Simeon, Eric Hollander and Lisa Cohen

College of Physicians and Surgeons, Columbia University, New York
State Psychiatric Institute, NY, USA

Introduction

On the basis of shared features with obsessive compulsive disorder
(OCD), such as clinical symptoms, associated features (age of onset,
clinical course and comorbidity), presumed etiology, familial transmission, and response to selective pharmacological or behavioral treatments,
the notion of obsessive compulsive related disorders (OCRD) has
emerged (1). This overlap provides evidence to support a relationship
between OCD and Ocrds, but does not establish a definitive relationship. Alternatively, the dimension of compulsivity and impulsivity may
be viewed as a spectrum of disorders having in common the inability to
delay repetitive behaviors or to resist urges to carry out repetitive behaviors. If one conceptualizes a dimension of harm avoidance, compulsive
risk-aversive disorders occupy one endpoint, whereas impulsive risk-
seeking disorders occupy the other endpoint.

This chapter briefly reviews and presents state-of-the-art findings on a
number of Ocrds. These disorders are characterized by obsessive
thoughts or preoccupations with body weight (anorexia nervosa), body
appearance (body dysmorphic disorder), or the self (depersonalization
disorder); or by stereotypic, ritualistic or driven behaviors such as
Tourette's syndrome, sexual compulsions, pathological gambling, or
impulsive personality disorders. In other words, Ocrds span various
categories of psychiatric disorders, such as somatoform, eating, dissociat-
ive, impulse control, psychotic, and personality disorders.

Of particular interest is pharmacological dissection which may support

Current Insights in Obsessive Compulsive Disorder. Edited by E. Hollander, J. Zohar,
D. Marazzati and B. Olivier
© 1994 John Wiley & Sons Ltd

or refute a relationship between OCD and OCRDs. Potent serotonin reuptake inhibitors (SRIs) such as clomipramine, fluoxetine, fluvoxamine, paroxetine, and sertraline are effective in up to 60% of OCD patients. Treatment studies of the OCRDs are less well characterized than those of OCD, and for the most part consist of open clinical series. Compulsive-style disorders such as OCD, body dysmorphic disorder, depersonalization, and anorexia appear to respond preferentially to SRIs. However, it remains to be seen whether impulsive-style disorders, such as pathological gambling, sexual compulsions and paraphilias, and impulsive personality disorders have an equal responsivity to this treatment approach. In addition, most studies of OCRDs and SRIs have focused on clomipramine and fluoxetine. These two medications may not be effective or tolerable for all such patients, and therefore the emergence of newer SRIs such as fluvoxamine is expected to expand the repertory of pharmacological options available to clinicians in treating such disorders (2).

Large-scale phenomenological, biological, and treatment studies are still needed to definitively characterize this spectrum of fascinating disorders. In addition, response to antiobsessional agents is not sufficient to document a link between disorders, since depression, panic, and social phobia also respond to SRIs. Therefore, a preferential response to serotonin rather than norepinephrine (noradrenaline) reuptake blockers, coupled with phenomenological and biological similarities, would better define this spectrum.

Anorexia nervosa

Anorexia nervosa is a serious psychiatric disorder, predominant in women, characterized by the relentless pursuit of thinness and obsessive fears of being fat. As presented by Kaye et al (3), four lines of evidence support a relationship between anorexia and OCD.

First, there are phenomenological similarities between the two. Patients with anorexia are typically described as rigid, perfectionistic, restrained, and compliant–defiant, traits that may precede or continue after the episodes of anorexia, and are reminiscent of obsessive compulsive symptomatology. In addition, anorexics score higher than normals on inventories measuring obsessive compulsive features, such as the Yale–Brown Obsessive–Compulsive Scale, demonstrating obsessions and compulsions outside of the eating disorder (4).

Second, patients presenting with OCD may have an increased incidence of prior anorexia nervosa (5), or may score higher than normals on eating disorder psychopathology (6).

Third, as in OCD, the serotonergic system has been implicated in the pathogenesis of anorexia. Animal studies show that serotonin mediates satiety. Neurochemical studies of patients previously suffering from anorexia but restored to normal weight have revealed preliminary findings similar to OCD. Both elevated cerebrospinal fluid (CSF) 5-hydroxyindoleacetic acid (5-HIAA) (7) and a blunted response to the partial serotonin agonist *meta*-chlorophenyl piperazine (mCPP) (3) have been reported. However, in contrast to OCD, the behavioral response to mCPP challenge consisted of reduced obsessionality and body weight concerns (3).

Fourth, open trials of SRIs in patients with anorexia have suggested a therapeutic response. In an open trial of fluoxetine by Kaye et al (8), 27 out of 31 patients had a good or partial response over a 1-year follow-up period. Of interest, restrictor-type anorexics did significantly better than bulimic-type anorexics, possibly suggesting that fluoxetine was beneficial via its antiobsessional properties. However, there is not a specific response to SRIs in anorexia, since some studies have documented improvement with tricyclic and monoamine oxidase inhibitor (MAOI) antidepressants as well. Controlled trials comparing response to SRIs and non-SRIs are needed for more definitive conclusions.

Body dysmorphic disorder

Body dysmorphic disorder (BDD) is characterized by a grossly excessive preoccupation with an imagined or greatly exaggerated defect in appearance other than body weight. As with anorexia, several lines of evidence suggest a very close relationship to OCD, and some investigators have argued that BDD may even comprise a subtype of OCD.

Symptomatically, patients with BDD are obsessively preoccupied with various bodily foci such as the face, hair, torso, extremities or sexual parts. Similarly to OCD patients, those with BDD may engage in various ritualistic behaviours which may transiently decrease anxiety, such as compulsive mirror-checking and excessive, ritualized grooming and dressing behaviors. Also similar is the age of onset and the usually chronic course of the two disorders. Phillips et al (9) have pointed out several differences between BDD and OCD: BDD preoccupations usually involve less insight, BDD rituals tend to be less anxiety relieving, and patients with BDD seem to suffer from greater social impairment and comorbid social phobia than OCD patients.

There is also significant comorbidity between OCD and BDD. The DSM-IV Field Trials for OCD found that 37% of OCD patients at one site also met criteria for BDD (E Hollander, unpublished data). Reversely, Phillips et al (9) reported that 21% of BDD patients had comorbid OCD. There is also a high rate of family histories of OCD in BDD patients.

Although very little work has been done so far on the neurochemistry of BDD, preliminary data from E Hollander et al (unpublished) suggest some overlap with OCD with regard to response to mCPP, neuropsychiatric impairment and regional blood flow on SPECT.

Controlled treatment studies have not been conducted in BDD. However, a review of both prospective and retrospective open trials reported in the existing literature reveals that the disorder is for the most part refractory to conventional pharmacotherapy, including tricyclics, MAOIs, benzodiazepines, and neuroleptics. Phillips et al (10) have reported a preferential response to SRIs in a large sample of patients with BDD. Fifty-six percent of SRI trials led to moderate improvement or remission, compared with 5% with all other medications (9). In our survey of the published literature of 35 treatment trials of clomipramine or fluoxetine for BDD or delusional disorder somatic type, 66% of patients showed a significant benefit (E Hollander, unpublished data). Our open treatment data with SRIs in 23 BDD patients also support this favorable treatment outcome: tricyclic antidepressants resulted in no change in BDD severity in 18 BDD patients, whereas clomipramine ($n = 15$), fluoxetine ($n = 14$), and fluvoxamine ($n = 6$) all resulted in much improved BDD severity (11).

Depersonalization disorder

Depersonalization disorder (DPD) is diagnosed, according to the DSM-IV, when an individual experiences persistent or recurrent depersonalization which is not purely secondary to another disorder. Depersonalization is the experience of detachment from one's own sense of self, body, cognitions, or affects, and is often accompanied by derealization. Previously viewed as a symptom that may accompany anxiety, panic, depression or psychosis, depersonalization is becoming increasingly recognized as an autonomous, although rare, syndrome with characteristic clinical characteristics, associated features, course and outcome (12).

Torch (13, 14) has described the phenomenological relationship between depersonalization and obsessive compulsive symptoms. He conceptualizes persistent depersonalization as a state in which the self becomes the obsessive focus of incessant and inexorable self-scrutiny. Patients with DPD engage in a ceaseless pattern of checking and rechecking separate observing and acting selves. In a systematic assessment of psychopathology in a small series of patients with primary DPD, Simeon and Hollander (15) reported comorbidity with OCD and obsessive compulsive personality disorder, as well as with borderline personality disorder and histories of childhood trauma.

Limited neurobiological correlations and findings have suggested serotonergic dysfunction in DPD, such as its association with marijuana and LSD use and with migraine headaches, and a case report of a DPD patient with hyperfrontality as is found in OCD (16). Pharmacological treatment studies may also suggest serotonergic involvement. Although DPD is typically refractory to medications, open trials have reported efficacy for SRIs (17). Simeon and Hollander (15) are conducting a controlled comparison of clomipramine and desipramine in primary DPD, and preliminarily report that clomipramine appears promising although difficult to tolerate, as these patients have a very heightened sensitivity to uncomfortable physical sensations.

The overlap of obsessive compulsive and psychotic symptoms

There are three major areas of overlap between obsessive compulsive and psychotic symptoms: delusional OCD, OCD with schizotypal personality, and schizophrenia with comorbid obsessive compulsive symptoms or OCD.

First, a minority of OCD patients lack any insight into the irrationality of their obsessions and compulsions, and thus have delusional OCD without other psychotic features (18). Such patients have not been found to differ from nonpsychotic OCD patients in illness course or demographic features (19).

Second, both retrospective and, more recently, prospective studies have determined that a percentage of OCD patients has comorbid schizotypal personality disorder, which is a predictor of poor pharmacological and behavioral OCD treatment outcome (20).

Third, the presence of comorbid obsessive compulsive symptoms or OCD in a proportion of patients with primary psychotic disorders, especially schizophrenia, has been very neglected until recently, even though there are data suggesting that schizophrenic patients with OC symptoms have a poorer long-term outcome than schizophrenic patients without OC symptoms (21). Reanalysis of the Epidemiologic Catchment Area Study data indicate that up to 26% of schizophrenic individuals may also meet criteria for OCD (22). Hwang et al (23) reported that schizophrenics with obsessive compulsive features have more negative symptoms, impaired abstraction, and stereotypic symptoms than schizophrenics without OC features. Sasson et al (24) presented the results of an open treatment trial demonstrating a beneficial effect of the addition of clomipramine to the ongoing neuroleptic regimen of schizophrenic patients with OC symptoms. There were substantial reductions in previously persistent OC symptoms, without exacerbation of psychosis. These findings await replication with double-blind trials. They emphasize the possible benefits of polypharmacy in subgroups of psychotic patients with obsessive compulsive symptomatology, and the importance of targeting symptom clusters rather than just syndromes in the treatment of chronic psychotic conditions.

Tourette's syndrome

There is a large literature regarding the presence of OCD symptoms in Tourette's syndrome (TS), and conceptual and methodological issues in studies comparing TS and OCD have been described (25). Leonard et al (26) followed patients with childhood onset OCD, but without tics, over a 2- to 7-year period, and found that 59% had tics at follow up, while eight males had developed TS. Patients with tics had a higher CSF 5-HIAA: homovanillic acid (HVA) ratio. Thus, OCD and TS may be alternative manifestations of the same underlying illness at least in some patients.

Recently, Leckman et al (27, 28) have turned their attention to the premonitory sensory and mental "just right" phenomena associated with compulsive behaviors in TS patients, as an area of investigation that may shed light on the relationship between TS and OCD. Out of 134 patients with TS, 23% had comorbid OCD and 46% had obsessive compulsive symptoms (OCS). Interestingly, a significantly higher proportion of the TS/OCD subjects had an urge to perform compulsions until they were "just right" compared to the subjects with TS/obsessive compulsive symptoms (OCS). As expected, the subjects with compulsive urges also had a significantly higher mean Yale–Brown Obsessive Compulsive Scale (Y-BOCS) score than those without, while they did not differ in tic severity. Most subjects could readily distinguish these "just right" mental urges from the bodily premonitory urges preceding tics. The investigators concluded that both tics and compulsions are frequently preceded or associated with the sudden intrusion of some type of urge, either to complete a muscular movement or to perform a specific task, respectively. Therefore, these urges may be evidence of a continuum linking the premonitory sensations of tics to the mental need for things to look "just right", supporting a relationship between TS and OCD.

Thus, there are phenomenological, familial, and comorbidity links between TS and OCD. While SRIs are effective in the treatment of obsessions, compulsions, and anxiety associated with TS, efficacy in treatment of the tics themselves has not been demonstrated. Clearly, neurotransmitters other than serotonin, particularly dopamine, may be critical in the pathogenesis of TS.

Sexual obsessions, addictions and paraphilias

Disorders of sexuality are phenomenologically very diverse, spanning the range of obsessions to paraphilias and nonparaphilic sexual addictions such as compulsive masturbation and promiscuity. It is believed that the overlap among individuals with paraphilias and nonparaphilic sexual addictions may be extensive (29). Pharmacotherapeutic dissection may offer one way to clarify the relationship between these various disturbances of sexuality.

Stein et al (30) and Stein and Hollander (31) retrospectively reviewed patients with various sexual disorders who were treated with SRIs (clomipramine, fluoxetine, or fluvoxamine). The most robust pharmacological response was observed in patients with ego-dystonic, intrusive sexual obsessions typical of OCD. Patients with paraphilias showed some improvement, but had a less robust pharmacological response. Finally, patients with nonparaphilic sexual addictions showed some improvement on low-dose SRIs but tended to worsen on higher doses, as may be more characteristic of patients at the impulsive end of the compulsive–impulsive spectrum. Similarly, Kafka and Prentky (32) have reported that patients with paraphilias respond favorably to open fluoxetine treatment at an average dose of 40 mg, without improvement on further dosage increase if relapse occurs. Controlled trials are needed to demonstrate whether SRI efficacy is selective for sexual disorders. In a small double-blind crossover study of clomipramine and desipramine, both medications resulted in a similar reduction in paraphilic urges and behaviors (33).

Pathological gambling

Pathological gambling (PG) is a common and frequently debilitating illness which is formally classified in the DSM-IV as an impulse control disorder. Although the neurobiology of PG has only recently started to receive more attention, the serotonergic and the noradrenergic systems have been implicated, in association with impulsivity and increased arousal, respectively. Furthermore, the repetitive and compulsive nature of the behavior, even when it becomes more ego-dystonic, raise the question of the relationship between OCD and PG.

In a preliminary series of patients with PG, DeCaria et al (34) found 9% to have comorbid OCD. On neuropsychiatric evaluation, the subjects were characterized by visuospatial impairment consistent with that found in OCD.

Preliminary neurochemical challenge studies and pharmacotherapy results have also suggested a relation to OCD. In one study of patients with PG, there was a blunted prolactin response to clomipramine (35). On the other hand, DeCaria et al (34) preliminarily reported an increased prolactin response to mCPP in pathological gamblers, coupled with decreased gambling urges, findings opposite from those in OCD. Preliminary results of a double-blind trial of clomipramine versus placebo in PG indicate that clomipramine may be a promising treatment, at least for some patients (36).

Impulsive personality disorders

There is an extensive literature linking impulsive and aggressive behaviors to central serotonergic dysfunction. Individuals with histories of suicide attempts, regardless of diagnoses other than bipolar disorder, have elevated CSF 5-HIAA (37). In completed violent suicides, reduced [^{3}H]imipramine binding and increased serotonin-2 (5-HT$_2$) receptor binding has been found in the frontal cortex (38). An inverse correlation has been found between CSF 5-HIAA and lifetime history of aggressive behaviors in patients with personality disorders (39). An inverse correlation has also been found between prolactin response to serotonin agonists (fenfluramine and buspirone) and impulsive aggression (40, 41). In addition, there is preliminary evidence suggesting that a reduction in 5-HT system function may be a familial inherited trait predisposing to impulsive aggression (42).

Thus, serotonergic dysregulation has been extensively implicated both at the impulsive and the compulsive end of the compulsive–impulsive spectrum. Accordingly, of interest is the finding that a subgroup of individuals with OCD in a large epidemiological sample also met criteria for antisocial personality disorder (E Hollander, unpublished data). Furthermore, preliminary small open trials have suggested that the SRI fluoxetine may be of benefit in treating the impulsive symptoms characteristic of borderline and related personality disorders (43, 44).

Coccaro et al (45) elaborated on the obscurities of the specific type of serotonergic dysfunction found in compulsive versus impulsive symptomatology. In the future, more specific probes will have to be systematically assessed for both populations, in order to determine presynaptic, postsynaptic, and net function at specific brain sites in compulsive and impulsive pathology.

Acknowledgments

This work was supported in part by a NARSAD Young Investigator Award (D. Simeon) and by a NIMH Research Scientist Development Award MH-00750 (E. Hollander).

References

1. Hollander E (ed.). Obsessive–Compulsive Related Disorders. American Psychiatric Press, Washington DC, 1993.
2. Hollander E, Cohen L, Stein DJ, Simeon D, Hwang M, DeCaria C. Fluvoxamine treatment of obsessive–compulsive related disorders. Ann Clin Psychiatry [in press].
3. Kaye WH, Weltzin TE, Hsu LKG. Is anorexia nervosa related to obsessive–compulsive disorder and/or altered serotinin activity? Presented at First

International Obsessive–Compulsive Disorder Congress, Capri, Italy, Mar 1993

4. Kaye WH, Weltzin T, Hsu LK, Bulik C, McConaha C, Sobkiewicz T. Patients with anorexia nervosa have elevated scores on the Yale–Brown Obsessive–Compulsive Scale. Int J Eating Disord 1992; 12: 57–62.

5. Kasvikis YG, Tsakiris F, Marks IM, Basoglu M, Noshirvani HF. Past history of anorexia nervosa in women with obsessive–compulsive disorder. Int J Eating Disorders 1986; 5: 1069–1075.

6. Piggott TA, Altemus M, Rubenstein CS et al. Symptoms of eating disorders in patients with obsessive–compulsive disorder. Am J Psychiatry 1992; 149: 1552–1557.

7. Kaye WH, Gwirtsman HE, George DT, Ebert MH. Altered serotonin activity in anorexia nervosa after long-term weight restoration: Does elevated CSF 5-HIAA correlate with rigid and obsessive behavior? Arch Gen Psychiatry 1991; 48: 556–562.

8. Kaye WH, Weltzin TE, Hsu LKG, Bulik CM. An open trial of fluoxetine in patients with anorexia nervosa. J Clin Psychiatry 1991; 52: 464–471.

9. Phillips KA, McElroy SL, Keck PE, Pope HG, Hudson JI. Body dysmorphic disorder: 74 cases of imagined ugliness. Presented at First International Obsessive–Compulsive Disorder Congress, Capri, Italy, Mar 1993.

10. Phillips KA, McElroy S, Keck PE, Pope HG, Hudson JI. Body dysmorphic disorder: 30 cases of imagined ugliness. Am J Psychiatry 1993; 150: 302–308.

11. Hollander E, Cohen L, Simeon D, Rosen J, DeCaria C, Stein DJ. Fluvoxamine treatment of body dysmorphic disorder [letter]. J Clin Psychopharm [in press].

12. Simeon D, Hollander E. Depersonalization disorder. Psychiatr Ann [in press].

13. Torch E. Review of the relationship between obsession and depersonalization. Acta Psychiatr Scand 1978; 58: 191–198.

14. Torch E. Depersonalization syndrome: A discussion of essential components and treatment. Psychiatr Q 1982; 36: 249–258.

15. Simeon D, Hollander E. Depersonalization disorder and self-mutilation. Presented at First International Obsessive–Compulsive Disorder Congress, Capri, Italy, Mar 1993.

16. Hollander E, Carrasco JL, Mullen LS et al. Left hemispheric activation in depersonalization disorder: a case report. Biol Psychiatry 1992; 31: 1157–1162.

17. Hollander E, Liebowitz MR, DeCaria CM et al. Treatment of depersonalization with serotonin reuptake blockers. J Clin Psychopharmacol 1990; 10: 200–203.

18. Insel TR, Akiskal HS. Obsessive–compulsive disorder with psychotic features: A phenomenologic analysis. Am J Psychiatry 1986; 143: 1527–1533.

19. Eisen J, Rasmussen SA. OCD with delusions. Presented at the 146th APA Annual Meeting, San Francisco, May 1993.

20. Jenike MA, Baer L, Minichiello WE, Ricciardi JN. Schizotypal personality disorder and OCD. Presented at the 146th APA Annual Meeting, San Francisco, May 1993.

21. Fenton WS, McGlasham TH. The prognostic significance of obsessive–compulsive symptoms in schizophrenia. Am J Psychiatry 1986; 143: 437–441.

22. Pato MT, Dowling FG, Jandorf L, Pato CN. Dual diagnosis: OCD and schizophrenia in the ECA study. Presented at the 146th APA Annual Meeting, San Francisco, May 1993.

23. Hwang MY, Hollander E, Stein DJ, Simeon D, DeCaria M. Schizophrenia

with obsessive compulsive features. Presented at the 146th APA Annual Meeting, San Francisco, May 1993.

24. Sasson Y, Dolberg O, Kindler S, Cohen R, Zohar J. Schizophrenia with obsessive–compulsive symptoms: pharmacological approach to treatment. Presented at the First International Obsessive–Compulsive Disorder Congress, Capri, Italy, Mar 1993.

25. Hollander E, Liebowitz MR, DeCaria C. Conceptual and methodological issues in studies of obsessive–compulsive and Tourette's disorders. Psychiatr Devel 1989; 4: 267–296.

26. Leonard HL, Lenane MC, Swedo SE, Rettew DC, Gershon ES, Rapoport JL. Tics and Tourette's disorder: A 2- to 7-year follow-up of 554 obsessive-compulsive children. Am J Psychiatry 1992; 149: 1244–1251.

27. Leckman JF, Walker DE, Cohen DJ. Premonitory urges in Tourette's syndrome. Am J Psychiatry 1993; 150: 98–102.

28. Leckman JF, Walker DE, Goodman WK, Rasmussen SA, Pauls DL, Cohen DJ. "Just right" perceptions associated with compulsive behavior in Tourette's syndrome and obsessive compulsive disorder. Presented at First International Obsessive–Compulsive Disorder Congress, Capri, Italy, Mar 1993.

29. Kafka MP, Prentky R. A comparative study of nonparaphilic sexual addictions and paraphilias in men. J Clin Psychiatry 1992; 53: 345–350.

30. Stein DJ, Hollander E, Anthony DT et al. Serotonergic medications for sexual obsessions, sexual addictions, and paraphilias. J Clin Psychiatry 1992; 53: 267–271.

31. Stein D, Hollander E. Lust, gluttony, jealousy, and OCD. Presented at First International Obsessive–Compulsive Disorder Congress, Capri, Italy, Mar 1993.

32. Kafka MP, Prentky RA. Fluoxetine treatment of nonparaphilic sexual addictions and paraphilias in men. J Clin Psychiatry 1992; 53: 351–358.

33. Kreusi MJP, Fine S, Valladares L, Phillips RA, Rapoport JL. Paraphilias: A double-blind crossover comparison of clomipramine versus desipramine. Arch Sex Behav 1992; 21: 587–593.

34. DeCaria CM, Stein DJ, Cohen L, Simeon D, Hwang M, Hollander E. Psychobiology of pathological gambling. Presented at First International Obsessive–Compulsive Disorder Congress, Capri, Italy, Mar 1993.

35. Moreno I, Saiz-Ruiz J, Lopez-Ibor JJ. Serotonin and gambling dependence. Human Psychopharmacol 1991; 6 (suppl): 9–12.

36. Hollander E, Frenkel M, DeCaria CM, Trungold S, Stein DJ. Treatment of pathological gambling with clomipramine [letter]. Am J Psychiatry 1992; 149: 710–711.

37. Asberg M, Schalling D, Traksman-Bendz L, Wagner A. Psychobiology of suicide, impulsivity, and related phenomena. In: Psychopharmacology: Third Generation of Progress (ed Meltzer HY). Raven Press, New York, 1987.

38. Stanley M, Viggilio J, Gershon S. Tritiated imipramine binding sites are decreased in the frontal cortex of suicides. Science 1982; 216: 1337–1339.

39. Brown GL, Ebert MH, Goyer PF et al. Aggression, suicide and serotonin: Relationships to CSF amine metabolites. Am J Psychiatry 1982; 139: 741–746.

40. Coccaro EF, Siever LJ, Klar H et al. Serotonergic studies in affective and personality disorder patients: correlates with suicidal and impulsive aggression. Arch Gen Psychiatry 1989; 43: 587–599.

41. Coccaro EF, Gabriel S, Siever LJ. Buspirone challenge: Preliminary evidence for a role for central 5-HT-1a receptor function in impulsive aggressive behavior in humans. Psychopharm Bull 1990; 26: 393–405.

42. Coccaro EF, Silverman JM, Klar HM, Horvath TH, Siever LJ. Familial correlates of reduced central 5-HT function in DSM-III personality disorder patients. Arch Gen Psychiatry [in press].

43. Coccaro EF, Astill JL, Schut AG. Fluoxetine treatment of impulsive aggression in DSM-III-R personality disorder patients. J Clin Psychopharm 1990; 10: 373–375.

44. Markovitz PJ, Calabresse JR, Schulz SC, Meltzer HY. Fluoxetine in the treatment of borderline and schizotypal personality disorders. Am J Psychiatry 1991; 148: 1064–1067.

45. Coccaro EF, Kavoussi RJ. Neurotransmitter correlates of impulsive spectrum behaviors. Presented at First International Obsessive–Compulsive Disorder Congress, Capri, Italy, Mar 1993.

PART II
ASSESSMENT AND EPIDEMIOLOGY

6 DSM-IV AND ICD-10 DIAGNOSTIC CRITERIA FOR OBSESSIVE COMPULSIVE DISORDER: SIMILARITIES AND DIFFERENCES

Edna B Foa and Michael J Kozak
Medical College of Pennsylvania, Philadelphia, PA, USA

Introduction

Over its long history, the conceptualization of obsessive compulsive disorder (OCD) has undergone significant changes. The DSM-III-R (1) criteria for OCD reflect this history by having incorporated current views about the phenomenology of the disorder, as well as having retained some aspects of traditional conceptualizations and symptom definitions. The compromise between past and current views has resulted in some internal inconsistencies and ambiguities that have been addressed in DSM-IV. In this chapter, we will consider the issues that led to revisions of the criteria. Some of the revisions were intended to clarify the existing criteria. Others were more substantive and required empirical justification. We will summarize the results of a study that was designed to address some of these issues. Finally, we will compare the criteria for obsessive compulsive disorder in DSM-III-R and DSM-IV with those of the International Classification of Diseases (ICD-10).

We will begin by reviewing the DSM-III-R criteria for OCD. According to the DSM-III-R, to be diagnosed with OCD, an individual must have either obsessions or compulsions. Obsessions are defined as (1 p. 245):

Current Insights in Obsessive Compulsive Disorder. Edited by E. Hollander, J. Zohar, D. Marazzati and B. Olivier
© 1994 John Wiley & Sons Ltd

persistent thoughts, impulses, or images that are experienced at least initially as intrusive and senseless. . . . The person attempts to ignore or suppress such thoughts or impulses or to neutralize them with some other thought or action. The person recognizes that the obsessions are a product of his or her own mind, and are not imposed from without . . .

Compulsions are defined as (1 p. 245):

repetitive, purposeful, and intentional behaviors that are performed in response to an obsession, according to certain rules, or in a stereotyped fashion. The behavior is designed to neutralize or to prevent discomfort or some dreaded event or situation. However, either the activity is not connected in a realistic way with what it is designed to neutralize or prevent, or it is clearly excessive . . . The person recognizes that his or her behavior is excessive or unreasonable (this may not be true for young children and may no longer be true for people whose obsessions have evolved into overvalued ideas) . . .

Three traditional views have influenced the language of the DSM-III-R. However, some of the traditional concepts are questionable in light of recent work on OCD.

Obsessions and compulsions defined

The first tradition is that obsessions are *covert* mental events such as thoughts, images, or impulses, whereas compulsions are observable, *overt* behaviors such as washing, checking, repeating actions, or ordering. This distinction between obsessions and compulsions on the basis of their mode of expression contradicts a second, more current, tradition that emphasizes a dynamic functional relationship between obsessions and compulsions. According to this view, obsessions are mental events that elicit distress, such as thoughts of contamination, thoughts of being responsible for a disaster, unacceptable impulses, or blasphemous images. In contrast, compulsions are viewed as consisting of either overt behaviors or mental acts that are performed to reduce distress associated with the obsessions.

According to the more current concept of OCD, thoughts which are designed to neutralize other thoughts or impulses constitute compulsions. Compulsions can thus be overt behavior such as washing to offset distress about contamination, *or* covert rituals such as silent praying to neutralize a blasphemous thought. Either behaviors or thoughts can function to reduce obsessional distress and, therefore, both can be considered compulsions. Distress-reducing thoughts are termed cognitive compulsions.

Two problems in the DSM-III-R are related to the issue of how to conceptualize obsessions and compulsions. The view that compulsions function to reduce obsessional distress assumes that obsessions are distressing. A problem arises, however, in that the DSM-III-R is ambiguous about whether obsessions are necessarily distressing. This assumption was expressed *indirectly* in the definition of obsessions and only by implication in the definition of compulsions. Specifically, obsessions were not explicitly defined as distressing, but it was stated that the individual attempts to "ignore, suppress, or neutralize" them. Compulsions were defined as "repetitive, purposeful, and intentional behaviors that are performed in response to an obsession", and are "designed to neutralize or prevent discomfort". This issue was clarified in the DSM-IV, which specifies that obsessions "cause marked anxiety or distress".

A second problem with the DSM-III-R stems from the conflict between the traditional view that obsessions are mental and compulsions are behavioral, and a current view that certain thoughts are designed to neutralize other thoughts or impulses and therefore constitute compulsions. The way in which the conflict between traditional and current views was resolved in DSM-III-R is confusing. The second criterion for obsessions states that "the person attempts to ignore or suppress such thoughts [obsessions] or impulses, or to neutralize them with some other thought or action" (1 p. 247). It follows that there are two types of obsessive thoughts: the kind that a person tries to suppress, and the kind with which a person attempts to neutralize another thought. However, the compulsions criteria do not mention neutralizing thoughts. Thus, the concept of mental rituals is introduced through the definition of obsessions, rather than that of compulsions.

Perhaps because the distinction between obsessions and compulsions has not been delineated clearly, studies of cognitive compulsions were unavailable. A field trial (2) including 431 obsessive compulsives at five sites, and designed to examine questions pertinent to proposed revisions of the DSM-III-R, investigated mental compulsions. Specifically, this study examined whether mental compulsions exist and, if so, whether they are intended to neutralize harm or reduce distress in the same way that behavioral compulsions are.

To answer these questions the Yale–Brown Obsessive–Compulsive Scale (Y-BOCS) checklist (2) was used to determine the number of subjects who had behavioral rituals only, mental rituals only, and both. The results indicated the presence of mental compulsions in the majority of the sample: 79.5% reported having both behavioral and mental compulsions; 20.3% had behavioral compulsions without mental compulsions; and only 0.2% had mental compulsions without behavioral compulsions. These results clearly indicate that compulsions can be either behavioral or mental acts, and that mental rituals are quite prevalent among individuals with OCD. Consequently, in the DSM-IV, compulsions are defined as "repetitive behaviors (e.g., hand washing, ordering, checking) or mental acts (e.g., praying, counting, repeating words silently)".

To examine whether mental and behavioral rituals have the same functional relationship with obsessions, subjects whose primary rituals were mental were compared with those whose primary rituals were behavioral on the basis of the following question: "Most of the time your compulsions: 1) are intended to prevent harm (e.g. disease, fire, poison), 2) have nothing to do with harm, they just reduce discomfort, 3) are done automatically without purpose, 4) relationship between obsessions and compulsions is unclear." Categories 1 and 2 indicate a functional relationship between obsessions and compulsions; categories 3 and 4 indicate functional independence between obsessions and compulsions. The results revealed that 90.4% of the primary behavioral rituals, and 80.7% of the mental rituals, were functionally related to obsessions. Thus, mental rituals resemble behavioral rituals in that, for the most part, both are functionally related to obsessions.

Recognizing obsessions and compulsions as senseless

A third tradition that has been reflected in the DSM-III-R and is somewhat in conflict with both early and current views of OCD is that individuals with the disorder recognize obsessions as "intrusive and senseless" and compulsions as "excessive and unreasonable". Early descriptions of OCD noted that patients' thinking is characterized by irrationality and insanity (4). However, the influence of Janet (5) and Schneider (6), who argued that obsessions are recognized by patients as absurd and ego-alien, strongly influenced various versions of the DSM criteria for OCD. The lack of such recognition, sometimes observed in OCD, received little attention. More recently, there has been renewed acknowledgment in the literature that at least some individuals with OCD do not recognize their obsessions or compulsions as senseless [(7, 8), L Solyom, D Sookman, C Solyom and L Morton, unpublished data, 1985]. This observation was accommodated in the DSM-III-R in that obsessions were said to be experienced as intrusive and senseless "at least initially" and may not be experienced as senseless if they have "evolved into overvalued ideas".

The DSM-III-R assertion that most people with OCD perceive their symptoms as senseless is not supported by the two studies of this issue (8, 9). Rather, the data indicate substantial variability between individuals in the extent to which they recognize their obsessions and compulsions as senseless. Because these data were based on a small number of subjects, the DSM-IV field trial (2) further examined insight in OCD. If one can conclude that there is a broad range of insight among individuals with OCD, then the idea that obsessions are viewed as senseless by individuals with OCD appears to be overemphasized in the DSM-III-R.

In the field trial (2), subjects were interviewed to assess their insight into the senselessness of their obsessive compulsive fears. Individuals whose obsessions included fear that some disastrous consequence would occur if they did not ritualize were asked how strongly they believed this. Strength of obsessive compulsive belief was broadly distributed. Only 13% were certain that their feared consequence would *not* occur, 27% were mostly certain, 30% were uncertain, 25% were mostly certain that the consequence *would* occur, and 4% were completely certain that it *would* occur. These data converged with previous results and with clinical observations that individuals with OCD exhibit a range of insight.

It is clear that many individuals with OCD do not recognize their obsessions and compulsions as senseless, and that the DSM-IV criteria should reflect this reality. A continuum, however, cannot be expressed as a diagnostic criterion. To alert clinicians to the range of insight that characterizes individuals with OCD, the subtype "with poor insight" was introduced into DSM-IV. Inclusion of this subtype in the diagnostic criteria may also encourage researchers to explore the relationships between insight and other aspects of the psychopathology and treatment of OCD.

Distinction between obsession and worry

Clinicians have struggled to distinguish obsessions from other types of intrusive, unwanted thoughts, such as the ruminations in depression and the worries in generalized anxiety disorder. A review of the literature has indicated that the content of obsessions differs from that of excessive day-to-day worries (10). To alert clinicians to this issue, a criterion was added to the definition of obsessions: "the thoughts, impulses, or images are not simply excessive worries about real life problems".

Comparison of the DSM-III-R and DSM-IV

The differences between DSM-III-R and DSM-IV are summarized below:

1. In the DSM-III-R, obsessions are defined as "intrusive and senseless", whereas in the DSM-IV, they are defined as "intrusive and inappropriate, and cause marked anxiety or distress". These changes correct the omission of the notion that obsessions are aversive, and de-emphasize insight as a characteristic of obsessions.
2. In DSM-IV, a criterion specifying that obsessions "are not simply excessive worries about real life problems" was introduced to help distinguish the obsessions of OCD from the worries of generalized anxiety disorders.
3. In DSM-IV, the definition of compulsions was expanded to include

mental compulsions, that is "mental acts (e.g., praying, counting, repeating words silently)".

4. In the DSM-IV, the emphasis of DSM-III-R on recognition of senselessness of the symptoms was softened. This was accomplished through the introduction of a new criterion that requires insight "at some point during the course of the disorder", but *not* during the current episode.

5. To accentuate further the lack of recognition of the senselessness of OCD symptoms, a new subtype, with "poor insight", was introduced into DSM-IV. This subtype is indicated if "for most of the time during the current episode, the person does not recognize that the obsessions and compulsions are excessive or unreasonable".

Comparison of DSM-IV and ICD-10

As might be expected, the International and American classification schemes are on the whole convergent for OCD. Both require the presence of obsessions or compulsions (the ICD-10 requires the symptoms to be of at least 2 weeks' duration; there is no duration requirement in the DSM-IV). Despite the overall agreement between the two nosologies, there are some divergences, which we will discuss below.

The above-mentioned difficulties with the issue of recognition of senselessness in OCD are reflected in some divergence between the DSM-IV and ICD-10 criteria. As mentioned above, the DSM-IV does not require current insight but does require some history of insight. The ICD-10, on the other hand, requires that "at least one obsession or compulsion must be present that is acknowledged as excessive or unreasonable". Although there are formal differences in how the two schemes handle insight, they converge in that both allow individuals who lack insight to be diagnosed with OCD.

Another point of divergence between the DSM-IV and ICD-10 lies in the explicit requirement in the ICD-10 that "at least one obsession or compulsion must be present which is unsuccessfully resisted". No such requirement is specified in the DSM-IV, but the idea is implied by the definition of obsessions as "intrusive" and by the requirement that the person "attempts to ignore or suppress" them. Thus, again, despite formal differences, the two classifications appear compatible.

The ICD-10 devotes an entire criterion to specifying that pleasurable experiences can not be obsessions or compulsions. In this way, the ICD-10 scheme effectively excludes sexual deviations and addictions from the diagnosis of OCD. The DSM-IV does not have a general exclusion for pleasurable activities. Rather, it handles this issue by listing a number of symptoms involving appetitive excesses that do not constitute OCD.

Two apparently more substantial differences between the DSM-IV and ICD-10 criteria are evident. One lies in the conceptualization of obsessions and compulsions. The ICD-10 construes obsessions and compulsions as functionally equivalent, distinguishing them only according to their mode of expression: obsessions are covert symptoms, and compulsions overt. Consequently, there is no room for mental compulsions in the ICD-10 scheme. As discussed above, the DSM-III-R and DSM-IV were influenced by the view that obsessions are distressing and compulsions are aimed at preventing or reducing distress. Because of this distinction, the DSM-IV has separate criteria for obsessions and compulsions, and compulsions can be either mental or behavioral.

A second substantive difference between the two nosologies lies in their subtyping schemes. The "poor insight type" of the DSM-IV, which we have already discussed, is not present in the ICD-10. The ICD-10 specifies five subtypes, two of which are "residual" categories: "other obsessive compulsive disorders", and "obsessive compulsive disorder, unspecified". The remaining three ICD-10 subtypes are distinguished from one another by the constellation of OCD symptoms: "predominantly obsessional thoughts and ruminations", "predominantly compulsive acts", and "mixed obsessional thoughts and acts". The DSM-III-R did not include such subtypes.

Because of an interest in promoting compatibility between the International and American classifications, the DSM-IV OCD field trial (2) examined whether there are natural groupings of OCD symptoms that parallel these three ICD-10 subtypes. To examine the ICD-10 subtypes of (a) predominantly obsessions, (b) predominantly compulsions, and (c) mixed obsessions and compulsions, three analyses were conducted.

The Y-BOCS severity scores for obsessions and compulsions were calculated separately and compared. The ratio of obsession severity to compulsion severity for each subject was calculated and the frequency distribution of these ratios was determined. A unimodal distribution was obtained, rather than the trimodal distribution that would have been expected if the three ICD-10 subcategories represent natural groupings. The mode (52% of subjects) was at the point of equivalent severity of obsessions and compulsions. Because a trimodal distribution did not emerge, we divided the range of the distribution into three equal segments and examined the percentage of subjects who fell into each segment. A large majority (91.0%) fell into the "mixed obsessions and compulsions" category; a minority (8.5%) fell into the "predominantly obsessions" category; very few (0.5%) fell into the "predominantly compulsions" category.

The ICD-10 subtypes were also examined by cross-tabulating the results of the clinician's categorization. Three categories were available: 1, predominantly obsessions; 2, predominantly compulsions; 3, obsessions and compulsions. We found that 29.6% fell into the category of predominantly obsessions; 21.1% predominantly compulsions, and 49.3% mixed obsessions and compulsions. Thus, the two analyses yielded different patterns of results. The analysis of Y-BOCS severity scores for obsessions and compulsions indicated that the vast majority of individuals (over 90%) fell into the mixed obsessions and compulsions group. On the other hand, when provided with the three ICD-10 categories, a greater proportion of individuals with OCD identified themselves as being bothered predominantly by obsessions or predominantly by compulsions.

Several problems limit the conclusions that can be drawn from these data about subtypes. The obvious problem is that an inconsistent picture emerges in the two analyses. This probably stems from the different measures used. The first analysis was based on a continuous measure; the second analysis was based on a categorical measure. When raters are forced to rate on three categories, it is likely that three categories will emerge in the data. We therefore believe that the continuous measure offered a more valid estimate of the actual pattern of symptoms in OCD. It should be noted, however, that even the results based on the continuous measure are subject to question on methodological grounds. Specifically, although obtaining a trimodal distribution on the continuous measure would have supported the hypothesis of three underlying categories, its absence is not conclusive. This is because a continuous measure may show a unimodal distribution *despite* three underlying categories.

A convention adopted in considering revisions of the DSM-III-R was that modifications would not be made in the absence of strong empirical support. Because such support was not evident for the ICD-10 subtypes, they were not adopted in DSM-IV.

The International and American classifications are sufficiently similar for one to expect substantial concordance between diagnoses based on the two systems. However, the different conceptualizations of obsessions and compulsions underlying the two systems could have important implications for understanding the psychopathology of OCD, and consequently for choice of treatment. In particular, because the DSM-IV criteria recognize a functional relationship between obsessions and compulsions, these criteria can accommodate learning-based theories of the psychopathology of OCD, and therefore can provide a conceptual foundation for the choice of behavioral techniques that have been found differentially effective with obsessions and compulsions. Specifically, obsessions are effectively treated with prolonged exposure, and compulsions with ritual prevention. The ICD-10 distinction between obsessions and compulsions, based on mode of expression, could be misleading, because it views mental compulsions as obsessions.

References

1. American Psychiatric Association. Diagnostic and Statistical Manual of Mental Disorders. 3rd ed—revised. American Psychiatric Association, Washington DC, 1987.
2. Foa EB, Kozak MJ. DSM-IV Field Trial: Obsessive compulsive disorder. Am J Psychiatry [in press].
3. Goodman WK, Price L, Rasmussen S. The Yale–Brown Obsessive–Compulsive Scale (Y-BOCS): Past development, use, and reliability. Arch Gen Psychiatry 1989; 46: 1006–1016.
4. Westphal C. Zwangsvor stellungen. Arch Psychiatr Nervenkr 1878; 8: 734–750.
5. Janet P. Les Obsessions et la Psychosthenie, 2nd ed. Baillière, Paris, 1908.
6. Schneider K. Schwangs zus tande un Schizophrenie. Arch Psychiatr Nervenkrankheiten 1925; 74: 93–107.
7. Kozak MJ, Foa EB. Obsessions, overvalued ideas, and delusions in obsessive compulsive disorder. Behav Res Ther 1994; 33: 343–353.
8. Insel TR, Akiskal H. Obsessive–compulsive disorder with psychotic features: A phenomenologic analysis. Am J Psychiatry 1986; 12: 1527–1533.
9. Lelliott PT, Noshirvani HF, Basoglu M, Marks IM, Monteiro WO. Obsessive–compulsive beliefs and treatment outcome. Psychol Med 1988; 18: 697–702.
10. Turner SM, Beidel DC, Stanley MA. Are obsessional thought and worry different cognitive phenomena? Clin Psychol Rev 1992; 12: 257–270.

7 RATING SCALES FOR OBSESSIVE COMPULSIVE DISORDER

Michele Tortora Pato, Jane L Eisen and Carlos N Pato

Department of Psychiatry and Human Behavior, Brown University, Providence, RI, USA

Introduction

The rapid growth in the understanding and treatment of OCD has been facilitated by the systematic use of reliable and valid rating scales, both rater-administered and self-rated. However, to be truly valid, these instruments must be used in the context of a well-founded understanding of the nature of OCD. As early as 1968, Orme noted that severity of OCD was not related simply to frequency of symptoms but to the level of interference and/or avoidance experienced by the patient (1). More than 25 years later this continues to be good advice to heed in rating patients with OCD. In addition, the occurrence of OCD is often part of a constellation of disorders including depression as well as other anxiety disorders, such as panic disorder. So it becomes essential to measure change in these disorders separately from OCD (2).

Self-rating scales for OCD

Self-rating scales have several benefits over rater-administered scales. These scales give access to the patient's inner state, which can be particularly important in a secretive illness like OCD. In addition, self-rating saves on professional time and expense; in particular, minimal rater training is required, since the patient is the rater. The major limitation of self-rating is its dependence on the accuracy of the patient's self percep-

Current Insights in Obsessive Compulsive Disorder. Edited by E. Hollander, J. Zohar, D. Marazzati and B. Olivier
© 1994 John Wiley & Sons Ltd

tion (3). The problem of inaccurate self-perception is of particular relevance in OCD, in which doubt and a sense of incompleteness can be hallmarks of the illness. Furthermore, in some cases the ratings may become a ritual in themselves (4). Patients with obsessional doubt can also find it difficult to decide between rating items such as moderate, much, and severe, and obsessional slowness or need to check may prevent patients from completing the form or lengthen the time for completion to such a degree that it becomes impractical. As Insel and Akiskal (5 p. 610) comment, "Some patients consistent with the rigidity that may be seen in compulsive character disorder, resist changing self-ratings until long after clinical improvement was noted by observers". Mindful of these issues, we will briefly review the primary self-rating scales available.

There are three self-rated instruments that were used extensively in the 1970s and 1980s for studying OCD. These are the Leyton Obsessional Inventory (LOI), the Maudsley Obsessive Compulsive Inventory (MOCI), and the Hopkins Symptom Checklist (HSCL and SCL-90). However, given the pitfalls of self-rating by OCD patients, and the release of the well-studied, Yale–Brown Obsessive–Compulsive Scale (Y–BOCS— described later in this chapter) in the late 1980s, these self-rating scales have figured less in treatment studies, though they may still have some value of screening instruments in mixed samples.

LEYTON OBSESSIONAL INVENTORY

The LOI was originally developed as part of a study aimed at assessing the daily interactions and activities of very young children at home. As the study progressed a group of mothers were observed who were described as "house proud" or "perfectionistic in their approach to housework and child rearing" (6). The inventory was developed to explore these obsessional traits and attitudes. Thus, the goal of the LOI was to be sufficiently sensitive to differentiate between normals, house-proud housewives, and obsessional patients (6).

The original inventory consisted of two sets of yes–no questions, 46 symptom-related questions and 23 trait-related questions. There are 10 categories of symptom questions: 1, unpleasant recurring thoughts; 2, checking; 3, dirt and contamination; 4, dangerous objects; 5, personal cleanliness and tidiness; 6, household cleanliness and tidiness; 7, order and routine; 8, repetition; 9, over conscientiousness and lack of satisfaction; and 10, indecision. The trait questions are divided into eight categories: 1, hoarding; 2, cleanliness; 3, meanness; 4, irritability and nervousness; 5, rigidity; 6, health (bowels); 7, regularity and method; and 8, punctuality (7). Each yes response is followed by two questions, one for resistance and one for interference, each scored on a 0–3 scale.

The scale has demonstrated some construct validity and test–retest reliability, but there are some problems with content validity (2). To guard against making this scale offensive to housewives to whom it was administered (6), unpleasant obsessional thoughts like blasphemous, obscene, and violent obsessive thoughts, as well as more florid bizarre symptoms, were excluded. Leaving out these items compromises the scale's content validity because these are potentially important symptoms in OCD patients. Similarly many of the questions are oriented toward the home, cleaning, and tidiness, and females in general; this makes it less valid for males. As Allen and Rack note, ''. . . it seems justifiable to use the mean Leyton score as evidence that a given group of patients falls into the obsessional compulsive clinical category, but not as sole indicator of severity, nor of improvement in studies designed to compare alternative methods of treatment'' (8 p. 43). The latter point has also been formally tested by Kim et al (9) (see later).

MAUDSLEY OBSESSIVE COMPULSIVE INVENTORY

Initially the MOCI was developed not as a diagnostic instrument but rather as a questionnaire for ''assessing the existence and extent of different obsessional–compulsive complaints'' and as an outcome measure in treatment research (10 p. 389). It was hoped that differentiating among the different types of OC symptoms might have some ''theoretical and practical implications''. Thus, the 30 questions of the MOCI were designed to be scored as a total score and as four subscale scores (11). A typical score in patients meeting DSM-III criteria for OCD is approximately 18 out of 30 (12).

The questions are balanced for true and false answers to guard against acquiescent response sets. Since individual patients often scored high on more than one of these subscales, the value of defining these subscales is questionable. Hodgson (10) noted that one potential use of the MOCI is to ensure that most common symptoms of OCD are explored and to reassure the patient that the therapist has an understanding of their obsessional problems. A recent report (12) looked at the predictive validity of the MOCI using a semistructured interview, the Anxiety Disorders Interview Schedule (ADIS), based on DSM-III guidelines. Eleven individuals out of 579 who scored in the upper 2% on MOCI were compared with 11 individuals who scored at the 50th percentile; the latter acted as a control group. Nine of the 11 scoring high on the MOCI were correctly categorized with the ADIS, and all 11 of the control group were correctly categorized. Thus the results supported the notion that the MOCI is a valid instrument for identifying obsessions and compulsions in a nonclinical sample, and that the identification of symptoms was stable over time (6–7 months).

An assessment of construct validity was done to determine the MOCI as a measure of change. Pre- and post-treatment MOCI total scores were compared with global assessment of improvement by both the clinicians and the patients. The global assessment consisted of a simple three-point scale: 1 = not improved, 2 = slight improvement, and 3 = much improvement. Correlations between two therapists' global scores and the MOCI were higher (0.67 and 0.74) than the correlation between patient global scores and the MOCI (0.53) (10, 11). The superior correlation between the two clinicians' global assessment and the MOCI than that between the patient's global assessment and the MOCI is significant because it highlights the problem of self-ratings made by OCD patients. Perhaps this poor correlation is related to patients' tendencies to underestimate their improvement (5).

As a self-rated scale, it is not reasonable to talk of MOCI inter-rater reliability. But reliability can be partially assessed by looking at consistency of patient response on six pairs of questions, four pairs (2/8, 3/7, 10/12, 17/21) that should be answered similarly and two pairs (6/22, 16/26) that should be answered oppositely. Taken together, a consistent response should score a 6, 1 point for each pair answered correctly. Any score of 3 or less is considered an indicator of inconsistency and the rating should be considered suspect (10).

There are a number of disadvantages in using either of these rating scales. They are a poor choice for outcome studies because they rely on specific symptom sets. Therefore, any item that does not appear in the MOCI or the LOI is not reflected in the total scores. This is a particular problem if one of the patient's chief obsessions or compulsions does not appear on the checklist. On both the MOCI and the LOI, it is the number of symptoms that increases the score, not the degree of interference or avoidance the symptom causes. One of the further disadvantages of the MOCI is that the responses are dichotomous (true or false) and can not be graded. The LOI is better than the MOCI in this sense, because one can use interference and resistance to grade the intensity of the symptoms. However, data on the reliability and validity of these subcomponents of the LOI are inconclusive.

HOPKINS SYMPTOM CHECKLIST

The HSCL is designed for use as a measure of outpatient symptomatology in clinical settings and in research (13, 14). Its intended uses include: outpatient screenings in psychiatric outpatient settings, obtaining symptom information in nonpsychiatric settings, and a repeated measure in treatment studies (14). Like other self-report scales, it is economical on professional time and gives an assessment of the inner state of the patient (15). But it also has the same pitfalls of other self-report measures.

The HSCL comes in two forms. The original HSCL is a 58-item questionnaire, with five symptom dimensions. An expanded version, the SCL-90, contains 90 items, and nine symptom dimensions (3, 14). The five HSCL symptom dimensions include: obsessive compulsive (OC), anxiety, depression, somatization, and interpersonal sensitivity. The four added dimensions in the SCL-90 are hostility, phobic anxiety, paranoid ideation, and psychoticism (13, 14). Each item is assessed on a 0–4 scale of distress: 0 = not at all, and 4 = extreme distress in frequency and/or intensity.

The OC dimension includes eight items in the HSCL: trouble remembering things, worry about sloppiness or carelessness, feeling blocked or stymied in getting things done, having to do things very slowly in order to be sure you are doing them right, having to check and double check what you do, difficulty making decisions, your mind going blank, and trouble concentrating. There are two additional items in the SCL-90: unwanted thoughts that won't leave your mind, and having to repeat the same actions (16). Thus the focus of the OC scale is on thoughts, impulses, and actions, experienced as unremitting and irresistible, ego dystonic, and unwanted (14), and as such fits well with the clinical syndrome and DSM-III-R diagnosis. The two items that seem least specific for OCD are "your mind going blank" and "trouble concentrating".

There are some data on the reliability and validity of these Hopkins scales, more for the HSCL because it has been in use longer. Internal consistency, test–retest reliability, and inter-rater reliability have all been good (16). But Steketee and Doppelt (16) found poor discriminant and convergent validity comparing the scores for outpatients with OCD and for a mixed group of other psychiatric disorders. More specifically their findings did not support this instrument as having value as a measure of change in symptoms. As Steketee and Doppelt (16) note, factor analyzed scales such as the SCL-90 and the Comprehensive Psychopathological Rating Scale (CPRS; to be discussed later) present an additional problem with validity because they simply represent a high-frequency clustering of items. Co-occurrence of items in a long checklist of symptoms does not mean that those symptoms encompass a single conceptual entity. Because depression and anxiety often coexist with OCD, it is not surprising that items related to these disorders show up on the OC subscales. But including those items more common to depression or other anxiety disorders compromises the validity of these scales and their use as a measure of change in OC symptoms.

Rater-administered scales

YALE–BROWN OBSESSIVE–COMPULSIVE RATING SCALE

The Y-BOCS has become the gold standard for measuring severity of OCD. It was developed specifically as a measure of the severity and not as a diagnostic measure. It is assumed in administering this scale that the diagnosis of OCD by DSM-III-R has already been made (17, 18). By being sensitive to severity, rather than type, or frequency, of symptoms, this scale provides a better measure of change in OC symptoms, especially in the study of treatment efficacy. Unlike the other scales already discussed, the Y-BOCS has an added benefit. It is a rater-administered scale, rather than a self-rated scale, which eliminates the issues of insight and reliability inherent in self-rating scales done by OCD patients themselves (4, 5).

The Y-BOCS is a 16-item scale, but the core of the scale is comprised of the first 10 questions. The sum of these 10 items is reported as the total Y-BOCS score. To date, the data obtained on reliability and validity are for these 10 questions. The other six questions (numbers 11–16) are under investigation as to their usefulness, both clinically and for research. These six items include insight, avoidance, indecisiveness, sense of responsibility, slowness, and pathological doubt.

The first 10 questions are divided into two balanced sets, five for obsessions and five for compulsions. The first question of each set assesses the time spent on obsessions and the time spent on compulsions. Then obsessions and compulsions, each as a separate item, are each rated for interference, distress, resistance, and control. Each of the 10 questions is rated on a 0–4 scale: 0 corresponds to no symptoms, and 4 to extreme symptoms. All questions are structured so that the higher the score, the more severe the symptoms. Thus the maximum score is 40. Scores between 20 and 35 are typical for untreated OCD outpatients.

A good clinical interview is essential for a valid score on the Y-BOCS. While the scale does not record types of OC symptoms in order to make an accurate clinical assessment of the time spent on obsessions and compulsions, and the interference they cause, an understanding of the features of the illness in the particular OCD subject being rated is important. To assist in this process the Y-BOCS symptom checklist was developed (19). This checklist includes 70 examples of obsessions and compulsions, and can facilitate identification of symptoms for later severity rating. Originally designed as a rater-administered checklist, both L Baer and J Greist have transformed these into self-administered checklists with good success (19). One of the greatest assets of the Y-BOCS is that it allows for severity comparison between subjects, regardless of the form of their obsessions or compulsions. The Y-BOCS was specifically designed to rate adult OCD patients; however, a child form of the Y-BOCS (CY-BOCS), using simpler language, is available. Unpublished data from Riddle (1992) and Ciba Geigy (1990) (19) support the reliability and validity of this child version.

One fundamental construct of this scale that should be noted is how the originators of the scale view resistance, because it differs from other scales. Other scales besides the Y-BOCS have noted the importance of resistance. Resistance is the urge or effort made willfully to stop an obsessive thought or compulsive act. Both the LOI and the NIMH global OC scale contain aspects of resistance. But in these two scales, the more effort made to resist, the more severe the patient's illness. Using the LOI a patient receives a score of 3 if the response is "I try very hard to stop", and in the NIMH global OC he receives a severe score in the 10–12 range if he responds, "may spend full time resisting symptoms". The Y-BOCS reverses and elaborates this concept and equates less effort to resist with more severe illness. The rationale behind this bears some explanation. In the LOI and the NIMH global OC the assumption is made that the urge to resist is intensified with the severity of the illness because resistance is related to the severity of the distress and the lack of control the patient feels over his symptoms. Thus distress, resistance, and control are evaluated as a single item. But the Y-BOCS separately assesses these three items: distress, resistance, and control. This results in a different and more sensitive scoring measure.

This focus on severity irrespective of the number of symptoms gives the Y-BOCS a major advantage over the MOCI and the LOI, which tend to assume that number of symptoms is directly associated with severity. In fact, recent data in two separate studies by Kim et al (9, 20) have born out this benefit. In a 1990 study by Kim et al (9), the Y-BOCS was compared with the LOI and global ratings of improvement ($n = 28$). The correlations between the Y-BOCS change scores and the global ratings were significantly greater than correlations between the LOI and global scores. Kim et al concluded that the Y-BOCS was a better measure of clinical change than the LOI. In a similar study in 1992, Kim et al compared the SCL-90 with the Y-BOCS and global ratings ($n = 23$). Correlations were high and statistically significant between the Y-BOCS and the National Institute of Mental Health Global Obsessive–Compulsive Scale (NIMH-GOCS). In contrast, the correlation of the SCL-90 with both these measures was poor. Based on these findings, both the SCL-90 and the LOI do not appear to be good instruments for assessing change in OC symptoms.

In their own studies of the reliability and validity of the Y-BOCS, Goodman et al (17, 18) showed that the Clinical Global Improvement–Obsessive Compulsive Scale (CGI-OC) showed consistently significant, high correlation in OCD patients in comparison with the Y-BOCS. The NIMH-GOCS was compared with the Y-BOCS in a limited group of OCD patients and showed good correlation. On the other hand, the MOCI showed inconsistent correlation with the Y-BOCS. In a small sample ($n = 10$) in which both the CGI-OC and the NIMH-GOCS were compared with the MOCI, both failed to show significant correlation with the MOCI. In addition, Y-BOCS scores pre- and post-fluvoxamine treatment were compared with MOCI and CGI-OC scores pre- and post-treatment. Both total Y-BOCS and CGI-OC showed significant change between pre- and post-treatment measures. The MOCI did not show any significant change pre- and post-treatment. In addition, the Y-BOCS and the

CGI-OC scores post-treatment were strongly correlated ($r = 0.89$, $p < 0.0001$, $n = 21$), but the MOCI was not correlated with either the Y-BOCS or the CGI-OC post-treatment. This illustrates how the true and false format of the MOCI is insensitive to change in OC symptoms, while even a global rating such as the CGI-OC is sensitive to change despite lacking the specificity of the Y-BOCS.

For the first 10 questions of the Y-BOCS, inter-rater reliability was also assessed by both Pearson product moment correlation coefficients ($r = 0.0974–0.982$, $p < 0.0001$) and interclass correlation coefficients (ICC) ($r = 0.98$, $p < 0.0001$) indicating inter-rater reliability (17). Internal consistency between the first 10 items was also very high and significant as measured by Cronbach's α coefficient ($\alpha = 0.98$, $p < 0.001$). Finally, test–retest reliability was assessed by comparing baseline scores 6–8 weeks apart during the placebo phase of the study; no significant change in scores was noted.

Given the extensive use of the Y-BOCS, as well as the available data on its reliability and validity, it is truly the gold standard against which all other measures of severity should be compared.

COMPREHENSIVE PSYCHOPATHOLOGICAL RATING SCALE

Like the Y-BOCS, the CPRS is designed to "measure change in the severity of psychiatric illness" using a clinical interview (21, 22). The CPRS, however, is a factor-analyzed scale, and its intent is to cover a wide range of psychiatric signs and symptoms in its 65 subscales.

The OCD subscale (CPRS-OC) of the CPRS has eight items. It was derived by administering the full CPRS to only 13 OCD patients during a placebo washout phase of a research study. The items in the scale were then rank ordered according to frequency and magnitude of the scores. These summed ranks were again rank ordered and the eight highest ranks became the CPRS-OC (22). The eight questions of the CPRS-OC are rituals, inner tension, compulsive thoughts, concentration difficulties, worry over trifles, sadness, lassitude, and indecision. Each item is scored on a 0–3 severity scale: $0 =$ no symptoms, $1 =$ occasional, $2 =$ frequent, and $3 =$ extreme.

This scale has several weaknesses, mostly based on its construction by use of factor analysis. Four of the eight items on the scale are also found on the subscale for depression (inner tension, concentration difficulties, sadness, and lassitude). This can be easily attributed to the frequency with which depression and OCD coexist. This inclusion probably compromises the disciminant validity of the scale, though formal analysis of discriminant validity is not available. Overall, this scale has not been well studied for its psychometric properties because there are no reliability data other than inter-rater reliability. The items of rituals and compulsive thoughts show good summed inter-rater reliability ($r = 0.87$, $p < 0.001$), but the narrow 0–3 scale for severity makes it difficult to rate patients sensitively. These shortcomings make the CPRS-OC a less powerful instrument for measuring change in OC symptoms (23).

Global scales: self- and rater-administered

Global assessment ratings by either the patient or clinician have shown good sensitivity to treatment effects (24). Sensitivity is improved by including seven or more categories from which to make the assessment (24). The problem with global scales is that they lack specificity. Moreover, the general assumption made in these scales is that they are based on objective clinical assessment, on the part of the rater or the subject who is doing the rating. As has already been noted in the case of self-ratings in OCD patients, this objectivity is suspect (4, 5).

There are two basic types of global assessment. One type asks for an assessment of global change and lacks specificity. The second type focuses on specific symptoms in OCD and again asks for a global assessment of severity of symptoms, interference, and resistance. This type of global assessment is common in treatment studies using cognitive behavioral treatment.

NIMH GLOBAL OBSESSIVE–COMPULSIVE SCALE

The NIMH-GOCS is one example of a global scale. Following the model of global subscales in depression (3, 4) the NIMH-GOCS is a rater-administered point scale (1–15 points) rating patients only in regard to OC symptoms. Thus, it is a bit more specific than the CGI-OC which measures "improvement" in general. The scale is split into five groups: 1–3, minimal, within normal; 4–6, subclinical OC behavior; 7–9, clinical OC behavior; 10–12, severe OC behavior; 13–15, very severe OC behavior. Within each of the five groups there is a description of the interference and resistance aspects of OCD for that level of severity. A score above 6 is considered to be clinically significant severity. Thus, as in the LOI, it is on the basis of interference and resistance that the assessment is made. Similar to the LOI, the greater the resistance, the more severe the OC symptoms are considered to be. This is in contrast to the position taken in the Y-BOCS (17, 18).

CLINICAL GLOBAL IMPROVEMENT

The Clinical Global Improvement (CGI) scales come in many varieties. One common scale uses a 1–7 rating: 4, no change; 1, severely worse; 7, markedly improved. Other CGI scales record similar data on a 100 mm line, analog scale. This may be somewhat easier for the patient to complete, since issues around indecision and doubt do not have to be resolved as they do in deciding on a finite number. As noted earlier, the CGI-OC has shown good correlation with other OC measures like the Y-BOCS and the NIMH-GOCS (9, 17, 18, 20).

INDIVIDUAL SELF-RATING SCALE

A global assessment of specific symptoms, the Individual Self-Rating Scale (ISS) (22), is commonly used in behavioral studies in which certain symptoms are targeted (25). These scales reflect change as a general construct, and not along specific dimensions such as time spent, interference, resistance, distress, or avoidance, as in the Y-BOCS or the LOI. Change is expressed as a single number, or line length in the case of visual analog scales. Thus, as in other global scales, it lacks specificity, but is able to measure change. An additional deficit of the ISS, however, is that because it targets specific symptoms, it may miss change that has taken place in other symptoms if they have not been targeted. This is especially true in its use for behavioral therapy where easily observable symptoms, such as hand washing or checking, are monitored and obsessions are not.

Other OC scales

There are several other scales that are worth mentioning; most are institution specific and have not gained wide use but may be promising for the future.

THE BROWN ASSESSMENT OF BELIEFS SCALE

This scale has been developed to deal with the increasing awareness in the diagnosis and treatment of OCD that patients have variable insight into the senselessness of their symptoms. As defined by DSM-III-R, patients with OCD are *aware* of the senselessness of their obsessions and need to perform compulsions (26). Yet, OCD patients with varying degrees of insight have been described in the literature (5, 27–31). Foa (28) has used the term "over-valued ideas" in describing a continuum of insight in OCD in which obsessions are firmly maintained as being reasonable but are not held with complete conviction. Insel and Akiskal (5) described four patients who developed delusional conviction about their obsessions. They postulated that insight in OCD may exist on a continuum ranging from good insight, in which patients clearly recognize the excessiveness and/or senselessness of their concerns, to delusional conviction, in which the obsessions are felt to be realistic and reasonable. In addition to a range of insight between patients, clinicians have observed clear fluctuations in patients' certainty about the accuracy of their obsessional fears depending on the proximity to the feared situation (32).

The distinction between good insight, overvalued ideas, and delusions seems to depend on a number of dimensions that determine the degree of tenacity with which patients embrace their obsessions. However, there are no generally accepted conventions, with which to make this differentiation between degrees of insight, that have proven validity and inter-rater reliability. Lelliott et al (29) used an interview to evaluate obsessions on a number of dimensions, including fixity, bizarreness, resistance and degree of control. The fixity dimension included several constructs: strength of belief in the feared situation, how the patient thought others viewed his/her belief, and the patient's response to evidence that contradicted the obsession. They found a full range of responses in the 43 patients assessed. More recently, the question of degree of insight in OCD was addressed during the field trial conducted in connection with DSM-IV (32). Patients were asked if they feared consequences other than anxiety if they did not perform their compulsions. Fifty-eight percent believed that harmful consequences would occur. The degree of certainty that their obsessions were reasonable ranged across the entire spectrum of insight: the majority of patients were uncertain whether they actually needed to perform their compulsions in order to avoid harm. However, 4% were certain, and 25% were mostly certain. Again, this finding supports the notion that OCD patients do not always maintain good insight but rather have varying degrees of insight.

Most recently, Eisen and Phillips developed the BABS, which is a semistructured interview composed of eighteen items with specific probes and anchors (33). These items are: 1, conviction—how certain is the patient that his/her obsessions are accurate; 2, perception of other views—do others view these beliefs as reasonable; 3, fixity—can the patient be persuaded that the belief is excessive or unreasonable; 4, time spent preoccupied with obsessions; 5, time free from obsessions; 6, distress caused by obsessions; 7, degree of functional impairment caused by beliefs/obsessions; 8, resistance—does the patient try to dismiss his/her concerns; 9, degree of control—is the patient able to turn attention away from the obsessions; 10, pressure—does the patient try to convince others that the obsessions are reasonable; 11, ego-syntonicity—do the obsessions feel like a part of the patient or alien; 12, insight—what has caused the patient to have obsessions; 13, plausibility/bizarreness; 14, coherence; 15, fluidity of ideas—does the patient's certainty about the accuracy of the obsessions fluctuate on a daily basis; 16, extension—how many areas of the patient's life are affected by the obsessions; 17, ideas/delusions of reference—do others take special notice of the patient;

and 18, explanation of differing views—how does the patient explain the disparity between his/her view and how do others view the accuracy of the beliefs/obsessions. All items are answered with scores from 0 (least symptomatic) to 4 (most symptomatic). Specific anchors are given for every possible answer. Several of the items focus on what are considered the core features of "delusionality": conviction, perception of others views, fixity of beliefs, fluidity of beliefs, "ego-syntonicity", and insight. Another group of items addresses the degree of preoccupation and impairment the beliefs cause. Several other items (pressure, bizarreness, coherence, extension, and ideas of reference) are derived from the literature on delusions.

In an initial pilot study of the scale, the BABS was administered to 46 patients: 18 patients with OCD, 18 patients with body dysmorphic disorder (BDD), and 10 patients with psychotic disorders (33). Inter-rater reliability was determined by three clinicians independently rating 10 taped interviews. Using Spearman correlations on all items except for the last three experimental items, inter-rater reliability showed good to excellent agreement between raters. The Cronbach's α coefficient on all items was 0.829, indicating homogeneity of the BABS items. Factor analysis was performed to extract statistically independent factors. Factor analysis yielded three factors (*core features*, *severity*, and *degree of psychosis*) accounting for 67% of the variance. A larger inter-rater reliability and validity study of the BABS is currently underway.

Degree of insight may be an important predictor of treatment response in OCD. Foa (28) reported that patients with overvalued ideas did not respond well to behavior therapy. However, a more recent report (29) reported that patients with high conviction about their obsessions and need to perform compulsions responded just as robustly to behavioral intervention as those patients with good insight. There are virtually no pharmacological treatment data related to the question of insight. One methodological limitation in pursuing this important area is lack of agreement on precisely what is meant by good and poor insight. The BABS, as a rating scale designed to address insight in a systematic way, should further our understanding of the relationship between obsessions and delusions and of its potential value in predicting outcome.

CHALLENGE SCALES

Most of the scales we have addressed so far have been designed to measure change in symptoms over days or weeks. The Y-BOCS for instance was designed to be used at weekly intervals (17, 18). Yet, as research proceeds in OCD, a number of researchers are using brief intense exposures with pharmacological agents or environmental stimuli to try to rapidly exacerbate or diminish OCD symptoms. Because of the short time intervals in the challenge studies, the scales need to be easy to administer, quickly completed, and very sensitive to change. Researchers have tried to address these rating issues by using a combination of global assessments, particularly visual analog scales, both self- and rater-administered (34–37). Zohar et al (36, 37) also used a modified version of the CPRS 8, called the CPRS 5 that excluded the items of sadness, inner tension, and worrying about trifles, as a repeated measure with good results in the challenge setting.

Conclusions

The past 5 years have seen the Y-BOCS emerge as truly being the gold standard for measuring change in OCD symptoms. Done in combination with the Yale-Brown symptom checklist, in order to insure an adequate clinical interview which does not miss any major symptoms, the Y-BOCS gives a well-rounded picture of the severity of illness in OCD. Yet, there will always remain problems of reliability and validity in any OCD rating instrument, because of the ritualistic and secretive nature of the illness and its poorly demarcated interface with both depression and anxiety disorders.

Despite their lack of specificity, global ratings such as the CGI-OC or NIMH-GOCS are easy to administer and have shown sensitivity to change (24), as well as good correlation with the Y-BOCS (9, 17, 18, 20). Finally, in an assessment of OCD, avoidance and its relation to symptom severity should not be overlooked, both in the baseline measures and over time. In using the Y-BOCS, avoidance can be incorporated both into overall severity as well as the measure of interference for both obsessions and compulsions.

Given the comorbidity of OCD with other anxiety disorders and depressive illness, there will always be a problem in rating both frequency and severity of symptoms to tease these disorders apart. Probably the best way to differentiate change over time in OCD symptoms versus depression and other anxiety symptoms is to incorporate scales that also measure these non-OCD symptoms into any rating battery. In this way, a better assessment of all that is changing over time can be made.

References

1. Orme J. Are obsessionals neurotic or are neurotics obsessional? Br J Med Psychol 1968; 41: 415.
2. Philpott R. Recent advances in the behavioral measurement of obsessional illness: Difficulties common to these and other measures. Scot Med J 1975; 20: 33.
3. Murphy D, Pickar D, Alterman J. Methods for the quantitative assessment of depression and manic behavior. In: The Behavior of Psychiatric Patients:

Quantitative Techniques for Evaluation (eds Burdock E, Sudilovsky A, Gershon S). Marcel Dekker, New York, pp 355–392.

4. Insel T, Murphy D, Cohen R, Atterman I, Kilts C, Linnoila M. Obsessive compulsive disorder: A double-blind trial of clomipramine and clorgyline. Arch Gen Psychiatry 1983; 40: 605.

5. Insel TR, Akiskal HS. Obsessive compulsive disorder with psychotic features: a phenomenological analysis. Am J Psychiatry 1986; 143: 1527–1533.

6. Cooper J. The Leyton obsessional inventory. Psychiatr Med 1970; 1: 48.

7. Cooper J, Kelleher M. The Leyton obsessional inventory: A principal component analysis on normal subjects. Psychiatr Med 1973; 3: 204.

8. Allen J, Rack P. Changes in obsessive–compulsive patients as measured by the Leyton inventory before and after treatment with clomipramine. Scot Med J 1975; 20: 41.

9. Kim S, Dysken M, Kuskowski M. The Yale–Brown obsessive compulsive scale: A reliability and validity study. Psychiatric Res 1990; 34(1): 94–106.

10. Hodgson R, Rachman S. Obsessional compulsive complaints. Behav Res Ther 1977; 15: 384.

11. Rachman S, Hodgson R. Obsessions and Compulsions. Prentice Hall, New York, 1980.

12. Sternberger LG, Burns GL. Maudsley Obsessional–Compulsive Inventory: Obsessions and compulsions in a nonclinical sample. Behav Res Ther 1990; 28(4): 337–340.

13. Derogatis L, Lipman R, Covi L. The SCL-90: An outpatient psychiatric rating scale. Psychopharmacol Bull 1973; 9: 13.

14. Guy W. ECDEU assessment manual for psychopharmacology. Publication 76-338. U.S. Department of Health, Education and Welfare, US Government Printing Office, Washington, DC, 1976.

15. Derogatis L, Lipman R, Rickels K, Wilemhuth E, Covi L. The Hopkins symptom checklist (HSCL): A self-report symptom inventory. Behav Sci 1974; 19: 1.

16. Steketee G, Doppelt H. Measurement of obsessive compulsive symptomatology: Utility of the Hopkin's symptom checklist. Psychiatry Res 1986; 19: 135–145.

17. Goodman W, Price L, Rasmussen S, Mazure C et al. The Yale–Brown Obsessive Compulsive Scale (Y-BOCS): Part I. Development, use and reliability. Arch Gen Psychiatry 1989; 46: 1006–1011.

18. Goodman W, Price L. Rasmussen S et al. The Yale–Brown Obsessive Compulsive Scale (Y-BOCS): Part II. Validity. Arch Gen Psychiatry 1989; 46: 1012–1016.

19. Goodman W, Price L. Assessment of severity and change in obsessive compulsive disorder. Psychiatr Clin North Am 1992; 15(4): 861–869.

20. Kim S, Dysken M, Kuskowski M. The symptom checklist—90 Obsessive compulsive subscales: A reliability and validity study. Psychiatry Res 1992; 41(1): 37–44.

21. Asberg M, Montgomery S, Perris C, Schalling D, Sedvall G. A comprehensive psychopathological rating scale. Acta Psychiatr Scand 1978; 271 (suppl): 5.

22. Thoren P, Asberg M, Cronholm P, Jornestedt L, Trachman L. Clomipramine treatment of obsessive compulsive disorder. A controlled clinical trial. Arch Gen Psychol 1980; 37: 1281.

23. Montgomery S, Asberg M, Jornestedt L et al. Reliability of the clinical psychopathological rating scale between the disciplines of psychiatry, general practice, nursing, and psychology in depressed patients. Acta Psychiatr Scand 1978; 271 (suppl): 29.

24. McNair D. Original investigations self-evaluations of antidepressants. Psychopharmacology 1974; 37: 281.
25. Marks IM, Stern RS, Mawson D et al. Clomipramine and exposure for obsessive–compulsive rituals. Br J Psychiatry 1980; 136: 1–25.
26. American Psychiatric Association. Diagnostic and Statistical Manual of Mental Disorders, 3rd edn—revised. American Psychiatric Association, Washington DC, 1987.
27. Eisen JL, Rasmussen SA. Obsessive–compulsive disorder with psychotic features. J Clin Psychiatr 1993; 54(10): 373–379.
28. Foa EB. Failures in treating obsessive compulsives. Behav Res Ther 1979; 17: 169–176.
29. Lelliott PT, Noshirvani HF, Basogiu M, Marks IM, Monteiro WO. Obsessive–compulsive beliefs and treatment outcome. Psychol Med 1988; 18: 697–702.
30. Solyom L, DiNola VF, Phil M et al. Is there an obsessive psychosis? Aetiological and prognostic factors of an atypical form of obsessive–compulsive neurosis. Can J Psychiatry 1985; 30: 372–374.
31. Stengel E. A study of some clinical aspects of the relationship between obsessional neurosis and psychotic reaction types. J Ment Sci 1945; 41: 166–187.
32. Kozak MJ, Foa EB. Obsessions, over-rated ideas and delusions in obsessive compulsive disorder. Behav Res Ther [in press].
33. Eisen JL, Phillips KA, Beer D, Rasmussen SA, Goodman WK. Assessment of Insight in Obsessions and Delusions. New Research APA, San Francisco, 1993.
34. Charney D, Goodman W, Price L et al. Serotonin function in obsessive–compulsive disorder. A comparison of the effects of tryptophan and m-chlorophenylpiperazine in patients and healthy subjects. Arch Gen Psychiatry 1988; 45: 177–185.
35. Rauch SL, Jenike MA, Alpert NA et al. Regional cerebral blood flow measured during symptom provocation in obsessive–compulsive disorder using oxygen 15-labeled carbon dioxide and positron emission tomography. Arch Gen Psychiatry 1994; 51: 62–70.
36. Zohar J, Mueller E, Insel T, Zohar-Kadouch R, Murphy D. Serotonergic responsivity in obsessive compulsive disorder: Comparison of patients and healthy controls. Arch Gen Psychiatry 1987; 44: 946–951.
37. Zohar J, Insel T, Zohar-Kadouch R, Murphy D. Serotonergic responsivity in obsessive compulsive disorder: Effects of chronic clomipramine treatment. Arch Gen Psychiatry 1988; 45: 167–172.

8 THE EPIDEMIOLOGY OF OBSESSIVE COMPULSIVE DISORDER

Jules Angst
Psychiatric University Hospital Zurich, Research Department, Zurich, Switzerland

Introduction

This chapter will deal with the methodological problems of research on obsessive compulsive disorder (OCD) epidemiology and with the findings of modern community studies. Problems in sampling, interview techniques, and case definition will be covered. Findings will include the prevalence rates, symptoms, comorbidity, age of onset, and course of OCD and of subthreshold obsessive compulsive syndromes (OCS).

The review will be confined to community studies which have been carried out since 1980, when operational diagnostic criteria for OCD were introduced by DSM-III. From a traditional clinical viewpoint, OCD is a rare, chronic, severely disabling disorder. The diagnostic criteria were developed on clinical grounds and can be validated by modern epidemiological studies by means of treatment rates, subjective suffering and disability, as well as course and family history. Evidence from child and adult studies suggests that the current diagnostic threshold derived from clinical practice may be too high and in need of revision.

Methodology

SAMPLING

Most epidemiological studies are based on *random community samples* and a single cross-sectional investigation. The large Epidemiological Catchment Area (ECA) Study carried out in the USA recruited subjects by the household method and from institutions (1). Such studies are very

Current Insights in Obsessive Compulsive Disorder. Edited by E. Hollander, J. Zohar, D. Marazzati and B. Olivier
© 1994 John Wiley & Sons Ltd

representative; however, most studies rely on the household method only. The Zurich Study (2) and the Iceland Study (3) both dealt with *cohorts*, aged 19–20 and 55–57, respectively. Cohorts that are followed up prospectively have the advantage of being relatively homogeneous and suitable for repeated prospective assessments, allowing study of the course and outcome of psychiatric disorders and longitudinal comorbidity and the testing of causal models. However, when dealing with very large populations, they are less representative than community studies.

SCREENING

Faced with the low prevalence of OCD, some community studies have used a two-stage design in order to enrich risk cases. Flament et al (4) used the 20-item Leyton Obsessional Inventory–Child Version (LOI-CV) as a screening instrument, forming two different kinds of substrata, defined by a cut-off of at least 15 points on the "yes" score and at least 20 points on the "interference" score. Combining the two scores, the authors achieved a good degree of sensitivity (88%) and specificity (77%). As a result, very few false negatives but a larger number of false positives were picked up for a second-stage interview, allowing, in addition, identification of subclinical cases. There is an inherent limitation in the LOI-CV in that it accounts for current psychopathology only, so that cases who have recovered may be lost.

Khanna et al (5) used the OCD section of the Screening for Anorexia Nervosa (SCAN) as a Screening instrument and the Yale–Brown Obsessive–Compulsive Scale (Y-BOCS) and the full version of the SCAN for case identification.

A two-stage design was also chosen in the Zurich Cohort Study (2), a general risk of psychopathology being defined by a high score on the Symptom Checklist 90-R of Derogatis (6).

CASE DEFINITION

All the studies reviewed here are based on operational case definitions and deal with random samples from the community. The modern criteria for case definition are derived from DSM-III, DSM-III-R, or the International Classification of Diseases (ICD-10).

Nevertheless, a valid case definition remains a problem. There is little doubt as to the existence of a spectrum of OCD manifestations, ranging from transitional symptoms through subclinical mild transient syndromes with a good prognosis to clinical nonrecurrent, recurrent, and even chronic cases. The relationship of OCD to obsessive compulsive personality disorder remains unclear (5). According to Flament et al (4), the subclinical group is both sizeable and intriguing. In childhood and adolescence, the subclinical group is characterized by abrupt onset and discrete symptoms, to which the subjects appear to adapt themselves. The findings of the longitudinal Zurich Study of young adults from the age of 20 years to 30 years over a ten year period, likewise point clearly to a sizeable group of healthy symptom carriers (30%), but also strongly suggest the existence of a clinically relevant OCS at subthreshold level (2).

Because the Diagnostic Interview Schedule [DIS, by Robins et al (7)] does not match DSM-III criteria exactly [also pointed out by Rasmussen and Eisen (8)], the prevalence rates yielded by this method are very probably higher than strict DSM-III or DSM-III-R criteria would allow. However, this discrepancy may not be critical: as the Zurich Study has clearly demonstrated, a slightly softer definition, giving annual prevalence rates comparable to the DIS definition, identifies a significant proportion of subjects suffering from a clinically relevant OCS. From this viewpoint, strict DSM-III criteria have to be questioned, for they appear to exclude many subclinical cases.

INTERVIEWS

The main interviews used for data collection were the DIS of Robins et al (7), the Diagnostic Interview for Children and Adolescents (DICA) of Herjanic and Campbell (9), and the structured psychopathological interview and rating of the Social Consequences of Psychic Disturbances for Epidemiology (SPIKE) (10) (Table 8.1).

INTERVIEWERS

Prevalence rates may be overestimated by lay interviewers; they may also be underestimated because of the patients' reluctance to discuss their symptoms, or because these may be masked by anxiety or depression (8). In addition, there is a tendency for lay interviewers to normalize findings. For these reasons, it is preferable for interviews to be conducted by trained psychologists or by psychiatrists.

Incidence and prevalence rates

Crum and Anthony (19) reported incidence data derived from a 1-year follow up of the ECA Study. They found an annual incidence of 7.5 new cases of OCD per 1000 persons. Using multiple logistic regression models, they identified as risk factors the use of cocaine and marijuana (relative risk of 7.2), and a number of psychiatric disorders, with the following estimated relative risks: bipolar disorder, 8.2; panic disorder, 4.6; phobic disorder, 3.4; major depression or grief reactions, 2.4; schizophrenic

Table 8.1 Lifetime prevalence rates of obsessive compulsive disorder (DIS/DSM-III criteria) in epidemiological studies*

Authors	Year	Reference	Criteria	Location	Rate (%)
Yeh et al	1985	11	DIS	Two Chinese townships	0.5
Khanna et al	1993	5	SCAN Y-BOCS	India	0.6
Yeh et al	1985	12	DIS	Taipei (Taiwan)	0.9
Wittchen and von Zerssen	1988	13	DIS	Munich	2.0
Lindal and Steffanson	1993	14	DIS	Iceland	2.0
Wells et al	1989	15	DIS	Christchurch (NZ)	2.2
Karno et al	1988	16	DIS	Epidemiological Catchment area (USA)	2.6
Henderson and Pollard	1988	17	ASI	St. Louis (USA)	2.8
Canino et al	1987	18	DIS	Puerto Rico	3.2
Degonda et al	1993	2	SPIKE	Zurich	5.5

*ASI, Anxiety Symptoms Interview; DIS, Diagnostic Interview Schedule; SCAN, SPIKE, Social Consequences of Psychic Disturbances for Epidemiology; Y-BOCS, Yale–Brown Obsessive–Compulsive Scale.
†Personal communication.

disorders, 2.3; alcohol use disorders, 2.2. The elevated risk is most clearly established for bipolar disorder and phobic disorder. The following sociodemographic variables did not correlate with incidence: race–ethnicity, educational level, marital status, a score for job prestige, or age (in years).

Lifetime prevalence rates of OCD vary considerably between countries, even when comparable methods are used (Table 8.1). The lowest rates were observed in Taiwan (11, 12), varying between 0.5 and 0.9%, and in India (5), where the rate was 0.6%. In North and Central America, on the other hand, studies which, like the Taiwan study, applied the DIS resulted in lifetime prevalence rates of between 2.6 and 3.2%. Applying strict DSM-III criteria in two interviews over three years, the Zurich Cohort Study (2) identified a prevalence rate of only 1%. Flament et al (4) found a raw point-prevalence rate of 0.35% among high school students, which, in view of the early age of onset, gives an estimated point-prevalence of 1% and a lifetime prevalence rate of 1.9% for an adolescent population.

The ECA study (20) found a 1-year prevalence rate of 1.65% for OCD; the Zurich Study found 1-year prevalence rates for an OSC varying between 1 and 3%, depending on the age of the cohort. The Zurich Study found a lifetime prevalence rate of 5.9%, including subclinical OCSs, accumulated by four interviews of subjects over 10 years between ages 20 and 30.

Table 8.2 gives 6-month prevalence rates from four studies, ranging between 1.0 and 1.8%. These figures are close to the lifetime prevalence rates based on the DIS in Table 8.1 (0.5–3.2%) which is somewhat suspect.

The studies reveal, on the one hand, genuinely low prevalence rates in the Far East and, on the other, relatively high rates in Western countries. Furthermore, the prospective Zurich Study shows that, because most of the syndromes do not persist in severity over the diagnostic threshold but fluctuate or sometimes even remit, the lifetime prevalence rates are considerably increased by repeated assessments (2).

Table 8.2 Six-month prevalence rates of OCD (DIS/DSM-III criteria) in epidemiological studies*

Authors	Year	Reference	Criteria	Location	Rate (%)
Oakley–Browne et al	1989	21	DIS	Christchurch (NZ)	1.0
Bland et al	1988	22	DIS	Edmonton (USA)	1.6
Canino et al	1987	18	DIS	Puerto Rico	1.8
Wittchen and von Zerssen	1988	13	DIS	Munich (D)	1.8

*DIS, Diagnostic Interview Schedule.

Sociodemographic factors

In children and adolescents Flament et al (4) found no correlation between race, socioeconomic status, grade-point average, religious affiliation, or current physical health and OCD. This finding is consistent with other studies carried out on adults (20, 23).

A mild female preponderance was repeatedly found among OCD cases (24) and was explained by interfering sociodemographic variables (20). The large study by Flament et al (4) detected no such sex differences among children and adolescents suffering from OCD (25).

Symptoms

Obsessive compulsive disorder symptoms appear to be independent of age. Both in the community and in clinics, children and adolescents manifest the same symptoms as adults (4). Symptoms are also similar across cultures (26–28). The partial integration of OCD symptoms into religious activity in Nepal (29) is an example of the need to take the cultural frame into account.

In an interesting study conducted in India, Khanna et al (30) carried out a cluster analysis of the symptoms of 160 psychiatric outpatients diagnosed as suffering from OCD according to ICD-9 (31). Applying two methods of cluster analysis of symptoms, the authors distinguished four main groups of patients, with manifestations of checking, washing, urges for embarrassing behavior, and obsessional thoughts of the past.

Sanavio (32) carried out a factor analysis of the Padua Inventory (PI), with 60 items administered to a community sample of 967 subjects in northeastern Italy. The four factors which emerged were: "impaired control over thoughts and mental imagery" (obsessions), "becoming contaminated" (washing, cleaning), "checking behaviors", and "urges of a violent and antisocial nature and losing control over motor behavior" (killing, damaging, stealing, etc.).

The St. Louis (USA) community study by Henderson and Pollard (17) revealed a high prevalence of checking and washing and of other compulsions such as counting, repeating, or collecting. Only a minority of subjects in the study suffered from obsessive symptoms without compulsions. In adolescents, Flament et al (7) found virtually no subjects with obsessions in isolation; 35% showed a fear of contamination, 30% a fear of hurting themselves or others. The ECA Study is alone in describing, in contrast to patient studies, a low overlap (8.6%) of OCD subjects with both obsessions and compulsions.

Little is known about the longitudinal change of symptoms in the community, even though there is evidence for such change in patients (33).

Age at onset and course

AGE AT ONSET

The ECA Study found a mean age of onset of OCD symptoms of between 21 and 25 years (16). The study also shows that the symptoms manifested in childhood in 20% and in adolescence in 29% of cases (20). The Edmonton Study found an average age of onset of 21.4 years (22), with median ages of 20 (males) and 19 (females). For one-third to one-half of OCD patients, the onset is in childhood (34). Studies of adolescents confirm an early age of onset, i.e. between 9 and 18 years (4, 35, 36). In 1986 Rapoport reported that in about 50% of adult cases symptoms were already manifest by the age of 15 years (37). In 70% of the subjects with an OCS in the Zurich Cohort Study (2), symptoms had appeared before the age of 20 years. The median age of onset for males was 17 and for females 19 years. This earlier age of onset in males is congruent with the literature survey by Rasmussen and Eisen (8).

The onset of OCD is more often gradual than sudden and is frequently unlinked to any precipitating events. In the findings of Flament et al (4), a previous history of head injury was over-represented.

COURSE

The course of OCD may be chronic or fluctuating. All earlier studies of the disorder, summarized by Insel and Murphy (38), were retrospective and therefore less conclusive; they stress chronicity, describing an episodic course pattern or recovery in a minority of cases. The ECA Study, too, stresses chronicity, but here again assessment is in retrospect (20). Prospective follow-up studies of community samples over 2 years (39) and over 9 years (2) show that OCD symptoms are commonly still present at follow up, but that adolescents and adults frequently no longer meet the diagnostic criteria. Whether this is due to a "second interview effect" (7) or spontaneous fluctuations remains an open question. Of particular interest is the finding of a 2-year follow-up study of adolescents that subclinical cases did not deteriorate (39). The Edmonton and Christchurch studies showed a 60–70% recovery rate from the present OCD episode at the end of 1 year. Thus, "OCD appears to be a disorder that waxes and wanes but from which recovery is possible even without treatment" (40).

The Zurich Cohort Study, consisting of four interviews over 10 years, showed that while there was considerable fluctuation in obsessive compulsive symptoms and no great stability of the DSM-III diagnosis, in many cases symptoms persisted. It was suggested that, over time, some subjects learn to cope and to live with their symptoms and cease to be impaired in daily life (2).

Comorbidity

Comorbidity rates of OCD resulting from the ECA Study were first published by Karno et al (16). On the basis of 468 cases of OCD, the authors found the following rates of overlap of the disorder: with phobia, 46.5%; with major depressive episodes, 31.7%; with panic disorder, 13.8%; with schizophrenia, 12.2%; with schizophreniform disorder, 1.3%; with alcohol abuse or dependence, 24.1%; with other drug abuse or dependence, 17.6%. They concluded that there was no specific diagnostic association for the disorder, the risk of comorbidity not being distinctive. In the majority of the associated cases, schizophrenia, panic disorder, or phobia emerged as the first and OCD as the second disorder (20); substance abuse tended to follow the onset of OCD, suggesting "that these disorders may develop from efforts at self-medication of distressing obsessive and compulsive symptoms" (16). Odds ratios of the association were unfortunately not published by the authors.

Crum and Anthony (19) found, in a 1-year follow-up of the ECA Study, that subjects actively using cocaine and marijuana had an increased relative risk of 7.2 for OCD.

In their study of children and adolescents, Flament et al (4) found OCD associated with anxiety disorders in 35% of cases, with affective disorders in 25%, with bulimia in 15%, and with obsessive compulsive personality disorder in 15% of cases. Fifteen out of 20 adolescent subjects (75%) had at least one other lifetime psychiatric diagnosis. In another study of adolescents, Hollander et al (41) found an unexpected association between OCD and certain behavioral symptoms (lying, stealing, trouble at school, fights, etc.). Moreover, adolescents with OCD displayed more antisocial symptoms and elevated rates of attempted suicide over a lifetime (15.0 vs 3.6%).

In the longitudinal Zurich Study of young adults (2), a significant association between OCS and major depressive disorder was found in females but not in males (odds ratios 2.5 and 1.2, respectively), whereas in both sexes the association was clear between OCS and panic disorder, social phobia and agoraphobia (odds ratio 2.3), dysthymia (2.8), and recurrent brief anxiety (1.9). Lifetime suicide attempts were found in 16.1% of subjects, with an odds ratio of 1.9 (42).

Conclusions

From an epidemiological viewpoint, OCD research is still in its infancy. Very many questions are still unanswered, while others have not even been formulated. The current case definitions contained in DSM, DSM-III-R, and ICD-10 are probably too rigorous. As we have seen, there exists a wide spectrum of OCD symptoms and syndromes in the community. Studies of OCD in childhood, adolescence and in adults demonstrate a substantial prevalence of subclinical cases that are characterized by a relatively good prognosis. Indeed, subclinical cases seem to form a clinically valid subgroup, which can be treated successfully but which modern classification systems fail to recognize. Moreover, in prospective studies of adults, OCD cases appear to fluctuate in severity around the diagnostic threshold, raising yet more doubts about the threshold. Application of strict diagnostic criteria results in low prevalence rates, i.e. under 1%, whereas a slightly softer definition (as for instance introduced by the DIS or the SPIKE) increases the lifetime prevalence rates of OCS to 2.0% (one assessment) or to 5.5% (four assessments).

There is a dearth of prospective studies conducted over several years with repeated assessments, with the consequence that our understanding of the course of OCD and OCS is still sketchy. For a substantial number of cases in the community the prognosis may be fairly good, owing perhaps to the development of coping strategies, which also await proper description. Severe and chronic cases probably form only one end of the spectrum and are probably not representative of the disorder itself.

To date, the epidemiological studies of OCD have largely been descriptive, and there has been no community study dealing with causal models based on repeated assessments in order to test the effect of personality, risk factors, or interfering variables on the natural history of the disorder.

Obsessive compulsive disorder has an early onset, with the symptoms frequently occurring in childhood or adolescence. While, transculturally, the symptoms of OCD appear to be rather stable, there is evidence to suggest that the disorder is considerably less prevalent in Indian and Chinese cultures.

The current classification of OCD as an anxiety disorder is not grounded on sufficient evidence. One study (42) described a relatively strong association between OCS and a number of anxiety disorders, as well as depression and attempted suicide. The ECA Study (16), on the other hand, found no specific associations. Even more intriguing are the findings regarding adolescents (41) and adults (32), which suggest that OCD is associated with behavioral symptoms (lying, stealing, trouble at school, fights, etc.) and with suicide attempts.

Acknowledgment

This project was supported by grant 32-33580-92 from the Swiss National Science Foundation.

References

1. Leaf PJ, Meyers JK, McEvoy LT. Procedures used in the epidemiologic catchment area study. In: Psychiatric Disorders in America. The Epidemiologic Catchment Area Study (eds Robins LN, Regier DA) The Free Press, New York, pp 11–32.

2. Degonda M, Wyss M, Angst J. The Zurich Study. XVIII. Obsessive–compulsive disorders and syndromes in the general population. Eur Arch Psychiatr Clin Neurosci 1993; 243: 16–22.
3. Stefansson JG, Lindal E, Bjoernsson JK, Guomundsdottir A. Lifetime prevalence of specific mental disorder among people born in Iceland in 1931. Acta Psychiatr Scand 1991; 84: 142–149.
4. Flament MF, Whitaker A, Rapoport JL et al. Obsessive compulsive disorder in adolescence: an epidemiological study. J Am Acad Child Adolesc Psychiatry 1988; 27: 764–771.
5. Khanna S, Gururay G, Sriram TG. Epidemiology of obsessive C disorder in India. Presented at First International Obsessive–Compulsive Disorder Congress, Capri, Italy, Mar 1993.
6. Derogatis LR. SCL-90. Administration, Scoring, and Procedures Manual-I for the R (revised) version and other instruments of the Psychopathology Rating Scales Series. Johns Hopkins University School of Medicine, Chicago, 1977.
7. Robins L. Epidemiology: reflections on testing the validity of psychiatric interviews. Arch Gen Psychiatry 1985; 42: 918–924.
8. Rasmussen SA, Eisen JL. Epidemiology of obsessive compulsive disorder. J Clin Psychiatry 1990; 51 (suppl): 10–13.
9. Herjanic B, Campbell W. Differentiating psychiatrically disturbed children on the basis of a structured psychiatric interview. J Abnorm Child Psychol 1977; 5: 127–135.
10. Angst J, Dobler-Mikola A, Binder J. The Zurich Study. A prospective epidemiology study of depressive, neurotic and psychosomatic syndromes. Eur Arch Psychiatry Neurol Sci 1984; 234: 13–20.
11. Yeh E-K, Hwu H-G, Chang L-Y, Yeh Y-L. Lifetime prevalence of mental disorders in a Chinese metropolis and two townships. Proceedings of the International Symposium on Psychiatric Epidemiology, 1985, Taipei City, Republic of China.
12. Yeh EK, Rin H, Yeh C-C, Hwu H-G. Prevalence of mental disorders. Proceedings of the International Symposium on Psychiatric Epidemiology, 1985, Taipai City, Republic of China.
13. Wittchen HU, von Zerssen D. Verläufe behandelter und unbehandelter depressionen und angststörungen. Eine klinisch-psychiatrische und epidemiologische verlaufsuntersuchung. Springer, Berlin, Heidelberg, New York, 1988.
14. Lindal E, Stefansson JG. The lifetime prevalence of anxiety disorders in Iceland as estimated by the US National Institute of Mental Health Diagnostic Interview Schedule. Acta Psychiatr Scand 1993; 88: 29–34.
15. Wells JE, Bushnell JA, Hornblow AR, Joyce PR, Oakley-Browne MA. Christchurch psychiatric epidemiology study, part i: methodology and lifetime prevalence for specific psychiatric disorders. Aust NZJ Psychiatry 1989; 23: 315–326.
16. Karno M, Golding JM, Sorenson SB, Burnam MA. The epidemiology of obsessive-compulsive disorder in five US communities. Arch Gen Psychiatry 1988; 45: 1094–1099.
17. Henderson JG, Pollard A. Three types of obsessive compulsive disorder in a community sample. J Clin Psychol 1988; 44: 747–752.
18. Canino GJ, Bird HR, Shrout PE, Rubio-Stipec M, Bravo M, Martinez R, Sesman M, Guevara LM. The prevalence of specific psychiatric disorders in Puerto Rico. Arch Gen Psychiatry 1987; 44: 727–735.
19. Crum RM, Anthony JC. Cocaine use and other suspected risk factors for obsessive–compulsive disorder: a prospective study with data from the

Epidemiologic Catchment Area surveys. Drug Alcohol Depend 1993; 31: 281–295.

20. Karno M, Golding JM. Obsessive compulsive disorder. In: Psychiatric Disorders in America. The Epidemiologic Catchment Area Study (eds Robins LN, Regier DA) The Free Press, Macmillan, London, 1991, pp 204–219.

21. Oakley-Browne MA, Joyce PR, Wells JE, Bushnell JA, Hornblow AR. Christchurch psychiatric epidemiology study, part II: six month and other period prevalences of specific psychiatric disorders. Aust NZJ Psychiatry 1989; 23: 327–340.

22. Bland RC, Newman SC, Orn H. Age of onset of psychiatric disorders. Acta Psychiatr Scand 1988; 77 (suppl 338): 43–49.

23. Burnam MA, Hough RL, Escobar JI et al. Six-month prevalence of specific psychiatric disorders among Mexican Americans and non-hispanic whites in Los Angeles. Arch Gen Psychiatry 1987; 44: 687–694.

24. Rasmussen SA, Tsuang MT. Epidemiology and clinical features of obsessive–compulsive disorder. In: Theory and Management (eds Jenike MA, Baer L, Minichello WE). Littleton, MA, 1986, pp 23–24.

25. Whitaker A, Johnson J, Shaffer D et al. Uncommon troubles in young people: Prevalence estimates of selected psychiatric disorders in a nonreferred adolescent population. Arch Gen Psychiatry 1990; 47: 487–496.

26. Akhtar S, Wig NN, Varma VK, Pershad D, Verma SK. A phenomenological analysis of symptoms in obsessive-compulsive neurosis. Br J Psychiatry 1975; 127: 342–348.

27. Khanna S, Channabasavanna, SM. Towards a classification of compulsions in obsessive compulsive neurosis. Psychopathology 1987; 20: 23–28.

28. Hinjo S, Hirano C, Murase S et al. Obsessive–compulsive symptoms in childhood and adolescence. Acta Psychiatr Scand 1989; 80: 83–91.

29. Sharma BP. Obsessive–compulsive neuroses in Nepal. Transcult Psychiatr Res 1968; 5: 38–45.

30. Khanna S, Kaliaperumal VG, Channabasavanna SM. Clusters of obsessive–compulsive phenomena in obsessive–compulsive disorder. Br J Psychiatry 1990; 156: 51–54.

31. ICD-9 International Classification of Diseases. Manual of the International Statistical Classification of Diseases, Injuries, and Causes of Death. Based on the recommendations of the Ninth Revision Conference, 1975, and adopted by the Twenty-ninth World Health Assembly. World Health Organization, Geneva, 1977.

32. Sanavio E. Obsession and compulsions: The Padua inventory. Behav Res Ther 1988; 26: 169–177.

33. Mavissakalian MR. Functional classification of obsessive compulsive phenomena. J Behav Assess 1979; 1: 271–279.

34. Rapoport JL. The walking nightmare: An overview of obsessive compulsive disorder. J Clin Psychiatry 1990; 51 (suppl): 25–28.

35. Berman L. The obsessive compulsive neurosis in children. J Nerv Ment Dis 1942; 95: 26–39.

36. Hollingsworth CE, Tanguay PE, Grossman L, Pabst P. Long-term outcome of obsessive–compulsive disorder in childhood. J Am Acad Child Psychiatry 1980; 19: 134–144.

37. Rapoport JL. Childhood obsessive compulsive disorder. J Child Psychol Psychiatry 1986; 27: 289–296.

38. Insel TR, Murphy DL. The psychopharmacological treatment of obsessive–compulsive disorder: A review. J Clin Psychopharmacol 1981; 1: 304–311.

39. Berg CZ, Rapoport JL, Whitaker A et al. Childhood obsessive–disorder: A

two-year prospective follow-up of a community sample. J Am Acad Child Adolesc Psychiatry 1989; 28: 528–533.
40.   Freeman CP. What is obsessive compulsive disorder? The clinical syndrome and its boundaries. Int Clin Psychopharmacol 1992; 7 (suppl 1): 11–18.
41.   Hollander E, Greenwald S, Neville D, Hornig C, Johnson J, Weissman M. Uncomplicated and comorbid obsessive–compulsive disorder in an epidemiological sample. Am J Psychiatry [in press].
42.   Angst J. Comorbidity of anxiety, phobia, compulsion and depression. Int Clin Psychopharmacol 1993; 8 (suppl 1): 21–25.

9 GENETIC STUDIES OF OBSESSIVE COMPULSIVE DISORDER

Steven A Rasmussen

Brown University School of Medicine, Butler Hospital, Providence, RI, USA

Introduction

Both Freud (1) and Janet (2) thought it likely that constitutional or genetic factors were important in the pathogenesis of obsessive compulsive (OC) symptoms. Although for the most part their evidence was anecdotal and descriptive, over the next several decades it stimulated a series of more systematic family studies in obsessive compulsive disorder (OCD). The potential significance that genetic studies have in contributing to our understanding of the pathogenesis of the disorder has become increasingly clear with recent advances in molecular biology. The evidence that genotypic factors are important in the phenotypic expression of psychiatric symptoms has been gathered from four basic sources: twin studies, family studies, adoption studies, and genetic linkage studies. There have been no adoptive studies in OCD, and linkage studies have only just begun. This chapter will critically review existing family and twin studies. It will also focus on the methodological implications of the heterogeneity and comorbidity of OCD for future family and genetic linkage studies.

Twin studies

Anecdotal reports of concordance in OCD twins were reviewed by Rasmussen and Tsuang in 1986 (3). Thirty-two of 51 (63%) monozygotic (MZ) twins reported in this series were concordant for OCD. These

Current Insights in Obsessive Compulsive Disorder. Edited by E. Hollander, J. Zohar, D. Marazzati and B. Olivier
© 1994 John Wiley & Sons Ltd

reports were mostly single case studies and, because no data from dizygotic (DZ) twins were available, definitive conclusions could not be made. However, the concordance rates for the MZ twins were consistent with those reported for other anxiety and affective disorders (4, 5).

Carey and Gottesman (6) studied a sample of 30 twin pairs (15 MZ and 15 DZ) identified by one of the twins having sought clinical treatment. The majority of the other MZ co-twins who had sought psychiatric treatment did so for OC symptoms. The rates of diagnosable OCD were not significantly different in the MZ and the DZ twins. However, if one included subclinical OCD (obsessional features) in the analysis, 87% of the MZ twin pairs were concordant compared with 47% of the DZ pairs. As in many of the twin and family studies, there were no clear criteria that distinguished OCD from subclinical OCD.

Clifford et al (7) completed an analysis of data collected from 419 pairs of unselected twins who had been given the Leyton Obsessional Inventory (8) and the Eysenck Personality Questionnaire. Multivariate analyses led to a heritability estimate of 0.47 for obsessional symptoms. Andrews et al (9) completed structured interviews of 446 pairs of adult twins, focusing on specific anxiety and mood-related symptoms. There was no evidence that these MZ twin pairs were significantly more concordant than DZ pairs for depression, dysthymia, OCD, social phobia, panic/agoraphobia, or generalized anxiety disorder (GAD). However, there did appear to be a genetic contribution to overall neuroticism.

Torgerson (10) came to similar conclusions in a study of a large sample of same-sex Norwegian twins. The sample was identified by a retrospective review of outpatient mental health records. At least one member of the pair had been treated for a neurotic condition. The twins were interviewed using the Present State Examination. Best estimate diagnoses were made from case synopses that were reviewed by independent psychiatrists. There was no significant difference in the concordance rates of the MZ twin pairs and the DZ twin pairs for obsessive neurosis. This may have been secondary to the fact that the OCD sample was very small. However, there was a significantly higher concordance rate for neurosis among MZ than among DZ twin pairs. Interestingly, the greatest risk for relatives was found for patients who were at the extreme of the severity spectrum.

In summary, the twin data support the existence of a heritable factor for neurotic anxiety. Some studies support the hypothesis that there is a heritable factor for OCD, while others do not. Since none of the concordance rates in MZ twins were 1.0, it can be safely concluded that environmental factors play at least some role in the phenotypic expression of symptoms. The discrepancies between studies may be due to limited sample sizes or differences in diagnostic criteria or thresholds. A systematic study of a large sample of OCD twins is needed to resolve these discrepancies.

Family studies

A series of family studies that were completed prior to 1970 found that OC symptoms occurred more frequently among biological relatives of patients than one would expect by chance (11–19). Unfortunately these studies suffered from one or more methodological shortcomings including: the lack of diagnostic criteria, the failure to use direct structured interviews of family members and probands, no control families interviewed, the lack of follow-up interviews.

While there was general agreement across studies that there was an increased risk of OC symptoms in first-degree family members, not all studies showed evidence for familiality. Differences in rates between studies may have been secondary to how cases were diagnosed. For example, Rosenberg reported that only two out of 547 relatives were affected with OCD (16). However, in order to qualify as having OCD in the Rosenberg study, patients needed to have been hospitalized for the disorder. McKeon and Murray (19) also reported no differences in the rate of OCD in the relatives of patients and those of controls. However, these investigators did report a higher rate of depression and anxiety disorders as a whole among the relatives of OC patients. These data support the previously reviewed twin studies that support the hypothesis that OCD is part of a broader inherited spectrum of neurotic anxiety.

Over the last 5 years, five additional family studies of OCD have been completed that have improved upon the methodological shortcomings of previous findings. All utilized standard diagnostic criteria and direct structured interviews of relatives and probands. Morbid risks for first-degree relatives varied significantly between these studies (see Table 9.1), but the majority support the hypothesis that there is a familial basis to the disorder.

Lenane et al (20) interviewed 145 first-degree relatives of 46 children and adolescents with severe OCD. Structured diagnostic interviews were conducted on both patients and relatives. Ninety-seven percent of the first-degree relatives completed the study battery. The investigators defined three separate categories of affected relatives and probands: OCD, subthreshold OCD, and compulsive personality. This standardized categorization eliminated a significant methodological weakness of previous investigations. Obsessive compulsive personality (OCP) symptoms were defined as a pervasive pattern of rigidity, indecisiveness, and perfectionism that interfered with social and occupational function. Subthreshold OCD was defined as traits or symptoms of OCD that were not severe enough to meet DSM-III criteria.

Twenty-five percent of the fathers and 9% of the mothers had OCD. An additional 13% of fathers and mothers had subclinical OCD. It is worth noting that 20% of the fathers and 2% of the mothers had OCP. Rates for affective disorder in family members also appeared to be elevated above

Table 9.1 Family studies of obsessive compulsive disorder (OCD) [adapted from Black et al (22)]

Authors	Year	Reference	Probands with OCD	No. of first-degree relatives	Diagnostic criteria	Controls	Blind to proband status	Structured interview	Rate of OCD in first-degree relatives (%)
Lewis	1936	11	50	306	No	No	No	No	28.1
Brown	1942	12	20	96	No	Yes	No	No	7.3
Rudin	1953	13	130	580	No	No	No	No	3.2
Kringlen	1956	14	91	182	No	No	No	No	2.0
Lo	1967	15	88	485	No	No	No	No	6.5
Rosenberg	1967	16	144	547	No	No	No	No	0.5
Insel et al	1983	17	27	54	DSM-III	No	No	No	0
Rasmussen and Tsuang	1986	18	44	88	DSM-III	No	No	No	10.2
McKeon and Murray	1987	19	50	149	RDC	Yes	No	No	0.6
Lenane et al	1990	20	46	145	DSM-III	No	Yes	Yes	17.0
Black et al	1992	23	32	120	DSM-III	Yes	Yes	Yes	2.6
Riddle et al	1993	21	21	42	DSM-III	No	Yes	Yes	16.2
Bellodi et al	1993	22	92	281	DSM-III	No	Yes	Yes	3.4
Pauls et al	1993	24	100	571	DSM-III	Yes	Yes	Yes	10.3
Fyer et al	1993	25	50	148	DSM-III	Yes	Yes	Yes	7.0

the figures that have been reported in the general population. This was not the case for the major anxiety disorders. The age-corrected risk for OCD and subthreshold OCD combined for all first-degree relatives was 35%. One significant shortcoming of this study was the failure to include a control group. While the rates of OCD and other Axis I disorders can be compared with the rates obtained in epidemiological studies, there has been no epidemiological study to date that will allow a meaningful comparison of the rates for subclinical OCD.

In a second family study of 21 child and adolescent OCD probands and their relatives, direct structured interviews were obtained (21). Fifteen of 42 patients (35.7%) received a diagnosis of clinical or subclinical OCD. No data were reported on rates of compulsive personalities found in either the probands or relatives. No comparisons were made with a matched control sample in this study.

L Bellodi et al (personal communication) studied the families of 92 adult patients with OCD. Probands were assessed for Axis I diagnoses using the Diagnostic Interview Schedule–Revised (DIS-R), and for Axis II diagnoses using the Structured Interview Diagnosis of Personality-Revised (SID P-R). Direct interviews were obtained in 73.3% of 281 first-degree relatives. No control sample was interviewed. No distinction was made between OCD and subthreshold OCD. The rate of OCD among first-degree relatives was 3.4%. However, it should be noted that when probands were separated on the basis of age at onset, the rates were significantly higher among relatives of probands who had an age at onset of less than 14 years. The risk for OCD among relatives of those with onset at less than 14 years was 8.8%.

Black et al (22) studied the families of 32 adult OCD probands and 33 normal controls. They utilized direct structured interviews of all first-degree family members. Diagnoses were made by independent raters who were blind to proband status, using best estimate diagnoses. Age-corrected morbidity risks were determined for OCD, subsyndromal OCD, compulsive personality, mood disorder, anxiety disorders, and substance abuse. The risk for OCD was 2.6% for first-degree relatives of OCD probands and 2.4% for the relatives of controls. The risk for subsyndromal OCD was 17.5% for OC relatives and 12.5% for control relatives. Interestingly, in spite of the fact that there were no significant differences in relative risks for all relatives of OC probands and those of controls in this study, the risk of morbidity for mothers of OC probands was 21% compared with 4.3% of the mothers of control subjects. The rates of anxiety disorders were significantly increased among relatives of obsessional probands compared with the relatives of controls.

Pauls et al (personal communication) studied 100 consecutive OCD probands and 466 first-degree relatives using direct structured interviews. Thirty-three normal controls and 113 first-degree relatives of the controls were also interviewed using an identical battery. Best estimate diagnoses were made by two independent raters who were blind to the proband status. Diagnoses were made for both OCD and subclinical OCD. Subclinical OCD was diagnosed when an individual met all criteria for OCD except that symptoms were reported to occur for less than 1 hour a day, met all criteria for OCD except ego-dystonicity and insight, or met all criteria for OCD except for interference and distress. One problematic aspect of the study was that only 228 out of the 571 relatives were interviewed directly. The rate of OCD in the relatives of the OCD probands (10.3%) was significantly higher than the rate in the control relatives (1.9%). A significant difference for subclinical OCD among relatives of OCD probands was also found between OC relatives (7.9%) and control relatives (2.0%). The relative risks for OCD and subthreshold OC symptoms was 18.2% compared with 4.0% among controls. The rate of OCD and subclinical OCD was approximately two times higher among the relatives of the probands aged less than 14 years at onset. Interestingly, 50% of the proband sample showed no familial transmission. This strongly suggests possible heterogeneity in the proband sample.

Fyer et al (23) reported on 148 first-degree relatives of OC probands. Patients were interviewed with the SADS-LA and a neurological soft sign battery. Lifetime rates of OCD, subthreshold, and other anxiety disorders in OC relatives were compared to those of the relatives of never mentally ill controls. Diagnostic categorizations were completed by blind independent raters using best estimate methodology. The relatives of OC probands had a significantly higher rate of both OCD (7% vs 2%) and subthreshold OC (9% vs 0%) than relatives of never-ill controls ($n = 56$). The rates of anxiety disorders and major depression did not differ between the groups. Interestingly, a higher but nonsignificant level of neurological soft signs was found in the relatives of OCD probands than in those of controls.

In summary, the majority of studies have supported the hypothesis that OCD is familial. The Black et al and Bellodi et al studies are two recent exceptions. Both studies used structured direct interviews of relatives. Blind independent raters were also used in both studies. The low rates of OCD that were found could be explained by several factors. First, best estimate diagnoses were made using all available information (both direct interview and multiple informant family history reports) in the studies by Pauls et al, Fyer et al, Lenane et al, and Riddle et al. In contrast, diagnosticians in the Black et al study relied on direct interviews. It may be that the best estimate method overestimates the true risk, or that direct interview underestimates the true risk. Obsessive compulsive disorder is a secretive disorder. Patients often expend a great deal of effort on concealing their illness from other family members. On the other hand, patients may deny symptoms when asked about them directly. Thus, it is important to also obtain information from multiple informants who may have observed obsessive and compulsive symptoms in the subject.

Second, there may be differences in how the severity of the obsessions and compulsions and their impact on social and occupational function are rated across studies. None of the studies used the Yale–Brown Obsessive Compulsive Scale (Y-BOCS) or NIMH Global Obsessive Compulsive ratings, the two most widely used measures of OC symptoms severity. None of the studies used quality-of-life measures and little effort was expended in measuring the degree of impairment in specific areas of social and occupational function.

Third, there may be differences in clinical characteristics of the probands that affect risk in the relatives. For example, in the study by Bellodi et al, 80% of the probands had an onset after the age of 14 years. In 82% of the probands in the study by Paul et al onset was before the age of 18 years. Differences in the willingness of the Iowa subjects (Black's study) and New England subjects (Paul's study) to divulge symptoms might explain some of the variance.

Methodological improvements that should be considered for future family studies should include the following:

1. Standardized diagnostic criteria.
2. A structured diagnostic interview that includes sections on Tourettes and tics, trichotillomania, hypochondriasis, eating disorders, delusional disorders, dysmorphophobia, and compulsive personality.
3. Measures of OC severity (Y-BOCS) in probands and relatives.
4. Data that is corroborated from both direct interviews as well as interviews with relatives.
5. Best estimate diagnoses made by blind independent raters.
6. Interviews of matched controls and relatives.
7. Clear definitions of OCD, subthreshold OC, and compulsive personality.
8. Quality-of-life measures.
9. Follow-up interviews to ascertain stability of diagnoses over time.

Diagnostic thresholds and OC related disorders

The importance of making accurate and reliable diagnoses over time in genetic linkage analysis has been amply demonstrated by the longitudinal Amish bipolar family study. Changes in the diagnosis of one or two members of a pedigree can have a drastic effect on the lod scores in genetic linkage analysis (24). In comparison with either schizophrenia or depression, OCD is quite a homogeneous diagnosis. None the less, it seems probable that it is a heterogeneous disorder with multiple genetic and environmental determinants. Experience in medical conditions such as cystic fibrosis has shown that after the abnormal gene is identified, many individuals who were never previously suspected of carrying the gene were found to have previously undiagnosed forms of subthreshold illness (personal communication). The accuracy of diagnoses in the comparatively heterogeneous psychiatric disorders is almost certain to make the interpretation of linkage analysis hazardous. This underscores the importance of long-term follow-up studies of OCD that have a family component, to determine the long-term stability and reliability of diagnoses. The phenomenological heterogeneity and extensive comorbidity of OCD with other Axis I and Axis II disorders has been well established (18). The major challenge now facing diagnosticians and geneticists is whether to include subthreshold OCD and the so-called OC-related disorders as OCD.

The basic problem in diagnosing subthreshold disorder is where to make the diagnostic cut-off on what seems to be a continuous range of severity of illness. Rachman and deSilva (25) pointed out that there was no qualitative difference between the obsessive thoughts of normal college students versus those of obsessive patients in terms of content. The difference appeared to be in the ability of individuals to dismiss their thoughts, and in the amount of time and anxiety that they experienced due to the obsessive beliefs. To make a diagnosis of OCD, DSM-III-R requires that ego-dystonic symptoms be present for at least a 6-month period of time, that they cause significant distress, and that they significantly interfere with social and occupational function. Variables that could lead to a diagnosis of subthreshold OCD could include ego-syntonic symptoms, symptoms with a duration of less than 6 months, symptoms that don't cause significant distress, and symptoms that don't interfere with social and occupational function. There are many potential combinations of these variables that could qualify for a diagnosis of subthreshold OCD. All of the permutations of these variables need to be considered when defining what constitutes subthreshold disorder. What constitutes significant distress or anxiety? Additional measures of social and occupational impairment with proven reliability and validity and that are not too time consuming to be administered are needed. Quantitative measures of distress, such as items 3 and 8 of the Y-BOCS, should be used on a routine basis. More work needs to be done on defining the longitudinal course of these disorders, and in particular if subthreshold symptoms continue to remain subthreshold or if they become more problematic over time. Leonard et al (26) have shown that in adolescents there is considerable movement from subclinical OCD to OCD and vice versa over time.

Determining which of the so-called OC-related disorders should be subsumed under the diagnosis of OCD is even more problematic. First, there is no established diagnostic criteria for what constitutes an OC related disorder. Disorders that are frequently mentioned as being part of this categorization include such diverse diagnoses as Tourette's syndrome, dysmorphophobia, hypochondriasis, the monosymptomatic delusional disorders, trichotillomania, impulse control disorders, and even anorexia nervosa. Without pre-existing knowledge of the pathophysiology of these conditions, we must rely on clustering of similarities in the course of illness, clinical features, family histories, biological markers, and treatment response, to formulate educated hypotheses about these disorders' relationships to one another. Some investigators have adopted the approach of seeing whether adding a particular diagnostic group such as OCD to the segregation analysis of, for example, Tourette's syndrome improves the fit of an autosomal dominant, single gene locus hypothesis (27). Others have criticized this approach as putting the cart before the horse. Recent evidence supports the hypothesis that OCD is a heterogeneous diagnosis.

In illnesses as complex as psychiatric syndromes like OCD or schizophrenia, diagnostic uncertainty may be the limiting factor in the success or lack of success of genetic linkage analysis. Valid and reliable measures of symptom severity, impairment of social and occupational function, and diagnosis will prove particularly critical in this regard. The next generation of family studies should pay particular attention to the careful definition of subthreshold syndromes, heterogeneity, and comorbidity.

References

1. Freud S. Obsessive actions and religious practices. In: The Standard Edition of the Complete Psychological Works of Sigmund Freud, vol 9 (ed Strachey J). Hogarth, London, 1952, pp 115–127.
2. Janet P. Les Obsessions et la Psychasthenie, 2nd edn. Baillière, Paris, 1904.
3. Rasmussen SA, Tsuang MT. DSM-III obsessive compulsive disorder: clinical characteristics and family history. Am J Psychiatry 1986; 143: 317–322.
4. Kendler KS, Health AC, Martin NG, Eaves LJ. Symptoms of anxiety and symptoms of depression. Arch Gen Psychiatry 1987; 44: 451–457.
5. Carey G. Big genes, little genes, affective disorders and anxiety. Arch Gen Psychiatry 1987; 44: 486–491.
6. Carey G, Gottesman II. Twin and family studies of anxiety, phobic and obsessive disorders. In: Anxiety: New Research and Changing Concepts (eds Klien DF, Rabkin J). Raven Press, New York, 1981, pp 117–136.
7. Clifford CA, Murray RM, Rulker DW. Genetic and environment influences on obsessional traits and symptoms. Psychol Med 1984; 14: 791–800.
8. Cooper J. The Kettib Obsessional Inventory. Psychiatr Med 1970; 1: 48–52.
9. Andrews G, Stewart G, Allen R, Henderson AS. The genetics of six neurotic disorders: A twin study. J Aff Disord 1990; 19: 23–29.
10. Torgerson S. Genetic factors in anxiety disorders. Arch Gen Psychiatry 1983; 40: 1085–1089.
11. Lewis A. Problems of obsessional illness. Proc R Soc Med 1936; 36: 325–336.
12. Brown FW. Heredity in the psychoneuroses. Proc R Soc Med 1942; 35: 785–790.
13. Rudin E. Ein Beitrag zur Frage der Zwangskrankheit. Arch Psychiat Nervenkr 1953; 191: 14–15.

14. Kringlen E. Obsessional neurotics: a long term follow-up. Br J Psychiatry 1965; 111: 709–722.
15. Lo WH. A follow-up study of obsessional neurotics in Hong Kong Chinese. Br J Psychiatry 1967; 113: 823–832.
16. Rosenberg CM. Familial aspects of obsessional neurosis. Arch Gen Psychiatry 1967; 113: 405–413.
17. Insel TR, Hoover C, Murphy DL. Parents of patients with obsessive–compulsive disorder. Psychol Med 1983; 13: 807–811.
18. Rasmussen SA, Tsuang MT. Clinical characteristics in family history in DSM-III obsessive–compulsive disorder. Am J Psychiatry 1986; 143: 317–322.
19. McKeon P, Murray R. Familial Aspects of Obsessive Compulsive Neurosis. Br J Psychiatry 1987; 151: 528–534.
20. Lenane MC, Swedo SE, Leonard H et al. Psychiatric disorders in first degree relatives of children and adolescents with obsessive–compulsive disorder. J Am Acad Child Adolesc Psychiatry 1990; 29: 407–412.
21. Riddle MA, Schaill L, King R et al. Obsessive compulsive disorder in children and adolescents: Phenomenology and family history. J Am Acad Child Adolesc Psychiatry 1990; 29: 766–772.
22. Black DW, Nayes R, Goldstein RB, Blum N. A family study of obsessive compulsive disorder. Arch Gen Psychiatry 1992; 49: 362–368.
23. Fyer A, Mannuzza S, Chapman TF, Liebowtz MR, Aronowitz B, Klein DF. Familial transmission of obsessive compulsive disorder. Presented at First International Obsessive–Compulsive Disorder Conference, Capri, Italy, 12–13 Mar 1993, p 98.
24. Pauls DL, Alsobrook SP, Goodman WK, Rasmussen SA, Leckman JL. A family study of obsessive compulsive disorder. Am J Psychiatry [in press].
25. Rachman S, DeSilva P. Abnormal and normal obsessions. Behav Res Ther 1978; 16: 233–248.
26. Leonard HL, Swedo SE, Lenane MC et al. A 2- to 7-year follow-up study of 54 obsessive compulsive children and adolescents. Arch Gen Psychiatry 1933; 50: 429–439.
27. Pauls DI, Leckman JF. The inheritance of Gilles de la Tourette's syndrome and associated behaviors. N Engl J Med 1986; 315: 993–997.

PART III
PATHOPHYSIOLOGY

10 ANIMAL MODELS OF OBSESSIVE COMPULSIVE DISORDER: A REVIEW

Thomas R Insel*, Jan Mos[+] and Berend Olivier[+‡]

*Laboratory of Neurophysiology, NIHM, Poolesville, MD, USA
[+]Department of CNS-Pharmacology, Solvay Duphar BV, Weesp, The Netherlands
[‡]Department of Psychopharmacology, Faculty of Pharmacy, University of Utrecht, Utrecht, The Netherlands

Introduction

Any attempt to develop an animal model of obsessive compulsive disorder (OCD) ultimately has to confront a fundamental question about the nature of this syndrome. Is this a disorder of aberrant thoughts—laden with aggression, guilt, and doubt—and often associated with secondary compulsive rituals? Or is this a disturbance of primitive motor circuits involving grooming and checking, with a secondary preoccupation with contamination or doubt generated by the patient's need to explain the stereotyped, automatic motor behavior? Both perspectives are well represented in the current clinical literature on OCD (1, 2).

Clearly, however, animal models of the "aberrant thoughts" view of OCD are not verifiable. Even among our closest primate relatives, the great apes, the existence of reprehensible aggressive thoughts or pathological guilt may be surmised by careful observation [see, for instance, Goodall (3)], but cannot be rigorously proved. It may be relevant in this regard that one of the neuroanatomical regions most frequently implicated in the pathophysiology of OCD is the prefrontal cortex, a mysterious region that comprises 30% of the human neocortex (4). This region, which is comparatively rudimentary in other primates, appears to be specifically important for anticipation (worry), temporal sequencing

Current Insights in Obsessive Compulsive Disorder. Edited by E. Hollander, J. Zohar, D. Marazzati and B. Olivier
© 1994 John Wiley & Sons Ltd

(doubt), and judgment (or guilt) in humans. Although the evolution of prefrontal cortex is an area of considerable controversy in the anatomical literature, anthropological data using cranial endoplasts demonstrate that a large prefrontal lobe was probably not present in hominid fossils before approximately 100 000 years ago [reviewed by MacLean (5)]. Based on this fossil evidence, one might conclude that the comparative study of OCD would be about as rewarding as the comparative study of dyslexia or aphasia.

Rather than ending this review on this somber conclusion, we will consider the second perspective of OCD—the repetitive motor circuit model—which has its anatomical representation in the phylogenetically ancient basal ganglia and may be evident in the stereotypic behaviors of virtually all vertebrates. It is important to note at the outset that the behaviors in question are motorically normal, but they are exhibited excessively or in a context that is inappropriate. A great number of such behaviors might be considered in reference to OCD, from the displacement behaviors of birds or mammals to the stereotypies observed during experimental studies of neurosis and frustration. The focus of this review will be to consider how any such behavior might be validated as either a "model" of OCD or a "minimodel" of some aspect of OCD pathology.

Validation of an animal model

Building on the original review of McKinney and Bunney (6), Willner (7) suggested three forms of validating criteria for assessing animal models of depression: predictive validity, face validity, and construct validity.

Predictive validity requires that treatments that reduce the symptoms of the illness affect the model behavior without errors of omission or commission. Ideally, potency in the model behavior should correlate with clinical potency. For predictive validity, the animal model need not resemble the clinical disorder except in terms of treatment response—the model basically serves as a behavioral assay for screening potential therapeutic agents. Mouse-killing behavior of rats (muricide) is such a model of depression, in that the behavior is reduced by several (although not all) classes of antidepressants.

In contrast, face validity requires, in addition to similar treatment response, a similarity in phenomenology. After olfactory bulbectomy, rats typically show irritability, hyperactivity, and hypercortisolemia—features also common in some forms of depression. As all of these effects in rats are reduced by antidepressants (most potently by serotonin (5-hydroxy tryptamine, 5-HT) reuptake inhibitors—SSRIs), olfactory bulbectomy has been suggested as a model of depression with a claim to face validity.

Finally, construct validity requires not only similarities in treatment response and phenomenology, but also a theoretical relationship to the disorder in question. Psychiatry has few such models, although no shortage of etiologic theories for its various disorders. In the case of depression, learned helplessness, separation distress, and "behavior despair" have all been touted as models with construct validity.

Predictive validity

There is a reasonable possibility of achieving predictive validity with an animal model of OCD because OCD responds to both pharmacological and behavioral treatments selectively. In terms of pharmacological approaches, thus far, the potent SSRIs (e.g. clomipramine, fluoxetine, and fluvoxamine) appear to be the only consistently effective treatments. In addition to this remarkable selectivity, almost every selective SSRI that has been tested appears to show some anti-obsessional potency (exceptions include zimelidine) (8, 9). Although one might screen for novel anti-obsessional agents simply by testing for the blockade of 5-HT uptake in platelets, the use of an animal model provides for checks on bioavailability, active metabolites, and responses to chronic vs acute treatment.

One such model is the isolation call of the rat pup. Prior to 14 days of age (when the eyes open), rat pups emit ultrasonic "distress" calls when they are isolated from social contact. These calls, which are a powerful stimulus for maternal retrieval, are outside of the range of auditory perception for humans and many predators (10, 11). Serotonin reuptake inhibitors (clomipramine 5.0 mg/kg, paroxetine 1.0 mg/kg, citalopram 1.0 mg/kg, or fluvoxamine 1 mg/kg) decrease these calls, whereas catecholamine uptake inhibitors (desipramine 5.0 mg/kg, mazindol 0.5 mg/kg, nortriptyline 1.0 mg/kg, or maprotiline 10 mg/kg) consistently increase them (12–16). The acute response thus appears to distinguish consistently between those antidepressants that are anti-obsessional and those that are not. Clomipramine reduces ultrasonic calls without affecting temperature, activity, or coordination (12). However, ultrasonic calls are also decreased by several compounds that are not clearly anti-obsessional (including benzodiazepines, opiates, and yohimbine) (10, 11). In addition, chronic administration of clomipramine (limited by the 2-week ontogenetic window during which these calls occur) is not effective in reducing isolation calls (12).

Matching the selectivity of pharmacological response is the selectivity of response to behavioral treatments in OCD. Several interventions that are effective for the reduction of phobias are ineffective in OCD, whereas the specific interventions of exposure and response prevention have been shown to confer long-term benefits. While these treatments clearly are based on the empirical foundation of habituation in the animal learning literature, we know of no specific model which responds selectively to these interventions and not to other behavioral treatments.

Face validity

The repetitive, stereotyped cleaning and checking rituals of OCD patients suggest several analogs in the realm of both naturalistic and experimental animal behavior. Naturalistic examples include displacement behaviors, such as the digging, grooming, and hoarding rituals found across vertebrate species faced with either frustration or conflict. Holland (17) was perhaps the first to point out the phenomenological similarities between displacement behavior and compulsive rituals. Stereotypies include both simple and complex repetitive motor acts that can be caused by experimental contingencies (e.g. adjunctive behaviors), by drug administration (e.g. psychomotor stimulants), or by unknown factors (e.g. "zoo behavior" in various carnivores). Finally, maze behavior, examining spontaneous alternation strategies, has been recently suggested as a model of obsessional perseveration. Each of these will be discussed below.

DISPLACEMENT BEHAVIOR

Displacement behaviors frequently show a curious automatic sequence of behavior, termed a "fixed action pattern", which suggests simple neural coding into an "all or nothing" signal. The behavior may appear excessive (e.g. hoarding) or inappropriate (e.g. the bird which in a territorial display pecks at the nonexistent worm), but may have some communicative value by virtue of either the formal pattern of the display or the number of times the display is repeated (18). While there are clear similarities between obsessional hoarding, washing, and checking and some of the most common displacement behaviors of other vertebrates, the extent to which these behaviors in OCD patients can be attributed to conflict or threat remains highly speculative. Moreover, it seems unlikely that OCD rituals have a communicative role, as patients are notoriously secretive about their rituals and rarely perform them in a social context.

There is a considerable literature on the pharmacology of grooming (19), but most of this is only remotely relevant to displacement. In a preliminary attempt to compare the response to clomipramine and desimipramine in a paradigm eliciting displacement grooming, Winslow and Insel (11) examined the frequency of grooming bouts of the intruder in a mouse resident–intruder test. A male mouse was placed in the scent-marked cage of an unfamiliar aggressive resident. When the resident was absent (in the anticipatory phase), the intruder's grooming was unaffected by clomipramine (5.0 mg/kg, i.p.), but nearly doubled by desimipramine (5.0 mg/kg, i.p.). When the resident was present (displacement phase), the intruder's grooming was decreased by more than half by clomipramine (5.0 mg/kg, i.p.), but unaffected by desimipramine (5.0 mg/kg, i.p.). These results would seem to suggest predictive as well as face validity for displacement grooming. Several additional studies will need to be done, however, to demonstrate the selectivity of this effect and to determine whether chronic treatment with a SSRI would be effective.

STEREOTYPIES—ADJUNCTIVE BEHAVIOR

Adjunctive behavior is spontaneous, repetitive behavior observed in experimental animals between regularly scheduled presentations of reward. Falk (20) was the first to describe how hungry rats exposed to periodic presentations of small pellets of food following a regular temporal delay would begin to drink excessively. This excessive drinking could not be attributed to a physiological demand nor was it due to the "superstitious" pairing of drinking with food delivery (21, 22). Recently, Woods et al (23) found that chronic selective SRIs (clomipramine, fluoxetine) inhibited schedule-induced polydipsia (SIP), whereas chronic desipramine, haloperidol, or diazepam had no influence, thereby suggesting that SIP may be a relevant animal model predictive for the treatment of OCD. Adjunctive behaviors are not limited to drinking; depending on the "releasing" stimuli, excessive wheel running, foraging, and aggression have all been elicited.

Altemus et al (24) have recently studied the pharmacology of one form of adjunctive behavior. Rats were fed for 90 minutes per day. This schedule is sufficient for maintaining body weight, but if the animal has access to a running wheel, he will begin to run excessively and may die of malnutrition within 2 weeks. Chronic treatment with fluoxetine (either 5.0 or 2.5 mg/kg i.p. for 5 weeks) but not imipramine (5.0 mg/kg i.p. for 5 weeks) decreased wheel running and weight loss while increasing food intake relative to saline-treated controls. Treatment with a 5-HT depleting agent (PCPA) actually increased wheel running and weight loss relative to controls. As fluoxetine presumably increased and parachlorophenylalanine (PCPA) decreased forebrain 5-HT, these results implicate 5-HT in the regulation of adjunctive wheel running and support both the predictive and face validity for this model. It should be noted that previous reports have described the role of mesolimbic dopamine pathways in the regulation of other forms of adjunctive behavior (25) and that the one region, the nucleus accumbens, that appears to mediate these dopaminergic effects (26) is also the region with one of the most dense concentrations of serotonin uptake sites (i.e. 5-HT terminals) in the primate forebrain (27, 28).

A very interesting and putative potential model for OCD has recently been introduced in one of our laboratories (JM, BO). When rats are trained on a Differential Reinforcement of Low Rates (DRL 18 s) schedule, their performance increases considerably when some manipulandum is present in the Skinnerbox (in this case a chain was suspended in the middle of the cage with a woodblock at the end). It appears that each individual animal develops its own "stereotypic" behavior in the waiting period (18 s) before a new response on the lever delivers a food reward. Animals show individual specific stereotypies (mostly chain gnawing and woodblock gnawing), which are constant over lengthy time periods (several months). Preliminary pharmacological experiments with SSRIs and neuroleptics show promising results, although much more work is needed to assess the status of the model as a putative OCD model.

STEREOTYPIES — ZOO BEHAVIOR

Zoo behavior is the label given to a diverse collection of poorly understood stereotypies observed in animals that are confined, isolated, or chronically frustrated (29, 30). These behaviors can range from scratching, hair pulling, or masturbation, to complex motor acts such as prolonged pacing rituals. Foraging mammals, particularly carnivores, appear most susceptible to these behaviors when confined.

One form of zoo behavior observed in certain breeds of dog may have particular relevance for OCD. Canine acral lick dermatitis (ALD) involves "compulsive" licking of a patch of skin on a paw or leg, leading initially to loss of fur and ultimately to a chronic abrasion of the underlying skin. This syndrome is also known as neurodermatitis, lick granuloma, or psychogenic alopecia (31), and is well known to veterinarians as a chronic, treatment-refractory, behavioral disorder. It seems to combine face, predictive and construct validity. Goldberger and Rapoport (32) were the first to describe the possible link between OCD and acral lick disorder (ALD).

Animals, mostly dogs or cats, repetitiously and without obvious purpose lick, scratch, or bite specific parts of their body. In dogs it is found most commonly in large breeds; in cats most often in oriental breeds (31). This stereotypic behavior is often so extreme that it results in skin lesions (dogs) or baldness (cats). Often secondary bacterial infections develop (32). Interestingly, skin lesions (dermatitis) have also been reported secondary to compulsive washing in human beings (33).

Stereotypic purposeless behavior resembling the one described by Goldberger and Rapoport (32) has also been reported by Brown in the dog (34), Dodman et al in the horse (35), dog (36), and stallion (37), and Korsgaard et al in the cebus monkey (38).

As in OCD patients (39, 40), benzodiazepines are not effective in ALD (34). However, SSRIs have been reported to be more successful in treating this condition (32). Again, as in OCD, clomipramine but not desipramine reduces the stereotypies. In a more extensive study, Rapoport et al (41) treated 37 afflicted dogs in 5-week crossover trials comparing either clomipramine (2.4–3.6 mg/kg) with desipramine (1.2–3.7 mg/kg), fluoxetine (0.55–1.36 mg/kg) with fenfluramine (0.55–1.36 mg/kg), and sertraline (2.7–4.3 mg/kg) with placebo. All drugs were given orally and clinical change was measured by each dog's owner (owners were trained and monitored, but inter-rater reliability was not assessed in this study). The results were remarkably analogous to what one expects in a clinical OCD population: the placebo response was nonexistent, each of the SSRIs (clomipramine, fluoxetine, and sertraline) were significantly better than their comparison agents, improvement evolved gradually over 5 weeks, and the mean maximal improvement was about 50% (somewhat less with sertraline). Moreover, like OCD patients, animals suffering from ALD relapse after stopping therapy with selective SSRIs.

A few clear relationships do exist between OCD and ALD, demonstrating:

1. Stress enhances the stereotypic/compulsive behavioral patterns both in animals with ALD (35, 36), and in OCD patients (42, 43).
2. In OCD (44–46) and in ALD (34, 36, 37) hereditary factors play a role. The etiological background of ALD is uncertain, but it has often been suggested that confinement, loneliness, and isolation in separate cages play an important role (31, 32, 35, 38). About the etiology of OCD even less is known but the same factors may also play a role here (47–52).

Interestingly a few years ago, isolation was reported to induce specific behavioral patterns in so-called tethered sows (53–55). Because this condition also seems to have face and construct validity for OCD, it will be discussed briefly. The predictive validity of this model still has to be investigated.

In sows purposeless, stereotypic behaviors develop after tethering. Interindividual variation in the stereotypic behavior is strikingly large, whereas the intraindividual variation is extremely small (53, 54). Sometimes the stereotypic behavior pattern of one animal consists only of three elements performed in a rigid sequence over and over again, for example bar nibbling (A), bar biting (B), and chewing (C) in a sequence ABC, ABC, etc. (53). Large interindividual variation and small intraindividual variation is also striking in the compulsive behavior of OCD patients; "Patients have to do the same thing over and over again until they feel it is right" (42 p. 129).

Various factors support the construct validity of this model, viz.

1. Hereditary factors probably play a part in the development of stereotypic behaviors in response to tethering, since stereotypies only develop in specific strains of pigs (Wiepkema PR, personal communication). Hereditary factors also play a role in OCD (46, 56).
2. In tethered sows the morphology of stereotyped acts may alter over

time. Initially, the stereotypies are directed at features in the external environment, e.g. chains, bars, etc. Over time they develop into self-directed stereotypies, e.g. chewing or mouth stretching (53, 54). Cronin (53 p. 21) describes this in the following way; "The form of an abnormal stereotyped behavior in an older animal may provide little insight into what the earlier forms of the stereotypy looked like". In OCD patients the same has been observed. Swedo et al (43, 51) mentioned that in 90% of cases the symptoms had changed over time. Most young patients had a single obsession or compulsion at onset, continued this for months to years and gradually acquired different thoughts or rituals [see also Rapoport (42)].

3. In tethered sows it is claimed that the stereotypies are plainly associated with conflict: for example restrains and/or confinement in an unstimulating and socially unbalanced environment (53, 55). Lack of certain factors in the environment, or loss of the ability to control the environment with one's own actions play a very important role in the etiology of the stereotypies (53, 54). It is tempting to speculate that OCD patients, who lack self-confidence and are in doubt and ambivalent about almost everything (57, 58), have a severe doubt about their control of the environment: "they will not risk making definite decisions or committing themselves to a point of view or course of action in case it turns out to be the wrong one" (52 p. 55). Jenike (57 p. 117) puts it this way: "One of the rules of OCD patients is that 'danger is imminent'". Like the sows that are claimed to rebuild a new environment that they can control through the performance of stereotypies (53, 54), perhaps the homology of the rituals and striving for perfection seen in OCD patients should be viewed as an attempt to control one's internal and external world: "Patients have the illusion that in this way they can make the world safe and secure" (57 p. 114). In other words, the ritualistic behavior may be a way to cope with a deep underlying uncertainty.

With regard to predictive validity very limited information is available; only naloxone, an opiate receptor antagonist, and haloperidol have been tested in the tethered sow model.

In the 2 hours following the administration of naloxone, time occupied by stereotypies was significantly reduced (33% of time) compared with that following saline administration (86% of time) (53). It should be noted that naloxone in the dosage used (≤ 1 mg/kg) did not affect the performance of exploratory behavior in nontethered sows. Brown et al (34) and Dodman et al (35–37) also have reported positive effects of opiate antagonists (naloxone and naltrexone) in animals performing ALD-like behavior. In OCD patients naloxone has only been used in case studies, with inconsistent results: Sandyke (59) reported positive effects, whereas Insel and Pickar (60) actually found a worsening rather than an improving effect. Like naloxone, haloperidol (250 mg i.m.) reduced stereotyped activities in pigs in the 4 days after treatment, without affecting the overall physical activities (61). There are also questions about the face validity of ALD, as dogs with this syndrome show no evidence that the licking behavior is aversive nor do they show associated avoidant behavior (41). In addition, it should be noted that this is not an experimental model, but a clinical veterinary disorder which currently is even less understood than OCD. Nevertheless, this initial study promises that ALD could be a useful model for studying not only the treatment but also the pathophysiology of a disorder with many of the features of OCD. One might wonder, for instance, about the developmental and genetic aspects of ALD as well as the environmental factors that reduce or enhance the symptoms. Elucidating the neural substrates of ALD by postmortem study may prove extremely helpful for telling us where to look for neurochemical and neuroanatomical pathology in OCD.

SPONTANEOUS ALTERNATION

The need for mini-models, mimicking some specific aspect of a clinical syndrome, has become more apparent in recent years. One such mini-model focusing on the perseveration and pathological doubt of some OCD patients has been recently described in a test of "spontaneous alternation" by Yadin et al (62). Food-deprived rats were run in a maze in which a black and a white goal box were equally baited with a small amount of chocolate milk. Each rat was given seven trials every other day, during which it was placed in the start box and allowed to make a choice. After a number of training trials, rats generally learn to alternate their choices rather than repetitively returning to the same arm. In this model, the dependent variables of interest are the number of repeated choices until an alternation occurs and the time spent in the choice area. A 5-HT receptor agonist 5-methoxy-N,N-dimethyl-tryptamine (5-MeODMT) (1.25 mg/kg, i.p.) delayed spontaneous alternation (the animals made more repeated choices), and this effect was blocked by chronic treatment with fluoxetine (2 × 5 mg/kg for 21 days). Although 5-MeODMT is a nonselective agonist, similar results were obtained with the 5-HT$_{1A}$ receptor agonist 8-hydroxy-2-(di-n-propylamino) tetralin (8-OH-DPAT). In subsequent studies using a four-arm maze, neither acute treatment with fluoxetine nor chronic treatment with desipramine (10 mg/kg, i.p.) affected the 5-HT agonist-induced delay.

This model posits an overactive serotonergic drive in OCD (presumably the 5-HT agonist increases "perseveration"), which is reduced by chronic treatment with SRIs. Several questions remain about the effects of other anti-obsessional compounds and the face validity of this model (is there an aversive component to the behavior?), but the finding of a response to chronic but not acute treatment with fluoxetine is important. Note, however, that 5-HT agonists alter both feeding and arousal, so the extent to which the delay in spontaneous alternation reflects perseveration rather than more general changes in other behavioral parameters still needs to be addressed.

Construct validity

As noted earlier, there are few animal models with construct validity in psychiatry. Ideally, construct validity should rest on a theory of etiology. In spite of remarkable advances in the treatment of OCD, the etiology of this syndrome remains as mysterious now as it was for Janet at the beginning of this century. Some important clues about etiology may be garnered from those rare patients who appear to develop OCD as a consequence of a neurological disorder. The presence of obsessional symptoms in a patient with an orbital–frontal meningioma (63) or in patients with basal disease [reviewed by Rapoport and Wise (64)] suggest obvious possibilities for the development of animal models using either lesion or stimulation techniques.

Perhaps the most exciting new development in the search for an etiology for OCD is the observation by Swedo et al (65) that children with Sydenham's chorea develop OCD at a higher rate than children with other forms of *Streptococcus* infection. More recently, this same group has observed correlations in caudate size on MRI scan within individual patients with Sydenham's chorea as the obsessive compulsive symptoms wax and wane (J Rapoport, personal communication, 1993). These results suggest that anticaudate antibodies generated in response to the *Streptococcus* infection directly lead to the symptoms of OCD. This is a hypothesis that can be tested rigorously in a nonhuman primate, in which the entire sequence from infection to behavior to neuropathology can be experimentally controlled. Such an experiment should provide an animal model with construct validity. Of course, one should not presume that many of the cases of OCD will be traced to an infectious/autoimmune cause. Nevertheless, by elucidating the pathophysiology of one rare form of OCD, we should learn what changes are necessary and sufficient for the development of this syndrome.

A ROLE FOR DOPAMINE AND 5-HT IN OCD?

Apart from the serotonergic involvement in OCD, it is sometimes suggested that the dopaminergic system in the basal ganglia is also affected in these patients [(66), see also Goodman et al (67)].

Since the animal models mentioned above show striking similarities between the animal condition and OCD, it is tempting to compare the effects of dopaminergic drugs in OCD patients and in animals with ALD [in the tethered sows, only one study showing the positive effects of the anti-dopaminergic drug haloperidol (see earlier) has been published]. Table 10.1 summarizes the results.

Dopamine (DA) receptor antagonists have positive effects on ALD (Table 10.1) and, despite the general belief of clinicians that these drugs are ineffective in OCD when given alone (67, 83), some case reports demonstrate positive effects in these patients (Table 10.1). In addition, DA receptor antagonists on top of ongoing therapy with SRIs potentiate the therapeutic effect of the latter drugs (Table 10.1) (73).

It has been suggested that positive effects of DA receptor antagonists occur especially in an OCD subgroup with comorbid tic spectrum disorders or schizotypal personality disorders (67, 73, 83). Positive effects of DA receptor antagonists have also been observed in OCD patients (Table 10.1) without these additional symptoms (70, 72).

Except for the results obtained by Insel et al (77), increasing the DA activity has been shown to result in an exacerbation of already existing OCD symptoms (Table 10.1). Only McDougle et al (75, 76) observed this effect in a patient with additional tic disorder. Leonard and Rapoport (74) and Rapoport (42) report exacerbation in a patient without these additional symptoms. Interestingly, in animals suffering from ALD, the symptoms also worsen after enhancing the DA activity (34). Enhancing the dopaminergic activity may induce OCD (78–80). Likewise, in animals, enhanced DA activity may elicit stereotypies (Table 10.1)

Finally, the close interaction between the 5-HT and DA systems as seen in OCD (73) (Table 10.1) exists also in DA induced stereotypies; Yamaguchi et al (1989) (Table 10.1) showed potentiation of stereotyped behaviors induced by methamphetamine and apomorphine when 5-HT is depleted.

The data given in Table 10.1 are not completely consistent. Insel et al (77) did not observe an exacerbation of OCD after enhancing DA activity, and no double blind drug/placebo controlled studies, but only case reports, exist on the DA involvement in OCD. Nevertheless, these data strongly suggest, together with 5-HT, an involvement of this neurotransmitter in both OCD and ALD (66, 67, 83). Dopamine hyperactivity in OCD, as hypothesized by these authors, would explain the positive effects of receptor antagonists and the exacerbations seen after DA receptor agonists. It is tempting to suggest that especially the DA system in the striatum is involved; this would explain the high metabolic rates for glucose observed in the striatum of OCD patients (84–87). It is even more tempting to hypothesize that especially the ventral part of the striatum is involved. This part of the striatum not only receives serotonergic input from the raphe nucleus (88) but also receives input from the anterior cingulate cortex and lateral orbital–frontal cortex (89, 64). The latter parts

Table 10.1 Effects of drugs that affect the dopamine (DA) system on obsessive compulsive disorder (OCD) and acral lick dermatitis (ALD)

Drugs	Humans			Animals	
	Effect*	Tic/schizoid personality disorder†	Reference	Effect	Reference
DOPAMINE (DA) ANTAGONISTS					
(Effect on already existing OCD/ALD)	→	?	68	→	34
	→	+	69	→	38
	→/0	−	70		
	→/0	?	71		
	→	±	72		
(DA Antagonists in addition to SSRIs)	→	+	73		
ENHANCEMENT OF DA ACTIVITY	↑	−	42	ALD ↑	34
	↑	−	74		
(Effect on already existing OCD/ALD)	↑	+	75, 76		
	→/0	?	77		
ENHANCEMENT OF DA ACTIVITY	↑		78	Stereotypies ↑	81
	↑		79	Stereotypies ↑	82
(Induction of OCD or stereotypies)	↑		80		

*↑, Enhancement or induction of OCD/ALD; ↓, reduction of OCD/ALD; 0, no effect; ↓/0, in some patients reduction of OCD but no effect in some patients.
†+, Tic/schizoid personality disorder; −, no tic/schizoid personality disorder; ?, no information about personality; ±, some patients have tics/schizoid personalities but others do not.

of the brain are involved in OCD, for stereotactic lesions have been shown to decrease OCD symptoms (66, 90), and PET scans have shown high glucose metabolism in the orbital frontal cortex and anterior cingulate gyrus (84, 87, 91), of these patients. In addition, the ventral striatum projects back to these cortical areas, respectively, through the substantia nigra pars reticulate (SNR)/globus pallidus (GP) and thalamus (89). Assuming a hyperactive DA system in the ventral striatum, this would result in hyperactivity of the excitatory thalamocortical projections because of the double inhibitory GABA-ergic (gamma-amino-butyric acid) (striatum–SNR/GP and SNR/GP–thalamus) connections in between [see also Rapoport and Wise (64), Modell (92)]. This high thalamocortical activity would explain the high rates for glucose metabolism in the orbital–frontal and anterior cingulate gyrus mentioned above. This involvement of the corticostriatal-thalamocortical system is also suggested by Leckman et al (93).

Conclusions

Much is not known about the pathology and therapy of OCD. Although the 5-HT system seems to play a very important role, other transmitter systems like the dopaminergic and perhaps even the opiate system are also involved. In order to learn more about the underlying pathology and therapy of this disabling disorder, animal models are needed. No good animal model exists, but both ADL and stereotypies in tethered sows are promising, combining predictive validity with face and construct validity.

This brief review has noted some of the recent attempts to develop an animal model of OCD. There is no single model that is ideal, but several do look promising for characterizing specific aspects of this syndrome (Table 10.2). The reader should be aware of two fundamental problems in

Table 10.2 Summary of proposed animal models of obsessive compulsive disorder

Proposed model	Predictive validity	Face validity	Construct validity
Pup isolation calls	Yes	No	No
Displacement grooming	Possibly	Yes	No
Adjunctive behavior	Yes	Yes	No
Canine acral lick	Yes	Yes	No ?
Tethered sows	Yes	Yes	Yes ?
Spontaneous alternation	Possibly	Possibly	No
DRL 18 s	Possibly	Yes	?

DRL 18 s = Differential Reinforcement of Low Rates 18 seconds.

this area. First, the nature of this clinical disorder precludes the development of a single satisfying model. One might argue that resistance and reprehensible thoughts are fundamental to OCD and that our inability to study these in other animals makes the use of animal models pointless. On the other hand, many of the features of compulsive behavior can be elicited in other species and, as we have seen, such "mini-models" may have both predictive and face validity. A more careful ethological approach to the phenomenology of both the clinical and animal behavior should prove helpful in establishing further face validity.

A second problem endemic to this area of research is the tendency to validate the model by pharmacological responsiveness. Species differ in their responsiveness to a given drug, based on differences in absorption, distribution, metabolism, and receptor localization. The last of these variables appears to show especially marked differences in comparative studies of serotonin receptors. Thus responses to chronic selective SSRIs in one species may not always extrapolate to responses in another. But even ignoring such species differences, there is a troubling circularity to using response to a SSRI as a criterion for a model of OCD. Not all OCD patients respond to SSRI and there remains the possibility that other compounds will prove effective (94). The conservative approach is to use pharmacological response to establish predictive validity and not as a criterion of face validity. The behavioral pharmacology of serotonergic compounds will no doubt provide many interesting parallels to ritualistic behavior in OCD patients. The reader should note, however, that careful physiological studies in cats have yielded little evidence for a relationship between a specific behavior and single cell activity in the dorsal raphe nucleus (95, 96). The one exception to this rule is a small cluster of cells in the dorsal raphe nucleus, which are activated when a cat licks, chews, or grooms with its mouth (95, 96). While such observations are intriguing, one should not presume that the neuropharmacology of serotonin will necessarily enlighten the neurochemical basis of OCD.

Finally, animal models for OCD will certainly become even more important in the future as we learn more about the pathophysiology of this disorder. The ability of lesions, toxins, and antibodies to alter specific neural pathways should provide vital tests of specific etiological theories of OCD. Before embarking on such studies, we will need to know which species to use, which behaviors to measure, and which criteria to adopt for recognizing the syndrome in a nonverbal animal.

References

1. Rapoport J. Recent advances in obsessive–compulsive disorder. Neuropsychopharmacology 1991; 5: 1–10.
2. Insel T. Has OCD research gone to the dogs? Neuropsychopharmacology 1991; 5: 13–17.

3. Goodall J. The Chimpanzees of Gombe: Patterns of Behavior. Harvard University Press, Cambridge, MA, 1986.
4. Goldman-Rakic PS. Circuitry of primate prefrontal cortex and regulation of behaviour by representational memory. In: Handbook of Physiology. A Critical Comprehensive Presentation of Physiological Knowledge and Concepts. Section 1: The Nervous System, vol V. Higher Functions of the Brain, Part I, American Physiological Society, Bethesda, 1987.
5. MacLean P. Triune Brain in Evolution. Plenum, New York, 1991.
6. McKinney W, Bunney W. Animal models of depression: review of evidence and implications for research. Arch Gen Psychiatry 1969; 21: 240–248.
7. Willner P. The validity of animal models of depression. Psychopharmacology 1984; 83: 1–16.
8. Insel TR, Mueller EA, Gillin JC, Siever LJ, Murphy DL. Biological markers in obsessive–compulsive and affective disorders. J Psychiatr Res 1984; 18: 407–425.
9. Insel TR, Zohar J, Benkelfat C, Murphy DL. Serotonin in obsessions, compulsions, and the control of aggressive impulses. Ann N Y Acad Sci 1990; 600: 574–586.
10. Winslow J, Insel T. The infant rat separation paradigm: A novel test for novel anxiolytics. Trends Pharm Sci 1991; 12: 402–404.
11. Winslow J, Insel T. Neuroethological models of OCD. In: The Psychobiology of Obsessive–Compulsive Disorder (eds Zohar J, Hollander E, Insel T). Springer, New York, 1991, pp 208–226.
12. Winslow J, Insel T. Serotonergic and catecholaminergic reuptake inhibitors have opposite effects on the ultrasonic isolation calls of rat pups. Neuropsychopharmacology 1990; 3: 51–59.
13. Mos J, Olivier B. Separation induced ultrasounds in rat pups as a model for anxiety disorders; psychopharmacological profile. In: Stress, Biological Rhythms and Psychiatric Disorders (ed Westenberg HGM). Medical Didactic Systems, Houten, 1989, pp 89–96.
14. Mos J, Olivier B. Ultrasonic vocalizations by rat pups as an animal model for anxiolytic activity: effects of serotonergic drugs. In: Behavioural Pharmacology of 5-HT (eds Bevan P, Cools AR, Archer T). Lawrence Erlbaum, Hillsdale, New Jersey, 1989, pp 361–367.
15. Olivier B. Animal models in obsessive–compulsive disorder. Int Clin Psychopharmacol 1992; 7 (suppl 1): 27–30.
16. Van der Poel AM, Molenwijk HE, Mos J, Olivier B. Enhancement of ultrasonic distress vocalizations in infant rats: effects of direct and indirect noradrenergic receptor antagonists and 5-HT$_2$ receptor antagonists. In: Destructive Drives and Impulse Control. Preclinical Consideration (eds Olivier B, Manceaux A). Medidact, Houten, 1992, pp 49–56.
17. Holland HC. Displacement activity as a form of abnormal behavior in animals: Obsessional states. Methuen Press, London, 1974, pp 161–174.
18. Tinbergen N. Social Behaviour in Animals. Theissen, Chapman and Hall, London, 1953.
19. Colbern DL, Gispen WH. Neural Mechanisms and Biological Significance of Grooming Behavior. New York Academy of Science, New York, 1988.
20. Falk JL. Production of polydipsia in normal rats by an intermittent food schedule. Science 1961; 133: 195–196.
21. Falk JL. The origins and functions of adjunctive behavior. Anim Learn Behav 1971; 5: 325–355.
22. Falk JL. Conditions producing psychogenic polydipsia in animals. Ann NY Ac Sci 1969; 151: 569–593.

23. Woods A, Smith C, Szewczak M, Dunn RN, Cornfeldt M, Corbett R. Selective setotonin re-uptake inhibitors decrease schedule-induced polydipsia in rats: a potential model for obsessive compulsive disorder. Psychopharmacology 1993; 112: 195–198.
24. Altemus M, Glowa J, Murphy D. Attenuation of food restriction induced running by chronic fluoxetine treatment. Psychopharm Bull [in press].
25. Sanger DJ. Effects of drugs on schedule-controlled behavior. In: Experimental Psychopharmacology (ed. Dourish C). Humana Press, Clifton, NJ, 1987.
26. Robbins TW, Koob GF. Selective disruption of displacement behaviour by lesions of the mesolimbic dopamine system. J Pharmacol Exp Therap 1980; 285: 409–412.
27. Insel T. Toward a neuroanatomy of obsessive–compulsive disorder. Arch Gen Psychiatry 1993; 49: 739–744.
28. Parent A. Serotonergic innervation of the basal ganglia. J Comp Neurol 1990; 299: 1–16.
29. Berkson G. Abnormal stereotyped motor acts. Comparative Psychopathology. Grune and Stratton, New York, 1967.
30. Hediger H. Studies of the Psychology and Behavior of Captive Animals in Zoos and Circuses. Criterion Press, New York, 1955.
31. Conroy JD. Circumscribed neurodesmatitis (Lichen simplex chronicus). In: Spontaneous Animal Models of Human Disease, vol 2 (eds Andrews EJ, Ward BC, Altman NH). Academic Press, New York, 1979, pp 19–21.
32. Goldberger E, Rapoport JL. Canine acral lick dermatitis; response to the anti-obsessional drug clomipramine. J Am Anim Hosp Assoc 1991; 27: 179–182.
33. Katz RJ, Landau P, de Veaugh-Geiss J, Hakkarainen H. Pharmacological responsiveness of dermatitis secondary to compulsive washing. Psychiatry Res 1990; 34: 223–226.
34. Brown SA, Crowell DS, Macolm T, Edwards P. Naloxone response tail chasing in a dog. Am J Vet Med Assoc 1987; 190: 884–886.
35. Dodman N, Shuster L, Court MH, Dixon R. Investigation into the use of narcotic antagonists in the treatment of a stereotypic behaviour pattern. Am J Vet Res 1987; 48: 311–319.
36. Dodman N, Shuster L, White S, Court M, Parker D, Dixon R. Use of narcotic antagonists to modify stereotypic self-lick, self-chewing, and scratching behavior in dogs. J Am Vet Med Assoc 1988; 193: 815–819.
37. Dodman NH, Shuster L, Court M, Patel J. Use of narcotic antagonist (nalmefene) to suppress self mutilative behaviour in a stallion. J Am Vet Med Assoc 1988; 192: 1585–1587.
38. Korsgaard S, Poolsen UJ, Randrup A. Effects of apomorphine and haloperidol on spontaneous stereotyped licking behaviour in cebus monkeys. Psychopharmacology 1985; 85: 240–243.
39. March JS, Gutzman LD, Jefferson JW, Griest JH. Serotonin and treatment of obsessive compulsive disorder. Psychiatry Devel 1989; 1: 1–18.
40. Teeuwisse JM, Nolen WA. De rol van medicatie in de behandeling van de obsessief compulsive stoornis. Ned Tijdschr Geneeskd 1989; 133: 2605–2608.
41. Rapoport J, Ryland D, Kriete M. Drug treatment of canine acral lick: An animal model of obsessive–compulsive disorder. Arch Gen Psychiatry 1992; 49: 517–521.
42. Rapoport JL. The Boy Who Couldn't Stop Washing. Dutton, New York, 1989.
43. Swedo SE, Leonard HL, Rapoport JL. Childhood onset obsessive compulsive disorder. In: Obsessive Compulsive Disorder, Theory and Management (eds

Jenike MA, Baer L, Minichiello WE). Year Book Medical Publishers, Chicago, 1990, pp 28–39.

44. Pauls DL, Leckman JF. The inheritance of Gilles de la Tourette's syndrome and associated behaviour; evidence for autosomal dominant transmission. N Engl J Med 1986; 315: 993–997.

45. Pauls DL, Towbin KE, Leckman JF, Zahner JE, Cohen DL. Gilles de la Tourette's syndrome and obsessive compulsive disorder. Arch Gen Psychiatry 1986; 43: 1180–1182.

46. Riddle MA, Scahill L, King R, Hardin M, Towbin KE, Ort SI, Leckman JF, Cohen DE. Obsessive compulsive disorder in children and adolescents; phenomenology and family history. J Am Acad Child Adol Psychiatry 1990; 26: 766–772.

47. Jenike MA. Illness related to obsessive compulsive disorders. In: Obsessive Compulsive Disorders: Theory and Management (eds Jenike MA, Baer L, Minichiello WE). Year Book Medical Publishers, Chicago, 1990, pp 39–61.

48. Swedo SE, Leonard HL, Rapoport JL, Lelane MC, Goldberger EL, Cheslow DL. A double blind comparison of clomipramine and desipramine in the treatment of trichotillomania (hair pulling). New Engl J Med 1989; 321: 497–501.

49. Swedo SE, Rapoport JL. Annotation: Trichotillomania. J Child Psych Psychiatry 1991; 32: 401–409.

50. Hamdan-Allan G. Trichotillomania in childhood. Acta Psychiatr Scand 1991; 83: 241–243.

51. Swedo SE, Rapoport JL, Leonard H, Lenane M, Cheslow D. Obsessive compulsive disorder in children and adolescents: Clinical phenomenology of 70 consecutive cases. Arch Gen Psychiatry 1989; 46: 335–341.

52. Salzman L. Psychoanalytic therapy of the obsessional patient. Curr Psychiatry Ther 1983; 9: 53–59.

53. Cronin GM. The development and significance of abnormal stereotyped behaviours in the tethered sows. PhD thesis, University of Wageningen, Holland, 1985.

54. Stolba A, Bakker N, Woodgush DGM. The characterization of stereotyped behaviour in stalled sows by informational redundancy. Behaviour 1983; 87: 157–182.

55. Rushen J. Stereotyped behaviour, adjunctive drinking and the feeding periods of tethered sows. Anim Behav 1984; 32: 1059–1067.

56. Rasmussen SA, Eisen JL. Epidemiology and clinical features of obsessive compulsive disorders. In: Obsessive Compulsive Disorder, Theory and Management (eds Jenike MA, Baer L, Minichiello WE). Year Book Medical Publishers, Chicago, 1990, pp 10–28.

57. Jenike MA. Psychotherapy of the obsessional patient. In: Obsessive Compulsive Disorders; Theory and Management (eds Jenike MA, Baer L, Minichiello WE). Year Book Medical Publishers, Chicago, 1986, pp 113–125.

58. Jenike MA. Psychotherapy of obsessive compulsive disorders. In: Obsessive Compulsive Disorders: Theory and Management (eds Jenike MA, Baer L, Minichiello WE). Year Book Medical Publishers, Chicago, 1990, pp 295–306.

59. Sandyke R. Naloxone abolishes obsessive compulsive behaviour in Tourette's syndrome. Int J Neurosci 1987; 35: 93–94.

60. Insel T, Pickar D. Naloxone administration in obsessive–compulsive disorder. A report of two cases. Am J Psychiatry 1983; 80: 1219–1220.

61. Von Borell E, Hurnik JF. The effect of haloperidol on the performance of sterotyped behaviour in sows. Life Sci 1991; 49: 309–314.

62. Yadin E, Friedman E, Bridger W. Spontaneous alternation behavior: an animal model for obsessive–compulsive disorder. Pharmacol Biochem Behav 1991; 40: 311–315.
63. Eslinger PJ, Damasio AR. Severe disturbance of higher cognition after bilateral frontal lobe ablation: Patient EVR. Neurol 1985; 35: 1731–1741.
64. Rapoport J, Wise SP. Obsessive compulsive disorder, evidence for basal ganglia dysfunction. Psychopharmacol Bull 1988; 24: 380–385.
65. Swedo SE, Rapoport JL, Cheslow DL et al. High prevalence of obsessive–compulsive symptoms in patients with Sydenham's chorea. Am J Psychiatry 1989; 146: 246–249.
66. Pitman RK. Animal models for compulsive behaviour. Biol Psychiatry 1989; 26: 189–198.
67. Goodman W, McDougle ChJ, Price LH, Riddle MA, Pauls DL, Leckman JF. Beyond the serotonin hypothesis: A role for dopamine in some forms of obsessive compulsive disorder. J Clin Psychiatry 1990; 51 (suppl 8): 36–43.
68. Flament MF, Koby E, Rapoport JL, Berg CL, Zahn Th, Cox Ch, Denckla M, Lenane M. Childhood obsessive compulsive disorder; a prospective follow-up study. J Child Psychol Psychiatry 1990; 31: 363–380.
69. Rivers-Bulkely N, Hollander MH. Successful treatment of obsessive compulsive disorder with loxapine. Am J Psychiatry 1982; 139: 1345–1346.
70. O'Regan JB. Treatment of obsessive compulsive neurosis with haloperidol. Can Med Assoc J 1970; 103: 167–168.
71. Hussain MZ, Ahad A. Treatment of obsessive compulsive neurosis. Can Med Ass J 1970; 103: 650–651.
72. Altschuler M. Massive doses of trifluoperazine in the treatment of obsessive rituals. Am J Psychiatry 1962; 119: 367–368.
73. McDougle ChJ, Goodman WK, Price LH, Delgado PL, Krystal JR, Charney DS, Heninger GR. Neuroleptic addition in fluvoxamine refractory obsessive compulsive disorder. Am J Psychiatry 1990; 147: 652–654.
74. Leonard HL, Rapoport JL. Relief of obsessive compulsive symptoms by LSD and psilocin. Am J Psychiatry 1987; 144: 1239–1240.
75. McDougle ChJ, Goodman WK, Price LH et al. Neuroleptic addition in fluvoxamine refractory obsessive compulsive disorder. Am J Psychiatry 1989; 147: 652–654.
76. McDougle ChJ, Goodman WK, Delgade PL, Price LH. Pathophysiology of obsessive compulsive disorder. Am J Psychiatry 1989; 146: 1350–1351.
77. Insel ThR, Hamilton JA, Gutmacher LB, Murphy DL. D-Amphetamine in obsessive compulsive disorder. Psychopharmacology 1983; 80: 231–235.
78. Jenike MA. Obsessive compulsive disorders; a question of a neurological lesion. Comp Psychiatry 1984; 25: 298–304.
79. Koizumi HM. Obsessive compulsive symptoms following stimulants. Biol Psychiatry 1985; 20: 1322–1337.
80. Satel SL, McDougle ChJ. Obsessions and compulsions associated with cocaine abuse. Am J Psychiatry 1991; 148: 947.
81. Randrup A, Munkvad I. Stereotyped activities produced by amphetamine in several animal species and man. Psychopharmacology 1967; 11: 300–310.
82. Yamaguchi K, Nabeshima T, Kameyama T. Potentiation of the phencyclidine induced dopamine behaviours in rats after pretreatment with serotonin depletors. J Pharmacobiodyn 1986; 9: 479–489.
83. McDougle ChJ, Goodman WK. Obsessive compulsive disorders; pharmacotherapy and pathophysiology. Curr Opin Psychiatry 1991; 4: 267–272.
84. Baxter LR, Schwarz JM, Fuze BH, Bergman K, Szuba MP. PET imaging in obsessive compulsive disorder with and without depression. J Clin Psy-

chiatry 1990; 51: 61–69.

85. Benkelfat C, Nordahl ThE, Semple WE, King C, Murphy DE, Cohen RM. Local cerebral glucose metabolic rates in obsessive compulsive disorder. Arch Gen Psychiatry 1990; 47: 840–848.

86. Khanna S. Obsessive compulsive disorder: Is there a frontal lobe dysfunction? Biol Psychiatry 1988; 24: 602–613.

87. Swedo SE, Shapiro MB, Grady ChL et al. Cerebral glucose metabolism in childhood onset of obsessive compulsive disorder. Arch Gen Psychiatry 1989; 46: 518–523.

88. Hillegaart V, Hjorth S, Ahlenius S. Effects of 5-HT and 8-OH-DPAT on forebrain monoamine synthesis after local application into the medical and dorsal raphe nuclei of the rat. J Neural Transm 1990; 81: 131–145.

89. Alexander GE, De Long MR, Strick PL. Parallel organization of functionally segregated circuits linking basal ganglia and cortex. Annu Rev Neurosci 1986; 9: 357–381.

90. Chiocca A, Martuza RL. Neurosurgical therapy of obsessive compulsive disorder. In: Obsessive Compulsive Disorders, Theory and Management (eds Jenike MA, Baer L, Minichiello WE). Year Book Medical Publishers, Chicago, 1990, pp 283–295.

91. Baxter LR, Phelps ME, Mazziotta JC, Fuze BH, Schwarz JM, Selm CE. Local cerebral glucose metabolic rates in obsessive compulsive disorder: a comparison with rates in unipolar depression and in normal controls. Arch Gen Psychiatry 1987; 44: 211–218.

92. Modell JG, Mountz JM, Curtis GC, Greden JF. Neurophysiological dysfunction in basal ganglia/limbic striatal and thalamocortical circuits as pathogenic mechanism of obsessive compulsive disorder. J Neuropsychiatry 1989; 1: 27–36.

93. Leckman JF, Knorr AM, Rasmussen AM, Cohen DJ. Basal ganglia research and Tourette's syndrome. Trends Neurosci 1991; 14: 94.

94. Goodman W, McDougle C, Price L. The role of serotonin and dopamine in the pathophysiology of obsessive-compulsive disorder. Int Clin Psychopharmacol 1992; 7 (suppl 1): 35–38.

95. Jacobs B, Fornal C, Wilkinson L. Neurophysiological and neurochemical studies of brain serotonin neurons in behaving animals. Ann N Y Acad Sci 1990; 600: 260–271.

96. Jacobs B, Wilkinson L, Fornal C. The role of brain serotonin: A neurophysiologic perspective. Neuropsychopharmacology 1990; 3: 473–479.

11 PHARMACOLOGICAL CHALLENGES

Ruth Gross-Isseroff, Seth Kindler, Moshe Kotler,
Yehuda Sasson, Orna Dolberg, Talma Hendler and
Joseph Zohar
Division of Psychiatry, The Chaim Sheba Medical Center, Tel Hashomer,
Israel

Introduction

Specific pharmacological challenges have been proved to be a fruitful approach to the study of the neurobiological bases of psychiatric syndromes. Direct activation or inhibition of a specific neurotransmitter system or receptor subsystem may elucidate the role of the challenged target in the pathophysiology of the disorder [for a review, see Goodman et al (1)].

A variety of such pharmacological challenges have been used in the study of obsessive compulsive disorder (OCD). This chapter will attempt to review these studies and to comment on their contribution to our understanding of this disorder, on their limitations and on future directions. The presentation will be organized according to the independent variable studied, that is, the neurotransmitter system, and the dependent variable, that is, the type of response observed.

Serotonergic challenges

SEROTONIN

The serotonergic system is the major neurotransmitter system implicated in both the etiology and pharmacological treatment of OCD (2). This system originates in the raphe nuclei located in the midline brainstem.

Current Insights in Obsessive Compulsive Disorder. Edited by E. Hollander, J. Zohar,
D. Marazzati and B. Olivier
© 1994 John Wiley & Sons Ltd

These cells innervate all other structures of the mammalian brain through relatively long ascending axons (3). The past 20 years have witnessed an immense surge in molecular and pharmacological studies of this system (4, 5). To date, seven subdivisions of the G-protein coupled serotonin (5-hydroxy tryptamine, 5-HT) receptor family have been defined: 5-HT_1, 5-HT_2, 5-HT_4, 5-HT_5, 5-HT_6, 5-HT_7, and a seventh as yet unidentified subdivision (4–6). Of these, members of the fourth subfamily have not been cloned. The first, second and fifth subfamilies are further subdivided into several receptor subtypes. The first subfamily consists of the 1A, 1B (1Dβ), 1Dα, 1E, and 1F subtypes, the second of the 2A(2), 2B(2F), and 2C(1C) subtypes, and the fifth of the 5A and 5B subtypes [see Branchek (5) and references therein]. An eighth class of 5-HT receptors (5-HT_3) is a ligand-gated ion channel (5).

ENDOCRINE RESPONSES TO SEROTONERGIC CHALLENGES IN OCD

Serotonin has been implicated in the regulation of some endocrine responses, such as prolactin secretion and the hypothalamic–pituitary–adrenal (HPA) axis. Therefore, plasma levels of prolactin, corticotropin and cortisol are considered indices of central serotonergic function.

The most widely used agent in studies of serotonergic involvement in OCD is *meta*-chlorophenyl-piperazine (mCPP), a breakdown product of the antidepressant trazodone. This substance binds with high affinity to 5-HT_{1C} receptors (7). It also binds with comparable affinities to 5-HT_2, 5-HT_{1A}, 5-HT_{1D} and α_2-adrenergic receptors, with lower affinity to α_1-adrenergic, β-adrenergic, dopamine, and muscarinic cholinergic receptors in human brain. *Meta*-chlorophenyl-piperazine is practically inactive at benzodiazepine receptors and 5-HT uptake sites (8). While predominantly a 5-HT agonist, mCPP may also have antagonist effects at 5-HT_2 and 5-HT_3 sites, and thus is considered a partial agonist.

In healthy human subjects, mCPP is associated with an elevation in plasma prolactin and cortisol concentrations. The effect of mCPP on prolactin secretion in OCD patients is in dispute. While one study found no difference between untreated OCD patients and controls (9), others (10, 11) found that the prolactin response to mCPP was blunted in OCD patients compared with healthy controls. Chronic treatment (4 months) with clomipramine does not alter the mCPP-induced elevation in plasma prolactin concentrations in OCD patients; however, it causes a significant increase in baseline prolactin levels (12), and chronic fluoxetine treatment partially normalizes the blunted prolactin response to mCPP (13). Metergoline, a potent nonspecific serotonin antagonist, blocks the mCPP-induced increase in plasma prolactin levels in OCD patients (14).

The cortisol response following mCPP administration is blunted in untreated OCD patients compared with healthy controls (9, 11), and is not affected by chronic treatment with clomipramine (12), fluoxetine (13) or by administration of metergoline (14).

Fenfluramine, a potent serotonin agonist, induces an increase in prolactin and cortisol secretion in healthy human subjects. The cortisol response in OCD patients is similar (11, 15, 16). The findings on prolactin are less decisive. Thus, while some studies (11, 15, 17) found the prolactin response in OCD patients to be similar to the response observed in healthy controls, others (16) reported a blunted prolactin response to fenfluramine in OCD patients. This blunting of fenfluramine-induced prolactin secretion is present in female patients only, and is reversed by treatment with clonazepam, but not by treatment with clomipramine, clonidine, or diphenhydramine (16).

Tryptophan, the serotonin precursor, induces an increase in prolactin secretion in OCD patients, which is enhanced by fluvoxamine treatment (17).

Ipsapirone, a selective 5-HT_{1A} ligand, induces increased corticotropin and cortisol levels in healthy human subjects. It has a similar effect on the HPA axis in OCD patients (18), and chronic treatment with fluoxetine decreases the ipsapirone-induced HPA activation in OCD patients (19).

A 5-HT agonist that binds with high affinity to 5-HT_{1B}, 5-HT_{1C}, and 5-HT_2 receptors in rodents, MK-212 [6-chloro-2-(1-piperazinyl)-pyrazine], induces a dose-dependent increase in plasma cortisol and prolactin concentrations in healthy human subjects (20). The MK-212 induced increase in cortisol and prolactin levels is blunted in untreated OCD patients (21).

Table 11.1 summarizes the effects of serotonergic challenges on neuroendocrine responses in OCD patients. Assuming that 5-HT_{1C} and 5-HT_2 receptors mediate prolactin and cortisol secretion, these data suggest 5-HT_{1C} and 5-HT_2 hyposensitivity in the hypothalamus in OCD patients.

PHYSIOLOGICAL RESPONSES TO SEROTONERGIC CHALLENGES IN OCD

Serotonin has been implicated in thermoregulation (4), and therefore body temperature is frequently used as an index of central serotonergic function.

Both in healthy human subjects and in unmedicated OCD patients, mCPP induces an increase in body temperature (9). Chronic clomipramine treatment blocks the hyperthermic effect of mCPP in OCD patients (12). However, the effect of clomipramine on mCPP-induced hyperthermia in healthy or non-OCD controls has not been tested.

Similarly, ipsapirone, a specific 5-HT_{1A} agonist, induces hyperthermia in OCD patients as well as healthy human subjects (19). This effect is blocked by chronic treatment with fluoxetine (19, 22).

Table 11.1 Summary of neuroendocrine responses to serotonergic challenges in patients compared with healthy controls

Response/challenge*	Decrease (No. of patients)	No effect (No. of patients)	Reference
Prolactin			
mCPP		12	9
	21		10
	20		11
	42		15
MK-212	17		21
Metergoline	6		14
Fenfluramine		14	17
		14	11
		42	15
	26		16
Cortisol			
mCPP	12		9
		20	11
	42		15
MK-212	17		21
Ipsapirone		12	18
Metergoline		6	14
Fenfluramine		20	11
		42	15
		26	16

*mCPP, Meta-chlorophenyl-piperazine; MK-212, 6-chloro-2-(1-piperazinyl)-pyrazine.

The effect of serotonergic medications on the hyperthermic effects of mCPP and ipsapirone is consistent with the hypothesis that chronic treatment with specific serotonergic reuptake inhibitors (SSRIs) induces adaptive downregulation of postsynaptic 5-HT receptors (23).

BEHAVIORAL RESPONSES TO SEROTONERGIC CHALLENGES IN OCD

Psychiatric disorders express themselves through anomalies in behavior. It is not surprising, then, that clinicians and scientists alike rely heavily on behavioral criteria in their definition of OCD and on behavioral measures in assessment of symptom severity (24–28).

Administered orally, mCPP caused a marked and transient exacerbation in obsessive compulsive symptoms in untreated OCD patients (9, 11, 12, 14, 15, 28). However, mCPP administered intravenously does not reliably replicate these behavioral findings (10, 29, 30). Pretreatment with metergoline blocked orally administered mCPP-induced exacerbation of OC symptoms (14) and chronic treatment with clomipramine or fluoxetine reduced it (12, 15).

A variety of other serotonergic challenges were used. Ondansetron, a 5-HT_3 antagonist, induced decreased anxiety and obsessive compulsive (OC) symptoms in OCD patients (30). Administration of MK-212 (21) or ipsapirone (21) to OCD patients did not measurably affect OC symptoms. Tryptophan (the 5-HT precursor) loading did not affect OC symptoms (10), nor did tryptophan depletion (31, 32). Metergoline did not affect OC symptoms in OCD patients in one study (9).

Different studies have reported varying findings regarding the effects of fenfluramine on OC behavior. Hollander et al (11, 15) did not find any behavioral differences, though one study (15) reported an elevation in self-rated mood. In a different study, fenfluramine was reported to reduce obsessions, but did not affect compulsions in OCD patients (17).

Challenge studies use various self-administered or rater-administered scales for rating OC symptoms. The Yale–Brown Obsessive–Compulsive Scale (Y-BOCS) is one of the most frequently used. The evaluation of OC symptoms is problematic, as noted by the authors of the Y-BOCS (1 p. 167).

Another problem with the evaluation of obsessive–compulsive behavior is that, unlike a mood state, OCD severity cannot be assessed during a single, brief slice of time. In fact, one of the major components of measuring symptom severity in OCD is the determination of how much time is occupied by the symptoms. Thus, the shorter the sampling time over which the symptoms are rated, the less confident one can be about the reliability of the ratings. In our experience, a 60-minute interval represents the shortest time period over which obsessive–compulsives can be rated without seriously compromising reliability.

Another limiting factor in measuring behavioral responses is the inter-rater reliability for the behavioral ratings performed. Thorough familiarity with patients' current and past condition prior to the challenge might increase inter-rater reliability values.

Taking all the studies together, OC symptom severity in response to mCPP has been assessed in approximately 100 OCD patients. The total number of patients who have received other types of challenges is much smaller, ranging from 12 to 21 (Table 11.2). As shown in Table 11.2, about half of the studied patients responded with exacerbation of OC symptoms, while the other half were not similarly affected. Differences in the

Table 11.2 Summary of obsessive compulsive symptom severity in response to serotonergic challenges

Challenge*	Exacerbation (No. of patients)	Decrease (No. of patients)	No effect (No. of patients)	Reference
mCPP (5-HT$_{1C}$, 5-HT$_2$, 5-HT$_{1A}$, 5-HT$_{1D}$, α_2-adrenergic)	11	1		9
	6			14
			21	10
	24		18	15
	10		17	29
Total	51		56	
Ipsapirone (5-HT$_{1A}$)			12	18
MK-212 (5-HT$_{1C}$, 5-HT$_2$, 5-HT$_{1D}$)			17	21
Fenfluramine (5-HT release, uptake blocker)			7	11
		14		17
Trytophan loading			18	10
Tryptophan depletion			7	31
Metergoline			12	14

*mCPP, *Meta*-chlorophenyl-piperazine; 5-HT, 5-hydroxy tryptamine (serotonin); MK-212, 6-chloro-2-(1-piperazinyl)-pyrazine.

mode of administration and behavioral rating procedures could explain some of these discrepancies. Studies of the effect of mode of administration suggest that the rate at which mCPP arrives at its target site is relevant to its behavioral effect; the data, though, are inconclusive (10, 29). Only one study (11) reported inter-rater reliability values, and to the best of our knowledge, it is also the only study that has used more than one rater. Careful assessment of inter-rater reliability and of the intercorrelations between different scales might help in clarifying some of the discrepancies between the studies.

Nonserotonergic challenges

There have been relatively few studies of pharmacological challenges to OC using nonserotonergic agents. Such studies could help in assessing the specificity of serotonergic effects, and in evaluating the case for alternative etiological mechanisms.

NORADRENERGIC AGENTS

The study of serotonergic challenges in OCD arises from clinical observations of the specific role of serotonergic medications in this disorder. In contrast, the study of noradrenergic challenges in OCD has been inspired by the DSM classification of this disorder, which groups OCD with the group anxiety disorders (25). Also, a recent epidemiological study has suggested a high frequency of comorbidity between panic disorder and OCD (33).

Clonidine is an α_2-adrenergic agonist which decreases noradrenergic function by binding to the autoreceptor. Growth hormone release in response to clonidine challenge was blunted in one study of OCD patients (34) but not in another (35). Clonidine also reduced symptoms in OCD patients (28), and this effect was found to be correlated to the amount of clonidine-induced growth hormone release. Since enhancement of noradrenergic transmission may ameliorate OC symptoms, one might expect that blocking of adrenergic function would exacerbate symptoms. Yohimbine, an α_2-adrenergic antagonist, was found to affect OCD patients and healthy controls in the same fashion, inducing anxiety in both groups to the same degree (36), but it did not affect severity of OC symptoms.

Although these results do not suggest a valid case for noradrenergic involvement in OCD, we cannot, at present, rule out the possibility that some of the effects obtained using mCPP are due to high-affinity binding of mCPP to α_2-adrenergic receptors (6). Further elucidation of the effects of adrenergic substances on OCD depends upon obtaining more precise data regarding the effective site of action of the agents used.

ANXIOGENIC CHALLENGES

Several studies have used different challenges to determine whether a common mechanism underlies OCD, anxiety, and panic disorders. Sodium lactate, which has anxiogenic effects in panic disorder patients, failed to induce panic attacks in OCD patients (37), while caffeine increased anxiety but not OC symptoms in OCD patients (9). Pentagastrin, a cholecystokinin tetrapeptide (CCK_4) analog, which has been shown to induce panic attacks in panic disorder patients also induced panic-like attacks in OCD patients without affecting OC symptom rating (38). The results of these studies suggest that OCD patients, in contrast to patients with panic disorder, are not vulnerable to these anxiogenic challenges.

Conclusions

Results of the studies reviewed in this chapter, together with the clinical findings that SSRIs are to date the only medications that appear to be therapeutically effective in OCD [e.g. see Benkelfat et al (39)], implicate the serotonergic system in OCD. The findings of this review suggest that this system does not respond as a homogenous synchronized system. Different segments of the system are implicated in different functions (prolactin release, HPA axis, mood, thermoregulation, anxiety, obsessions, compulsions, sleep, eating behavior, etc.). A possible way of partitioning the serotonergic system is by its receptors. Thus one would expect $5\text{-}HT_{1A}$ receptors to serve one type of function (thermoregulation, anxiety) while $5\text{-}HT_{1C}/5\text{-}HT_2$ receptors would have regulatory effects on neuroendocrine function, and the $5\text{-}HT_{1D}$ would be responsible for another function (OC symptoms, response inhibition). A recent study (40), which compared prolactin, cortisol and behavioral effects of mCPP in healthy subjects as a function of age, is in line with the "uncoupling" of neuroendocrine effects and behavioral effects in the serotonergic system. In this study, the behavioral effects of mCPP declined with age, while its neuroendocrine effects were not affected.

Studies of the effects of different variables on the mapping of brain serotonin receptors lend further support to the hypothesis that the serotonergic system does not react monolithically. Age, sex, psychotropic drugs, and psychopathology each have different effects on the distribution of various serotonin receptors [see Dillon et al (41) and Gross-Isseroff et al (42) and references therein]. Advances in brain imaging techniques (single photon emission computerized tomography and positron emission tomography) and the development of specific radiolabelled serotonergic ligands will soon enable the in vivo visualization of structure–function relationships in this system (43, 44).

Moreover, preclinical pharmacological studies and molecular pharmacology studies have shown that many of the challenges used in psychiatric research so far actually affect several neurohumoral systems. There is an abundance of basic research demonstrating opioid–serotonergic interactions [e.g. see Graur et al (45) and references therein] and dopaminergic–serotonergic interactions (46) to name but two of the more prominent examples. The clinical implications of such interactions warrant further research.

References

1. Goodman WK, Price LH, Woods SW, Charney DS. Pharmacologic challenges in obsesseive compulsive disorder. In: The Psychobiology of Obsessive–Compulsive Disorder (eds Zohar J, Insel T, Rasmussen S). Springer Verlag, New York, 1991, pp 162–186.
2. Zohar J, Zohar-Kadouch RC, Kindler S. Current concepts in the pharmacological treatment of absessive–compulsive disorder. Drugs 1992; 43: 210–218.
3. Azmitia EC, Gannon PJ. The primate serotonergic system: a review of human and animal studies and a report on *Macaca fascicularis*. In: Advances in Neurology (eds Fahn et al). Raven, New York, 1986, pp 407–467.
4. Peroutka SJ (ed). Serotonin Receptor Subtypes: Basic and Clinical Aspects. Wiley-Liss, New York, 1991.
5. Branchek T. More serotonin receptors? Curr Biol 1993; 3: 315–317.
6. Peroutka SJ. The molecular pharmacology of 5-hydroxytryptamine receptor subtypes. In: Serotonin Receptor Subtypes: Basic and Clinical Aspects (ed Peroutka SJ). Wiley-Liss, New York, 1991, pp 65–80.
7. Hoyer D, Pazos A, Probst A et al. Serotonin receptors in the human brain. II. Characterization and autoradiographic localization of $5-HT_{1C}$ and $5-HT_2$ recognition sites. Brain Res 1986; 376: 97–107.
8. Hamik A, Peroutka SJ. 1-(m-Clorophenyl)piperazine (m-CPP) interactions with neurotransmitter receptors in the human brain. Biol Psychiatr 1989; 25: 569–575.
9. Zohar J, Mueller EA, Insel TR. Serotonin responsivity in obsessive compulsive disorder. Arch Gen Psychiatry 1987; 44: 946–951.
10. Charney DS, Goodman WK, Price LH, Woods SW, Rasmussen SA, Heninger GR. Serotonin function in obsessive–compulsive disorder. Arch Gen Psychiatry 1988; 45: 177–185.
11. Hollander E, DeCaria CM, Nitescu A et al. Serotonergic function in obsessive–compulsive disorder. Arch Gen Psychiatry 1992; 49: 21–28.
12. Zohar J, Insel TR, Zohar-Kadoush RC, Hill JL, Murphy DL. Serotonergic responsivity in obsessive–compulsive disorder: Effects of clomipramine treatment. Arch Gen Psychiatry 1988; 45: 167–172.
13. Hollander E, DeCaria C, Gully R et al. Effects of chronic fluoxetine treatment on behavioral and neuroendocrine responses to meta-chlorophenylpiperazine in obsessive–compulsive disorder. Psychiatr Res 1991: 36: 1–17.
14. Pigott TA, Zohar J, Hill JL et al. Metergoline blocks the behavioral and neuroendocrine effects of orally administered m-chlorophenylpiperazine in patients with obsessive–compulsive disorder. Biol Psychiatry 1991; 29: 418–426.
15. Hollander E, Cohen L, DeCaria C, Stein D, Simeon D, Hwang M. Pharmacological challenges in OCD. Presented at First International Obsessive–Compulsive Disorder Congress, Capri, Italy, 12–13 Mar 1993.

16. Hewlett WA, Martin K. Fenfluramine challenges and serotonergic functioning in obsessive compulsive disorder. Presented at First International Obsessive–Compulsive Disorder Congress, Capri, Italy, 12–13 Mar 1993.

17. Price LH, Charney DS, Delgado PL, Anderson GM, Heninger GR. Effects of desipramine and fluvoxamine treatment on the prolactin response to tryptophan: Serotonergic function and the mechanism of antidepressant action. Arch Gen Psychiatry 1989; 46: 625–631.

18. Lesch KP, Hoh A, Disselkamp-Tietze J, Weismann M, Osterheider M, Schulte HM. 5-Hydroxytryptamine$_{1A}$ (5-HT$_{1A}$) receptor responsivity in obsessive–compulsive-disorder: comparison of patients and controls. Arch Gen Psychiatry 1991; 48: 540–547.

19. Lesch KP. 5-HT$_{1A}$ receptor responsivity in OCD: Attenuation during long-term treatment with the selective 5-HT reuptake inhibitor (SSRI) fluoxetine. Presented at First International Obsessive Compulsive Disorder Congress, Capri, Italy, 12–13 Mar 1993.

20. Lowy MT, Meltzer HY. Stimulation of serum cortisol and prolactin secretion in humans by MK-212. Biol Psychiatry 1988; 23: 818–828.

21. Bastani B, Nash F, Meltzer H. Prolactin and cortisol responses to MK-212, a serotonin agonist, in obsessive–compulsive disorder. Arch Gen Psychiatry 1990; 47: 946–951.

22. Lesch KP, Hoh A, Osterheider M, Schulte HM, Muller T. Long-term fluoxetine treatment decreases 5-HT$_{1A}$ receptor responsivity in obsessive–compulsive disorder. Psychopharmacology 1991; 105: 415–420.

23. Whamsley KJ, Byerley WF, McCabe RT, McConnell EJ, Dawson TM, Grosser BI. Receptor alterations associated with serotonergic agents: An autoradiographic analysis. J Clin Psychiatry 1987; 48 (suppl): 19–25.

24. American Psychiatric Association. Diagnostic and Statistical Manual (DSM-III-R). American Psychiatric Association, Washington, 1987.

25. Goodman W, Price L, Rasmussen S et al. The Yale–Brown Obsessive-Compulsive Scale (Y-BOCS): Part I. Development, use and reliability. Arch Gen Psychiatry 1989; 46: 1006–1011.

26. Goodman W, Price L, Rasmussen S et al. The Yale–Brown Obsessive-Compulsive Scale (Y-BOCS): Part II. Validity. Arch Gen Psychiatry 1989; 46: 1012–1016.

27. Hodgson R, Rachman S. Obsessional compulsive complaints. Behav Res Ther 1977; 15: 384.

28. Hollander E, Fay M, Cohen B, Campeas R, Gorman JM, Liebowitz MR. Serotonergic and adrenergic sensitivity in obsessive–compulsive disorder: Behavioral findings. Am J Psychiatry 1988; 145: 1015–1017.

29. Pigott TA, Hill JL, Grady TA et al. A comparison of the behavioral effects of oral versus intravenous mCPP administration in OCD patients and the effect of metergoline prior to i.v. mCPP. Biol Psychiatry 1993; 33: 3–14.

30. Pigott TA, Murphy DL, Brooks A. Pharmacological probes in OCD: support for selective 5-HT dysregulation. Presented at the First International Obsessive Compulsive Disorder Congress, Capri, Italy, 12–13 Mar 1993.

31. Delgado PL, Charney DS, Price LH et al. Behavioral effects of acute tryptophan depletion in depressed and obsessive compulsive disorder (OCD) patients. Society of Neuroscience Abstracts, Toronto, Canada, 13–18 Nov 1988.

32. Barr LL, Goodman WK, McDougle LJ et al. Tryptophan depletion in obsessive–compulsive disorder patients responding to serotonin reuptake inhibitors. Arch Gen Psychiatry [in press].

33. Breier A, Charney DS, Heninger GR. Agoraphobia and panic disorder:

Development, diagnostic stability and course of illness. Arch Gen Psychiatry 1986; 43: 1029–1036.

34. Siever LJ, Insel TR, Jimerson DC et al. Growth hormone response to clonidine in obsessive–compulsive patients. Br J Psychiatry 1983; 142: 184–187.

35. Hollander E, DeCaria L, Nitescu A et al. Noradrenergic function in obsessive–compulsive disorder: behavioral and neuroendocrine response to clonidine and comparison to healthy controls. Psychiatry Res 1991; 37(2): 161–177.

36. Rasmussen SA, Goodman WK, Woods SW, Heninger GR, Charney DS. Effects of yohimbine in obsessive compulsive disorder. Psychopharmacology 1987; 93: 308–313.

37. Gorman JM, Liebowitz MR, Fyer AJ et al. Lactate infusion in obsessive–compulsive disorder. Am J Psychiatry 1985; 142: 864–866.

38. Den Boer JA, De Leeuw AS, Westenberg HGM. Pentagastrin challenge in obsessive compulsive disorder: A pharmacological probe for the dissociation of anxiety and obsessive compulsive disorder. Presented at First International Obsessive–Compulsive Disorder Congress, Capri, Italy, 12–13 Mar 1993.

39. Benkelfat C, Murphy DL, Zohar J, Hill JL, Grover G, Insel TR. Clomipramine in obsessive–compulsive disorder. Arch Gen Psychiatry 1989; 46: 23–28.

40. Lawlor BA, Sunderland T, Hill JL et al. Evidence for a decline with age in behavioral responsivity to the serotonin agonist, m-chlorophenylpiperazine, in healthy human subjects. Psychiatr Res 1988; 29: 1–10

41. Dillon KA, Gross-Isseroff R, Israeli M, Biegon A. Autoradiographic analysis of serotonin 5-HT$_{1A}$ receptor binding in the human brain postmortem: effects of age and alcohol. Brain Res 1991; 554: 56–64.

42. Gross-Isseroff R, Salama D, Israeli M, Biegon A. Autoradiographic analysis of age-dependent changes in serotonin 5-HT$_2$ receptors of the human brain postmortem. Brain Res 1990; 519: 223–227.

43. Insel TR. Toward a neuroanatomy of obsessive–compulsive disorder. Arch Gen Psychiatry 1992; 49: 739–744.

44. Hollander E, Cohen LJ, Prohovnik I, Hwang M, Decaria CM, Liebowitz MR. M-CPP Effects on cortical blood flow in OCD. Abstr Am Psychiatr Assoc, 1993, p 133, NR292.

45. Grauer SM, Tao R, Auerbach SB. Morphine induces an increase in extracellular serotonin in the rat diencephalon. Brain Res 1992; 599: 277–282.

46. Rajda F, Descarriers L, Dewar KM, Reader TA. Serotonin 5-HT$_1$ and 5-HT$_2$ receptors in adult rat brain after neonatal destruction of nigrostriatal dopamine neurons: a quantitative autoradiographic study. Brain Res 1993; 606: 273–285.

12 BIOLOGICAL DISSECTION OF OBSESSIVE COMPULSIVE DISORDER

Donatella Marazziti[*], Joseph Zohar[†] and Giovanni B Cassano[†]

[*]Institute of Psychiatry, University of Pisa, Pisa, Italy
[†]Division of Psychiatry, The Chaim Sheba Medical Center, Tel Hashomer, Israel

Introduction

The synthesis of psychotropic drugs gave a strong impetus to biological research, so that most of the biological hypotheses in psychiatry have been based on the psychopharmalogical paradigm. This process, which had a revolutionary impact on clinical practice and renewed interest in diagnosis and nosology, permitted the identification of new entities such as panic disorder, but it also led to pitfalls via the over- or underestimation of major psychoses. It is now clear that "use of a drug as a tool" (1) cannot be the unique approach to the nosology and biology of a given psychiatric disorder.

This is particularly evident in the formulation of biological theories of obsessive compulsive disorder (OCD). The major hypothesis on the pathophysiology of this disorder postulates an involvement of 5-hydroxy tryptamine or serotonin (5-HT), on the basis of an almost exclusive response of OC patients to 5-HT reuptake inhibitors (SRIs) such as clomipramine, fluoxetine and fluvoxemine (2–5), while tricyclics with less marked activity on 5-HT uptake are less effective (6–8). However, because about 40% of patients do not respond to SRIs, it is conceivable that other mechanisms are involved (9). Moreover, SRIs are also effective in other

Current Insights in Obsessive Compulsive Disorder. Edited by E. Hollander, J. Zohar, D. Marazzati and B. Olivier
© 1994 John Wiley & Sons Ltd

psychiatric disorders, and this shared response raises the problem of the specificity.

Although OCD is currently classified as an anxiety disorder, there has been a long tradition linking OCD and affective illness (10). In modern times, phenomenological studies have demonstrated not only that depression is the most common complication of OCD (11, 12) but that obsessions are common in primary affective illness as well (11, 13). Moreover, the Epidemiologic Catchment Area (ECA) survey (14, 15), like earlier studies (12, 16), found a significant overlap between OCD and major depressive disorder.

In this chapter, we will review the biological abnormalities described in OCD, in an attempt to clarify those specific for the disorder and the possible relationship of OCD to other forms of psychopathology, mainly to major depressive disorder, anxiety disorders, and schizophrenia. The biological markers discussed will be the following: dexamethasone suppresion test (DST), rapid eye movement (REM) latency and density, growth hormone response to the α_2-adrenergic agonist clonidine, platelet markers (5-HT transporter, peripheral benzodiazepine receptor, sulfotransferase activity, 5-HT_2 receptor), and cerebrospinal fluid (CSF) measures of 5-hydroxy-indoleacetic acid (5-HIAA) and 3-methoxy-4-hydroxyphenyl-glycol (MHPG).

Neuroendocrine studies

THE HYPOTHALAMUS–PITUITARY–ADRENAL AXIS: DEXAMETHASONE SUPPRESSION TEST

Neuroendocrine studies continue to have an important place in the search for a rational neurobiology of psychiatric disorders.

In major depression, an increased serum concentration of cortisol is a common, although variable, finding. Most clinical research has employed the dexamethasone suppression test (17), but the original hope that this test would reflect the severity of the illness has not been fulfilled. However, recent data in this field have shown that the metabolism of dexamethasone itself may be a better correlate of clinical outcome than baseline cortisol or the axis response to dexamethasone (18).

The dexamethasone suppression test (DST) has been widely employed in OCD. In a study carried out in a mixed population of nondepressed inpatients and outpatients affected by OCD, about 25% had abnormally high cortisol levels following administration of 1 mg of dexamethasone given at 11 pm (19). This percentage of DST nonsuppression is somewhat more modest than other findings reporting 41% (20), 37.5% (21) and 30% (22), respectively. These heterogenous results probably reflect the different percentage of outpatients in the various studies. As outpatients were sampled for plasma cortisol at only one time point, the likelihood of finding an abnormality was considerably less for inpatients who were tested at three time points. A 25% incidence of nonsuppression approximates to the sensitivity of the DST for endogenous depression in some centers and is somewhat higher than the incidence of DST nonsuppression in normals. However, the significance of this test in OCD is diminished, as two reports described normal DST responses in OCD (23, 24).

When employed in a study of panic disorder (PD), the DST did not reveal any difference between patients and controls, the rate of nonsuppression ranging between 13 and 19% (25). The same observations apply also for schizophrenic patients (26).

In conclusion, while DST abnormalities suggest a link between OCD and major depression, a similarly high incidence of cortisol levels following administration of dexamethasone exists in a variety of other psychiatric syndromes, such as anorexia nervosa, Alzheimer's dementia, and alcohol withdrawal (20). Moreover, even healthy controls subjected to stress or of advanced age have a high incidence of DST nonsuppression (27). Hence, the physiological link between these conditions and DST nonsuppression remains unclear. In Cushing's syndrome, for instance, DST nonsuppression may result from pituitary, hypothalamic, or even pulmonary lesions. It is therefore premature to assume that all psychiatric patients with DST nonsuppression have the same abnormality.

Changes in glucocorticoid receptor binding in the pituitary have been invoked as a possible mechanism for the reduced dexamethasone suppression in depression, but the recent studies aimed at evaluating the lymphocyte glucocorticoid receptors in patients have been inconclusive, and no comparison with other psychiatric disorders has been performed (28). However, this is an interesting tool which deserves to be employed in future studies on this topic.

THE BRAIN–THYROID AXIS: THYROID-STIMULATING HORMONE RESPONSE TO THYROTROPIN-RELEASING HORMONE

Of the changes reported in the brain–thyroid axis in depression, a blunting of the thyroid-stimulating hormone (TSH) response to thyrotropin-releasing hormone (TRH) and an elevation of serum L-thyroxine (T_4) are the most consistent (29, 30).

A study carried out in drug-free OC patients showed that nine out of the total of 10 exhibited decreased TSH response to TRH provocation, whereas reduced TSH response was detected in two controls (31). The blunted TSH response to TRH stimulation indicates some dysfunctions of the hypothalamic–pituitary thyroid axis, and suggests a link between OCD and mood disorders. However, reduced TSH response to TRH have also been found in other neuropsychiatric disorders, including panic disorder (PD), eating disorders, personality disorders, mania, alcoholism, schizophrenia, and cocaine abuse (32), which questions the specifity of this test.

GROWTH HORMONE RESPONSE TO CLONIDINE CHALLENGE TEST

The clonidine-stimulated release of growth hormone (GH) allows us to evaluate dynamically the status of α_2-adrenoreceptor. In one study of nine OCP patients and nine healthy volunteers, the patients showed a significant blunted GH response following this challenge with clonidine; GH increases of greater than 3 ng/ml following clonidine were observed only in two (out of nine) patients with OCD, compared with five (out of nine) normal controls (33). However, baseline GH levels were not significantly different between the two groups.

These results with OCD subjects resemble previously reported results with depressives. However, the blunted GH response was not limited to subjects with secondary depression; of the five OCD subjects with 17-item Hamilton Rating Scale for Depression (HRSD) scores of less than 12, all but one had a blunted GH response to clonidine.

Similar to the DST, the question of the specificity of blunted GH response remains controversial, as nondepressed postmenopausal women and schizoaffective patients also show attenuation similar to that seen in depressives (34). In addition, direct measurement of α-adrenoreceptors with the ligand dihydroergotamine did not reveal any difference between OCD and depressed patients. This is a finding that requires replication.

Sleep electroencephalography studies

The triad of short REM latency, increased REM density, and disturbed temporal distribution of REM has been suggested as being specific to endogenous depressive illness (35).

In one study, patients with OCD had decreased REM latency compared with age-matched normal control and depressed patients, although in this study the OCD patients were, as a group, significantly less depressed ($p < 0.05$) than the primary affective group (36).

Feinberg et al (37) and Rush et al (38) have studied depressed patients with both DST and electroencephalography (EEG). More patients showed short REM latency, defined as less than 62 min by Rush et al (33), than showed dexamethasone nonsuppression, suggesting that REM latency might be a more sensitive test as a diagnostic marker of depression than is the DST. However, the specificity of shortened REM latency for depression remains controversial, as one report (39) described very short REM latencies in a group of carefully diagnosed schizophrenic patients.

The REM density in the OC patients was reported by Ruch et al to be identical to that of the normal and significantly different ($p < 0.05$ paired t test) from that of the depressed patients (38).

The extent to which these sleep variables are state dependent is not entirely clear. Hauri et al (40) reported normal REM latencies for unipolar patients in remission. Others have found increased REM density and even occasional nights with short REM latency in euthymic bipolar patients (41). Conceivably, increased REM density may reflect a vulnerability to affective illness, whereas REM latency may be more closely related to clinical state; thus far, however, the data are insufficient to confirm such a proposition.

In summary, patients with OCD resemble patients with major depressive disorder in only one variable, i.e. decreased REM latency, while they are identical to normal subjects on the other variable, i.e. increased REM density.

BLOOD AND PLATELET SEROTONIN CONTENT

Whole blood 5-HT content has been reported to be reduced in OCD (42), although this was not confirmed by Cottraux et al (43) or by Flament et al (44), who found no difference in the platelet 5-HT levels of OCD patients and healthy subjects. In the latter study, however, platelet 5-HT content appeared highest in patients who responded best to clomipramine treatment, suggesting that this measure may prove useful in predicting treatment response even if it is not valid as a diagnostic marker.

An initial study (45) in PD reported decreased plasma 5-HT levels, but this finding has not been replicated in subsequent studies of platelet 5-HT content (46, 47). On the contrary, schizophrenic patients showed increased 5-HT content, which has been considered a trait of the illness (48).

Although it is difficult to make conclusions as to the significance and/or specificity of these findings, it is noteworthy that patients concomitantly affected by PD and OCD had a significantly lower platelet 5-HT content than patients affected only by PD (47).

Platelet studies

Blood platelets show similarities with presynaptic serotonergic neurons and constitute a peripheral tool for investigating the serotonergic system. In particular, platelets possess a mechanism for active uptake of 5-HT, possibly modulated by [^{3}H]imipramine (^{3}H-IMI) binding sites (49, 50) similar to those present in the brain. Pharmacological studies in this field

(51–53) have shown heterogeneity of IMI binding sites when desipramine is used to define "specific" binding, which questions the adequacy of the platelet model (54). In platelets, as well as in the brain, desipramine-defined IMI binding appears to be constituted by two subpopulations: only that of protein nature, 5-HT-sensitive and sodium dependent would be present in serotonergic neurons and related to the 5-HT transporter (55, 56).

Insel et al (57) found no difference in either 5-HT uptake or ^{3}H-IMI binding in healthy controls and in OC patients, although there was a trend towards reduced ^{3}H-IMI binding sites in the OCP patients. However, much of this tendency resulted from two patients with very low values. These patients were the only ones included who had received clomipramine in the past (more than 3 months before the study). Removing them and their two matched controls from the sample abolishes the difference between the remaining 10 OCP patients and their 10 matched controls. Weizman et al (58) and Marazziti et al (59) observed normal 5-HT uptake coupled with a reduced number of ^{3}H-IMI binding sites. In contrast, Black et al (60) observed no change in ^{3}H-IMI binding, except a decrease in clomipramine-treated patients, while other studies have shown a decreased number of ^{3}H-IMI binding sites and a decreased affinity in 5-HT uptake (61), as well as an increased velocity of 5-HT uptake, with no change in ^{3}H-IMI binding (62). These contradictory results may be explained by methodological differences in platelet preparations or in IMI binding or 5-HT uptake assays (63). Other possible reasons may be different pharmacological wash-out periods, recruitment of patients at different stages of the illness, or heterogeneity of 5-HT function within OCP patients. Some authors (64) have proposed the existence of two forms of OCD based on the course of the disorder, pharmacological response, and even differential IMI binding.

Several studies have shown a reduction in the number of the uptake sites in platelets of depressed patients compared with healthy controls (65–67), while other studies have reported an increased uptake in PD (45). In depressed patients a decrease in the number of ^{3}H-IMI sites has been found by several groups (68–71), and this has been proposed as a biological marker (possibly state-dependent) for major depression (72, 73). However, subsequent replications of these findings in different psychiatric disorders, such as PD (74), eating disorders (75, 76), suicidal behavior (77), and OCD, make this suggestion questionable. The values found in our OC patients are quite low and are similar to those observed in bulimic patients and suicide attempters. While some bulimic patients did show OC personality traits, the close similarities of B_{max} may reflect a similar level of derangement of 5-HT function reflected by IMI binding, possibly relate to impulse dyscontrol. It is noteworthy that a negative correlation between obsessional features and B_{max} has been reported in a group of 46 major depressives (78). Therefore, it is now agreed that a low number of ^{3}H-IMI binding sites is suggestive of a dysfunction of the serotonergic system at the presynaptic level, possibly linked to a favorable response to tricyclics or SRIs (79). The study of the platelet 5-HT transporter appears extremely interesting in OCD, but in future studies the use of more specific ligands (e.g. paroxetine) is recommended, because the IMI binding performed with desipramine for the definition of the "specific" binding appears to give a reasonable, although overestimated, indication of that fraction coupled with the 5-HT uptake (54). Another possibility for future studies of this subject is offered by the recent cloning of the human 5-HT transporter (80), which might permit determination of the level of the observed alterations, as well as the design of new and specific therapeutic agents.

Platelets possess one type of benzodiazepine (BDZ) receptor, called peripheral, which is also found in kidneys, lungs, ovaries, testes, and adrenal cortex and is present in the central nervous system (CNS), in particular in glial cells (81, 82). Besides diazepam, the most specific ligands for this receptor are the 4'-chlordiazepam analog Ro5-4864 and, especially, an isoquinoline carboxamide derivative, PK-11195 (83). The peripheral BDZ receptor has been recently solubilized and cloned, and expressed (84), and it has been demonstrated that is localized in the mitochondrial outer membrane (82). Although for some time considered to be an acceptor site with no pharmacological activity (85), more recent data suggest that the peripheral BDZ receptor is involved in a variety of actions, such as control of cell proliferation, chemotaxis, and contractility of the myocardium (86–88), and that it fulfills all the requirements of a functional receptor. In addition, it has been shown that it is modulated by stress, hormones (89), or drugs (90). The most attractive hypothesis regarding the role of this receptor is the one suggesting a role in steroidogenesis because, in adrenal glands, it has been demonstrated that it mediates the translocation of cholesterol from the outer to the inner mitochondrial membrane and is also involved in the side-chain cleavage of cholesterol (91, 92). Thus, it is supposed that the peripheral BDZ receptor serves the same function in nonsteroidogenic tissues, in particular in glial cells, which are able to synthetize steroids, such as pregnenolone, progesterone, and its derivatives (93, 94), that strongly modulate the γ-aminobutyric acid (GABA) A-receptor complex and thereby the stress response (95). It is noteworthy that different stress paradigms in animals produce changes in peripheral BDZ receptors (96, 97).

Studies in humans have shown that stressing situations, such as sitting an exam (98) or undergoing a parachute training course (99), influence the density of the receptors: an acute stress seems to provoke upregulation, while a repeated stress provokes downregulation. The few studies in OCD have shown a decreased density of ^{3}H-PK-11195 binding sites in the episodic type of OCD (100), and no change in patients with a chronic course [(101); R Weizman, personal communication]. A reduced number (B_{max}) of peripheral BDZ receptors have been reported in patients with PD, when compared with both healthy controls or OC patients with no associated change in the dissociation constant.

Our results in patients with PD are at variance with the observation by Rocca et al (100) that there is no change in peripheral BDZ receptors in lymphocytes of patients with this condition. However, most of the patients included in the study by Rocca et al were also suffering from a mild to a moderate depression, so it is possible that the depression concomitant of PD might have masked eventual changes in peripheral BDZ receptors due to the anxiety disorder alone.

Patients with generalized anxiety disorder (GAD) have been reported to have a decreased number of peripheral BDZ receptors which, after treatment with BDZs, returns towards the normal values found in healthy controls (88, 90). In other anxiety disorders, such as social phobia and post-traumatic stress disorder, we have recently reported an increase in the density of this receptor (100).

Further studies in larger samples are needed to confirm this preliminary observation that different anxiety disorders, and possibly other psychiatric disorders, produce different changes in peripheral BDZ receptors.

Sulfotransferases (STs) (102, 103), enzymes that are involved in the sulfation of biogenic amines, are present in platelets, and are thought to be related to those present in the brain (although there is some controversy about this) (104). Two forms of STs may be found in platelets, as is the case in the CNS: one, which acts preferentially on monoamine substrates, is thermolabile (TL), while the other, which prefers phenol and phenolic compounds, is thermostable (TS) (105, 106). Although, principal catabolic pathways of biogenic amines are those catalyzed by monoaminoxidases and by catechol-O-methyl transferases, it is conceivable that a change in ST activity, although representing a minor degradative pathway, might affect the fine balance existing between different neurotransmitters, in particular sulfated dopamine, 5-HT and tyramine, which might be relevant for the pathophysiology of some psychiatric symptoms (107). There is only one study of ST in OCD, which showed an increased activity of both the two forms of the enzyme in the patients compared with matched controls (59). In schizophrenic and depressed patients, the data are inconsistent (108, 109). In 30 patients with PD and 10 bipolar patients in a depressed phase, we have found normal activity of the enzyme (unpublished data), but these data must be interpreted with caution and will have to be replicated by other groups before any firm conclusions can be drawn.

More recently, platelet 5-HT$_2$ receptor binding sites have been assessed in 20 patients with OCD, by means of the ligand [^{125}I]lysergic acid diethyl-amide, and no difference from controls has been reported (110).

On the contrary, different findings in platelets of depressed patients indicate that 5-HT$_2$ receptors are increased in this condition (111–113). It is a pity that, for a broader comparison, there are no further data on these receptors in other psychiatric disorders.

Cerebrospinal fluid studies

Two studies have looked at CSF levels of 5-HIAA in patients with OCD. Thoren et al (114) found a nonsignificant increase (19%) in CSF 5-HIAA levels in 24 pretreatment hospitalized patients with OCD compared with 37 healthy volunteers. In a cohort of eight patients with OCD, Insel et al (57) found that 5-HIAA levels were significantly elevated in comparison with 23 matched controls. The high variance in the patient sample was largely due to a single outlier, a 55-year-old, postmenopausal woman with a CSF 5-HIAA value of 200 pmol/ml. As there were no postmenopausal females in the control group, the data were reanalyzed excluding this subject. The patient mean decreased to 84.3 ± 13.7 pmol/ml. Correcting both patient and control values for height and weight did not abolish the significant difference between the groups. The patients were shorter than the controls; however, some of the increase that this height difference contributed to the 5-HIAA values was offset by the lower weights of the OCD subjects. Differences between patients and normals in other monoamine metabolites, such as homovanillic acid (HVA) and MHPG, were not significant (57,114).

The possibility of a type-1 error in the CSF study seems likely. Previous reports, both in normals and in other psychiatric groups, have found a large variance in CSF monoamine metabolites. Some investigators have described a bimodal distribution of CSF 5-HIAA (115), others have suggested that this variable may relate to particular clinical characteristics, such as impulsivity or aggression, that are not syndrome specific (116). With so much variance within diagnostic groups, large samples are usually required to demonstrate differences between groups.

Given the complexities of this variable, the CSF data should be interpreted very cautiously. Certainly the results for OCD patients do not suggest the lower CSF 5-HIAA previously reported for violent or psychopathic subjects (117–122). The higher levels of CSF 5-HIAA are of interest, as OC patients tend to be diametrically opposed to impulsive or violent patients.

Administration in OCD of anxiogenic challenges specific for PDs

Beside the above-mentioned biological markers, recent studies with the so-called "anxiogenic" challenges give further support to the distinction between OCD patients and patients with PD and agoraphobia. As detailed description and discussion of these pharmacological challenges are provided in Chapter 11, we will confine our remarks to what one might learn from these studies regarding the biological interaction between OCD and PD. For instance, in one study, lactate infusions were followed by a panic attack in only one of seven OC patients compared with 26 out of 48 PD patients with agoraphobia with panic attacks (123). Moreover, three of the patients with OCD actually reported feeling better than usual during the lactate infusion, a phenomenon that was "never seen" during lactate infusions in patients with PD and agoraphobia or in normal volunteers (123). Patients with OCD also fail to develop increased symptoms following yohimbine (124) or caffeine administration (125), in contrast to the anxious response of agoraphobic patients following these challenges. Hence, anxiogenic challenge studies have questioned the current linkage between OCD and other anxiety disorders, mainly PD.

Discussion and conclusions

On the basis of the biological markers reviewed in this chapter, which have been tested in different psychiatric disorders, it turns out that OCD is more similar to major depression than to PD and schizophrenia, although differences do exist, and suggest that it is a distinct psychiatric disorder.

The abnormalities shared by OCD and major depression are DST nonsuppression, blunted GH response to clonidine, decreased REM latency, and decreased platelet IMI binding. However, in major depression the increased REM density is coupled with decreased REM latency, while in OCD the decrease in REM latency is not associated with alteration in REM density. Similarly, the decreased IMI binding in major depression, at least in unipolar depressives (126), is accompanied by reduced 5-HT uptake, whereas in OCD the reduced IMI binding is not accompanied by diminished 5-HT uptake; however, this is a controversial matter. Moreover, some data suggest that platelet IMI binding may also be decreased in PD patients (74), while 5-HT uptake is increased (45). The lack of association of the changes in IMI binding and 5-HT uptake, from a pharmacological point of view, sustains the theory of the existence of multiple sites: only a subset of desipramine-defined IMI sites would be related to the 5-HT transporter (53, 55). Clinically, it suggests that the degree of severity in the impairment of the 5-HT transporter varies with different psychiatric disorders and further emphasizes the biological differences, rather than the similarities, between OCD and other conditions.

The other two biological markers similar in OCD and major depression are neuroendocrine biological markers (DST, GH response to clonidine, and TSH response to TRH). All are present in a variety of psychiatric and nonpsychiatric conditions and thus they do not appear to be specific.

Another marker, the elevated CSF 5-HIAA level in patients with OCD, is opposite to the reduced or normal CSF 5-HIAA levels usually reported in major depression. Taken together the findings with biological markers do not support a direct linkage between OCD and major depression. Furthermore, the natural courses of these two illnesses are different; OCD is usually chronic in contrast to primary depression, which tends to be episodic. The age at onset is younger for OCD than for major depression, and the male:female ratio is different for the two disorders (lower for depression). Moreover, in contrast to major depression, only clomipramine and SRIs appear to be relatively effective in reducing OC symptoms (3), while in major depression all the tricyclic antidepressants appear to be equipotent.

The search for biological markers in OCD is relatively new, as most of the literature in this field has been produced in the past 5 years. Recent studies have focused on strategies to assess the functional state of neurotransmitters, neuroreceptors, and neuroendocrine axes, by means of research tools widely applied in other psychiatric disorders. Although the pathophysiology of OCD is still unclear, as well as its borders with major depression, PD, and schizophrenia, biological markers seem to indicate that OCD shares some abnormalities with major depression and, to a lesser extent, with PD, but is a separate psychobiological entity.

The shared dysfunctions in biological markers suggest common brain abnormalities which might be the reasons for similar symptoms present in different diseases. However, without doubt, future biological research in OCD should be directed towards the understanding in biological terms of the specific abnormalities that have been already described.

A new level of interpretation of receptor abnormalities has recently been offered by the shift from the studies of binding parameters to dynamic challenges and intracellular processes. Using an elegant approach, Lesch (127) has demonstrated that OCD is clearly different from major depression and PD, at least in the involvement of 5-HT_{1A} receptors. In fact, depressed patients show a blunted hypothermic response to ipsapirone, a 5-HT_{1A} agonist, coupled with a blunted adrenocorticotropic hormone (ACTH)/cortisol response and elevated basal cortisol secretion. In patients with PD, the blunted hypothermic response and ACTH/cortisol response is accompanied by normal cortisol secretion, while patients with OCD are not different from healthy controls.

If we consider how many 5-HT receptors have been characterized to date, the coupling with different G-proteins and intracellular effectors, and the recent cloning of the human 5-HT transporter, we have to reconsider the simplistic serotonergic hypothesis of OCD, which is still the main hypothesis, to substantiate this theory with data derived from different lines of research, and to emphasize where might lie the uniqueness of this psychiatric disorder.

References

1. Hollister L. Psychopharmacology: the bridge between psychiatry and psychology. Clin Pharmacol Ther 1988; 44(2): 123–128.
2. Thoren P, Asberg M, Cronholm B. Clomipramine treatment of obsessive–compulsive disorder: a controlled clinical trial. Arch Gen Psychiatry 1980; 37: 1281–1289.
3. Zohar J, Insel TR. Drug treatment of obsessive–compulsive disorder. J Affect Dis 1987; 13: 193–202.
4. Goodman WK, Price LH, Rasmussen SA, Delgado PL, Heninger GL, Charney DJ. Efficacy of fluvoxamine in obsessive–compulsive disorder: a double-blind comparison. Arch Gen Psychiatry 1989; 46: 36–44.
5. Liebowitz MA, Hollander E, Schneier F et al. Fluoxetine treatment of obsessive–compulsive disorder: an open clinical trial. J Clin Psychopharmacol 1989; 9: 423–427.
6. Ananth J, Pecknold JC, Van Den Steen N, Engelsmann F. Double-blind comparative study of clomipramine and amitriptyline in obsessive neurosis. Prog Neurol Psychopharmacol 1981; 5: 25–62.
7. Volavka J, Neziroglu F, Yaryura Tobias JA. Clomipramine and imipramine in obsessive–compulsive disorder. Psychiatry Res 1985; 14: 83–91.
8. Zohar J, Insel TR. Obsessive–compulsive disorder: psychobiological approaches to diagnosis, treatment and pathophysiology. Biol Psychiatry 1987; 22: 667–687.
9. Goodman WK, McDougle CJ, Lawrence HP, Riddle MA, Pauls DL, Leckman JE. Beyond the serotonin hypothesis: a role for dopamine in some forms of obsessive–compulsive disorder. J Clin Psychopharmacol 1990; 51 (suppl 8): 36–43.
10. Maudsley H. The Pathology of the Mind. MacMillan, London, 1985.
11. Gittlesson N. The depressive psychosis in the obsessional neurotic. Arch Gen Psychiatry 1966; 112: 883–887.
12. Goodwin D, Guze S, Robins E. Follow-up studies in obsessional neurosis. Arch Gen Psychiatry 1969; 20: 182–187.
13. Vaughan M. The relationship between obsessional personality, obsessions in depression and symptoms of depression. Br J Psychiatry 1976; 129: 36–39.
14. Myers JK, Weissman MM, Tischler GL et al. Six-month prevalence of psychiatric disorders in three communities. Arch Gen Psychiatry 1984; 41: 959–971.
15. Robins LN, Helzer JE, Weissman MM et al. Lifetime prevalence of specific psychiatric disorders in three sites. Arch Gen Psychiatry 1984; 41: 949–958.
16. Lewis AJ. Problems of obsessional illness. Proc R Soc Med 1936; 29: 325–336.
17. Carroll BJ, Feinberg M, Greden JF et al. A specific laboratory test for the diagnosis of melancholia. Arch Gen Psychiatry 1981; 38: 15–22.
18. Devanand DP, Sackeim HA, Lo ES et al. Serial dexamethasone suppression tests and plasma dexamethasone levels. Arch Gen Psychiatry 1991; 48: 525–533.
19. Insel TR, Kalin HN, Guttmacher LB, Cohen RM, Murphy DL. The dexamethasone suppression test in patients with primary obsessive–compulsive disorder. Psychiatry Res 1982; 6: 153–158.
20. Asberg M, Thoren P, Bertilsson L. Clomipramine treatment of obsessive compulsive disorder—Biochemical and clinical aspect. Psychopharmacol Bull 1982; 18: 13–21.
21. Insel TR, Goodwin FK. The promises and problems of laboratory tests in

psychiatry: the dexamethasone suppression test as a case example. Hosp Commun Psychiatry 1983; 34: 1131–1138.

22. Cottraux JA, Bouvard M, Claustrat B, Juenet C. Abnormal dexamethasone suppression test in primary obsessive–compulsive patients—A confirmatory report. Psychiatry Res 1984; 13: 157–165.

23. Lieberman J, Kane JM, Sarantakos S et al. Dexamethasone suppression tests in patients with obsessive–compulsive disorder. Am J Psychiatry 1985; 142: 747–751.

24. Monterio W, Noshiruani H, Marks IM, Checkley S. Normal dexamethasone suppression test in OCD. Br J Psychiatry 1986; 148: 326–329.

25. Nesse RM, Curtis GC, Tyers BA, McCann DS, Hubersmith MJ, Knoff RF. Endocrine and cardiovascular responses during phobic anxiety. Arch Gen Psychiatry 1984; 41: 471–476.

26. Herz MF, Fava GA. Dexamethasone suppression test in newly hospitalised schizophrenic patients. Am J Psychiatry 1985; 142: 127–129.

27. Mullen PE, Linsell CR, Parker D. Influence of sleep disruption and calorie restriction on biological markers for depression. Lancet 1986; 2: 1051–1055.

28. Rupprect R, Kornhuber J, Wodarz N et al. Lymphocyte glucocorticoid receptor binding during depression and after clinical recovery. J Affective Disord 1991; 22: 31–35.

29. Loosen PT, Prange AJ Jr. The serum thyrotropin (TSH) response to thyrotropin-releasing hormone (TRH) in psychiatric patients: A review. Am J Psychiatry 1982; 139: 405–416.

30. Bauer MS, Whybrow PC. Thyroid hormones and the central nervous systems in affective illness: interactions that may have clinical significance. Integr Psychiatry 1988, 6: 165–175.

31. Weizman A, Hermesh H, Gilad I, Aizenberg D, Tyano ST, Laron Z. Blunted TSH response in obsessive compulsive disorder. Presented at the 70th Annual Meeting of the Endocrine Society, New Orleans, Louisiana, 1988 [abstr 792].

32. Khan AV. Sensitivity and specificity of TRH stimulation test in depressed and nondepressed adolescents. Psychiatry Res 1988; 25: 11–17.

33. Siever LJ, Insel TR, Jimerson DC et al. Growth hormone response to clonidine in obsessive–compulsive patients. Br J Psychiatry 1983; 142: 184–187.

34. Matussek N, Ackenheil M, Hippius H et al. Effect of clonidine on growth hormone release in psychiatric patients and controls. Psychiatry Res 1980; 2: 25–36.

35. Vogel EW. The relationship between endogenous depression and REM sleep. Psychiatry Ann 1981; 11: 423–428.

36. Insel TR, Gillin JC, Moore A, Mendelson WB, Loewenstein RJ, Murphy DL. The sleep of patients with obsessive–compulsive disorder. Arch Gen Psychiatry 1982; 39: 1372–1377.

37. Feinberg M, Gillin LC, Carroll BL, Greden LF, Zis AP. EEG studies of sleep in the diagnosis of depression. Biol Psychiatry 1982; 17: 305–316.

38. Rush AJ, Giles DE, Roffwarg HP, Parker CR. Sleep-EEG and dexamethasone suppression test findings in unipolar major depressive disorders. Biol Psychiatry 1982; 17: 327–341.

39. Hiatt JF, Floyd TC, Katz P, Feinberg M. A new look at abnormal NREM sleep in schizophrenia. In: New Research Abstracts of 136th APA Meeting, NR III, New York. American Psychiatric Association, Washington, DC, 1983, p 256.

40. Hauri P, Chernik D, Hawkins D, Mendels J. Sleep of depressed patients in remission. Arch Gen Psychiatry 1974; 31: 386–391.

41. Gillin JC. Sleep studies in affective illness: Diagnostic, therapeutic and pathophysiological implications. Psychiatry Ann 1983; 13: 367–383.
42. Yaryura-Tobias JA. Obsessive–compulsive disorders: A serotoninergic hypothesis. J Orthomolec Psychiatry 1977; 6: 317–326.
43. Cottraux J, Flachaire E, Renaud B. Dosage de la sérotonin plaquettaire dans les obsessions compulsions. Presse Med 1987; 16: 590–594.
44. Flament MF, Rapoport JL, Murphy DL, Berg CL, Lake CR. Biochemical changes during clomipramine treatment of childhood obsessive–compulsive disorder. Arch Gen Psychiatry 1987; 44: 219–225.
45. Norman TR, Sartor DM, Judd FK, Barrow GD, Gregory MS, McIntyre I. Platelet serotonin uptake and ₃H-imipramine binding in panic disorder. J Affect Disord 1989; 17: 77–81.
46. Balon R, Pohl R, Yeregani V, Rainey J, Oxenkrug GF. Platelet serotonin levels in panic disorder. Acta Psychiatr Scand 1987; 75: 315–317.
47. Servant D, Bailly D, Perret C, Vignau J, Parquet PJ. Platelet serotonin decreases in panic disorder with obsessive compulsive symptoms. Eur Psychiatry 1992; 7: 27–31.
48. Stahl SM. Hyperserotonemia and platelet serotonin uptake and release in schizophrenic and affective disorder patients. Am J Psychiatry 1983; 140: 26–30.
49. Wennogle LP, Meyerson LR. Serotonin modulates the dissociation of ³H-imipramine from human platelet recognition sites. Eur J Pharmacol 1984; 86: 303–307.
50. Meyerson LR, Ieni JR, Wennogle LP. Allosteric interaction between the site labelled by ³H-imipramine and the serotonin transporter in human platelets. J Neurochem 1987; 8: 560–565.
51. Ieni JR, Zukin SR, Van Praag HM. Human platelets possess multiple ³H-imipramine binding sites. Eur J Pharmacol 1985; 106: 669–672.
52. Marcusson JO, Baeckstroem I, Ross SB. Single-site model of the neuronal 5-hydroxytryptamine uptake and imipramine binding site. Mol Pharmacol 1986; 30: 121–128.
53. Hrdina PD. Differences between sodium-dependent and desipramine-defined ³H-imipramine binding in intact human platelets. Biol Psychiatry 1989; 25: 576–584.
54. Halbreich U, Rojansky N, Zander KJ, Barkai A. Influence of age, sex and diurnal variability on imipramine receptor binding and serotonin uptake in platelets of normal subjects. J Psychiatr Res 1991; 25: 7–18.
55. Marcusson JO, Fowler CJ, Hall H, Ross SB, Winblad B. "Specific" binding of ³H-imipramine to protease-sensitive and protease-resistant sites. J Neurochem 1985; 44: 705–711.
56. Severson JA, Woodward JJ, Wilcox RE. Subdivision of mouse brain ³H-imipramine binding based on ion dependence and serotonin sensitivity. J Neurochem 1986; 46: 1743–1754.
57. Insel TR, Mueller EA, Alterman I, Linnoila M, Murphy DL. Obsessive–compulsive disorder and serotonin: is there a connection? Biol Psychiatry 1985; 20: 1174–1188.
58. Weizman R, Carmi M, Hermesh H et al. High-affinity imipramine binding and serotonin uptake in platelets of eight adolescent and ten adult obsessive–compulsive patients. Am J Psychiatry 1986; 143: 335–339.
59. Marazziti D, Hollander E, Lensi P, Ravagli S, Cassano GB. Peripheral marker of serotonin and dopamine function in obsessive–compulsive disorder. Psychiatry Res 1992; 42: 41–51.
60. Black DW, Kelly M, Myers C, Noyes R Jr. Tritiated imipramine binding in

obsessive–compulsive volunteers and psychiatrically normal controls. Biol Psychiatry 1990; 27: 319–327.

61. Bastani B, Arora RC, Meltzer HY. Serotonin uptake and imipramine binding in the blood platelets of obsessive–compulsive disorder patients. Biol Psychiatry 1991; 30: 131–139.

62. Vitiello B, Shimon H, Behar D, Stoff D, Bridger WH, Friedman E. Platelet imipramine binding and serotonin uptake in obsessive–compulsive patients. Acta Psychiatr Scand 1991; 84: 29–32.

63. Severson JA, Schneider LS, Fredrickson ER. Methodological issues in the preparation and assay of platelet ^{3}H-imipramine binding. Psychiatry Res 1990; 33: 19–29.

64. Ravizza L, Rocca P, Maina G et al. An analysis of ^{3}H-imipramine binding in obsessive–compulsive disorder. Biol Psychiatry 1991; 29 (suppl): 440–441.

65. Tuomisto J, Tukiainen E. Decreased uptake of 5HT in blood platelets from depressed patients. Nature 1976; 262: 596–598.

66. Coppen A, Swade C, Wood K. Platelet 5-hydroxytryptamine accumulation in depressed illness. Clin Chim Acta 1978; 87: 165–168.

67. Meltzer HY, Arora RC, Baber R, Tricou BJ. Serotonin uptake by blood platelets of psychiatric patients. Arch Gen Psychiatry 1981; 38: 1322–1326.

68. Briley MS, Langer SZ, Raisman R, Sechter D, Zarifian E. Tritiated imipramine binding sites are decreased in platelets from untreated depressed patients. Science 1980; 209: 303–305.

69. Baron M, Barkai A, Gruen R, Kowalik S, Quitkin F. ^{3}H-Imipramine binding sites in unipolar depression. Biol Psychiatry 1983; 18: 1403–1409.

70. Lewis DA, McChesney C. Tritiated imipramine binding distinguishes among subtypes of depression. Arch Gen Psychiatry 1985; 42: 485–488.

71. Waegner A, Aberg-Wistedt A, Asberg M, Ekquist B, Martenson B, Montero D. Lower ^{3}H-imipramine binding in platelets from untreated depressed patients compared with healthy controls. Psychiatry Res 1985; 16: 131–139.

72. Suranyi-Cadotte BE, Wood PL, Nair NPV, Schwartz G. Normalisation of platelet ^{3}H-imipramine binding in depressed patients during remission. Eur J Pharmacol 1982; 85: 357–358.

73. Marazziti D, Perugi G, Deltito J et al. High-affinity ^{3}H-imipramine binding: A possible state-dependent marker for major depression. Psychiatry Res 1988; 23: 229–237.

74. Lewis DA, Noyes RJ, Coryell W, Clancy S. Tritiated imipramine binding to platelets is decreased in patients with agoraphobia. Psychiatry Res 1985; 16: 2–9.

75. Weizman R, Carmi M, Tyano S, Apter A, Rehavi M. High-affinity imipramine binding and serotonin uptake to platelets of adolescent females suffering from anorexia nervosa. Life Sci 1986; 38: 1235–1242.

76. Marazziti D, Macchi E, Rotondo A, Placidi GF, Cassano GB. Involvement of serotonin system in bulimia. Life Sci 1988; 43(25): 2123–2126.

77. Marazziti D, De Leo D, Conti L. Further evidence supporting the role of the serotonin system in suicidal behavior: A preliminary study in suicide attempters. Acta Psychiatr Scand 1989; 80: 322–324.

78. Theodoru AE, Katona CLE, Davies SL et al. ^{3}H-Imipramine binding to freshly prepared platelet membranes in depression. Psychiatry Res 1989; 29: 87–103.

79. Castrogiovanni P, Di Muro A, Marazziti D. Imipramine binding as predictor of clinical response in depression. Clin Neuropharmacol 1992; 15 (suppl 1B): 337.

80. Lesch KP, Wolozin BL, Murphy DL, Riederer P. Primary structure of the human platelet serotonin uptake site: identity with the brain serotonin transport. J Neurochem 1993; 60: 2319–2322.

81. Anholt RRH, Murphy KMM, Mack GE, Snyder SH. Peripheral-type benzodiazepine receptors in the central nervous system: Localization to olfactory nerves. J Neurosci 1984; 4: 593–603.

82. Anholt RRH, Aebi U, Pederson PL, Snyder SH. Solubilization and reassembly of the mitochondrial benzodiazepine receptors. Biochemistry 1986; 25: 2120–2125.

83. Marangos PJ, Patel J, Boulenger JP, Clark-Rosenberg R. Characterization of periphal type benzodiazepine binding sites in brain using ^{3}H-Ro-5-4864. Mol Pharmacol 1982; 22: 26–32.

84. Sprengel R, Werner P, Seeburg PH et al. Molecular cloning and expression of cDNA encoding a peripheral type benzodiazepine receptor. J Biol Chem 1989; 264: 20415–20421.

85. Richards JC, Mohler H, Haefely W. Benzodiazepine binding sites: receptors or acceptors. Trend Pharmacol Sci 1982; 3: 233–235.

86. Ruff MR, Pert CB, Weber RJ, Wahl LM, Wahl SM, Paul SM. Benzodiazepine receptor mediated chemotaxis of human monocytes. Science 1985; 229: 1281–1283.

87. Taupin V, Herbelin A, Descamps-Latscha B, Zavala F. Endogenous anxiogenic peptide, ODN-diazepam binding inhibitor, and benzodiazepine enhance the production of interleukin-1 and tumor necrosis factor by human monocytes. Lymph Cytok Res 1991; 10: 7–13.

88. Ferrarese C, Apollonio I, Bianchi G et al. Benzodiazepine receptors and diazepam binding inhibitor: A possible link between stress, anxiety and the immune system. Psychoneuroendocrinology 1993; 18: 3–22.

89. Drugan RC, Basile AS, Crawley JN, Paul SM, Skolnick P. Inescapable shock reduces (^{3}H)-Ro 5-4864 binding to "peripheral-type benzodiazepine receptor" in the rat. Pharmacol Biochem Behav 1986; 24: 1673–1677.

90. Weizman R, Tanne Z, Granek M et al. Peripheral benzodiazepine binding sites on platelet membranes are increased during diazepam treatment of anxious patients. Eur J Pharmacol 1987; 138: 289–292.

91. Muhkin AG, Papadopoulos V, Costa E, Krueger KE. Mitochondrial benzodiazepine receptors regulate steroid biosynthesis. Proc Natl Acad Sci USA 1989; 86: 9813–9816.

92. Papadopoulos V, Muhkin AG, Costa E, Krueger KE. The peripheral-type benzodiazepine receptor is functionally linked to Leydig-cell steroidogenesis. J Biol Chem 1990; 265: 3772–3779.

93. Hu ZY, Jung-Testas I, Robel P, Baulieu EE. Neurosteroids: Steroidogenesis in primary cultures of rat glial cells after release of aminoglutethimide blockade. Biochem Biophys Res Commun 1989; 161: 917–922.

94. Jung-Testas I, Hu ZY, Baulieu EE, Robel P. Neurosteroids: biosynthesis of pregnenolone and progesterone in primary cultures of rat glial cells. Endocrinology 1989; 125: 2083–2091.

95. Purdy RH, Morrow AL, Moore PH, Paul SM. Stress-induced elevation of GABA-A receptor-active 3 alpha-hydroxysteroids in the rat brain. Soc Neurosci Abstr 1990; 16: 289.

96. Drugan RC, Basile AS, Crawley JN, Paul SM, Kolnick P. Peripheral benzodiazepine binding sites in Maudsley reactive rats: Selective decrease confined to peripheral tissues. Brain Res Bull 1987; 18: 143–145.

97. Okun F, Weizman R, Katz Y, Bomzon A, Youdim MBH, Gavish M. Increase in central and peripheral benzodiazepine receptor following surgery. Brain

Res 1988; 458: 31–36.

98. Karp L, Weizman A, Tyano S, Gavish M. Examination stress, platelet peripheral benzodiazepine binding sites, and plasma hormone levels. Life Sci 1989; 44: 1077–1082.

99. Dar DE, Weizman A, Karp L et al. Platelet peripheral benzodiazepine receptors in repeated stress. Life Sci 1991; 48: 341–346.

100. Rocca P, Ferrero P, Gualerzi A et al. Peripheral-type benzodiazepine receptors in anxiety disorders. Acta Psychiatr Scand 1991; 84: 537–544.

101. Marazziti D, Diamond BI, Rotondo A, Borison RL, Cassano GB. Peripheral benzodiazepine receptors in anxiety disorders. Biol Psychiatry 1993; 33 (suppl 6e): 50.

102. Butler PR, Anderson RJ, Venton DL. Human platelet phenol sulphotransferase: Partial purification and detection of two forms of the enzyme. J Neurochem 1983; 41: 630–639.

103. Young WF Jr, Okazaki H, Laws ER Jr, Weishilboum RM. Human brain phenol sulfotransferase: Biochemical properties and regional localization. J Neurochem 1984; 43: 706–715.

104. Young WF Jr, Laws ER Jr, Sharbrough FW, Weishilboum RM. Human phenol sulfotransferase: correlation of brain and platelet activities. J Neurochem 1985; 44: 1131–1137.

105. Rein G, Glover V, Sandler M. Multiple forms of phenolsulphotransferase in human tissues: Selective inhibition by dichloronitrophenol. Biochem Pharmacol 1982; 31: 1893–1897.

106. Reiter C, Weinshilboum R. Acetyloaminophen and phenol: substrates for both a thermostable and a thermolabile form of human platelet phenol sulphotransferase. J Pharmacol Exp Ther 1982; 221: 43–51.

107. Rensker KJ, Feor KD, Roth JA. Sulfation of dopamine and other biogenic amines by human brain phenol sulfotransferase. J Neurochem 1980; 34: 1362–1368.

108. Bonham Carter SM, Glover V, Sandler M, Gillman PK, Bridges PK. Human platelet phenolsulphotransferase: Separate control of the two forms and activity in depressive illness. Clin Chim Acta 1980; 117: 333–344.

109. Reveley AM, Bonham Carter SM, Reveley MA, Sandler M. A genetic study on platelet phenolsulphotransferase activity in normal and schizophrenic twins. J Psychiatr Res 1983; 17: 303–307.

110. Pandey SC, Kim SW, Davis JM, Pandey GN. Platelet serotonin-2 receptors in obsessive–compulsive disorder. Biol Psychiatry 1993; 33: 367–373.

111. Biegon A, Weizman A, Karp L, Ram A, Tyano S, Wolff M. Serotonin-2 receptor binding on blood platelets: A peripheral marker for depression? Life Sci 1987; 4: 2485–2492.

112. Arora RC, Meltzer HY. Increased serotonin-2 receptor binding as measured by (^{3}H)-lysergic acid diethylamide (^{3}H-LSD) in blood platelets of depressed patients. Life Sci 1989; 44: 726–734.

113. Pandey GN, Pandey SC, Janicak PG, Marks RC, Davis JM. Platelet serotonin-2 receptor binding sites in depression and suicide. Biol Psychiatry 1993; 28: 215–222.

114. Thoren P, Asberg M, Bertilsson L, Mellstrom B, Sjoqvist F, Traskmah L. Clomipramine treatment of obsessive compulsive disorder, II, biochemical aspects. Arch Gen Psychiatry 1980; 37: 1289–1294.

115. Post RM, Ballenger JC, Goodwin FK. Cerebrospinal fluid studies of neurotransmitter function in manic and depressive illness. In: Neurobiology of Cerebrospinal Fluid (ed Wood JE). Plenum Press, New York, 1980, pp 685–695.

116. Jimerson DC, Berrettini W. Cerebrospinal fluid amine metabolite studies in depression: Research update. In: Pathochemical markers in major psychoses (eds Beckmann E, Riederer P). Springer Verlag, Berlin, 1985, pp 129–143.
117. Asberg M, Ringberger V, Sjoqvist F, Thoren P, Traskman L, Tuck R. Monoamine metabolites in the cerebrospinal fluid and serotonin uptake inhibition during treatment with chlorimipramine. Clin Pharmacol Ther 1977; 21: 201–207.
118. Traskman L, Asberg M, Bertilsson L, Sjostrand L. Monoamine metabolites in CSF and suicidal behaviour. Arch Gen Psychiatry 1981; 38: 631–636.
119. Van Praag HM. Neurotransmitters and CNS disease depression. Lancet 1982; ii: 1259–1269.
120. Brown GL, Ebert MH, Goyer PF et al. Aggression, suicide, and serotonin: Relationships to CSF amine metabolites. Am J Psychiatry 1982; 139: 741–746.
121. Linnoila M, Virkkunen M, Scheinin M, Nuutila A, Rimon R, Goodwin FK. Low cerebrospinal fluid 5-hydroxy-indoleacetic acid concentration differentiates impulsive from nonimpulsive violent behaviour. Life Sci 1983; 33: 2609–2614.
122. Roy A, Linnoila M. Suicidal behavior, impulsiveness, and serotonin. Acta Psychiatr Scand 1988; 78: 529–535.
123. Gorman JM, Liebowitz MR, Fyer AJ et al. Lactate infusions in obsessive–compulsive disorder. Am J Psychiatry 1985; 142: 861–866.
124. Rasmussen SA, Goodman WK, Woods SW, Heninger GR, Charney DS. Effects of yohimbine in obsessive–compulsive disorder. Psychopharmacology 1987; 93: 308–313.
125. Zohar J, Mueller EA, Insel TR, Zohar-Kadouch RC, Murphy DL. Serotonergic responsivity in obsessive–compulsive disorder: Comparison of patients and healthy controls. Arch Gen Psychiatry 1987; 44: 946–951.
126. Marazziti D, Lenzi A, Cassano GB. Serotonergic dysfunction in bipolar disorder. Pharmacopsychiatry 1991; 5: 164–168.
127. Lesch KP. Modulation of receptor G-protein complex function by psychotropic drugs and glucocorticoids: Implications for anxiety disorders and depression. Eur Neuropsychopharmacol 1991; 3: 340–343.

13 NEUROPSYCHIATRY OF OBSESSIVE COMPULSIVE DISORDER

Dan J Stein, Eric Hollander and Lisa Cohen

Mount Sinai School of Medicine, NY, USA

Introduction

Clinicians have long noted an association between obsessive compulsive disorder (OCD) and neurological disorders. Furthermore, in recent years a growing body of neuropsychiatric studies has documented impairment in cognitive and sensory–motor functions in OCD. Together with imaging studies and neurosurgical research, this work has contributed to the development of neuroanatomical models of OCD. These models have focused on reciprocal connections between frontal cortex and basal ganglia (1–5). In this chapter we review the association between OCD and neurological disorders as well as research on neurological soft signs, neuropsychological tests, and electrophysiological findings in OCD.

Obsessive compulsive disorder in neurological disorders

Several authors have argued that there is an association between OCD and neurological disorders. There are reports of OCD symptoms in seizure disorder (6–13), head trauma (14, 15), cerebral infarction (16, 17), brain tumors (18–23), herpes simplex encephalitis (24), developmental disorders (25, 26), diabetes insipidus (27), multiple sclerosis (28), and acute intermittent porphyria (29). Furthermore, an early study demonstrated that 19.4% of 104 obsessive patients had associated neurological

Current Insights in Obsessive Compulsive Disorder. Edited by E. Hollander, J. Zohar, D. Marazzati and B. Olivier
© 1994 John Wiley & Sons Ltd

disorders such as encephalitis, meningitis, and seizure disorder (30). Other early studies found an association between birth trauma and OCD (31), although more recent work has not confirmed this (32, 33). The incidence of OCD following head injury also remains unclear (34, 35).

The 1915–26 pandemic of viral encephalitis lethargica provided early evidence of a specific neurological basis for OCD. The outbreak was followed by the presentation of numerous patients with a somnolent-like state and parkinsonian features. von Economo (36) documented various focal brain lesions in these cases, including involvement of the basal ganglia. In addition, von Economo detailed associated obsessive compulsive symptoms and tics. Subsequently, a series of authors (37) has confirmed these associations.

Research on neurological disorders associated with OCD provides further evidence for a link between OCD and movement disorders with basal ganglia pathology. Grimshaw (30) found that six of 103 OCD patients had histories of Sydenham's chorea. Symptoms of obsessive compulsive disorder have also been reported in Huntington's disease (38, 39), Parkinson's disease (40, 41), spasmodic torticollis (42), and in basal ganglia lesions of various etiologies (43–49). Early studies suggested a link between Sydenham's chorea and OCD symptoms (50, 51), and a recent controlled study by Swedo et al (52) demonstrated that rheumatic fever patients with Sydenham's chorea had significantly greater scores on the Leyton Obsessional Inventory than those without chorea. Khanna (24) has found that this association between OCD and Sydenham's chorea is also present in India.

Some of the most promising research on the association between OCD and a movement disorder is work on the relationship of OCD and Tourette's Syndrome (TS). Gilles de la Tourette's (53) initial description of the syndrome included a patient with tics, vocalizations, and perhaps obsessions. While there has been some dispute about the association of OCD with TS (54), there is increasing evidence that a subgroup of TS patients also have OCD (55). Conversely, a subgroup of OCD patients has tics (56–58). Furthermore, family studies demonstrate a high rate of OCD and/or tics in relatives of TS patients, and a high rate of TS and/or tics in relatives of OCD patients (56, 59–61).

In so far as movement disorders implicate basal ganglia pathology, a role for these structures in the mediation of OCD is suggested. A number of studies are, however, also compatible with involvement of the frontal lobe (12, 14, 15, 17–21) or other regions (6, 9, 11, 12, 22, 27). Further research is required to dissect out genetic and other contributions to frontal lobe–basal ganglia dysfunction. Understanding the genetic mechanisms that lead to TS or the immunological processes involved in Sydenham's chorea with associated obsessive compulsive symptoms may, for example, provide insights into the pathogenesis of OCD.

Neurological soft signs

The term "neurological soft signs" refers to various neurological phenomena that occur in the absence of evidence of gross neurological disease. These include involuntary movements, a variety of apraxias, difficulties in performing rapid alternating movements, and difficulties in discerning double simultaneous stimulation and dysgraphesthesia (62). Neurological soft sign examination appears reliable (63) and stable (64). Neurological soft signs have been linked to childhood asocial schizophrenia and emotionally unstable character disorder (65), as well as childhood hyperactivity and minimal brain dysfunction (66, 67). These were not nonspecific findings, since several psychiatric groups, including non-asocial schizophrenics and patients with affective disorders and other personality disorders, did not show them (65). In prospective studies, increased soft signs at 7 years of age were associated with adolescent (62) and adult (68) anxiety and affective disorders, including OCD.

In his early paper, Schilder (69) suggested that subtle neurological abnormalities were present in about a third of OCD cases. In a small study of seven adolescents with OCD, neurodevelopmental examination yielded a high frequency of age-inappropriate synkinesias and left hemibody signs (70). In a larger study, 54 children and adolescents with OCD were examined with a standard neurological examination and with the revised Physical and Neurological Examination for Soft-Signs (71). Of the 54 patients, 44 had abnormal neurological findings, and only 10 had no evidence of neurodevelopmental abnormalities. Compared with normal controls, left hemisyndrome OCD patients were most impaired on spatial tests, such as the Money Road Map and Stylus Maze Learning tests, with the choreiform patients intermediate between these groups.

Hollander et al (72) administered a 20-item neurological soft sign examination to 41 adult OCD patients and 20 normal controls, matched for age, sex, and handedness. The OCD patients had significantly more total soft signs than normals, with abnormalities in fine motor coordination, involuntary and mirror movements, and visual spatial dysfunction. Increased neurological soft signs were associated with greater symptom severity (72), increased ventricular volume (73), and with treatment resistance (74). Soft signs correlated positively with impairment on a measure of visual memory (the Benton Visual Retention Test), but negatively with a measure of set-switching (Trials B-A) (75). Although soft signs are non-localizing, abnormal and choreiform movements are consistent with basal ganglia dysfunction, while visual spatial deficits are consistent with right hemispheric dysfunction. Patients without increased soft signs may, however, have frontal impairment as suggested by impaired set-switching.

Bihari et al (76) evaluated 39 OCD patients and normal and patient controls with a neurological soft sign examination. The OCD patients on medication ($n = 14$) did not differ in soft signs from medication-free OCD patients. Patients with OCD had increased soft signs over both normal controls and a combined group of patients with non-OCD anxiety disorders and seasonal affective disorder.

Hymas et al (77) studied 59 patients with OCD, 17 of whom had obsessional slowness. In this subgroup, patients had increased subtle neurological abnormalities compared with normal controls. Although examination was not blind to diagnosis, and a few patients had neurological disorders or were on medication, prevalence of abnormalities similar to those rated by Hollander et al (72) was equivalent across the two studies. However, there was no significant correlation between motor abnormalities and obsessionality.

Khanna (78) has also reported increased soft signs in OCD patients. Analysis of individual items indicated that deficits were predominantly in complex motor tasks.

Thomson and Jensen (79) compared 61 child and adolescent OCD patients with 177 matched control patients for organic features as assessed by neurological signs, electrophysiological abnormalities, specific developmental disorder, and attention deficit. Significantly more OCD patients were assigned to the organic class than were controls. Neurological soft signs were the most sensitive and specific indicator of organicity. Behavioral problems and loss of temper were significantly more frequent in the nonorganic class, whereas symptoms of phobia and depression were more often present in the organic class. Like a number of other studies discussed in the section, this research on soft signs suggests several avenues for future empirical study of the clinical and neurobiological heterogeneity of OCD.

Neuropsychology

For the purposes of summarizing the growing literature on the neuropsychology of OCD, we will divide neuropsychological tests into tests of visual spatial function [e.g. performance IQ:verbal IQ ratio on the Weschler Adult Intelligence Scale (WAIS)], tests of set-shifting ability (e.g. the Wisconsin Card Sort Test, verbal fluency), and tests that involve both functions (e.g. the Money Road Map Test, the Stylus Learning Test) (80). It may be suggested that tests of visual spatial function reflect right hemisphere function, while tests of set-shifting ability reflect frontal lobe function.

However, several limitations to this kind of attempt to localize neurological deficits using neuropsychological tests should be noted. First, neuropsychological impairment on any particular test cannot readily be related to a single brain area. Thus, impairment on tests of frontal lobe function may also be seen in basal ganglia disease. Second, the absence of neuropsychological impairment does not imply the absence of neurological deficits. Neurological deficits may be too subtle to lead to neuropsychological impairment. Third, neuropsychological dysfunction does not allow assessment of a particular process as primary or secondary. Neuropsychological impairment may for example represent a compensatory strategy.

Flor-Henry et al (81) studied 11 adult OCD patients with a neuropsychological test based on Reitan's battery. Ten of the patients were said to show bilateral frontal dysfunction, left hemisphere greater than right. However, the tests used to ascertain dominant frontal lobe dysfunction (the Digit Span and Digit Symbol subscales of the WAIS) may not be valid measures of this. The OCD patients did, however, have impaired performance on the Tactile Performance Test, a measure of visual spatial function. Nevertheless, results may have been confounded by lower IQ in patients relative to archived controls, as well as the inclusion of patients with depression.

Insel et al (82) studied 18 adult OCD patients using the WAIS and the Halstead-Reitan Battery. There was no impairment on the Digit Span and Digit Symbol subtests, although there was some evidence that OCD patients were generally impaired on the performance subtests. There was no overall impairment on the Halstead–Reitan Battery, but more than half the subjects were impaired on visual spatial function (the Tactile Performance Test). These findings were noted to be consistent with right hemisphere dysfunction. However, the authors also suggested that depression, obsessional slowness, and fear of contamination from the testing apparatus may have been confounding factors.

Rapoport et al (83) reported no difference between nine adolescent OCD patients and normal controls in sustained attention and reaction time tasks. However, later studies demonstrated specific deficits in OCD subjects on Money's Road Map Test and on Stylus Maze Learning, measures of directional orientation and trial and error learning that may be frontally mediated (84, 85). There was also evidence of lower performance IQ and impaired performance on the Wisconsin Card Sort.

Behar et al (70) studied 16 adolescent OCD patients and 16 normal controls with a neuropsychological battery. The OCD patients were impaired on Money's Road Map Test and the Stylus Maze Learning Task. The OCD patients were not impaired on measures of attention. On the Rey–Osterreith Complex Figure Test, patients used immature strategies for completion. Neuropsychological deficits did not correlate with ventricular : brain ratios on computerized tomography. The authors noted that a high rate of secondary depression in their sample may have been a confounding factor.

Harvey (86) found that OCD patients were impaired on the Nelson's Modified Wisconsin Card Sorting Test. Impairment on this test, and on a verbal fluency task, correlated with obsessional characteristics on the Leyton Obsessional Inventory. Malloy (87) and Martinot et al (88) have also found impairment on set-shifting tasks in OCD patients.

Head et al (80) found that, compared with normal controls, OCD patients had lower performance on Block Design but not the Line Orientation Test (tests of visual spatial ability), impairment on some verbal fluency tests, and deficits on Money's Road Map Test but not the Stylus Maze Learning Task.

Hollander et al (89) found that on the Matching Familiar Figures Test (MFFT), which has been used to study impulsive and reflective behavioral styles, and which may be a measure of both visual spatial and set-shifting function, OCD patients tended to be fast and inaccurate or slow and accurate in comparison with the control group's intermediate latency and low error rate. Results on the MFFT were correlated with neurological soft signs, behavioral response to pharmacological challenge with the partial serotonin agonist meta-chlorophenyl-piperazine (mCPP) and treatment response to serotonin reuptake inhibitors (SSRIs). Preliminary conclusions were that the patients fell into two groups. One group tended to have fast and inaccurate responses on the MFFT, a high number of soft signs, behavioral nonresponsiveness to mCPP, and a poor response to SSRIs. A second group had slow and accurate responses on the MFFT, a moderate number of soft signs, behavioral responsiveness to mCPP, and a good treatment response.

Boone et at (90) studied 20 nondepressed OCD patients and 16 normal controls using a battery designed to measure frontal lobe function, memory and attention, and visual spatial skills. There were deficits only in visual spatial and visual memory functioning (as measured by performance IQ, the Hooper Visual Organizational Test and the Rey–Osterreith Complex Figure Test). Patients with a family history of OCD were more compromised on these measures than those without such a history. The authors suggested that these findings are consistent with right hemisphere disturbance. However, the authors noted that they may also suggest basal ganglia lesions.

Zielinski et al (91) studied 21 patients with OCD and 21 controls on indices of attention, memory, perseveration, and fluency. Patients had impairment on tests of visual spatial function (Recurring Figures Test, Corsi's Blocks). Impairment did not significantly correlate with anxiety. Patients did not have impaired performance on most verbal tasks and measures of frontal lobe functioning (e.g. the Wisconsin Card Sort Test).

Christensen et al (92) tested 18 OCD patients and normal controls on verbal abilities, visual spatial reasoning, recent verbal memory, recent nonverbal memory, and executive function. There were significant differences between OCD patients and normal controls on recent nonverbal memory function (assessed by delayed recall on Wechsler Memory Scale (WMS) Visual Reproduction and the designs portion of the Continuous Paired Associates Test). This was not the function of immediate nonverbal memory deficit (assessed by Block Tapping). Although there were no group differences in visual spatial tests on multivariate analysis, OCD patients were impaired on Block Design in a univariate contrast.

Martin et al (93) found that OCD patients were not dysfunctional on tests that are typically impaired in Huntington's disease. Measures included the WAIS-R Vocabulary and Block Design subtests, the Road Map Test, verbal fluency, Simple and Choice Visual Reaction Time, a visual search task, and The California Verbal Learning Test. They concluded that perhaps only a subgroup of OCD patients have clinical slowness and cognitive impairment.

Overall, there has been some agreement between different studies, but the implications of dysfunction on specific neuropsychological tests in OCD are not readily interpretable. It has been hypothesized that there is often a significant verbal/performance IQ split on the WAIS in OCD and this has been repeatedly documented and supported by evidence of visual spatial deficits (70, 80, 82, 84, 89–91). These may indicate right hemisphere abnormalities. However, they may also be consistent with basal ganglia dysfunction (16). In addition, several studies have suggested impairment on tests of frontal lobe function (80, 84, 86, 87, 89), although this finding is more controversial (90–93).

Furthermore, impairment on many of the measures used to assess frontal lobe function (e.g. Money's Road Map, Stylus Maze Learning) may simply reflect visual spatial abnormalities. They may also reflect comorbid depression (70, 81, 82). Finally, deficits on neuropsychological tests may reflect secondary rather than primary deficits. This possibility gains some support from several studies that have shown no correlation between symptoms and neuropsychological deficits.

Electrophysiology

There have been reports of seizure disorder patients with pre-ictal, ictal, or interictal OCD symptoms (6–13). On the basis of electrical stimulation studies, Grey-Walter (94) argued that overactivity of the cingulate system led to obsessive compulsive symptoms, a conclusion that was given some support by later work (95). Varying rates of EEG abnormalities were reported in early studies of obsessional patients, ranging from less than 10 to over 60% (96–100).

Flor-Henry et al (81) reported predominantly left hemisphere temporal and parietal abnormalities of variability on power spectral EEG analysis of 10 OCD patients. In support of temporal findings, Bingley and Persson

(101) reported increased frontotemporal theta activity in five of 35 OCD patients, Jenike and Brotman (102) found that four of 12 OCD patients had EEG abnormalities over the temporal lobes, and Epstein and Bailine (103) reported similarities between sleep EEGs in three OCD patients and those of temporal lobe epilepsy. However, Insel et al (104) found EEG abnormalities in only two of 18 adults with OCD, and Behar et al (70) found only mild EEG abnormalities in three of 16 adolescents with OCD. Sleep EEG in adults with OCD differed from controls but was similar to that seen in age-matched depressives (104). Similarly, sleep EEG in adolescents with OCD resembled that of depressed patients (83).

Rapoport et al (83) also compared visual (VEPs) and auditory (AEPs) evoked potentials in adolescent OCD patients and matched controls. While P100 to VEPs differed between the two groups, values were within normal limits. The OCD patients showed shorter latencies and less decrease in latency with increasing stimulus intensity for N120.

Beech et al (105, 106) found shortened latencies and reduced negativity of late event-related potentials (ERPs N220 and N350) to visual stimuli in a group of eight OCD patients. Differences from controls were greater during a more complex visual spatial task. The authors noted that shortened latencies, but not reduced negativity, were consistent with enhanced arousal in OCD.

Shagass et al (107) studied early and middle latency evoked potentials to somatosensory, auditory, and visual stimuli. Compared with normal and psychiatric controls, OCD patients had greater negativity of N60 somatosensory evoked potentials (SEPs). The OCD patients also had lower early peak amplitudes on VEPs and AEPs, while later peak amplitudes were higher. These findings were again thought consistent with hyperarousal. In a subsequent study, Shagass et al (108) factor analyzed the peak amplitude of SEPs across 14 leads and found that factor scores of OCD patients differed from those of other groups. In view of (a) lower left SEP P90 contralateral factor scores and higher right SEP P90 contralateral factors, and (b) higher N130 anterior factor scores and lower P130 posterior and contralateral factor scores, the authors noted that these findings were also consistent with left anterior dysfunction. Khanna et al (109) found that middle latency AEPs and VEPs in 50 OCD patients did not differ significantly from normal controls. Like Beech et al, the authors noted that increased complexity of cognitive tasks may be necessary in order to demonstrate deficits in OCD.

Towey et al (110) elicited late brain ERPs in 10 OCD and normal controls using an auditory "oddball" task. They found that OCD patients had shorter latencies in the regions of N200 and P300 during the difficult discrimination condition. For both levels of task difficulty, OCD patients also showed greater negativity in the N200 and slow-wave region, especially over the left hemisphere. These findings were replicated with a larger sample (J Towey, personal communication). The findings of briefer latency of N200 and P300 components in OCD patients differ from those in other psychiatric disorders such as schizophrenia and depression. Cortical arousal may result in a speeding of cognitive processing and shortening of latency, while overaroused and overfocused attention may result in increased negativity of late ERP latency. Lateral asymmetry for ERPs may be consistent with increased left hemisphere responsiveness in OCD.

Stefanis et al (111) studied patients with OCD, patients with generalized anxiety disorder, and normal controls during a presentation of the Stroop test. The OCD patients had significantly longer latencies and greater negativity on N100 as compared with both normal subjects and patients with generalized anxiety disorder. There were, however, no differences between groups in P200 and P300.

A number of studies have focused on slow potentials and the Bereitschaftpotential in OCD. Timsit-Berthier et al (112) found prolonged postimperative negativity in OCD patients. Several workers have reported a higher amplitude of the late component of the contingent negative variation (112–114). Khanna (24) found decreased onset in latency and increase in amplitude in Bereitschaftpotential in OCD patients. Khanna (24) also found that in Sydenham's chorea, subjects with comorbid OCD had increased abnormalities in morphology of bereitschaftspotentials.

Rapoport et al (83) found a significant decrease in right ear advantage in a dichotic test in adolescents with OCD compared to normal controls. Wexler and Goodman (115) also found significantly decreased right ear advantage in adult OCD patients compared to controls. This abnormality was more pronounced in patients with more severe illness. These findings are consistent with decreased left hemisphere function. Wexler and Goodman (115) also found that OCD patients tended to be consciously aware of hearing fewer emotion-related words (positive and negative) than healthy controls. Decreased perceptual awareness of emotion-related disorders predicted increased likelihood of response to SSRIs.

Conclusions

Neuropsychiatric research on OCD has addressed the nature and specificity of neuropsychiatric deficits in OCD, as well as the possibility of discrete neuropsychiatric subgroups within OCD.

Localization of neuropsychiatric deficits in OCD is suggested by imaging studies, which have documented involvement of the frontal lobe and basal ganglia in OCD (Hoehn-Saric and Benkelfat, this volume). Comorbidity of OCD with neurological disorders provides substantial further evidence for involvement of basal ganglia, but also indicates that damage to other areas of the brain may lead to OCD. Neurological soft signs are perhaps too nonspecific to point to any particular brain area, although increased involuntary movements are consistent with basal ganglia involvement in OCD. Further work needs to be done to document whether these soft sign findings are selective for OCD, or whether they are also found in OCD spectrum disorders and other anxiety disorders.

Neuropsychological testing provides some evidence for visual spatial and set-shifting deficits in OCD, and electrophysiological work has provided partial evidence for hyperarousal. Neither neuropsychological nor electrophysiological research has clearly demonstrated specific neurological lesions in OCD. Nevertheless, this work is broadly consistent with the involvement of frontal lobe–basal ganglia circuits in OCD (24). Further work is necessary to construct comprehensive cognitive processing models of OCD (116, 117).

The research reviewed in this chapter does not allow a determination of whether frontal lobe dysfunction in OCD is an antecedent or a consequence of basal ganglia impairment. Further research is also necessary to determine the etiopathology of impairment in patients who have OCD without comorbid neurological disease. The finding of links between infectious disease and OCD suggests that work in neuroimmunology may be particularly relevant. It will also be interesting to ascertain whether etiological mechanisms that are important in OCD are also present in related disorders such as trichotillomania.

The possibility of specific subgroups within OCD is raised by phenomenological differences within OCD, variation in response to pharmacological challenges, and treatment response differences. Only a small subgroup of OCD patients has a clear comorbid neurological disorder, but a larger subgroup of OCD patients may have a genetic link with TS. Small subgroups of OCD patients have also been shown to have very high neurological soft signs, widespread neuropsychological deficits, or marked electrophysiological abnormalities. While the relevance of these findings to the majority of OCD patients is unclear, they support the importance of researching the neurobiological basis of OCD.

Evidence for subgrouping the remainder of OCD patients on the basis of neuropsychiatric findings remains preliminary. Nevertheless, there is already some evidence that this work may have both pharmacological and psychological (74, 115) implications. These findings encourage further research in this direction. There is a need to standardize neuropsychiatric methodology to allow more direct comparisons between research in different groups and countries. It may also be useful to combine soft sign examination, neuropsychological testing, or electrophysiological investigation with other methodologies, such as brain imaging. Such work may contribute to better delineation and differentiation of subgroups of OCD patients, which in turn may have an impact on treatment.

References

1. Insel TR. Toward a neuroanatomy of obsessive–compulsive disorder. Arch Gen Psychiatry 1992; 49: 739–744.
2. Khanna S. Obsessive–compulsive disorder: Is there a frontal lobe dysfunction? Biol Psychiatry 1988; 24: 602–613.
3. Baxter LR. PET studies of cerebral function in major depression and obsessive compulsive disorder: The emerging prefrontal cortex consensus. Ann Clin Psychiatry [in press].
4. Wise SP, Rapoport JL. Obsessive–compulsive disorder: Is it basal ganglia dysfunction? In: Obsessive–Compulsive Disorders in Children and Adolescents (ed Rapoport JL). American Psychiatric Press, Washington DC, 1989, pp 327–344.
5. Modell JG, Mountz JM, Curtis GC et al. Neurophysiologic dysfunction in basal ganglia/limbic striatal and thalamocortical circuits as a pathogenic mechanism of obsessive–compulsive disorder. J Neuropsychiatry 1989; 1: 27–36.
6. Brickner RM, Rosen AA, Munro R. Physiological aspects of the obsessive state. Psychosom Med 1940; 2: 369–383.
7. Garmany G. Obsessional states in epileptics. J Ment Sci 1947; 93: 639–643.
8. Penfield W, Jasper H. Epilepsy and the Functional Anatomy of the Human Brain. Churchill, London, 1954.
9. Bear DM, Fedio P. Quantitative analysis of interictal behavior in temporal lobe epilepsy. Arch Neurol 1977; 34: 454–467.
10. Yaryura-Tobias JA, Neziroglu FA. Obsessive–compulsive disorders. Marcel Dekker, New York, 1983.
11. Kettl PA, Marks M. Neurological factors in obsessive compulsive disorder: Two case reports and a review of the literature. Br J Psychiatry 1986; 149: 315–319.
12. Ward CD. Transient feelings of compulsion caused by hemispheric lesions: Three cases. J Neurol Neurosurg Psychiatry 1988; 51: 266–268.
13. Levin B, Duchowny M. Childhood obsessive–compulsive disorder and cingulate epilepsy. Biol Psychiatry 1991; 30: 1049–1055.
14. McKeon J, McGuffin P, Robinson P. Obsessive–compulsive disorder following head injury: A report of four cases. Br J Psychiatry 1984; 144: 190–192.
15. Khanna S, Narayanan HS, Sharma SD, Mukundan CR. Post-traumatic obsessive–compulsive disorder: A single case report. Ind J Psychiatry 1985; 27: 337–340.
16. Laplane D, Levasseur M, Pillon B et al. Obsessive–compulsive and other behavioral changes with bilateral basal ganglia lesions. Brain 1989; 112: 699–725.
17. Paunovic VR. Obsessional syndrome with organic brain disease. Ann Med Psychol 1984; 142: 379–382.
18. Minski L. The mental symptoms associated with 58 cases of cerebral tumor. J Neurol Psychopath 1933; 13: 330–343.
19. Eslinger PJ, Damasio AR. Severe disturbance of higher cognition after bilateral frontal lobe ablation: patient EVR. Neurology 1985; 35: 1731–1741.
20. Cambier J, Masson C, Benammou S et al. La graphomanie, activite graphique compulsive manifestation d'un gliome fronto-calleux. Rev Neurol 1988; 144: 158–164.
21. Seibyl JP, Krystal JH, Goodman WK, Price LH. Obsessive–compulsive symptoms in a patient with a right frontal lobe lesion. Neuropsychiatry Neuropsychol Behav Neurol 1989; 1: 295–299.

22. Caplan R, Comair Y, Shewmon DA, Jackson L, Chugani HT, Peacock WJ. Intractable seizures, compulsions, and coprolalia: A pediatric case study. J Neuropsychiatry Clin Neurosci 1992; 4: 315–319.

23. Paradis CM, Friedman S, Hatch M, Lazar RM. Obsessive–compulsive disorder onset after removal of a brain tumor. J Nerv Ment Dis 1992; 180: 535–536.

24. Khanna S. Neuropsychiatry of obsessive–compulsive disorder: Organic basis and organic etiologies. Presented at First International Obsessive–Compulsive Disorder Conference, Capri, Italy, 1993.

25. Vitiello B, Spreat S, Behar D. Obsessive–compulsive disorder in mentally retarded patients. J Nerv Ment Dis 1989; 177: 232–236.

26. Stein DJ, Keating J, Zar HJ, Hollander E. Compulsive and impulsive symptoms in Prader-Willi Syndrome. Presented at the Annual Meeting of the American Psychiatric Association, San Francisco, 1993.

27. Barton R. Diabetes insipidus and obsessional neurosis. Am J Psychiatry 1976; 133: 235–236.

28. George MS, Kellner CH, Fossey MD. Obsessive–compulsive symptoms in a patient with multiple sclerosis. J Nerv Ment Dis 1989; 177: 304–305.

29. Hamner MB. Obsessive–compulsive symptoms associated with acute intermittent porphyria. Psychosomatics 1992; 33: 329–331.

30. Grimshaw L. Obsessional disorder and neurological illness. J Neurol Neurosurg Psychiatry 1964; 27: 229–231.

31. Capstick N, Seldrup U. Obsessional states. A study in the relationship between abnormalities occurring at birth and subsequent development of obsessional symptoms. Acta Psychiatr Scand 1977; 56: 427–439.

32. Thomsen PH, Jensen J. Latent class analysis of organic aspects of obsessive compulsive disorder in children and adolescents. Acta Psychiatr Scand 1991; 84: 391–395.

33. Buka SL, Tsuang MT, Lipsitt LP. Pregnancy/delivery complications and psychiatric diagnosis. Arch Gen Psychiatry 1993; 50: 151–156.

34. Hillbom E. After-effects of brain injuries. Acta Psychiatr Neurol Scand 1960; 35 (suppl): 125.

35. Lishman WA. Brain damage in relations to psychiatric disability after head injury. Br J Psychiatry 1968; 114: 373–410.

36. von Economo C. Encephalitis Lethargica: Its Sequellae and Treatment. Oxford University Press, London, 1931.

37. Hymas NFS, Prasad AJ. Obsessive–compulsive disorder: its clinical neurology and recent pharmacological studies. In: Biological Basis and Therapy of Neuroses (ed Prasad AJ). CRC Press, Boca Raton, FL, 1989, pp 41–79.

38. Dewhurst K, Oliver J, Trick KLK, McKnight AL. Neuro-psychiatric aspects of Huntington's diseases. Confin Neurol 1969; 31: 258–268.

39. Cummings JL, Cunningham K. Obsessive–compulsive disorder in Huntington's disease. Biol Psychiatry 1992; 31: 263–270.

40. Schwab RS, Fabing HD, Prichard JS. Psychiatric symptoms and syndromes in Parkinson's disease. Am J Psychiatry 1951; 197: 901–907.

41. Hardie RJ, Lees AJ, Stern GM. On–off fluctuations in Parkinson's disease. Brain 1984; 107: 487–506.

42. Bihari K, Hill JL, Murphy DL. Obsessive–compulsive characteristics in patients with idiopathic spasmodic torticollis. Psychiatry Res 1992; 42: 267–272.

43. Schuler P, Oyanguren H, Maturana V et al. Manganese poisoning. Industrial Med Surg 1957; 26: 167–173.

44. Mena I, Marin O, Fuenzalida S, Cotzias GC. Chronic manganese poisoning.

Neurology 1967; 17: 128–136.
45. Weilburg JB, Mesulam M-M, Weintraub S et al. Focal striatal abnormalities in a patient with obsessive–compulsive disorder. Arch Neurol 1989; 46: 233–235.
46. Durand MCh, Vercken JB, Goulon M. Syndrome extra-pyramidal apres incompetence cardio-circulatoire. Rev Neurol 1989; 145: 398–400.
47. Tonkonogy J, Barreira P. Obsessive–compulsive disorder and caudate-frontal lesion. Neuropsychiatry Neuropsychol Behav Neurol 1989; 2: 203–209.
48. Destee A, Gray F, Parent M et al. Comportement compulsif d'allure obsessionnelle et paralysie supranucleaire progressive. Rev Neurol 1990; 146: 12–18.
49. Trillet M, Croisile B, Tourniaire D, Schott B. Perturbations de l'activite motrice volontaire et lesions de noyaux caudes. Rev Neurol 1990; 146: 338–344.
50. Chapman AH, Pilkey L, Gibbons MJ. A psychosomatic study of eight children with Sydenham's chorea. Pediatrics 1958; 21: 582–595.
51. Freeman JH, Aron AM, Collard JE et al. The emotional correlates of Sydenham's chorea. Pediatrics 1965; 35: 42–49.
52. Swedo SE, Rapoport JL, Cheslow DL et al. High prevalence of obsessive–compulsive symptoms in patients with Sydenham's chorea. Am J Psychiatry 1989; 146: 246–249.
53. de la Tourette G. Etude sur une affection nerveuse caraterisee par de l'incoordination motrice accompagnee d'echolalie et de coprolie. Arch Neurol 1885; 9: 19–42, 158–200.
54. Shapiro AK, Shapiro E. Evaluation of the reported association of obsessive–compulsive symptoms or disorder with Tourette's disorder. Comp Psychiatry 1992; 33: 152–165.
55. Hollander E, Liebowitz MR, DeCaria C. Conceptual and methodological issues in studies of obsessive–compulsive and Tourette's Disorders. Psychiatric Dev 1989; 4: 267–296.
56. Rassmussen SA, Tsuang MT. Clinical characteristics and family history in DSM-III obsessive–compulsive disorder. Am J Psychiatry 1986; 143: 317–322.
57. Pitman RK, Green RC, Jenike MA et al. Clinical comparison of Tourette's disorder and obsessive–compulsive disorder. Am J Psychiatry 1987; 144: 1166–1171.
58. Swedo S, Rapoport J, Leonard H, Lenane M, Cheslow D. Obsessive compulsive disorder in children and adolescents. I. Clinical phenomenology of 70 consecutive cases. Arch Gen Psychiatry 1989; 46: 335–349.
59. Comings DE, Comings B. Hereditary agoraphobia and obsessive–compulsive behavior in relatives of patients with Gilles de la Tourette's syndrome. Br J Psychiatry 1987; 151: 1229–1241.
60. Pauls DL, Kruger SD, Leckman JF et al. The risk of Tourette's syndrome and chronic multiple tics among relatives of Tourette's syndrome patients obtained by direct interview. J Am Acad Child Psychiatry 1984; 23: 134–137.
61. Pauls DL, Towbin KE, Leckman JF et al. Gilles de la Tourette's syndrome and obsessive compulsive disorder: Evidence supporting a genetic relationship. Arch Gen Psychiatry 1986; 43: 1180–1182.
62. Shaffer D, Schonfeld IS, O'Connor PA et al. Neurological soft signs and their relationship to psychiatric disorder and intelligence in childhood and adolescence. Arch Gen Psychiatry 1985; 42: 342–351.
63. Stokman CJ, Shafer SO, Shaffer D, Ng SK-C, O'Connor PA, Wolff RR.

Assessment of neurological soft signs in adolescents: Reliability studies. Dev Med Child Neurol 1986; 28: 428–439.

64. Shafer SQ, Stokman CJ, Shaffer D, Ng SC, O'Connor PA, Schonfeld IS. Ten-year consistency in neurological test performance of children without focal neurological deficit. Dev Med Child Neurol 1986; 28: 417–427.

65. Quitkin FM, Rifkin A, Klein DF. Neurological soft signs in schizophrenia and character disorders: Organicity in schizophrenia with premorbid asociality and emotionally unstable character disorders. Arch Gen Psychiatry 1976; 33: 845–853.

66. Nichols PL. Minimal brain dysfunction and soft signs. In: The collaborative perinatal project in Soft Neurological Signs (ed Tupper ED). Grune & Stratton, New York, 1987, pp 179–199.

67. Denckla MB. Minimal brain dysfunction. In: Education and the Brain (eds Mirsky AF, Relage KJ). University of Chicago Press, Chicago, 1978.

68. Hollander E, DeCaria CM, Aronowitz B, Klein DF, Liebowitz MR, Shaffer D. A pilot follow-up study of childhood soft signs and the development of adult psychopathology. J Neuropsychiatry Clin Neurosci 1991; 3: 186–189.

69. Schilder P. The organic background of obsessions and compulsions. Am J Psychiatry 1938; 94: 1397–1414.

70. Behar D, Rapoport J, Berg C et al. Computerized tomography and neuropsychological test measures in adolescents with obsessive compulsive disorder. Am J Psychiatry 1984; 141: 363–369.

71. Denckla MB. Neurological examination. In: Obsessive Compulsive Disorder in Children and Adolescents (ed Rapoport JL). American Psychiatric Press, Washington DC, 1988, pp 107–115.

72. Hollander E, Schiffman E, Cohen B et al. Signs of central nervous system dysfunction in obsessive–compulsive disorder. Arch Gen Psychiatry 1990; 47: 27–32.

73. Stein DJ, Hollander E, Chan S, DeCaria CM, Hilal S, Liebowitz MR. Computerized tomography and neurological soft signs in obsessive–compulsive disorder. Biol Psychiatry 1992; 31: 268 (abstr).

74. Hollander E, DeCaria CM, Saoud JB, Klein DF, Liebowitz MR. Neurological soft signs in obsessive–compulsive disorder. Arch Gen Psychiatry 1991; 48: 278–279.

75. Hollander E, Cohen L, DeCaria CM. Neuropsychiatric studies of OCD. Presented at First International Obsessive–Compulsive Disorder Conference, Capri, Italy, 1993.

76. Bihari K, Pato MT, Hill JL, Murphy DL. Neurological soft signs in obsessive–compulsive disorder. Arch Gen Psychiatry 1991; 48: 278.

77. Hymas N, Lees A, Bolton D, Epps K, Head D. The neurology of obsessional slowness. Brain 1991; 114: 2203–2333.

78. Khanna S. Soft neurological signs in obsessive compulsive disorder. Biol Psychiatry 1991; 29 (suppl): 442.

79. Thomsen PH, Jensen J. Latent class analysis of organic aspects of obsessive compulsive disorder in children and adolescents. Acta Psychiatr Scand 1991; 84: 391–395.

80. Head D, Bolton D, Hymas NFS. Deficit in cognitive shifting ability in patients with obsessive–compulsive disorder. Biol Psychiatry 1989; 15: 929–937.

81. Flor-Henry P, Yeudall LT, Koles ZJ, Howarth BG. Neuropsychological and power spectral EEG investigations of the obsessive compulsive syndrome. Biol Psychiatry 1979; 14: 119–330.

82. Insel T, Donnelly EF, Lalakea ML, Alterman IS, Murphy DL. Neurological

and neuropsychological studies of patients with obsessive compulsive disorder. Biol Psychiatry 1983; 18: 741–751.

83. Rapoport J, Elkins R, Langer D et al. Childhood obsessive–compulsive disorder. Am J Psychiatry 1981; 138: 1545–1554.

84. Cox CS, Fedio P, Rapoport JL. Neuropsychological testing of obsessive–compulsive adolescents. In: Obsessive–Compulsive Disorder in Children and Adolescents (ed Rapoport JL). American Psychiatric Press, Washington DC, 1989, pp 73–85.

85. Flament MF. The neurobiology of childhood OCD. Presented at First International Conference on Obsessive–Compulsive Disorder, Capri, Italy, 1993.

86. Harvey NS. Neurological factors in obsessive–compulsive disorder. Br J Psychiatry 1986; 147: 567–568.

87. Malloy P. Frontal lobe dysfunction in obsessive–compulsive disorder. In: The Frontal Lobes Revisited (ed Malloy P). IRBN Press, 1987, pp 207–223.

88. Martinot JL, Allilaire JF, Mazoyer BM et al. Obsessive–compulsive disorder: A clinical, neuropsychological and positron emission study. Acta Psychiatr Scand 1990; 82: 233–242.

89. Hollander E, Liebowitz MR, Rosen WG. Neuropsychiatric and neuropsychological studies in obsessive–compulsive disorder. In: The Psychobiology of Obsessive–Compulsive Disorder (ed Zohar J, Insel T, Rasmussen S). Springer, New York, 1991, pp 126–145.

90. Boone KB, Ananth J, Philpott L, Kaur A, Djenderedjian A. Neuropsychological characteristics of nondepressed adults with obsessive-compulsive disorder. Neuropsychiatry Neuropsychol Behav Neurol 1991; 4: 96–109.

91. Zielinski CM, Taylor MA, Juzwin KR. Neuropsychological deficits in obsessive–compulsive disorder. Neuropsychiatry Neuropsychol Behav Neurol 1991; 4: 110–126.

92. Christensen KJ, Kim SW, Dysken MW, Hoover KM. Neuropsychological performance in obsessive–compulsive disorder. Biol Psychiatry 1992; 31: 4–18.

93. Martin A, Pigott TA, Lalonde FM, Dalton I, Dubbert B, Murphy DL. Lack of evidence for Huntington's disease-like cognitive dysfunction in obsessive–compulsive disorder. Biol Psychiatry 1993; 33: 345–353.

94. Grey-Walter W. The Neurological Foundation of Psychiatry. Blackwell, Oxford, 1966.

95. Talairach J, Bancaud J, Geir S et al. The cingulate gyrus and human behavior. Electroencephalogr Clin Neurophysiol 1975; 34: 415–452.

96. Pacella BL, Polatin P, Nagler SH. Clinical and EEG studies in obsessive–compulsive states. Am J Psychiatry 1944; 100: 830–838.

97. Rockwell FV, Simons DJ. The electroencephalogram and personality organization in the obsessive–compulsive reactions. Arch Neurol Psychiatry 1947; 57: 71–77.

98. Ingram IM, McAdam WA. The electroencephalogram, obsessional illness and obsessional personality. J Ment Sci 1960; 106: 686–691.

99. Inouye R. Electoencephalographic study in obsessive–compulsive states. Clin Psychiatry 1973; 15: 1071–1083.

100. Sugiyama T. Clinico-electroencephalographic study on obsessive compulsive neurosis. Bull Osaka Med School 1974; 20: 110–114.

101. Bingley T, Persson A. EEG studies on patients with chronic obsessive–compulsive neurosis before and after psychosurgery (stereotaxic bilateral anterior capsulotomy). Electroencephalogr Clin Neurophysiol 1978; 44: 691–696.

102. Jenike MA, Brotman AW. The EEG in obsessive compulsive disorder. J Clin Psychiatry 1984; 45: 122–124.
103. Epstein AW, Bailine SH. Sleep and dream studies in obsessional neurosis with particular reference to epileptic states. Biol Psychiatry 1971; 3: 149–158.
104. Insel TR, Gillin JC, Moore A, Mendelson WB, Loewenstein RJ, Murphy DL. Sleep in obsessive–compulsive disorder. Arch Gen Psychiatry 1982; 39: 1372–1377.
105. Ciesielski H, Beech HR, Gordon PK. Some electrophysiological observations in obsessional states. Br J Psychiatry 1981; 138: 479–484.
106. Beech HR, Ciesielski KT, Gordon PK. Further observations of evoked potentials in obsessional patients. Br J Psychiatry 1983; 142: 605–609.
107. Shagass C, Roemer RA, Straumanis JJ, Josiassen RC. Evoked potentials in obsessive–compulsive disorder. Adv Biol Psychiatry 1984; 15: 69–75.
108. Shagass C, Roemer RA, Straumanis JJ, Josiassen RC. Distinctive somato-sensory evoked potential features in obsessive compulsive disorder. Biol Psychiatry 1984; 19: 1507–1524.
109. Khanna S, Mukundan CR, Channabasavanna SM. Middle latency evoked potentials in obsessive compulsive disorder. Biol Psychiatry 1989; 25: 980–983.
110. Towey J, Bruder G, Hollander E et al. Endogenous event-related potentials in obsessive–compulsive disorder. Biol Psychiatry 1990; 28: 92–98.
111. Stefanis CN, Rabavilas AD, Papageorgiou Ch. Event-related potentials and selective attention in obsessive–compulsive disorder. Presented at First International Obsessive–Compulsive Disorder Conference, Capri, Italy, 1993.
112. Timsit-Berthier M, Delanoy J, Konnick N, Rousseau J. Slow potential changes in psychiatry. Electroencephalogr Clin Neurophysiol 1973; 28: 41–47.
113. McCallum WC, Walter WC. The effects of attention and distraction on the contingent negative variation in neurotic and normal subjects. Electro-encephalogr Clin Neurophysiol 1968; 25: 319–329.
114. Sartory G, Master D. Contingent negative variation in obsessional patients. Biol Psychiatry 1984; 18: 253–267.
115. Wexler BE, Goodman WK. Cerebral laterality, perception of emotion, and treatment response in obsessive–compulsive disorder. Biol Psychiatry 1991; 29: 900–908.
116. Stein DJ, Hollander E. Cognitive science and obsessive–compulsive disorder. In: Cognitive Science and Clinical Disorders (ed DJ Stein, JE Young). Academic Press, San Diego, 1992, pp 235–247.
117. Otto MW. Normal and abnormal information processing: A neuropsychological perspective on obsessive–compulsive disorder. Psych Clin North Am 1992; 15: 825–848.

14 STRUCTURAL AND FUNCTIONAL BRAIN IMAGING IN OBSESSIVE COMPULSIVE DISORDER

Rudolf Hoehn-Saric* and Chawki Benkelfat†

*The Hopkins Medical Institutions, Department of Psychiatry and Behavioral Sciences, The Henry Phipps Psychiatric Services, Baltimore, MD, USA

†Neurobiological Psychiatry Unit, Department of Psychiatry, McGill University, Montreal, QC, Canada

Introduction

Although the psychopathology of obsessive compulsive disorder (OCD) has fascinated psychiatrists for well over a century, little systematic research has been conducted until recently. This was in part because OCD has been, mistakenly, regarded to be an uncommon illness, and therefore difficult to study in appropriate numbers, and in part because appropriate investigational tools were not available. Obsessive compulsive disorder usually starts at an early age, its course is chronic and its symptoms appear bizarre and unexplainable even to the patient. The illness responds poorly to conventional psychotherapies and psychopharmacological interventions, except to antidepressants with serotonin reuptake inhibiting properties and behavioral therapy. Obsessive compulsive symptoms have been associated with illnesses or injuries that affect the basal ganglia of the brain. On the other hand, psychosurgery that disconnects orbitofrontal regions from limbic, thalamic, and possibly striatal structures improves patients symptomatically. Therefore, it has been suspected for a long time that organic changes in the frontal lobes or in the basal ganglia and, to a lesser extent, the limbic system are responsible for OCD's psychopathology.

Current Insights in Obsessive Compulsive Disorder. Edited by E. Hollander, J. Zohar, D. Marazzati and B. Olivier
© 1994 John Wiley & Sons Ltd

Recently developed brain imaging techniques have enabled us to explore in depth the brain correlates of OCD: computed tomography (CT) or magnetic resonance imaging (MRI) are used to depict structures of the brain, whereas 133-xenon inhalation imaging (Xe-Flow), single photon emission computerized tomography (SPECT) and positron emission tomography (PET) are used for functional imaging. The latter allows for the measurement of global and regional cerebral blood flow (rCBF) and glucose metabolism. It also can be used to estimate various components of brain neurotransmission in vivo, in patients, e.g. the regional neuronal uptake and rate of metabolism of monoamine precursors, neuroreceptor occupancy, enzyme activity, etc. These methods, their advantages and limitations, have been discussed in detail by Andreasen (1). Newer techniques, such as rapid-sampling echo-planar MRI ("functional MRI") or magnetic resonance spectroscopy (MRS) are in development and promise further refinements in imaging technique.

In this chapter we will successively review (a) results of studies that compared brain structures of OCD patients with those of normal controls, (b) studies that examined rCBF and glucose metabolism in patients at rest and during drug or behavioral challenges known to enhance OCD symptomatology, and (c) studies that measured changes in regional brain function during treatment. The remaining sections of the chapter discuss some methodological limitations, the significance of these studies in the light of the current neurobiological models of OCD, and suggestions for further research.

Brain imaging studies: summary of results

STRUCTURAL IMAGING

Because of the occasional presence of obsessive compulsive symptoms in illnesses and injuries that involve basal ganglia (2), it was hoped that new imaging techniques would disclose pathology in brain structures, e.g. the caudate nucleus, of OCD patients. Two brain CT studies of patients with an onset of OCD during childhood gave promising results (see Table 14.1): in one, OCD patients exhibited an increased ventricular-brain ratio when their scans were compared with those of controls (4); in the other, the volume of the caudate nucleus in OCD patients was decreased (5). However, Insel et al (3) found no differences on CT scans between 10 adult OCD patients and a matched group of controls, in spite of the fact that four of the OCD patients rated abnormally on the Halstead–Reitan Battery and two of the patients had abnormal EEGs. Garber et al (6) found no specific abnormalities in brain MRI scans of OCD patients. In this study, the authors used the controversial approach of T1 mapping: OCD patients had a prolonged spin-lattice relaxation time for right frontal matter as well as greater right-minus-left differences for frontal white

Table 14.1 Findings with structural imaging in obsessive compulsive disorder patients [modified from Insel (8)]*

Authors	Year	Reference	Method	Subjects	Findings
Insel et al	1983	3	CT	10 OCD 10 Controls	OCD = C
Behar et al	1988	4	CT	16 OCD (adolescents) 16 Controls	OCD > C: mean ventricular:brain ratio
Luxenberg et al	1988	5	MRI	10 OCD (childhood onset) 10 Controls	OCD < C: caudate nucleus volume
Garber et al	1989	6	MRI	32 OCD 14 Controls	OCD: no specific structural abnormalities OCD > C: R to L T_1, differences in frontal white matter
Kellner et al	1991	7	MRI	12 OCD 12 Controls	OCD = C
Harris et al†			MRI	24 OCD 21 Controls	OCD = C

*CT, Computerized tomography; MRI, magnetic resonance imaging; OCD > C, OCD more than controls; OCD < C, OCD less than controls; OCD = C, OCD equal to controls; R, right; L, left.
†Unpublished data.

matter. These findings were interpreted as being consistent with frontal–limbic–striatal pathology. Three other studies using MRI failed to find structural abnormalities in OCD patients [(7, 9); GJ Harris et al, unpublished data].

Differences between these studies may in part be attributable to differences in scanning techniques and/or image analysis procedures. On MRI the contrast between gray and white brain matter is sharper than on CT, and therefore MRI provides more accurate images of the brain. Newly developed volumetric image analyses also permit more accurate measures of the volume of basal ganglia (10). Another reason for differences between studies may be that OCD patients do not form a homogenous population (11). For instance, the underlying pathology of patients examined by Behar et al (4) and Luxenberg et al (5), whose clinical manifestations of OCD started in childhood, may differ from that of OCD patients with later onset. There may also be differences in pathology between OCD patients who do not exhibit neurological signs or abnormalities on neuropsychological examinations and patients with concomitant neurological changes (11).

FUNCTIONAL IMAGING

Studies at rest, including a continuous performance task

Thirteen studies have investigated cerebral blood flow, glucose metabolism and, in one case, dopaminergic neurotransmission, in patients with OCD symptoms, by means of PET or SPECT. Ten focused specifically on OCD patients and three on patients falling in the OCD spectrum, such as Tourette's syndrome or trichotillomania [(12, 13); BH Guze et al, personal communication]. One unpublished study has presented reanalysis of previously presented data (14). Table 14.2 summarizes the methods and findings of these studies.

Obsessive compulsive disorder

The studies differed in technique, patient populations and selection of control subjects. Thus, differences in results are not surprising. Some findings, however, occurred with sufficient regularity to suggest an association with at least some OCD pathology. Not all scanning techniques permit measures of absolute levels of cerebral blood flow. Therefore, only seven studies reported absolute levels of blood flow or glucose metabolism. Four of these studies reported no differences in global cerebral or cortical activity between OCD patients and normal controls. Two studies, both by the same investigators, found in OCD patients an increased, and one study, a decreased glucose metabolism. When absolute metabolic activity of regions of interest (ROI), namely activity of anatomically defined brain regions, was compared between patients and controls, three studies reported that patients had higher activity in prefrontal regions and two studies reported higher activity in both heads of the caudate. No difference between normal controls and patients with obsessive slowness could be found, on the basis of the accumulation and metabolism in the basal ganglia of [^{18}F]dihydroxy-phenylalanine ([^{18}F]DOPA), a tracer thought to connote presynaptic dopamine neurotransmission (21).

The measurement of absolute values of glucose metabolism or cerebral blood flow is subject to wide inter- and intraindividual variations (24), which render their statistical evaluation difficult. For these reasons, results are often "normalized", and expressed as unitless ratios representing the relationship between specific ROIs and global cerebral or cortical activity. In general, normalized regional CBF or glucose metabolic rates are fairly stable over time, within individual subjects.

In all 10 studies in which relatively "pure" OCD patients were examined, the normalized data showed differences in activity in prefrontal cortex between patients and controls, although the exact areas differed between studies. In eight of them, the activity was reported to be increased in OCD, while it was decreased in the remaining two (9, 15). Less consistent changes were found in basal ganglia: in studies in which an increase in caudate function was associated with OCD (16, 17), patient–control differences disappeared after normalization of the data. Increased normalized caudate activities were reported by Benkelfat et al (20) in the left basal ganglia, using PET and fluorodeoxyglucose (FDG) as tracer, and bilaterally decreased activity by Rubin et al (23), using SPECT and [^{99m}Tc]hexamethyl-propylene amine oxime ([^{99}Tc]HMPAO). No other systematically occurring differences between OCD patients and controls have been reported in other brain areas.

Obsessive compulsive spectrum (Tourette's syndrome and trichotillomania)

There is a considerable overlap between OCD and Tourette's syndrome (TS) (2). Depending on the survey, between 28 to 67% of Tourette's patients also suffer from OCD symptoms (25). Moreover, tics occur in childhood OCD far more frequently than one would expect by chance (2). In their treatment response, however, the two disorders differ considerably: obsessive compulsive symptoms respond primarily to serotonin reuptake inhibitors, while tics respond to neuroleptics (26). Therefore, it is of interest that in the study of George et al (13), TS patients both without and with concomitant OCD exhibited evidence of hyperfrontality, a finding often reported in OCD patients (see Table 14.2). The authors concluded that their findings indicated functional similarities between the two disorders. The failure to differentiate patients with TS from those with both TS and OCD symptoms on the basis of their regional brain function does not, however, exclude a relative regional specificity in the neural mediation of symptoms, with motor tics being preferentially mediated by pathways located in part in the basal ganglia, and OC symptoms or "resistance to symptoms" being preferentially prefrontal. The recent report (BH Guze et al, personal communication) of an increased regional glucose metabolism in the striatum, but not prefrontal cortex, of patients with TS but apparently free of OCD symptoms supports this view.

Another disorder that is often thought to fall within the OCD spectrum is trichotillomania. In a PET scan study conducted by Swedo et al (12), using FDG, patients with this disorder exhibited higher global metabolic rates than controls (see Table 14.2). After normalization, scans showed increased activity in the cerebellum and the right superior parietal cortex but, in contrast to OCD patients, not in prefrontal regions or in the basal ganglia. Patients with trichotillomania are less plagued by obsessive thoughts than OCD patients (27). Their hair pulling is often automatic or in response to an urge devoid of cognitive elaboration. The automatic nature of the disorder may explain the lack of prefrontal hyperactivity.

Table 14.2 Functional imaging in the unchallenged state [modified from Insel (8)]*

Source	Subjects	Medication	Method	Imaging resolution (mm)	Condition: eyes/task
Mindus et al 1986 (15)	5 OCD (severe chronic) 10 Controls	Medication-free	PET [^{11}C]-Glucose	7.6	Closed/ none
Baxter et al 1987 (16)	14 OCD (9 depressed) 14 Unipolar depressed 14 Controls	9 Medication-free	PET–FDG	11	Open/none
Baxter et al 1988 (17)	10 OCD (not depressed) 10 Controls	Medication-free for 2 weeks	PET–FDG	11	Open/none
Nordahl et al 1989 (18)	8 OCD (not depressed) 30 Controls	Medication-free for 3 weeks†	PET–FDG	6	Closed/ auditory continuous performance task
Swedo et al 1989 (19)	18 OCD (childhood onset) 18 Controls	Medication-free for 4 weeks†	PET-FDG	6	Closed/none
Benkelfat et al 1990 (20)	8 OCD 30 Controls	Drug-free for 2 weeks†	PET-FDG	6	Closed/auditory continuous performance task
Martinot et al 1991 (9)	16 OCD (not depressed) 8 Controls	6 Drug-free for 2 weeks†	PET–FDG	13	Closed/none
Sawle et al 1991 (21)	6 OCD (obsessive slowness) 6 Controls	3 Drug-free	a). PET: [^{15}O]CO$_2$ [^{15}O]O$_2$ [^{15}O]CO b). PET: [^{18}F]DOPA	8.5	Open/none

	Findings			
		Normalized values		
Absolute values	Normalization	Orbitofrontal	Basal ganglia	Other brain regions
	Region/transaxial section, containing region	OCD < C: L orbital gyrus	OCD = C	
OCD > C: L&R hemisphere OCD > C: Orbital gyri L&R head of caudate OCD > D: L&R hemisphere L&R head of caudate L orbital gyrus	Region/hemisphere	OCD > C: L orbital OCD = D: Orbital gyri	OCD = C	
OCD > C: L&R hemisphere L&R orbital gyrus L&R head of caudate	Region/hemisphere	OCD > C: L&R orbital gyri	OCD = C	
OCD = C	Region/global gray matter	OCD > C: L&R anterior R posterior, anterior, and medial orbital frontal cortex	OCD = C	OCD > C: R parietal L parietooccipital cortex
OCD = C: Whole brain, mean cortical matter OCD > C: L&R prefrontal L orbital frontal L premotor R sensorimotor R inferior temporal L paracentral R cerebellar R thalamus R&L anterior cingulate	Region/mean cortical gray matter	OCD > C: R prefrontal region	OCD = C	OCD > C: L anterior cingulate
OCD = C	Region/global gray matter	OCD > C: Infromedial frontal cortex R posterior R anterior frontal cortex	OCD > C: L caudate nucleus L anterior and posterior putamen	
OCD < C: All brain regions	Region/global cortical rate	OCD < C: Whole prefrontal lateral cortex	OCD = C	Premotor cortex
Not reported	Region/global cerebral rate	OCD > C: Orbital frontal midfrontal cortex	OCD = C	
OCD = C: All measures				*Continued overleaf*

Table 14.2. (*continued*) Functional imaging in the unchallenged state [modified from Insel (8)]*

Source	Subjects	Medication	Method	Imaging resolution (mm)	Condition: eyes/task
Machlin et al 1992 (22)	10 OCD (not depressed) 8 Controls	Medication-free for 4 weeks†	SPECT– HMPAO	16	Open/none
Rubin et al 1992 (23)	10 OCD (not depressed) 10 Controls	Medication-free for 4 weeks†	SPECT– ^{133}xenon inhalation SPECT– HMPAO	9.6	Open/none
Harris et al (in press, 14)	10 OCD (not depressed) 7 Controls	Medication-free for 4 weeks†	SPECT– HMPAO	16	Open/none
George et al 1992 (13)	10 TS + OCD 10 TS 8 Controls	Not stated	SPECT– HMPAO	9	Open/none
Swedo et al 1991 (12)	10 Trichotillomania 10 Controls	Medication-free for 4 weeks†	PET–FDG	6	Closed/none
Guze et al (Personal communication)	9 TS 18 Controls	Medication-free for 2 weeks†	PET–FDG	6.75	Open/none

*PET, Positron emission tomography; SPECT, single photon emission tomography; FDG, [^{18}F]deoxyglucose; HMPAO, [^{99m}Tc]hexamethyl-propylene amine oxime; [^{11}C]glucose, [^{11}C]9-glucose; [^{18}F]DOPA, [^{18}F]6-fluorodopa; OCD, obsessive compulsive disorder; TS, Tourette's syndrome; T, trichotillomania; D, unipolar depression; C controls; R, right; L, left.
†Number of weeks or more.

Activation studies conducted in the laboratory

Obsessive compulsive symptoms are not present continuously; they occur sporadically. Therefore, state-dependent changes in regional brain function might only be detected in OCD patients during times when symptoms actually occur. Several challenge procedures, namely procedures that activate obsessions and compulsions, have been developed. Table 14.3 summarizes the effects of three challenge studies on cerebral blood flow. In two, the challenges were of psychological, and in one, of pharmacological nature.

The first challenge study in OCD involving brain functional imaging

| | Findings | | | |
| Absolute values | Normalized values | | | |
	Normalization	Orbitofrontal	Basal ganglia	Other brain regions
	Region/whole cortex	OCD > C: Medial frontal cortex	OCD = C	
OCD = C: All measures				
	Region/cerebellum Region/cerebral cortex	OCD > C: L&R orbital frontal cortex L posterior frontal cortex	OCD < C: L&R head of caudate	OCD > C: L&R high dorsal parietal cortex
	OCD = C: Reanalysis of data from Machlin et al (21) using 3-dimensional analysis of subtractive SPECT combined with MRI images	OCD > C: Medial frontal R frontal cortex	OCD = C	OCD > C: Cerebellum OCD < C: R visual association cortex
	Region/visual cortex Region/whole brain activity	TS + OCD = TS TS > C: R frontal cortex	TS + OCD = TS TS = C	
T > C: Mean gray matter	Region/mean gray matter	T = C	T = C	T > C: R&L cerebellum R superior parietal cortex
	Region/ipsilateral hemisphere	TS = C	TS > C: L putamen L&R thalamus R internal globus pallidus	TS > C: L, R parietal lobes

was conducted by Zohar et al at the NIMH (28). Ten OCD patients with clearly identifiable contamination obsessions underwent scans that measured rCBF by use of 133-xenon inhalation as tracer. Patients were scanned under three conditions: 1, during relaxation, while listening to a taped "relaxation scene"; 2, during imaginal flooding, while listening to a brief, individually tailored tape which described the feared contamination; and 3, during the provocation stimulus, while listening to the same flooding tape as in condition 2 and, in addition, feeling a "contaminated" object placed on the dorsum of the right hand. The imaging technique was two-dimensional, that is, it yielded data on cortical perfusion but not on perfusion of subcortical structures. Compared to the state of relaxa-

Table 14.3 Functional imaging: response to challenge*

Author	Year	Reference	Method	Subjects	Challenge	Findings
Zohar et al	1989	28	^{133}Xenon inhalation Two-dimensional scan	10 OCD	(a) Relaxation (b) Imaginal flooding (c) In vivo exposure	Imaginal flooding: Slight increase of rCBF in temporal regions In vivo exposure: Marked decrease of rCBF in several cortical regions
Rauch et al	1994	29	PET, [^{15}O]CO$_2$ inhalation	8 OCD	(a) Resting (b) Control stimulus (c) Provocation stimulus	Provocative stimulus/control stimulus: Increased rCBF in R caudate nucleus, L anterior cingulate cortex, L&R orbitofrontal cortex
Hollander et al Personal communication			^{133}Xenon inhalation	14 OCD	mCPP	mCPP challenge: Responders > global CBF than nonresponders

*PET, Positron emission tomography; mCPP, *meta*-chlorophenyl-piperazine; CBF, cerebral blood flow; rCBF, regional cerebral blood flow; L, left; R, right.

tion, imaginal flooding slightly increased rCBF in temporal regions while the in vivo exposure lowered rCBF in several cortical regions.

A study by Rauch et al (29) built on the study by Zohar et al (28). Eight OCD patients, six with contamination phobia, one with checking obsession and one with violent obsessions, were scanned with a PET scanner using $[^{15}O]CO_2$ as tracer. They were examined under three conditions: 1, during rest; 2, while exposed to a control stimulus, for instance a clean rubber glove, placed on the left arm; and 3, the provocative stimulus, for instance the placement of a "contaminated" glove on the same location the "clean" glove had been placed previously. Images were normalized and analyzed by pairwise subtraction. In comparison with the resting condition, the provocative stimulus induced increased rCBF bilaterally in the orbitofrontal cortex, in the right caudate nucleus and the left anterior cingulate. The effect of the control stimulus on rCBF was not reported.

In the third study, Hollander et al (personal communication), used two-dimensional 133-xenon inhalation technique to examine the effects of *meta*-chlorophenyl-piperazine (mCPP) on rCBF; mCPP is a partial serotonin agonist that binds predominantly to serotonin, 5-HT$_{1C}$, receptors. Several (30, 31), but not all (32), studies reported that mCPP temporarily elicits or exacerbates obsessive compulsive symptoms, possibly through its serotonergic mechanisms. The investigators reported that patients who responded to the mCPP challenge with an exacerbation of OC symptoms had a greater increase of global CBF than nonresponders.

Given the differences in methodology, the results of the three studies are not readily comparable. They differ radically in imaging technique and procedure. However, as discussed below, these studies are stimulating and will, hopefully, lead to further research.

Effect of treatment on brain metabolism and blood flow

Another way of exploring the psychobiology of OCD is to examine changes occurring during successful treatment. The assumption here is that the careful examination of brain regional metabolic and/or perfusion changes as a result of treatment may help delineate further the functional neuroanatomy of OCD, as well as the mechanism of action of anti-OCD treatments.

Serotonin reuptake inhibiting antidepressants, behavior therapy, and psychosurgery have been found to decrease, but rarely totally suppress, obsessions or compulsions. Table 14.4 summarizes six studies that reported changes in rCBF or metabolism following psychosurgery, pharmacotherapy or behavior therapy.

Anterior capsulotomy (15), as well as treatment with clomipramine or fluoxetine, led to reduction of activity in prefrontal areas (20, 33, 35). Benkelfat et al (20) also noted a decrease in activity of the left caudate

Table 14.4 Functional imaging: effect of treatment [modified from Insel (8)]*

Authors	Year	Reference	Subjects	Method	Treatment	Findings	Correlations with treatment response
Mindus et al	1986	15	5 OCD (severe chronic)	PET [¹¹C]Glucose	Anterior capsulotomy (12 months after surgery)	Decreased activity in frontomedial cortex	None
Baxter et al	1987	16	10 OCD (includes depressed patients)	PET–FDG	Trazodone/monoamine oxidase inhibitors	Increased activity in R caudate nucleus	None
Benkelfat et al	1990	20	8 OCD	PET–FDG	Clomipramine (16 weeks)	Decreased activity in L caudate nucleus, R orbitofrontal cortex	With activity in L caudate nucleus
Hoehn-Saric et al	1991	33	6 OCD	SPECT HMPAO	Fluoxetine (12–16 weeks)	Decreased activity in medial frontal cortex	None
Baxter et al	1992	34	9 OCD	PET–FDG	Fluoxetine (10 weeks)	Decreased activity in R caudate nucleus, R cingulate cortex, L thalamus	With activity in R caudate nucleus
			9 OCD	PET–FDG	Behavioral therapy (10 weeks)	Decreased activity in R caudate nucleus	
Swedo et al	1992	35	13 OCD (childhood onset)	PET–FDG	Clomipramine/fluoxetine (12 months)	Decreased activity in R and L orbitofrontal cortex	With activity in R orbitofrontal cortex

*PET, Positron emission tomography; SPECT, single photon emission tomography; FDG, [¹⁸F]2-deoxyglucose; HMPAO, [⁹⁹mTC]hexamethyl-propylene amine oxime; [¹¹C]glucose, [¹¹C]9-glucose; R, right; L, left.

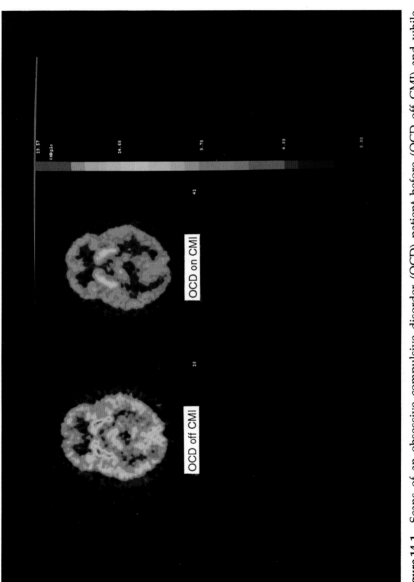

Figure 14.1 Scans of an obsessive compulsive disorder (OCD) patient before (OCD off CMI) and while (OCD on CMI) taking clomipramine (CMI)

nucleus after treatment with clomipramine (see Figure 14.1). In contrast, Baxter et al (34) found no changes in prefrontal activity in patients treated with fluoxetine or behavior therapy. Both treatments led to decreased activity in the right caudate nucleus. In addition, fluoxetine decreased activity in the right cingulate cortex and left thalamus. Only one study reported an increase in activity of the right caudate nucleus during treatment with trazodone alone or in combination with monoamine oxidase inhibitors (16). The population of that study, however, was to a large degree depressed. Moreover, neither trazodone nor monoamine oxidase inhibitors, while good antidepressants, have been found particularly helpful in the treatment of OCD (36, 37). Thus, changes reported by Baxter et al (16) may represent changes in depression rather than in OCD.

Significant correlations between regions do not necessarily represent functional connections. This being said, this correlational approach has been used to examine changes in the functional connectivity of the various nodes of the orbital frontal cortex (OFC)–caudate–thalamic–OFC loop in OCD patients while symptomatic, and during recovery: Baxter et al (34) contrasted normalized region of interest rank-order correlations (Kendall's τ) before and during treatment and reported that the right orbital cortex correlated significantly in treatment responder patients with the ipsilateral caudate before, but not after, treatment. Additional data collected in OCD patients treated with clomipramine (C Benkelfat et al, unpublished data) (see Figure 14.2) suggest that some degree of regional connectivity in the loop may also be reinstalled during treatment. Interestingly, both studies showed a significant correlation between caudate

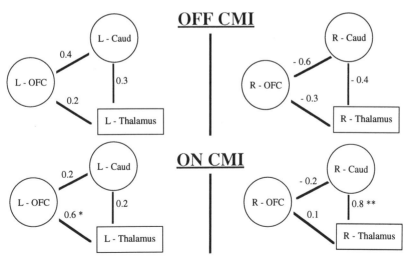

Figure 14.2 Normalized region of interest rank-order correlations (Kendall's τ) before and after clomipramine treatment. Caud, Caudate; L, left; OFC, orbital frontal cortex; R, right. *p < 0.05, **p < 0.01

and thalamus in the right hemisphere, which was absent in the unmedi-ated state. Collectively, these studies, although limited in size and num-ber, strongly suggest that treatment may not only affect regional brain function *per se*, but also regional connectivity. These effects on regional networking may lead to marked changes in information processing capa-bilities.

Significant correlations between clinical improvement and changes in regional brain function were found in three studies: Benkelfat et al (20) reported a positive correlation with activity in the left, Baxter et al (34) in the right caudate nucleus and Swedo et al (35) with activity in the right orbitofrontal cortex.

In summary, following treatment a reduction of activity in prefrontal cortical regions, including primarily the orbital frontal cortex, has been noted in four studies, and in the head of the caudate nucleus, in two. Reductions in orbital frontal cortex and caudate metabolism have been associated with clinical improvement in some but not all studies. Finally, very preliminary and limited findings suggest that treatment may modul-ate regional connectivity between nodes of the OFC–caudate–thalamic–OFC loop in both directions. In interpreting these studies, one should not overlook the possibility that such reductions in regional brain function could merely reflect the brain status of a less symptomatic patient.

Relating imaging studies to the psychopathology of OCD: problems and pitfalls

In spite of the growing number of brain imaging studies of OCD that have been conducted during the last decade, many questions remain unanswered. Comparisons between studies are difficult because the tech-nology of imaging is expanding and changing rapidly. Older, two-dimen-sional scans, using 133-xenon inhalation, have been replaced by scanners permitting examination of subcortical regions. The resolution of scanners has markedly improved: for example, the old NeuroECAT on which the original UCLA study (16) was carried out had an in-plane resolution of 11 mm, whereas the current scanner used by this group, the NeuroECAT III, has in-plane resolution half the original (6 mm) (34). Moreover, scanners like the MRI, which until recently have only been used to study structures of the brain, are becoming dynamic (echo-planar MRI) and soon will permit serial rCBF studies of greater precision than is possible with presently used scanners. A good example of what one can expect from new technology is shown in the work of Dager et al (38). Using MRS, Dager and his colleagues were able to measure changes in brain lactate levels in panic disorder patients and controls during sodium lactate infusion. They demonstrated higher lactate build up in the brains of patients who panicked during the infusion than in controls who received the same infusion but did not panic (39).

Any attempt to review critically the brain imaging literature in OCD rests upon a careful examination of the several methodological constraints and limitations, both technology-driven and clinical, likely to affect the interpretation of the data (for examples, see Table 14.2). Not meant to be exhaustive, the following is an account of several such examples, in which differences in methods of scanning and analysis may have accounted for some of the variance in the PET and SPECT literature on OCD.

TECHNICAL CONSIDERATIONS: RELEVANCE FOR PLANNING CLINICAL STUDIES

Selection of tracer for assessing brain function

The time necessary for the tracer to bind to brain tissue and duration of binding are known to affect measurements. The duration of the brain-uptake phase for FDG is approximately 30 min; once trapped in a brain cell, FDG does not undergo further metabolism. Therefore, the resulting image contains the sum of all brain activities that occurred during the uptake phase. Thus, FDG is useful in imaging "static" metabolic states but cannot capture transitory events. [^{11}C]Glucose also measures glucose metabolism but, because it undergoes metabolic changes in the brain, may underestimate glucose metabolism (40). The SPECT tracer for determining relative changes in cerebral blood flow, [^{11}Tc]HMPAO, enters the brain within 5 min, with most of the neuronal uptake occurring during the first 2 min. Once bound, however, it is hardly displaced during the following 8 h. Therefore, HMPAO can capture a fairly brief event. Moreover, it can be administered at a location away from the scanner. For instance, HPMAO can be given in a laboratory in which the patients perform tasks that cannot be performed in the area of the scanner or it can be given at locations which reliably induce symptoms. Unfortunately, SPECT scans with HMPAO do not permit the calculation of absolute levels of cerebral blood flow. 15-Oxygen has a half-life of 2 min and can be administered repeatedly, as serial intravenous boluses of [^{15}O]H$_2$O, during the same session. Therefore, it is at present the most useful tool for the examination of the effects of challenge tests during which a consecutive number of scans need to be obtained under different conditions.

Determination of "input" function and calculation of absolute glucose metabolism or cerebral blood perfusion

The calculation of absolute global brain glucose metabolic rates (MRS) relies upon the simultaneous dynamic measurements of the brain distribution of the tracer [^{18}F]FDG with PET and arterial plasma concentrations of [^{18}F]FDG and glucose ("input function"), as well as a knowledge of the various transfer rate constant values between the periphery and the central compartments (41). Variations between centers are known with respect to input function (arterial vs "arterialized" blood) or lumped constant value. For example, the UCLA group uses an arterialized venous blood sampling method, whereas both NIMH groups use arterial sampling, through a catheter installed in the radial artery. The former is known to change the shape of the time–radioactivity curves, thus affecting glucose MR measurements. The published values for the lumped constants used in the tracer kinetics of FDG in the NIMH and the UCLA studies were 0.418 and 0.52, respectively. Such differences of input function and lumped constant values may explain the marked differences between the two centers in their published values of absolute global glucose MRs (NIMH: 9.68 ± 1.42 vs UCLA: 4.87 ± 1.21 mg/100 g tissue/min).

Selection of neuroanatomical regions of interest for analysis of PET and SPECT images

The images obtained by PET and SPECT are artificial computer images which lack neuroanatomical definition. In order to extract regional information which refers to brain anatomy, investigators must trace manually or automatically, by means of a dedicated software, the boundaries of the cortical and subcortical subdivisions, thus defining the specific regions of interest (ROIs) to be analyzed. The methods to do so vary considerably between centers, depending on whether ROIs are drawn or positioned over the cortical rim, on the basis of a stereotactic brain atlas of reference, or using the subject's own individual brain CT or MRI scan. All FDG/PET studies to date have relied upon the manual drawing/positioning of ROIs, using pre-established standard templates: in the studies by Nordahl et al (18), Martinot et al (9), and Benkelfat et al (20), five "typical" brain planes were used, defining a total of 60–73 individual ROIs. In the studies by Swedo et al (19, 35), eight brain slices were used, defining 201 individual ROIs. In the reports by Swedo et al (19, 34) and Baxter et al (17), as well as that of Martinot et al (9), data were pooled across brain slices and expressed as metabolic rates *per brain structure*. Conceivably, such methodological differences in ROI tracing and definition could affect the results. Machlin et al (22) compared SPECT scans of OCD patients with those of controls by using a semicomputerized method, in which cortical circumferential profiles at the level of the basal ganglia and 1 cm above were analyzed for a total of 60 samples per slide. The normalized perfusion values of the ROIs were expressed as a percentage of the whole cortical mean value, calculated from the sum obtained from the circumferential profiles. Using this method of analysis, we (22) found increased perfusion of the medial frontal cortex but in no other brain areas in OCD patients. Recently, the same set of data (14) was reanalyzed by using a modification of the method described by Fox et al (42). Multiplanar reconstruction was used on both SPECT and the corresponding MRI scans from these subjects to reorient all image sets into the spatial reference of the Talairach atlas (43). The SPECT images were normalized to the "whole" brain count value, then averaged between subjects within groups. The average group brain images were subtracted between groups and analyzed for regions of significant differences. With this method, OCD patients showed higher activity in the medial frontal gyrus, right middle frontal gyrus, and lateral areas in the cerebellum, areas that have been associated with higher order functions, and lower activity in the right inferior and middle occipital gyrus, as well as the visual association cortex. The decrease in perfusion in visual association areas may represent the attentional focus of OCD patients on thoughts, manifesting themselves through increased perfusion in prefrontal areas, rather than in processing visual stimuli. Thus, areas of difference between patients and controls, which have not been noticed previously, were visualized with the advanced analysis. The analysis also avoided the *a priori* definition of ROIs, which differs considerably between investigators. Moreover, the superimposition of MRIs on corresponding SPECT or PET images helps avoid erroneous interpretations of extracranial activity as belonging to the brain (C Benkelfat et al, unpublished data).

An interesting analytical approach has been taken by Horwitz et al (44). The authors calculated correlations between normalized cerebral metabolic areas from PET FDG scans of 18 early onset OCD patients and 18 controls. Similar approaches have been used in calculating areas of synergistic activity in computerized EEG recordings. The authors found that the two regions with largest numbers of correlations, that differed significantly between OCD patients and controls, were the superior parietal region and anterior temporal area of the left hemisphere, which included the amygdala. Correlations involving the caudate showed no differences between the two groups. The anterior limbic/paralimbic regions had significantly larger numbers of positive correlations with frontal areas in OCD patients than in controls. These findings are interesting, because they suggest a linkage between limbic structures and frontal lobe regions in OCD. Such a linkage makes intuitive sense when one considers the strong emotional component present in OCD. On the other hand, more conventional analyses of scans failed to show differences in temporal cortex areas between OCD patients and controls. As interesting as the results are, they need to be treated with caution. The data have been obtained from scans using FDG as tracer. Therefore, each data point represents local brain activity covering a period of nearly 30 min and may include changes that had occurred in that brain region independently from OCD. Moreover, positive correlation between regions does not necessarily represent functional connection. With further development of imaging techniques, which permit the capture of short epochs of activity, however, correlation analyses may yield important information.

"Absolute" or "relative" brain glucose metabolic rates or blood perfusion?

As diverse as the definitions of ROIs, and the statistics used in the examination of their activity, are the means to calculate and express brain glucose metabolic rates or cerebral blood perfusion, either as absolute or relative levels. Ideally, one should compare absolute metabolic rates or levels of blood perfusion; yet, not all methods permit the calculation of absolute levels. In addition, the great intra- and intersubject variability of absolute values when rescanned makes statistical comparisons difficult. Therefore, investigators normalize their data by calculating the ratio between a defined region of interest and a larger section of the brain. As one can see from Table 14.2, almost every investigator uses a different method of normalization. In one case, the region of comparison is the activity of the same hemisphere, in other cases, it is the global activity of grey matter, the transaxial slide in which the ROI has been defined, the visual cortex or, in one study, the cerebellum. The authors of the last study (23) assumed that the cerebellum is not involved in the pathology of OCD. Recently, however, we (14) found increased activity in the cerebellum of OCD patients. If this finding is replicated, one cannot use the cerebellum for normalization in OCD patients. The method of normalization employed by Rubin et al (23) could also explain why only this group, and no other investigators, found decreased activity in the heads of both caudates of OCD patients.

CLINICAL CONSIDERATIONS: RELEVANCE FOR INTERPRETING PET AND SPECT STUDIES

Clinicometabolic correlations

Correlations between ratings of obsessive compulsive symptoms and regional brain function are inconsistent and often not present: glucose metabolic rates in the orbital frontal cortex correlated positively with clinical OCD severity in only one of four FDG/PET studies in OCD (19), and no correlation could be found between caudate function and clinical measures. This is not surprising if one considers that manifestations of OCD are not invariably present but occur intermittently. Scans capture a discrete moment of brain activity, which may or may not occur at times when symptoms are present. Therefore, in the case of "state"-related regional abnormalities in brain function, one would expect significant correlations to occur only when symptoms are present. This is not necessarily the case when patients are unchallenged or, because of the long brain uptake time, in scans using FDG as a tracer.

"State"- vs "trait"-related alterations in regional brain function in OCD

As increasing evidence supports a genetic vulnerability for some OCD patients, it is conceivable that regional alterations in brain function could contribute a particular phenotype of "familial OCD", pre-existing the onset of clinical symptoms ("trait"). In contrast to challenge studies designed to experimentally elicit specific behavioral states during scanning, the cross-sectional comparison of functional brain imaging data, between OCD patients and normal controls, cannot distinguish between state- and trait-related changes in brain function; nor can it determine whether these alterations, if and when present, are cause or consequence of the psychopathological disease process. Follow-up studies of OCD patients treated with either medications or behavior therapy, at various stages of recovery, while under treatment or in remission, at distance of treatment, may help address this problem. Collectively, most studies to date suggest some "correction" of the brain abnormalities with treatment, consistent with these "alterations" in regional brain function being "state-related". Significant correlations relating normalization of brain function to clinical improvement of OCD symptoms have been reported in several studies (see earlier). Yet, definite conclusions await the results of future studies, involving a larger sample size, the addition of several control groups, e.g. OCD patients treated with placebo, anxiety disorder patients treated with SSRIs and/or behavior therapy, longitudinal follow-up studies of OCD patients in clinical remission, studies of unaffected biological siblings of OCD patients, subject vulnerable for OCD, etc.

The problem of comorbidity with depression and anxiety

Generally, obsessive compulsive symptoms are accompanied by anxiety. Many OCD patients are also depressed to a more or lesser extent, although coexisting major depression is often an exclusion criterion in the most recent FDG/PET studies. Some patients, however, feel not anxious but irritated by their inability to control obsessive thoughts or compulsive actions (45). Other patients experience disgust, rather than anxiety, when they feel contaminated. Accompanying emotions are likely to affect functional scans. Generally, OCD is associated with hyperfrontality, while depression lowers prefrontal activity. Thus, a combination of OCD and depression may present images that differ from those of each disorder alone, even, potentially, in clinically nondepressed OCD patients. Baxter et al (46) reported reduced glucose MRs in the left prefrontal cortex, with a trend on the right, in unmedicated depressed OCD patients compared with nondepressed OCD patients. We (C Benkelfat et al, unpublished data) recently compared regional MRs in the left, medial, and right prefrontal cortex in unmedicated depressed ($n = 5$, CPRS-OC = 10.2 ± 0.8, HDRS17 = 16.6 ± 7.3, cortisol = 13.6 ± 14 ng/ml) and nondepressed OCD patients ($n = 8$, CPRS-OC = 8.4 ± 1.8, HDRS17 = 7.9 ± 3.1, cortisol = 7.8 ± 3 ng/ml): depressed OCD patients had significantly lower MRs in the medial and right prefrontal cortex than the nondepressed patients (see Figure 14.3). This and other similar results suggest that the comorbidity with depression is a significant covariate in functional brain imaging studies of OCD patients and should be taken into account while interpreting the data.

Changes in cerebral blood flow accompanying anxiety are complex and depend on the severity of anxiety and the presence or absence of cognitive elements. It appears that lower levels of anxiety increase, while higher levels decrease, cerebral blood flow (47, 48). The decrease in blood flow during high anxiety may be the consequence of decreased CO_2 pressure due to anxiety-induced hyperventilation or due to vasoconstriction which occurs during sympathetic activation (48, 49). Activity in frontal areas of the brain may be associated with ruminative anxiety, but may not be present in nonreflective anxiety responses. For instance, when snake phobics were exposed to visual phobic stimuli, their fear reaction was spontaneous, without cognitive elaboration. This response led to an increase of rCBF, measured using PET and [^{15}O]butanol injection, in the visual associative cortex but not in the prefrontal cortex (50). Thus, the state of the patient during the scan, the nature of the challenge procedure, and the resulting affective response significantly alter the

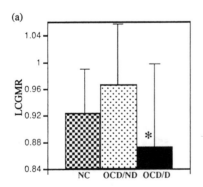
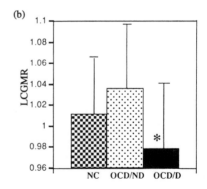

Figure 14.3 Reduction of normalized local cerebral glucose metabolic rate (LCGMR) in depressed versus nondepressed obsessive compulsive disorder (OCD) patients: prefrontal cortex (D plane). (a) Anterior medial frontal cortex (ANOVA $p < 0.04$). (b) Right anterior frontal cortex (ANOVA $p < 0.01$). NC, Normal controls; OCD/ND, nondepressed OCD; OCD/D, depressed OCD

subject's brain function and therefore the subsequent measurements of rCBF.

The problem of "artefacts"

Another source of erroneous interpretation of brain PET/SPECT data in OCD research includes activities that are unrelated to OCD but, because they occur during the tracer uptake phase, may show up in the scan. In a study by Goldenberg et al (55) using SPECT scans with HMPAO as tracer, spontaneously occurring mental visual images increased orbitofrontal CBF, while voluntary imagery led to increased rCBF in basal temporal regions of both hemispheres. Another study, using PET imaging with FDG as tracer, found that glucose metabolism increased in the left head of the caudate nucleus when individuals used visual images as a strategy to identify sequences of tones (52). Even apparent "resting states" are difficult to define. Measuring glucose metabolism with PET, using FDG as tracer, Mazziotta et al (53) found that overall glucose metabolism declined progressively with reduced sensory input. The relationship between metabolism of the frontal cortex to that of the parietal and occipital cortex progressively increased from the eyes-closed to the ears-closed to the eyes- and ears-closed state. Therefore, it is important that sensory or motor activities, as well as cognitive affective states, that are not relevant to the specific pathology, are absent during the uptake phase of the tracer.

Table 14.2 demonstrates how investigators tried to control such unwanted intrusion during the time of the administration of the tracer. Some investigators tried to eliminate all sensory inputs by taping patients' eyes in a quiet environment. Others, who believe that sensory deprivation may induce unwanted thoughts and feelings, used a dimly lit, quiet room in which patients kept their eyes open. It was thought that an environment subjecting individuals to weak sensory inputs would diminish the intrusion of thoughts with strong affective loading. A third group of investigators had their subjects perform simple repetitive tasks, such as the auditory continuous performance task, in which subjects pressed a button whenever they detected the lowest of three tones. Such tasks may preoccupy the mind of the subject sufficiently to block the intrusion of undesirable thoughts but may also affect brain activity. Yet, in all studies in which a continuous performance task was used, patients and controls engaged in exactly the same activities every time they were scanned and did not differ, in terms of task performance. Comparisons between scans conducted with different tasks, however, could lead to erroneous conclusions. We (54) compared SPECT scans of volunteers who performed the Stroop test, a test which creates an attentional conflict state, with scans obtained during a control condition. To avoid the potentially confounding effects of speech on an individual's physiological reactions and on the imaging data, subjects gave their answers to the task manually, by using a keyboard with their right hand. Our findings were similar to those of Pardo et al (55) whose subjects gave verbal responses, except that our scans also showed increased activity in the left precentral and motor areas, which reflected the use of the right hand in the performance of the task.

The fact that some studies reported changes in the right and others in the left caudate raises the question of what effect, if any, the site of manipulations performed during the scan (for instance, which hand and forearm were heated to obtain arterialized venous blood, on which side an arterial line was placed, or on what location the provocative stimulus was positioned) had on the scan. Manipulations that cause discomfort could increase muscular tension in the limb and be responsible for these discrepancies. The study by Rauch et al (29) took into account such problems. It used, as a control for the provocative stimulus condition, the placement of a physically identical but not "contaminated" object. Unfortunately, their article does not report the effects of the control condition on rCBF.

Clinical heterogeneity

Also of importance is the selection of patients. In spite of the high reliability of the diagnosis (56), OCD does not appear to be a homogenous disorder. Patients with onset during childhood may differ from patients in whom OCD reaches clinical levels at a later age. There also may be a difference between patients who are neurologically intact and patients who, in addition to OCD, exhibit soft neurological signs, tics, or disturbances affecting basal ganglia. Not accounting for such differences in patient populations may explain contradictory findings between studies. Finally, as Baxter et al (57) have pointed out, differences in criteria employed in the selection of control subjects affect the comparisons of patients with "normal" controls.

Conclusions

What can we learn about OCD from imaging studies? Presently favored neurobiological hypotheses of OCD assume that the disorder is caused by or associated with a disturbance in the cortico–striatal–thalamic–cortical circuit, with inputs from the limbic system. The main differences between the hypotheses are assumptions about functions of the subsystems thought to be responsible for the pathology. The hypothesis of Wise and Rapoport (58) places the emphasis on a disturbance of basal ganglia functions. It is based on the assumption that the basal ganglia are a repository of innate motor programs and, in addition, that the basal ganglia also function as a gating mechanism for sensory inputs. When these functions are disturbed, the activation of innate motor programs produces behavioral responses, for instance hand washing, even in the absence of sensory inputs signalling "dirt". The hypothesis also assumes that the cingulate cortex is involved in generating behavior in the absence of an appropriate sensory stimulus. Baxter et al (34) see the primary disturbance as being a deficit in caudate nucleus function, which leads to an inadequate "filtering" of orbital "worry" inputs. Modell et al (59) speculated that a dysfunction of neural circuits interconnecting the orbito-frontal cortex, basal ganglia/limbic striatum, and thalamus serves a critical role in the pathogenesis of OCD. After a critical review of imaging studies, Insel (8) suggested that the hyperactivity found in orbitofrontal regions of OCD patients is the most likely focus of disturbance.

Judging from the results of structural imaging, OCD patients do not exhibit visible anatomical brain abnormalities. This does not exclude changes that are not detectable by present methods. However, OCD patients with early childhood onset of symptoms may differ from patients with later onset. Systematic comparisons of patients with different time of illness onset, severity, and, above all, presence or absence of neurological signs are needed to clarify which OCD patient groups differ structurally from the norm.

As Insel (8) pointed out, imaging studies support the hypothesis that OCD is associated with prefrontal hyperactivity. All but two studies found OCD associated with prefrontal, generally orbitofrontal, hyper-activity. One of the two studies that reported hypoactivity (9) included medicated patients (10 out of 16); the other study (15) did not examine orbitofrontal regions. The latter also examined chronic patients who had not responded to treatment. Such patients may differ from those who respond to medications. Whether hyperfrontality represents the primary disturbance in OCD or a compensatory reaction to a disturbance else-where, for instance in the striatum, remains unknown. Also, the incon-sistency of locations of hyperactive regions in prefrontal cortex remains a puzzle. The hyperfrontality, however, is state related and diminishes during pharmacotherapy or after psychosurgery. Since it is also present in psychiatrically healthy individuals who were asked to recall a situation that would make them feel very sad (60) or to experience spontaneously occurring images at the time of the scan (51), but is absent in trichotillo-mania (12), it may reflect the cognitive–affective activation of the brain in OCD patients but not their repetitive activities.

Changes in basal ganglia are more difficult to integrate into a theoretical framework. Findings, whether obtained in baseline scans, during chal-lenges, or during treatment, are inconsistent. Baxter (34) raised the possibility that therapy may alter brain functions gradually. He pointed out that the study with the shortest interval between scans (34) found only caudate changes and the study with the longest interval (35) found only orbital changes, while a study of intermediate length (20) found both. However, a SPECT scan study that explored the effects of intermediate length treatment of OCD patients with fluoxetine found only a decrease in hyperfrontality and no changes in the activity of the basal ganglia (33). The possibility that factors not related to changes induced by treatment contributed to the observed changes in the head of caudate nuclei cannot be overlooked.

Thus, present data raise more questions than they answer. They also shed no light on the serotonin hypothesis of OCD. This hypothesis, which still awaits a clear formulation, is based primarily on the observation that serotonin reuptake inhibiting antidepressants, but not antidepressants with other pharmacodynamic properties, improve symptoms of OCD. While not universally accepted [for a critical review see Hantouche and Badoura (61)], it remains popular. Three studies (20, 33, 35) found fluoxetine or clomipramine to reduce hyperfrontality. Only one (34) reported no changes in prefrontal areas after treatment with fluoxetine. This finding could be interpreted in support of the hypothesis that OCD is caused by a disturbance of the serotonergic system, which is ameliorated through medications that alter its functions. However, we (62, 63) observed that serotonin reuptake inhibiting antidepressants can cause apathy, indifference and in some cases, a frontal lobe-like syndrome not only in OCD but also panic disorder and depressed patients. Moreover, clomipramine, given to OCD patients, decreased their autonomic responses to pathology-specific as well as nonspecific stressors (64). Such diminished responses have also been seen in patients with frontal lobe damage (65). Thus, the effect of serotonin reuptake inhibitors may be a nonspecific suppression of frontal lobe activity, rather than the correction of hypothetical serotonergic abnormalities in the brain functioning of OCD patients. Progress in the understanding of the role of putative serotonergic abnormalities in the neurobiology of OCD must wait until more specific in vivo brain imaging techniques of the serotonergic neurotransmission in man (66) are developed and tested in OCD patients.

To further advance our understanding of OCD using functional brain imaging techniques, more well-controlled studies are needed. Within-subject longitudinal studies, off and on treatment, and, during recovery, remission or relapse, should replace cross-sectional comparisons of patients and controls. Psychiatric control groups, including, for example, anxiety disorder patients (contamination-phobic patients) or patients with disorders of impulse control (pathological gamblers), also need to be compared with OCD patients with respect to regional brain function, psychopathology and treatment response. Moreover, because of the effects mental processes have on regional brain metabolism, precise information will be needed about patients' thoughts, emotions, and bodily sensations experienced at the time of the uptake phase. Challenge studies that elicit specific reactions will provide important information about brain functions in OCD, but they will have to be carefully controlled for not including changes in brain activities that are not relevant to the desired response. As in structural imaging studies, functional studies also need to compare "pure OCD" patients with patients who exhibit, in addition, tics, neurological signs, or concomitant neurological diseases. Since it is difficult to find a sufficient number of patients who differ from each other in all but one variable, Baxter (67) proposed experimental "triangulation" as a strategy for functional neuroimaging studies. This method examines one factor present in all patients belonging to two or more otherwise differing groups, for instance brain activities observable in all patients with depression, irrespective of their psychiatric diagnosis, or brain changes associated with improvement, when different treatments are being given to a homogenous patient population. This approach certainly will be useful in OCD research.

In spite of many methodological difficulties, imaging techniques should greatly enhance our knowledge of the functions of the brain. Most of the present difficulties can be attributed to the newness of imaging techniques, the rapid change of technology, and, above all, the scarcity of studies describing changes in regional brain activities during "normal" behavior. With expanding knowledge of "normal" physiological processes, we shall be better able to assess differences between normal and abnormal responses. As Insel (8) stated, "the real power of cerebral imaging lies not only in providing data on the pathophysiologic characteristics of diagnostic syndromes, but also in relating neural functions to specific mental processes". Obsessive compulsive disorder presents a unique opportunity to study such processes.

References

1. Andreasen NC. Brain Imaging: Applications in Psychiatry. American Psychiatric Press, Washington DC, 1989.
2. Rapoport JL. Obsessive compulsive disorder and basal ganglia dysfunction. Psychol Med 1990; 20: 465–469.
3. Insel TR, Donnelly EF, Lalakea ML, Alterman IS, Murphy DL. Neurological and neuropsychological studies of patients with obsessive–compulsive disorder. Biol Psychiatry 1983; 18: 741–751.
4. Behar D, Rapoport JL, Berg CJ et al. Computerized tomography and neuropsychological test measures in adolescents with obsessive–compulsive disorder. Am J Psychiatry 1984; 141: 363–368.
5. Luxenberg JS, Swedo SE, Flament MF, Friedland RP, Rapoport J, Rapoport SI. Neuroanatomical abnormalities in obsessive–compulsive disorder detected with quantitative X-ray computed tomography. Am J Psychiatry 1988; 145: 1089–1093.

6. Garber HJ, Ananth JV, Chiu LC, Griswold VJ, Oldendorf WH. Nuclear magnetic resonance study of obsessive–compulsive disorder. Am J Psychiatry 1989; 146: 1001–1005.

7. Kellner CH, Jolley RR, Holgate RC et al. Brain MRI in obsessive–compulsive disorder. Psychiatry Res 1991; 36: 45–49.

8. Insel TR. Toward a neuroanatomy of obsessive–compulsive disorder. Arch Gen Psychiatry 1992; 49: 739–744.

9. Martinot JL, Allilaire JF, Mazoyer BM et al. Obsessive–compulsive disorder: a clinical, neuropsychological and positron emission tomography study. Acta Psychiatr Scand 1990; 82: 233–242.

10. Harris GJ, Pearlson GD, Peyser CE, Aylward EH, Folstein SE. Putamen volume measures on MRI completely discriminate early Huntington's disease patients from controls. Ann Neurol 1992; 31: 69–75.

11. Hollander E, Schiffman E, Cohen B et al. Signs of central nervous system dysfunction in obsessive–compulsive disorder. Arch Gen Psychiatry 1990; 47: 27–32.

12. Swedo SE, Rapoport JL, Leonard HL, Schapiro MB, Rapoport SI, Grady CL. Regional ceebral glucose metabolism of women with trichotillomania. Arch Gen Psychiatry 1991; 48: 828–833.

13. George MS, Trimble MR, Costa DC, Robertson MM, Ring HA, Ell PJ. Elevated frontal cerbral blood flow in Gilles de la Tourette syndrome: A 99Tm-HMPAO SPECT study. Psychiatry Res Neuroimaging 1992; 45: 143–151.

14. Harris GJ, Hoehn-Saric R, Lewis RW, Pearlson GD, Streeter C. Mapping of SPECT regional cerebral perfusion abnormalities in obsessive compulsive disorder. Human Brain Mapping [in press].

15. Mindus P, Ericson K, Greitz T, Meyerson B, Nyman H, Sjogren I. Regional cerebral glucose metabolism in anxiety disorders studied with positron emission tomography before and after psychosurgical interventions. Acta Radiol 1986; suppl 369: 444–448.

16. Baxter LR, Phelps ME, Mazziotta JC, Guze BH, Schwartz JM, Selin CE. Local cerebral glucose metabolic rates in obsessive–compulsive disorder. A comparison with rates in unipolar depression and in normal controls. Arch Gen Psychiatry 1987; 44: 211–218.

17. Baxter LR, Schwartz JM, Mazziotta JC et al. Cerebral glucose metabolic rates in nondepressed patients with obsessive–compulsive disorder. Am J Psychiatry 1988; 145: 1560–1563.

18. Nordahl TE, Benkelfat C, Semple WE, Gross M, King AC, Cohen RM. Cerebral glucose metabolic rates in obsessive compulsive disorder. Neuropsychopharmacology 1989; 2: 23–28.

19. Swedo SE, Schapiro MB, Grady CL et al. Cerebral glucose metabolism in childhood-onset obsessive–compulsive disorder. Arch Gen Psychiatry 1989; 46: 518–523.

20. Benkelfat C, Nordahl TE, Semple WE, King C, Murphy DL, Cohen RM. Local cerebral glucose metabolic rates in obsessive–compulsive disorder. Patients treated with clomipramine. Arch Gen Psychiatry 1990; 47: 840–848.

21. Sawle GV, Hymas NF, Lees AJ, Frackowiak RSJ. Obsessional slowness. Functional studies with positron emission tomography. Brain 1991; 114: 2191–2202.

22. Machlin SR, Harris GJ, Pearlson GD, Hoehn-Saric R, Jeffery P, Camargo EE. Elevated medial–frontal cerebral blood flow in obsessive–compulsive patients: A SPECT study. Am J Psychiatry 1991; 148: 1240–1242.

23. Rubin RT, Villanueva-Myer J, Ananth J, Trajmar PG, Mena I. Regional Xenon

133 cerebral blood flow and cerebral Technetium 99m HMPAO uptake in unmedicated patients with obsessive–compulsive disorder and matched normal control subjects. Arch Gen Psychiatry 1992; 49: 695–702.

24. Parks RW, Crockett DJ, Tuokko H et al. Neuropsychological "systems efficiency" and positron emission tomography. J Neuropsychiatry 1989; 1: 269–282.

25. Singer HS, Walkup JT. Tourette syndrome and other tic disorders. Diagnosis, pathophysiology, and treatment. Medicine 1991; 70: 15–32.

26. Sandor P. Gilles de la Tourette syndrome: A neuropsychiatric disorder. J Psychosom Res 1993; 37: 211–226.

27. Stanley MA, Swann AC, Bowers TC, Davis ML, Taylor DJ. A comparison of clinical features in trichotillomania and obsessive–compulsive disorder. Behav Res Ther 1992; 30: 39–44.

28. Zohar J, Insel TR, Berman KF, Foa EB, Hill JL, Weinberger DR. Anxiety and cerebral blood flow during behavioral challenge. Dissociation of central from peripheral and subjective measures. Arch Gen Psychiatry 1989; 46: 505–510.

29. Rauch SL, Jenike MA, Alpert NM et al. Regional cerebral blood flow measured during symptom provocation in obsessive–compulsive disorder using oxygen 15-labeled carbon dioxide and positron emission tomography. Arch Gen Psychiatry 1994; 51: 62–70.

30. Zohar J, Mueller E, Insel T, Zohar-Kadouch R, Murphy D. Serotonergic responsivity in obsessive–compulsive disorder. Arch Gen Psychiatry 1987; 44: 946–951.

31. Hollander E, Fay M, Liebowitz M. Serotonergic and noradrenergic function in obsessive–compulsive disorder. Am J Psychiatry 1988; 145: 1015–1017.

32. Charney D, Goodman W, Price L, Woods S, Rasmussen S, Heninger G. Serotonin function in obsessive–compulsive disorder. Arch Gen Psychiatry 1988; 45: 177–185.

33. Hoehn-Saric R, Pearlson GD, Harris GJ, Machlin SR, Camargo EE. Effects of fluoxetine on regional cerbral blood flow in obsessive–compulsive patients. Am J Psychiatry 1991; 148: 1243–1245.

34. Baxter LR, Schwartz JM, Bergman KS et al. Caudate glucose metabolic rate changes with both drug and behavior therapy for obsessive–compulsive disorder. Arch Gen Psychiatry 1992; 49: 681–689.

35. Swedo SE, Pietrini P, Leonard HL et al. Cerebral glucose metabolism in childhood-onset obsessive–compulsive disorder. Revisualization during pharmacology. Arch Gen Psychiatry 1992; 49: 690–694.

36. DeVeaugh-Geiss J. Pharmacological treatment of obsessive–compulsive disorder. In: The Psychobiology of Obsessive–Compulsive Disorder (eds Zohar J, Insel T, Rasmussen S). Springer, New York, 1991, p 201.

37. Pigott TA, L'Heureux F, Rubenstein CS, Bernstein SE, Hill JL, Murphy DL. A double-blind, placebo controlled study of trazodone in patients with obsessive–compulsive disorder. J Clin Psychopharmacology 1992; 12: 156–162.

38. Dager SR, Steen RG. Applications of magnetic resonance spectroscopy to the investigation of neuropsychiatric disorders. Neuropsychopharmacology 1992; 6: 249–266.

39. Dager SR. Initial application of magnetic resonance spectroscopy to study the pathophysiology of anxiety disorders. Abstract, First International Obsessive Compulsive Disorder Conference, Capri, Italy, 12–13 Mar 1993, p 35.

40. Baxter LR. Neuroimaging studies of obsessive compulsive disorder. Psychiatr Clin North Am 1992; 15: 871–884.

41. Sokoloff L, Reivich M, Kennedy C et al. The [14C]deoxyglucose method for

the measurement of local cerebral glucose utilization: Theory, procedure and normal values in the conscious and anesthetized albino rat. J Neurochem 1977; 28: 897.

42. Fox PT, Mintun MA, Reiman EM, Raichle ME. Enhanced detection of focal brain responses using intersubject averaging and change-distribution analysis of subtracted PET images. J Cereb Blood Flow Metab 1988; 8: 642–653.

43. Talairach J, Tournoux P. Co-planar Sterotaxic Atlas of the Human Brain. Thieme, New York, 1988.

44. Horwitz B, Swedo SE, Grady CL et al. Cerebral metabolic pattern in obsessive–compulsive disorder: Altered intercorrelations between regional rates of glucose utilization. Psychiatry Res Neuroimaging 1991; 40: 221–237.

45. Marks I. Fears, Phobias, and Rituals. Oxford University Press, New York, 1987, pp 442–444.

46. Baxter LR, Schwartz JM, Phelps M et al. Reduction of prefrontal cortex glucose metabolism common to three types of depression. Arch Gen Psychiatry 1989; 46: 243–250.

47. Gur RC, Gur RE, Resnick SM, Skolnick BE, Alavi A, Reivich M. The effect of anxiety on cortical cerebral blood flow and metabolism. J Cereb Blood Flow Metab 1987; 7: 173–177.

48. Wilson WH, Mathew RJ. Cerebral blood flow and metabolism in anxiety disorders. In Biology of Anxiety Disorders (eds Hoehn-Saric R, McLeod DR). American Psychiatric Press, Washington DC, 1993, pp 1–59.

49. Jibiki I, Kurokawa K, Matsuda H, Fukushima T, Yamguchi N, Hisada K. Widespread reduction of regional cerebral blood flow during hyperventilation-induced EEG slowing ("buildup"). Neuropsychobiology 1992; 26: 120–124.

50. Fredrikson M, Wik G, Greitz T, Eriksson L, Stone-Elander S, Ericson K, Sedvall G. Regional cerebral blood flow during experimental phobic fear. Psychophysiology 1993; 30: 126–130.

51. Goldenberg G, Podreka I, Uhl F, Steiner M, Willmes K, Deecke L. Cerebral correlates of imaging colours, faces and a map. I. SPECT of regional cerebral blood flow. Neuropsychologia 1989; 27: 1315–1328.

52. Mazziotta JC, Phelps ME, Carson RE. Tomographic mapping of human cerebral metabolism: Subcortical responses to auditory and visual stimulation. Neurology 1984; 34: 825–828.

53. Mazziotta JC, Phelps ME, Carson RE, Kuhl DE. Tomographic mapping of human cerebral metabolism: Sensory deprivation. Ann Neurol 1982; 12: 435–444.

54. Rivera-Luna H, Camargo EE, Sostre S et al. (99m)-HMPAO SPECT imaging identifies cerebral activation changes during the Stroop test. Society of Nuclear Medicine 38th Annual Meeting, Cincinnati, Ohio, 11–14 June 1991 [abstr].

55. Pardo JV, Pardo PJ, Janer KW, Raichle ME. The anterior cingulate cortex mediates processing selection in the Stroop attentional conflict paradigm. Proc Natl Acad Sci USA 1990; 87: 256–259.

56. DiNardo PA, Moras K, Barlow DH, Rapee RM, Brown TA. Reliability of DSM-III-R anxiety disorder categories. Using the anxiety disorders interview schedule-revised (ADIS-R). Arch Gen Psychiatry 1993; 50: 251–256.

57. Baxter LR, Schwartz JM, Guze BH. Brain imaging: Toward a neuroanatomy of OCD. In: The Psychobiology of Obsessive–Compulsive Disorder (eds Zohart J, Insel T, Rasmussen S). Springer, New York, 1991, pp 101–125.

58. Wise SP, Rapoport JL. Obsessive–compulsive disorder: It is basal ganglia dysfunction? In: Obsessive–Compulsive Disorder in Children and Adoles-

cents (ed Rapoport JL). American Psychiatric Press, Washington DC, 1998, pp 327–344.

59. Modell JG, Mountz JM, Curtis GC, Greden JF. Neurophysiological dysfunction in basal ganglia/limbic striatal and thalamocortical circuits as a pathogenic mechanism of obsessive–compulsive disorder. J Neuropsychiatry 1989; 1: 27–36.

60. Pardo JV, Pardo PJ, Raichle ME. Neural correlates of self-induced dysphoria. Am J Psychiatry 1993; 150: 713–719.

61. Hantouche E, Baddoura C. Hypothèses biologiques dans la trouble obsessionnel–compulsif. L'Encephale 1990; 16: 241–249.

62. Hoehn-Saric R, Lipsey JR, McLeod DR. Apathy and indifference in patients on fluvoxamine and fluoxetine. J Clin Psychopharmacol 1990; 10: 343–345.

63. Hoehn-Saric R, Harris GJ, Pearlson GD, Cox CS, Machlin SR, Camargo EE. A fluoxetine-induced frontal lobe syndrome in an obsessive compulsive patient. J Clin Psychiatry 1991; 52: 131–133.

64. Hoehn-Saric R, McLeod DR, Zimmerli WD, Hipsley PA. Symptoms and physiological manifestations in obsessive–compulsive patients before and after treatment with clomipramine. J Clin Psychiatry 1993; 54: 272–276.

65. Damasio AR, Tranel D, Damasio HC. Somatic markers and the guidance of behavior: Theory and preliminary testing. In: Frontal Lobe Function and Dysfunction (eds Levin HS, Eisenberg HM, Benton AL). Oxford University Press, New York, 1991, pp 217–229.

66. Crouzel C, Guillaume M, Barre L, Lemaire C, Pike VW. Ligands and tracers for PET studies of the 5HT system: current status. Int J Radiat Appl Instrum 1992; 19: 857–872.

67. Baxter LR. Experimental "triangulation" as a strategy for functional neuroimaging studies of obsessive–compulsive disorder. First International Obsessive Compulsive Disorder Conference, Capri, Italy, 12–13 Mar 1993, p 45 [abstr].

PART IV
TREATMENT

15 PHARMACOLOGICAL TREATMENT OF OBSESSIVE COMPULSIVE DISORDER

Stuart A Montgomery

St Mary's Hospital Medical School, Academic Department of Psychiatry, London, UK

Introduction

As little as a decade ago any discussion of pharmacological approaches to treatment of obsessive compulsive disorder (OCD) would have been based on meagre data. This chapter reviews the substantial progress that has been made in recent years in establishing the efficacy of pharmacological treatments for obsessional illness.

Open trials of a number of medications from different psychoactive classes had been tried without systematic benefit before clomipramine was released in 1966. The first report that clomipramine might have particular advantages in treating patients with obsessional symptoms was published in 1967 (1) and was followed by further positive reports from open trials (2).

Clomipramine's efficacy in OCD, firmly established in numerous placebo-controlled studies, both large and small (3–11), and its potent serotonin reuptake inhibiting effects, generated hypotheses for the involvement of serotonin in OCD (12, 13). The studies that have attempted to elucidate the serotonergic basis of OCD have helped us recognize the complexities inherent in neurotransmission and neuromodulation (14). However, specific underlying abnormalities of the serotonin (5-hydroxy tryptamine, 5-HT) system have been hard to identify in OCD patients and

Current Insights in Obsessive Compulsive Disorder. Edited by E. Hollander, J. Zohar, D. Marazzati and B. Olivier
© 1994 John Wiley & Sons Ltd

the results from the small studies of probes of serotonin function have often been conflicting. Serotonin reuptake inhibition is clearly important in the pharmacological management of OCD, though the beneficial effects of serotonin reuptake inhibitors (SRIs) are usually partial and limited to the time for which they are continued. Adverse effects also limit the use of these medications in some patients.

Issues that need to be addressed are whether any of the pharmacological treatments have greater efficacy than others, whether efficacy can be increased by attempts at augmenting serotonergic activity, and whether there are subgroups of nonresponding OCD patients who may respond to different pharmacological approaches.

Efficacy of pharmacological treatments in OCD

A number of psychoactive medications have shown occasional benefit in case reports, but conclusions cannot be drawn about the strengths and limitations of putative treatments without evidence from controlled studies. Among biological treatments, potent SRIs have been most thoroughly studied and have consistently and convincingly been shown to be effective treatments for OCD.

CLOMIPRAMINE

Clomipramine has been the most thoroughly studied agent, having been available for 28 years, and its efficacy has been demonstrated with remarkable consistency. Five studies that included patients with varying degrees of depression found clomipramine to be superior to placebo, and four studies that excluded depression have shown that this effect was specifically anti-obsessional and not dependent on the known antidepressant effect of clomipramine (3–11).

SELECTIVE SEROTONIN REUPTAKE INHIBITORS

Trials of other potent and selective serotonin reuptake inhibitors (SSRIs) have also been uniformly positive, and these more selective compounds have the advantage of substantially less affinity for cholinergic, histaminergic, and α-adrenergic receptors, which results in a more favorable side effect profile.

Fluvoxamine was the earliest of the SSRIs to be investigated in OCD and there have been five placebo-controlled studies, all of which have produced positive results. Three of the earlier studies were relatively small (15–17), but two large multicenter studies have since confirmed that fluvoxamine is effective compared with placebo (18, 19).

In two large multicenter studies (20, 21), sertraline has been shown to be effective compared with placebo. One of these studies used a flexible dose and the other compared fixed dosages and found all the doses of sertraline tested to be effective. Fluoxetine has also been shown to be effective in OCD in three multicenter studies, one in Europe and two in the USA (22, 23). Paroxetine has also been shown to be effective in a multicenter placebo-controlled trial (24).

The SSRIs as a class appear to have anti-obsessional efficacy, all those that have been tested having been found to be effective.

ANTIDEPRESSANT OR ANTI-OBSESSIONAL EFFECT?

With the possible exception of clonazepam (25), all effective anti-obsessional agents are antidepressants, but it is clear that their efficacy in OCD is not mediated via an antidepressant effect. Clomipramine has been effective in studies that excluded patients with depression, as well as in studies that included patients with varying levels of depression. Similarly, with fluvoxamine efficacy did not depend on an antidepressant effect on depressive symptoms. Level of severity of depression at the start of the studies was not related to outcome (16), and depressive symptoms improved in parallel with the obsessional symptoms (15, 17, 26).

If the anti-obsessional effect were due to an antidepressant action, the whole range of antidepressants would be expected to be effective. In fact antidepressants that lack potent serotonin reuptake inhibiting action are not effective in OCD. Neither of the selective norepinephrine reuptake inhibitors tested, nortriptyline and desipramine, have been found to be effective (6, 7). The failure of desipramine was also seen in a small direct comparison with clomipramine (27) and also in a comparison with fluvoxamine (28). Imipramine and amitriptyline have been investigated but without finding positive anti-obsessional activity (29, 30). Trazodone, which has some serotonergic activity, was not significantly different from placebo in a small study, and this failure has been interpreted as related to the weakness of its serotonergic actions (31).

The position of monoamine reuptake inhibitors is still unclear. Although positive effects have been reported in open studies, including one in which 41% of nonresponders to clomipramine subsequently improved during treatment with tranylcypromine (32–34), controlled studies have not been encouraging. Clorgyline, for example, has not been found to be effective in a placebo-controlled trial (8) and, although no difference was found between clomipramine and phenelzine in one study, the numbers included were too small to provide an adequate test of equivalence (35).

Clinically relevant differences in response between OCD and depression or anxiety

Obsessive compulsive disorder differs from depression in the selectivity of response. Only serotonin reuptake inhibitors have been shown to be effective in OCD and all drugs of this class exhibit this effect. Agents lacking potent serotonin reuptake inhibiting activity are not effective.

Depression usually responds sooner than obsessive compulsive disorder, so that 6 weeks is often accepted as an adequate period to test the efficacy of a compound. In OCD a significant difference from placebo may appear early, within 5 weeks, but response continues incrementally over a much longer period. For this reason, trial treatment periods of 10–12 weeks are frequently advocated.

Higher daily doses of antidepressants have often been used in treatment of OCD than in treatment of depression, though the empirical data supporting this practice are scant. Fixed-dose studies of fluoxetine (22) and sertraline (20, 21) found no significant difference between high and low doses, although the effect size tended to be greater in both studies, with the highest dose (60 mg fluoxetine and 200 mg of sertraline). However, low doses of clomipramine have been shown to be effective in the study by Montgomery (3), which used clomipramine 75 mg, in the study by Thoren et al (6), which used 150 mg, and in the early part of the study by de Veaugh Geiss et al (11) before the dose had been fully titrated upwards. Moreover, Pato et al (36) showed that a group of patients who had responded to clomipramine in an average dose of 270 mg and relapsed when this medication was discontinued, responded when treatment with clomipramine was restarted at an average dose of only 165 mg daily.

All potent SRIs are effective in OCD while other antidepressants are not, but the net improvement for patients treated with SRIs is usually less than would be expected in depressed patients. The extent of improvement in OCD is usually partial (20–60% in different studies).

The response of OCD to placebo also differs from the response in depression. In depression, a 30% placebo response is usual and 50% is quite common. In OCD, the placebo response is much lower and rates of 5% were reported in the early studies (3, 11). This low placebo response rate permitted small population studies to identify substantial differences between effective treatments and placebo. Low placebo response rates coupled with the common chronicity of OCD, in which patients had often been continuously ill for a decade or more before entering controlled trials, made OCD among the most chronic mental illnesses. However, recent multicenter controlled trials of SSRIs have found larger placebo response rates (37). Larger populations and longer durations of treatment will probably be needed in OCD trials to avoid Type II errors.

Often OCD is accompanied by anxiety symptoms and is even misleadingly included in the anxiety disorders in DSM-III and DSM-IV. The anti-obsessional efficacy of effective treatments is, however, not mediated by an anxiolytic effect. If it were, one would expect other conventional anxiolytics to be effective, yet trials of neuroleptics and benzodiazepines have been discouraging (38–40).

One small study that was limited by not including a placebo control has suggested that clonazepam may be effective in OCD, though improvement plateaued at 3 weeks whereas the improvement with clomipramine continued (25). The effect seen might be due to the serotonergic activity of this drug, since clonazepam upregulates 5-HT_1 and 5-HT_2 sites in the frontal cortex (41) following acute administration.

A comparison of buspirone and clomipramine was unable to find a significant difference between these two drugs, though there was a trend for a better response with clomipramine (42). The small numbers and lack of a placebo control inhibit the drawing of conclusions from this study, and there is no other supportable evidence for the efficacy of buspirone.

Response in OCD differs from the anxiety disorders in the size of the drug effect and in the low placebo response rate but most importantly in the specificity of response for potent serotonergic drugs. This contrasts, for example, with panic disorder, in which a good response is seen with SSRIs, with imipramine, with preferential noradrenergic reuptake inhibitors such as desipramine, or with alprazolam.

Long-term treatment of OCD

Obsessive compulsive disorder is generally a chronic condition, with residual symptoms after patients have responded to treatment. It is important to know whether effective treatments remain effective when used in the longer term. It is also important to know whether patients who have responded to treatment remain well if treatment is discontinued. The evidence suggests that treatment should be continued.

High relapse rates have been shown for both clomipramine (36, 43) and fluoxetine (44). Two blind trials have shown that abrupt discontinuation of clomipramine treatment leads to rapid resurgence of symptoms. In one trial 89% of patients who were discontinued from clomipramine to placebo relapsed within 7 weeks, and in the other trial eight of nine patients discontinued from clomipramine to desipramine relapsed compared with only two of 11 who continued on clomipramine (36, 43). Pato et al (44) discontinued fluoxetine in five patients who had beneficial response to that medication. Four relapsed within 8–12 weeks, later than clomipramine-treated patients, presumably because of the longer half-life of fluoxetine and norfluoxetine. Clinical experience suggests that fluvoxamine- and sertraline-treated patients also experience high relapse rates when those medications are discontinued.

Resistant OCD

A major challenge in treating OCD is the substantial number of resistant patients. As with depression, the most common reason for failure of good response to medication is too little treatment for too short a time. A number of pharmacological approaches for those who fail to respond to an adequate course of treatment have been suggested.

Some patients have difficulty in tolerating the side effects of clomipramine, so an adequate dose may not be reached. Some clinicians have suggested the use of intravenous clomipramine in patients who are intolerant of oral doses. Patients who have previously been unresponsive may benefit and be able subsequently to continue on oral clomipramine. However, the clinical drawbacks of this procedure and the increased risks of serious adverse drug reactions, for example seizure, limit its use to only the seriously ill.

Lithium augmentation, which has shown a certain success in depression, does not appear to be helpful in OCD (45, 46). Adding buspirone to SSRIs to try to increase the effect at the 5-HT_{1A} receptor also appears unsuccessful (47, 48).

The only adjunctive treatment with evidence of extra efficacy is use of neuroleptics in addition to SSRIs (49). In examining the possible causes of nonresponse, there is some evidence suggesting a role for dopamine in OCD or in some patients with OCD. The association between OCD and certain disorders that are associated with basal ganglia dysfunction and the indication of basal ganglia involvement in OCD gained from positron emission tomography (PET) scanning studies suggest a possible neurological basis (50–53). Dopamine antagonists alone are ineffective in treating OCD but in the study in refractory OCD carried out by McDougle et al (49) response was seen when low-dose dopamine antagonists were added to ongoing SRI therapy in patients who had associated tics. Clinical experience, and an early negative controlled trial (38) strongly suggest that antipsychotics are not an effective treatment for uncomplicated OCD. Antipsychotics have the liability of extrapyramidal side effects and long-term risks of tardive dyskinesia. Nevertheless, the prominent and worthwhile response of antipsychotic augmentation in those suffering OCD and tics suggests that further investigation of these drugs is worthwhile.

Choice of treatment

The available evidence supports the anti-obsessional efficacy of potent SRIs. It is clear that pharmacotherapy is effective in treating both the obsessional ruminations and rituals of OCD, as can be seen from the good response of both types of symptoms in the large multicenter study of clomipramine (11).

The questions that arise are whether there are any clinical differences between these effective agents on which to base a choice and whether patients who do not respond to one drug may respond to another of the same class.

Clomipramine has been used in OCD over a longer period than other drugs and has the advantage of familiarity. It does, however, suffer the disadvantage of associated toxicity and unwanted side effects which many patients are unable to tolerate. The newer more selective drugs have a lesser side-effect burden and therefore offer a treatment more acceptable to patients.

The only suggestions of differential efficacy have come from open reports, which cannot of course provide unbiased answers (54). There have been few controlled studies that have made a direct comparison between clomipramine and a SSRI, but in those that have no difference efficacy has been demonstrated.

In choosing between effective treatments a relative risk–benefit assessment has to be made, and this assessment has to take account of the frequent unpleasant, and sometimes dangerous, side effects associated with clomipramine, particularly at the higher doses frequently used in OCD. The risk of seizures with clomipramine (1–2%) (55) is of particular concern, and the SSRIs, which have a seizure rate of only 0.1–0.5%, therefore seem to be an obvious first-choice treatment. The SSRIs are better tolerated and therefore offer a more acceptable treatment (56). The improved compliance that follows from a well-tolerated treatment is important, particularly in a long-term illness such as OCD.

Conclusions

Serotonin reuptake inhibitors are effective anti-obsessional agents. The response in OCD is mostly partial, and patients are left with some residual symptoms. The partial response is, nevertheless, reflected in substantial improvement in social and occupational functioning. The response levels with pharmacotherapy are similar to those reported with behavior therapy. It is, however, the experience of many clinicians that the best response is obtained when pharmacological treatment is combined with behavior therapy. There is certainly no evidence that the two types of treatment interfere with each other. Treatment with pharmacotherapy appears to be of greatest benefit in patients with severe OCD, and best effect may be obtained by initiating treatment with anti-obsessional drugs and then introducing behavioral treatments when a partial response begins to be seen.

Our inability to achieve full remission in any predictable way with present treatments provides a continuing stimulus both to refine present treatments and to study and understand the neurotransmitter systems through which they are mediated, so that still more effective treatments will be developed.

Acknowledgement

Dr John Greist, Chairman of the session on efficacy for his help in preparing this chapter.

References

1. Fernandez CE, Lopez-Ibor JJ. Monochlorimipramine in the treatment of psychiatric patients resistant to other therapies. Actas Luso Esp Neurol Psiquiatr Cienc 1967; 26: 119.
2. van Renygnghe de Voxvrie G. Use of anafranil (G34586) in obsessive neuroses. Acta Neurol Belg 1968; 100: 787.
3. Montgomery SA. Clomipramine in obsessional neurosis; a placebo controlled trial. Pharmaceut Med 1980; 1: 189.
4. Marks IM, Stern RS, Mawson D, Cobb J, McDonald R. Clomipramine and exposure for obsessive compulsive rituals. Br J Psychiatry 1980; 136: 1.
5. Marks IM, Lelliott P, Basoglu M et al. Clomipramine, self exposure and therapist aided exposure for obsessive compulsive rituals. Br J Psychiatry 1988; 152: 522.
6. Thoren P, Asberg M, Cronholm B, Jornestedt L, Traskman L. Clomipramine treatment in obsessive compulsive disorder, I a controlled clinical trial. Arch Gen Psychiatry 1980; 37: 1281.
7. Insel TR, Mueller EA, Alterman I, Linnoila M, Murphy DL. Obsessive compulsive disorder and serotonin: is there a connection. Biol Psychiatry 1985; 20: 1174.
8. Insel TR, Murphy DL, Cohen RM, Alterman I, Kilts C, Linnoila M. Obsessive compulsive disorder—A double blind trial of clomipramine and clorgyline. Arch Gen Psychiatry 1983; 40: 605.
9. Flament MF, Rapoport JL, Berg CJ. Clomipramine treatment of childhood OCD: A double-blind controlled study. Arch Gen Psychiatry 1985; 42: 977.
10. Mavissakalian M, Turner S, Michelson L, Jacob R. Tricyclic antidepressants in obsessive disorder: antiobsessional or antidepressant agents. Am J Psychiatry 1985; 142: 572.
11. de Veaugh Geiss J, Katz RJ, Landau P et al. Clomipramine in the treatment of patients with obsessive–compulsive disorder. Arch Gen Psychiatry 1991; 48: 730.
12. Yaryura-Tobias JA. Obsessive–compulsive disorders: A serotonergic hypothesis. J Orthomolec Psychiatr 1977; 6: 317.
13. Zohar J, Insel TR. Obsessive compulsive disorder: Psychobiological approaches to diagnosis, treatment and pathophysiology. Biol Psychiatry 1987; 22: 667.
14. Rauch SL, Jenike MA. Neurobiological models of obsessive–compulsive disorder. Psychosomatics 1993; 34: 20.
15. Perse TL, Greist JH, Jefferson JW, Rosenfeld JW, Dar R. Fluvoxamine treatment of obsessive compulsive disorder. Am J Psychiatry 1987; 144: 1543.
16. Goodman WK, Price LH, Rasmussen SA, Delgado PL, Heninger GR, Charney DS. Efficacy of fluvoxamine in obsessive compulsive disorder. Arch Gen Psychiatry 1989; 46: 36.

17. Cottraux J, Mollard E, Bouvard M et al. A controlled study of fluvoxamine and exposure in obsessive compulsive disorders. Int Clin Psychopharmacol 1990; 5: 17.
18. Montgomery SA, Manceaux A. Fluvoxamine in the treatment of obsessive compulsive disorder. Int Clin Psychopharmacol 1992; 7 (suppl 1): 5.
19. Greist JH. Fluvoxamine treatment of obsessive compulsive disorder. Biol Psychiatry 1991; 29 (suppl): 438 [abstr].
20. Chouinard, G, Goodman WK, Greist JH et al. Results of a double blind serotonin uptake inhibitor sertraline in the treatment of obsessive compulsive disorder. Psychopharmacol Bull 1990; 26(3): 279.
21. Chouinard G. Sertraline in the treatment of obsessive compulsive disorders: Two double-blind, placebo controlled studies. Int Clin Psychopharmacol 1992; 752: 37.
22. Montgomery SA, McIntyre A, Osterheider M et al. The Lilly European OCD Study Group: A double-blind, placebo-controlled study of fluoxetine in patients with DSM-III-R obsessive compulsive disorder. Eur Neuropsychopharmacol 1993; 3: 143.
23. Tollefson GD, Rampey AH, Potvin JH et al. A multicenter investigation of fixed-dose fluoxetine in the treatment of obsessive-compulsive disorder. Arch Gen Psychiatry 1994; 51(7): 559–567.
24. Wheadon D, Bushnell WD, Steiner M. A fixed dose comparison of 20, 40 or 60 mg of paroxetine to placebo in the treatment of obsessive-compulsive disorder. Poster, presented at American College of Neurophyschopharmacology meeting, Hawaii, 1993.
25. Hewlett WA, Vinogradov S, Agras WS. Clomipramine, clonazepam, and clonidine treatment of obsessive compulsive disorder. J Clin Psycopharmacol 1992; 12: 420.
26. Price LH, Goodman WK, Charney DS, Rasmussen SA, Heninger GR. Treatment of severe obsessive–compulsive disorder with fluvoxamine. Am J Psychiatry 1987: 144:1059.
27. Leonard HL, Swedo SE, Rapoport JL, Coffey M, Cheslow DL. Treatment of childhood obsessive compulsive disorder with clomipramine and desmethylimipramine; A double blind crossover comparison. Psychopharmacol Bull 1988; 24: 93.
28. Goodman WK, Price LH, Delgado PL et al. Specificity of serotonin reuptake inhibitors in the treatment of obsessive compulsive disorder: comparison of fluvoxamine and desipramine. Arch Gen Psychiatry 1990; 47: 577.
29. Foa E, Steketee G, Kozak M, Digger D. Imipramine and placebo in the treatment of obsessive compulsives: their effect on depression and obsessional symptoms. Psychopharmacol Bull 1987; 23(1): 8.
30. Ananth JV, Pecknold JC, Van den Steen N, Engelsmann F. Double-blind comparative study of clomipramine and amitriptyline in obsessive neurosis. Prog Neuropsychopharmacol Biol Psychiatry 1981; 5: 257.
31. Pigott TA, L'Heureux F, Rubenstein CS, Bernstein SE, Hill JL, Murphy DL. A double-blind placebo controlled study of trazodone in patients with obsessive–compulsive disorder. J Clin Psychopharmacol 1992; 12: 156.
32. Joel SW. Twenty month study of iproniazid therapy. Disord Nerv System 1959 20: 1.
33. Jenike MA, Surman OS, Cassem NH, Zusky P, Anderson WH. Monoamine oxidase inhibitors in obsessive–compulsive disorder. J Clin Psychiatry 1983; 44: 131.
34. Joffe RT, Swinson RP. Tranylcypromine in primary obsessive–compulsive disorder. J Anx Disord 1990; 4: 365.

35. Vallejo J, Olivares J, Marcos T, Bulbena A, Menchon JM. Clomipramine versus phenelzine in obsessive compulsive disorder. A controlled clinical trial. Br. J Psychiatry 1992; 161: 665.
36. Pato M, Zohar-Kadouch R, Zohar J, Murphy DL. Return of symptoms after discontinuation of clomipramine in patients with obsessive compulsive disorder. Am J Psychiatry 1988; 145: 1543.
37. Fineberg NA, Bullock T, Montgomery DB, Montgomery SA. Serotonin reuptake inhibitors are the treatment of choice in obsessive compulsive disorder. Int Clin Psychopharmacol 1992; 7 (suppl 1): 43.
38. Trethowan WH, Scott PAL. Chlorpromazine in obsessive–compulsive and allied disorders. Lancet 1955; 1: 781.
39. Orvin GH. Treatment of the phobic obsessive compulsive patient with oxazepam: an improved benzodiazepine compound. Psychosomatics 1967; 8: 278.
40. Rao AV. A Controlled trial with "Valium" in obsessive compulsive states. J Ind Med Assoc 1964; 42: 564.
41. Jenner P, Chadwick D, Reynolds EH, Marsden CD. Altered 5-HT metabolism with clonazepam, diazepam and diphenylhydantoin. J Pharmacol 1975; 27: 707.
42. Pato M, Pigott TA, Hill JL, Grover GN, Bernstein SE, Murphy DL. Controlled comparison of buspirone and clomipramine in obsessive–compulsive disorder. Am J Psychiatry 1991; 148: 127.
43. Leonard HL, Swedo SE, Lenane MC et al. A double-blind desipramine substitution during long-term clomipramine treatment in children and adolescents with obsessive compulsive disorder. Arch Gen Psychiatry 1991; 48: 922.
44. Pato M, Murphy DL, De Vane CL. Sustained plasma concentrations of fluoxetine and/or norfluoxetine four and eight weeks after fluoxetine discontinuation. J Clin Psychopharmacol 1991; 11: 224.
45. Pigott TA, Pato M, L'Heureux F. A controlled comparison of adjuvant lithium carbonate or thyroid hormone in clomipramine-treated OCD patients. J Clin Psychopharmacol 1991; 11: 245.
46. McDougle CJ, Price LH, Goodman WK et al. A controlled trial of lithium augmentation in fluvoxamine refractory obsessive–compulsive disorders lack of efficacy. J Clin Psychopharmacol 1991; 11: 175.
47. McDougle CJ, Goodman WK, Leckman JF et al. Limited therapeutic effect of addition of buspirone in fluvoxamine-refractory obsessive compulsive disorder. Am J Psychiatry 1993; 150: 647.
48. Grady TA, Pigott TA, L'Heureux F, Hill JL, Bernstein SE, Murphy DL. Double-blind study of adjuvant buspirone for fluoxetine-treated patients with obsessive compulsive disorder. Am J Psychiatry 1993; 150: 819.
49. McDougle CJ, Goodman WK, Leckman JF, Lee NC, Heninger GR, Price LH. Haloperidol addition in fluvoxamine-refractory obsessive-compulsive disorder: a double-blind, placebo-controlled study in patients with and without tics. Arch Gen Psychiatry 1994; 51: 302–308.
50. von Economo C. Encephalitis Lethargica: Its Sequelae and Treatment. Oxford University Press, London, 1931.
51. Swedo SE, Rapoport JL, Cheslow DL. High prevalence of obsessive–compulsive symptoms in patients with Sydenham's chorea. Am J Psychiatry 1989; 146: 246.
52. Baxter LR, Phelps ME, Mazziotta JC, Guze BH, Schwartz JM, Selin CE. Local cerebral glucose metabolic rates in obsessive–compulsive disorder—A comparison with rates in unipolar depression and in normal controls. Arch Gen

Psychiatry 1987; 44: 211.
53. Baxter LR, Schwartz JM, Mazziotta JC et al. Cerebral glucose metabolic rates in non depressed obsessive–compulsives. Am J Psychiatry 1988; 145: 1560.
54. Tamimi R, Mavissakalian M, Jones B, Olson S. Clomipramine versus fluvoxamine in obsessive–compulsive disorder. Ann Clin Psychiatry 1991; 3: 275.
55. Geltzer J. Limits to chemotherapy of depression. Psychopathology 1986; 19: 108.
56. Montgomery SA, Henry J, McDonald G et al. Selective serotonin reuptake inhibitors: Meta-analysis of discontinuation rates. Int Clin Psychopharmacol 1994; 9: 47.

16 MANAGEMENT OF TREATMENT-RESISTANT OBSESSIVE COMPULSIVE DISORDER: CONCEPTS AND STRATEGIES

Scott L Rauch and Michael A Jenike

Department of Psychiatry, Harvard Medical School and Massachusetts General Hospital, Charlestown, MA, USA

Introduction

The primary purpose of studying disease is to achieve improved under-standing and treatment, if not prevention or cure. Therefore, treatment resistance and its associated phenomena represent an obvious focus of future research. In this chapter, we will define treatment resistance with regard to obsessive compulsive disorder (OCD), scrutinize data as to its prevalence, review the assessment and management of treatment resist-ant OCD, and discuss challenges confronting researchers in this field.

Definitions

The terms "treatment resistant" and "treatment refractory" are often used interchangeably, and only rarely explicity defined. For the purposes of this chapter, we define treatment-resistant OCD patients as those who undergo adequate trials of first-line therapies, without deriving satisfac-tory response. In contradistinction, treatment-refractory patients are those who undergo an exhaustive array of therapies without deriving satisfac-tory response. It should be clear that for any given study of treatment

Current Insights in Obsessive Compulsive Disorder. Edited by E. Hollander, J. Zohar, D. Marazzati and B. Olivier
© 1994 John Wiley & Sons Ltd

Table 16.1 Adequate trials of first-line anti-obsessional therapies

Agent/method	Dose (mg/day)	Duration
Pharmacological*		
Clomipramine	Up to 250	> 10 weeks
Fluoxetine	Up to 80	> 10 weeks
Fluvoxamine	Up to 250	> 10 weeks
Sertraline	Up to 200	> 10 weeks
Paroxetine	Up to 40	> 10 weeks
Behavioral		
Exposure and response		
prevention		> 20 h

*First-line pharmacological treatment should typically proceed with one trial of clomipramine and one trial each of at least two different selective serotonin reuptake inhibitors.

resistance, the operational definitions of "adequate first-line therapies" and "satisfactory response" will substantially influence the findings.

Given the current state of the art in OCD therapy, first-line treatment entails pharmacotherapy with serotonin reuptake inhibitors (SRIs) and behavior therapy consisting of exposure and response prevention. Examples of adequate trials of these various therapies are depicted in Table 16.1. There exist several clinical instruments to measure symptom severity and gauge clinical improvement in OCD. Patients who have persisting symptoms coinciding with a residual Yale–Brown Obsessive Scale (Y-BOCS) (1, 2) score of at least 12, or who fail to have at least a 25% reduction in Y-BOCS score might be considered unsatisfactory responders.

Prevalence

To date, no studies have been performed to determine accurately the prevalence of treatment-resistant OCD. Rather, it is through inference from nonresponder rates in individual therapeutic efficacy trials that estimates of treatment resistance have been generated. From trials of SRIs, for instance, it is suggested that approximately 40% of subjects are nonresponders to monotherapy (3), though the variability in criteria of treatment response should be noted. At first glance, such estimates would be deemed overestimates, since a subpopulation of any cohort failing one first-line therapy might respond to another. Other considerations, however, suggest that these numbers could be underestimates. Among the OCD population at large, some individuals fail to present for treatment at all. Of those who do arrive for treatment, a portion refuse to participate in one or all recommended first-line therapies. Of those who agree to first-line therapies, a subset refuses to do so in the context of research protocols, or are excluded in the presence of comorbidity. Moreover, of those who participate in the research protocols, a number drop out. Finally, of those who respond robustly, some relapse. Therefore, research protocol participants who are completers represent a population that may not be representative of the overall OCD population.

Thus, although it is clear to clinicians who see large numbers of OCD patients that there exists a sizeable subpopulation who are treatment resistant, an accurate estimate of prevalence is not currently available. Furthermore, the subpopulation of OCD patients that "resist" seeking or following through treatment may be even greater, and certainly more difficult to ascertain.

Assessment of treatment resistance

When evaluating OCD patients with apparent treatment resistance consider the following.

Is the diagnosis of OCD correct?

Patients who are mistakenly diagnosed with OCD often suffer from other disorders which do not respond well to anti-obsessionals or behavioral therapies. The differential diagnosis of OCD includes major affective illness with ruminations, other anxiety disorders, psychotic illness with delusions, organic mental disorders (with intrusive thoughts, hallucinations, or stereotypies), habit disorders, impulse control disorders, eating disorder, substance abuse or dependence, borderline personality disorder (especially with ritualized self-injury which should not be considered OCD), or obsessive compulsive personality disorder.

Have adequate first-line therapies for OCD been tried?

It is important to assess pharmacotherapeutic trials for agent (SRIs), dose, duration (at least 10 weeks), and whether trials were discontinued primarily due to inefficacy or intolerance of side effects. Similarly, for behavior therapy, it is important to assess whether the treatment provided was true exposure and response prevention therapy, whether the patient participated in earnest, and the number of therapy hours actually conducted, as well as the patient's response.

Are there comorbid psychiatric diagnoses?

Symptoms of OCD are often unresponsive to treatment when a concurrent psychiatric condition remains untreated. Affective disorders, other anxiety disorders, organic mental disorders, substance abuse disorders, and personality disorders are prime offenders in this regard. Comorbid conditions, when present, must be treated as well, prior to abandoning first-line therapies for OCD.

Once treatment resistance has been established, and a patient's past treatment history reviewed, alternative treatment strategies can be entertained.

Strategies for the treatment-resistant patient

Before proceeding with this section, it is important to emphasize that the problem of treatment resistance and its management is greatly complicated by our lack of understanding of the underlying pathophysiology of OCD and the mechanisms by which different treatments produce their beneficial effects. Consequently, we are reduced to empirical trial and error. Advances in the phenomenology of which patients are most likely to respond (or not respond) to which treatments will represent a tremendous contribution to this field. In keeping with a medical model, the most reliable and valid predictors of treatment response will probably be ones that reflect underlying pathophysiology. Moreover, as data pertaining to the pathophysiology of OCD and the mechanism of effective treatments accrues, we may begin to develop new and more effective treatments.

PHARMACOLOGICAL TREATMENT

The mainstay of pharmacological treatment of OCD is the SRIs, which can be divided into the tricyclic SRI clomipramine and the so-called selective serotonin reuptake inhibitors (SSRIs), including fluoxetine, fluvoxamine, paroxetine, and sertraline. Clomipramine, due to its affinity for non-serotonergic receptors as well, is more likely to cause the side effects associated with anticholinergic and antiadrenergic action. None the less, as the most tried and true anti-obsessional agent, it is suggested that clomipramine might have the greatest anti-obsessional efficacy (4, 5). In contrast, there is evidence that SSRIs are better tolerated (6, 7), especially in patients who are most sensitive to anticholinergic or antiadrenergic effects (e.g. the elderly). Side effects due to serotonergic action seem to be comparable across SRIs (6, 7).

As noted above, first-line pharmacotherapy for OCD should usually entail trials of optimal doses of an SRI for up to 12 weeks. If one SRI fails, especially if the failure is due to side effect intolerance at a low, or submaximal dose, the next step is typically a trial of a different SRI. We recommend that at least one of these trials is with clomipramine, except in cases for which some strong contraindication exists. For patients who fail trials of three different SRIs, alternative pharmacological strategies should be considered (see Tables 16.1 and 16.2).

Table 16.2 Recommended alternative pharmacological strategies

Agent	Dose (mg/day)	Duration (weeks)
Augmentation of serotonin reuptake inhibitors		
Clonazepam	Up to 5	>4
Neuroleptics	Up to 3 (pimozide)*	>4
Fenfluramine	Up to 60	>8
Buspirone†	Up to 30	>8
Alternative agents for monotherapy		
Clonazepam	Up to 5	>4
Phenelzine‡	Up to 90	>10
Tranylcypromine‡	Up to 60	>10
Buspirone	Up to 60	>6
Alternative routes of administration		
Clomipramine, intravenously	Up to 350 mg/infusion × 14 infusions	

*The dose given is for pimozide; *equivalent* doses are appropriate for other neuroleptics. These strategies may be most effective in cases characterized by comorbid tics.
†Buspirone may have its best efficacy as an augmentor in combination with fluoxetine; a high rate of adverse results was observed when buspirone was added to clomipramine.
‡Monoamine oxidase inhibitors (MAOIs) may be indicated when comorbid panic disorder is present. Caution is essential to prevent dangerous adverse effects (e.g. hypertensive crisis or serotonergic syndrome resulting from combined MAOI and serotonin reuptake inhibitor treatment, or inadequate wash-out between trials).

AUGMENTATION STRATEGIES

Augmentation or combination therapy relies on the notion that addition of a second medication enhances the action of some primary agent, so that the combination yields greater efficacy than either agent alone.

Combinations of SRIs

Combinations of different SRIs have been tried (8), although there have been no controlled studies assessing this strategy. Simeon et al (8) reported a case series of six adolescents with clomipramine treatment-resistant OCD all of whom improved (five markedly and one moderately) after addition of fluoxetine. In these cases, and consistent with our clinical experience, patients are often able to tolerate a higher SRI effective dose (blood level) without intolerable side effects (such as undue sedation from clomipramine or agitation with fluoxetine) when agents are combined than when either agent is used in monotherapy. Indeed, since fluoxetine raises the blood levels of tricyclics (9), comparable or higher levels of clomipramine can be achieved at lower dosages.

Fenfluramine

Fenfluramine, an agent marketed as an anorectic, has pharmacological properties of serotonergic reuptake blockade and also causes selective synaptic release of serotonin. Case reports have described its effectiveness when added at doses of 30–45 mg/day to ongoing fluvoxamine therapy (10, 11). Hollander et al (12) published a series of seven OCD patients resistant to clomipramine ($n = 1$), fluoxetine ($n = 5$), and fluvoxamine ($n = 1$), who exhibited clinical improvement after addition of fenfluramine (20–60 mg/day). Reported side effects included tinnitus, impotence, and sexual impulsivity. No larger scale or placebo-controlled studies have been conducted to conclusively determine the efficacy of fenfluramine as an anti-obsessional agent, either as an augmentor or as monotherapy.

Benzodiazepines

There are several early reports in the literature suggesting efficacy of traditional benzodiazepines in the treatment of obsessional symptoms (13). Unfortunately, it is difficult to interpret these findings given the changes in nomenclature, diagnostic criteria, and instruments for the assessment of treatment response. More recently, investigators have reported seven cases of anti-obsessional efficacy with alprazolam (14–17), but no contemporary controlled studies have been conducted to assess the anti-obsessional efficacy of traditional benzodiazepines as either augmentors or monotherapies.

Clonazepam represents a special example in that there are mounting data to suggest that, unlike other benzodiazepines, it has preferential effects on the serotonergic system (18–21). Case reports and a double-blind crossover study have shown its efficacy when used alone as an anti-obsessional, comparing favorably with clomipramine, clonidine and diphenhydramine (22–25). Moreover, another controlled, double-blind study supported its role as an effective augmenting agent when combined with SRIs (26). Clonazepam is typically started at doses of 0.5 mg once or twice per day and may be advanced gradually to maximum doses of approximately 5 mg/day when used as an anti-obsessional. The time course of its anti-obsessional effects has not been specifically studied, but, unlike the SRIs, clinical improvement with clonazepam may occur in hours to days, rather than weeks. Because of its anxiolytic effects clonazepam should be considered early on in OCD patients for whom anxiety is prominent. Furthermore, because of its purported benefits in the treatment of Tourette's syndrome (TS) (27), clonazepam may be an especially prudent option in patients suffering from OCD plus tics or TS.

Neuroleptics

Neuroleptics (dopamine receptor antagonists) have been shown to be efficacious in the treatment of several disorders related to OCD, including TS (28) and body dysmorphic disorder (29, 30). Furthermore, Stein and Hollander (31) reported therapeutic benefit in six of seven patients with SRI-resistant trichotillomania upon addition of the neuroleptic pimozide (1–3 mg/day) to clomipramine or fluoxetine. McDougle et al (32) were the first to formally study the efficacy of neuroleptic augmentation of SRIs in OCD. They found that nine of 17 patients were responders after the addition of neuroleptic (pimozide, thioridazine, or thiothixene, for 2–8 weeks) to fluoxetine, with or without lithium. All 17 subjects were resistant to fluvoxamine, with or without lithium, prior to the trial of neuroleptic augmentation. In this cohort, a comorbid tic disorder was associated with positive response to neuroleptic augmentation. It is also important to acknowledge that the use of neuroleptics as monotherapies for OCD has not been definitively studied. Together, however, these findings suggest that neuroleptic augmentation should be considered for cases of treatment-resistant OCD, and especially in cases in which a tic disorder, body dysmorphic disorder, or trichotillomania is also present.

Antidepressants

Hollander et al (33) reported a case series describing the use of conventional tricyclic antidepressants (nortriptyline or desipramine) as augmentors added to fluoxetine in treatment-resistant OCD in the presence of comorbid depression. In an open trial of 10 subjects, they found that the addition of tricyclics yielded clinical improvement in both disorders. Again, no controlled trials assessing this strategy appear in the literature. More specifically, there is a lack of evidence to support the use of conventional tricyclic antidepressants as anti-obsessional augmentors in the absence of concurrent major depressive illness.

The atypical antidepressant *trazodone* has established antidepressant efficacy, perhaps with particular benefits in the elderly (34). An open trial of trazodone augmentation of fluoxetine for OCD suggested clinical improvement in only four of 13 subjects, and this combination was very poorly tolerated due to sedation in one-third of the cohort (35, 36). A double-blind placebo-controlled study (37) did not support efficacy to trazodone as a monotherapy for OCD. Controlled studies of trazodone as an anti-obsessional augmenting agent have not been performed.

Lithium

Lithium was first reported to be an effective augmenting agent when added to tricyclic antidepressants in the treatment of major depression (38). Subsequently, several case reports appeared in the literature describing therapeutic benefit in OCD when lithium was added to imipramine (39), clomipramine (40–42), desipramine (43), doxepin (42), or fluoxetine (44). In contrast, larger open and controlled trials of lithium augmentation have been disappointing. Hermesh et al (45) reported that only one of 10 patients responded to lithium augmentation when added to clomipramine in an open fashion. Similarly, Jenike et al (46) reported that only one of seven patients derived anti-obsessional benefit from the addition of lithium to fluoxetine in another open trial. McDougle et al (47) conducted a pair of double-blind placebo-controlled studies of lithium plus fluvoxamine, in cases of fluvoxamine-resistant OCD. A cohort of 20 subjects exhibited a statistically significant but clinically minimal improvement while receiving lithium augmentation for 2 weeks, whereas no statistically significant improvement was found in a cohort of 10 subjects receiving lithium augmentation for 4 weeks. Likewise, Pigott et al (48) found no therapeutic benefit from either lithium or L-tri-iodothyronine as augmentors added to clomipramine in a double-blind crossover study of eight OCD subjects who had already partially responded to clomipramine alone. Taken together, these data do not support the efficacy of lithium as an anti-obsessional augmenting agent.

Buspirone

Buspirone is a partial 5-HT$_{1A}$ agonist with a mild side-effect profile and weak anxiolytic properties. Trials of buspirone as monotherapy for OCD have yielded mixed results. Jenike and Baer (49) reported negative results in an open trial ($n = 10$) whereas Pato et al (50) found that buspirone alone had significant anti-obsessional efficacy, comparable with that of clomipramine, in a double-blind controlled trial. When interpreting the head-to-head comparison of clomipramine and buspirone conducted by Pato et al, it must be recognized that the short duration of the trial (6 weeks) probably did not allow for maximal response to clomipramine.

Open trials of buspirone as an augmentor of SRIs have been promising, but data form controlled studies have been unimpressive. In an open trial, Markovitz et al (51) studied the addition of buspirone (up to 30 mg/day) to ongoing fluoxetine ($n = 11$), and found that the combination led to further improvement from the baseline fluoxetine-alone condition. Allessi and Bos (52) reported a single case of buspirone augmentation (30 mg/day) of fluoxetine, with similarly beneficial results. Jenike et al (46) also found clinical improvement of OCD with buspirone augmentation of fluoxetine in 10 subjects compared with a control group receiving fluoxetine alone in an open trial. This difference reached statistical significance at 8, but not at 6, weeks after initiation of buspirone, suggesting a gradual or delayed improvement with this strategy.

More recently, however, Grady et al (53), in a double-blind crossover study of buspirone augmentation of fluoxetine, found no statistically significant benefit from this strategy. Only one of 14 subjects showed superior performance with buspirone vs placebo augmentation of fluoxetine. It is worth noting that this trial followed patients on augmentation for only 4 weeks in each of the placebo and buspirone condition. Therefore, these results are consistent with the earlier report of Jenike et al (46), if one accepts the notion that buspirone augmentation of fluoxetine requires more than 6, or at least 8, weeks to be of significant benefit. Although Grady et al (53) did not follow their subjects beyond 4 weeks, Pigott et al (54) have studied buspirone augmentation of clomipramine for 10 weeks in 14 subjects who were partial responders to clomipramine alone. They found no statistically significant improvement in OCD across the cohort using this strategy. Moreover, while four of 14 subjects had at least a 25% further improvement in symptoms with buspirone augmentation, three of 14 became more than 25% worse with this regimen.

Taken together, these data provide marginal support for the use of buspirone as an augmenting agent in combination with fluoxetine, acknowledging that benefits may not emerge until at least 8 weeks after combination therapy is initiated. Although a few patients may also benefit from the addition of buspirone to clomipramine, this combination is apparently more likely to cause an exacerbation of OCD than is buspirone plus fluoxetine. Augmentation of other SRIs with buspirone remains to be formally studied.

Tryptophan

L-Tryptophan, like lithium, was first used as an augmentor in combination with conventional antidepressants in the treatment of treatment-resistant major depression (55). There is a single case report describing the anti-obsessional efficacy of L-trytophan (6 g/day) augmenting ongoing partial response to clomipramine (40). Relapse was demonstrated with discontinuation of L-tryptophan and efficacy returned upon rechallenge, supporting the role of L-tryptophan as a critical factor in the patient's clinical improvement. No case series or controlled studies of L-tryptophan as an anti-obsessional augmenting agent have been conducted.

Clonidine

Clonidine has received attention as a treatment option for TS (27, 56, 57). In patients suffering from concurrent OCD and TS, clonidine has been reported to have anti-obsessional effects as well (57). Case reports have described anti-obsessional efficacy in OCD without TS for clonidine alone (58), and as an augmentor in combination with clomipramine (59). In contrast, Hollander et al (6) reported two cases in which the addition of clonidine to clomipramine was not effective. In our clinic (MA Jenike et al, unpublished data), we have found clonidine to be poorly tolerated, with side effects of sedation and ataxia leading to discontinuation by 50% of patients in less than 1 month. Furthermore, when used as an augmentor in combination with fluoxetine, anti-obsessional efficacy has been minimal. In an unpublished ongoing open trial, only three of the 17 patients treated with this regimen have showed any improvement, and none have derived clinically meaningful benefit.

ALTERNATIVE PRIMARY AGENTS

There is evidence to support some non-SRIs as candidates for consideration in cases of OCD that are resistant to both SRIs alone and SRIs plus augmentation.

Monoamine oxidase inhibitors

There has been a small case series suggesting anti-obsessional efficacy of monoamine oxidase inhibitors (MAOIs) as monotherapy for OCD in the context of concurrent panic disorder (61). But a controlled trial of the MAOI clorgyline for OCD without concurrent panic disorder demonstrated its inferiority to clomipramine, offering no significant benefit compared with placebo (62). More recently, a randomized double-blind trial was conducted, comparing the anti-obsessional efficacy of the MAOI phenelzine with that of clomipramine (63). Use of either agent was associated with a statistically significant improvement of OCD symptoms over the 12-week study period, and there was no significant difference in efficacy found between the two drugs.

It is important to emphasize that while trials of MAOIs may be worthwhile in otherwise treatment-resistant cases of OCD (perhaps especially in the presence of comorbid panic disorder), special attention must be paid to avoiding the severe adverse effects associated with the interaction between MAOIs and serotonergic medications. For instance, current guidelines suggest that MAOIs should not be combined with either SRIs or buspirone. Furthermore, adequate wash-out periods must be allowed between courses of these agents; (a) > 2 week wash-out after clomipramine before starting an MAOI; (b) > 5 week wash-out after fluoxetine before staring an MAOI; and (c) > 2 week wash-out after discontinuation of an MAOI before starting any serotonergic agent.

Clonazepam

Although several of the augmenting agents discussed so far have been reported to be effective as monotherapies in certain cases, it is worth restating that clonazepam may be a valuable monotherapy in patients with OCD who cannot tolerate SRIs. Indeed, a substantial body of data has accrued to support clonazepam's use as an alternative monotherapy for OCD (13, 22–25).

Dextroamphetamine

Interestingly, although psychostimulants have been observed to induce or exacerbate OCD symptoms in some individuals (64, 65), D-amphetamine has been reported to have anti-obsessional efficacy in others. Insel et al (66) reported the results of a double-blind cross-over study of 14 subjects suffering from OCD, comparing their response with single doses of D-amphetamine (30 mg) vs placebo. They found that 13 of 14 subjects exhibited improvement of their OCD symptoms after stimulant administration, and response to stimulant treatment was statistically superior to placebo for the entire cohort. Subsequently, Joffe et al (67) used a similar design to compare the anti-obsessional efficacy of D-amphetamine (30 mg) vs methylphenidate (40 mg) vs placebo. They also found that D-amphetamine provided a statistically significant anti-obsessional effect in comparison to placebo, whereas methylphenidate did not.

Although these studies converge to support the potential efficacy of D-amphetamine as an anti-obsessional, it is crucial to recognize that these were trials evaluating the effects of *acute* administration. No evidence is available to support the chronic administration of D-amphetamine or methylphenidate as an effective treatment for OCD.

ALTERNATIVE ROUTES OF ADMINISTRATION

In addition to alternative agents, some investigators have reported enhanced anti-obsessional efficacy by virtue of alternative routes of administration. Specifically, Warneke et al (68) reported that intravenous clomipramine infusion produced a reduction in OCD symptoms in a cohort of 30 subjects, with over 50% of subjects responding favorably. Fallon et al (69) subsequently studied five subjects suffering from treatment-refractory OCD using a regimen of 14 clomipramine infusions. They also reported promising preliminary findings from this small group; three subjects were much improved, one subject was minimally improved, and one subject was unchanged. Double-blind placebo-controlled studies of this treatment are needed.

Case reports have also described anti-obsessional efficacy after acute administration of intravenous clonidine (60). Now that clonidine is available in a transdermal preparation, one wonders whether this alternative mode of administration will provide any clinical benefits in OCD.

Behavioral treatment

The importance of behavior therapy in the treatment of OCD cannot be overemphasized. Despite the fact that this mode of therapy probably has the best efficacy and adverse effect profile, it remains underutilized. For instance, in a series of 15 consecutive patients referred to our clinic for review as intractable cases of OCD and potential candidates for cingulotomy, we found that seven of the 15 had not undergone an adequate trial of behavior therapy (SL Rauch, unpublished data). Indeed, with regard to behavior therapy, treatment resistance is often a consequence of resistance to the idea of behavior therapy, either on the part of the patient or the treating clinician.

The first step in overcoming misconceptions about behavior therapy is education. In many places, there are no clinicians who are knowledgeable about behavior therapy. Furthermore, some patients with OCD are reluctant to even discuss behavior therapy because of misconceptions about the provocative nature of exposure and response prevention. Consequently, self-help books represent an invaluable tool for education of patients, their families and friends, as well as clinicians (70, 71). In many communities, lay support groups for OCD can also be an important source of information, and in some cases offer structured self-exposure programs.

Salkovskis (72) has also advocated that clinicians adopt a cognitive framework for addressing the issue of treatment resistance and refusal of behavior therapy. According to this cognitive model, the patient's acceptance of the treatment hinges on his or her beliefs about the therapy. Therefore, after the rationale for behavior therapy has been explained by the clinician, it is important to explore the beliefs of the patient, especially misconceptions and idiosyncratic or irrational congnitions that might lead to noncompliance or treatment refusal. Once these key beliefs are elicited, they can be challenged, in keeping with a cognitive approach to therapy.

Several other techniques may be helpful in identifying or preventing potential sources of resistance (73) (see Table 16.3). First, the role that relatives play in facilitating treatment or impeding the patient's progress must be scrutinized thoroughly. It is often a challenge for relatives to withhold reassurance and abstain from ritualizing on behalf of the patient. Role-playing by relatives together with patients, when observed by the clinician, can help to illustrate helpful vs not helpful methods for the relative. Second, encouraging patients to keep a diary of self-exposure can

Table 16.3 Recommended strategies for behavioral treatment resistance

Adopt a cognitive framework to address treatment refusal
Assess the role of family members via supervised role-playing
Institute use of patient diaries
Be vigilant for subtle discounting, neutralizing, dissociating, or undoing
Consider home visits or other in situ therapy sessions

be helpful in monitoring progress through homework and can also identify trouble spots. Third, the clinician must be vigilant to the presence of subtle discounting, neutralizing, dissociating, or undoing maneuvers on the part of the patient.

In some instances, special settings are necessary to optimize the efficacy of exposure and response prevention therapy. For patients who need more time-intensive sessions, help with tolerating or following through with exposures, or compliance with response prevention, an inpatient setting may be warranted. In contrast, some patients only experience their symptoms in certain settings, such as in their homes, an indication for home visits.

Despite all of these considerations, some patients who earnestly participate in behavior therapy still do not derive a satisfactory amelioration of symptoms, even after more than 20 h of exposure and response prevention work. Foa (74) has suggested that such treatment resistance is most commonly associated with failure to habituate, comorbid affective illness, or overevaluation of ideas. Especially in such cases, a careful review of diagnostic considerations and pharmacotherapeutic strategies must be performed.

NEUROSURGICAL TREATMENT

In cases of chronic, severe and debilitating OCD for which thorough assessment and an exhaustive array of pharmacologic and behavior therapies have not yielded satisfactory response, neurosurgical treatment should be considered. For further discussion of neurosurgical treatment of OCD, see Chapter 17.

Challenges and direction for future research

Research pertaining to the management of treatment-resistant OCD represents a challenging field. The population to be studied is by definition atypical, probably quite heterogeneous, and often difficult to identify or reliably ascertain. We advocate that the following lines of inquiry be pursued in an effort to advance understanding and treatment of treatment-resistant OCD. First a standardized operational definition of treatment resistance will enhance communication between investigators and allow comparison between studies. Second, efforts must be redoubled in an attempt to discover the underlying pathophysiology of treatment-responsive OCD and associated disorders, such as TS, trichotillomania, and body dysmorphic disorder. Third, the mechanism of action by which first-line therapies confer their anti-obsessional efficacy needs to be determined. Fourth, OCD subtyping based on clinical phenomenology must be further explored, emphasizing aspects that provide predictive significance with regard to treatment response. Fifth, double-blind controlled studies of various promising pharmacological augmenting strategies must be conducted. Sixth, education of patients, their families, and clinicians must become a public health priority. Such education should emphasize both the nature of the disorder and the efficacy of available treatments.

Summary

Obsessive compulsive disorder is a common disorder for which currently available first-line treatments are often effective. Although there is no universally accepted definition of treatment resistance, and the prevalence of unsatisfactory treatment response is not known, it is clear that a substantial number of people with OCD fail to respond fully to first-line therapies. We have reviewed appropriate assessment of such patients and the available data pertaining to the efficacy of alternative treatment strategies. Lacking sufficient data from controlled studies, recommendations about the management of treatment-resistant OCD are necessarily tentative.

Based on the available data, failing behavioral therapy and adequate trials of three SRIs (including one trial of clomipramine), augmentation with clonazepam, fenfluramine, or neuroleptics (if tics are present) represent promising second-line pharmacological strategies. Buspirone augmentation of fluoxetine may also be effective, but probably requires at least 8 weeks to yield clinical benefits. Failing augmentation, alternative monotherapy trials of clonazepam, an MAOI (after adequate wash-out of serotonergic medications) or intravenous clomipramine might be considered. Education about behavior therapy as an effective first-line therapy, along with a cognitive approach to patient resistance, can optimize the likelihood of treatment response. We have reviewed several specific strategies for combating treatment resistance. Failing an exhaustive array of available behavioral and pharmacological treatments, neurosurgical intervention should be considered in the most severe cases of OCD.

Future research should seek to define criteria for treatment resistance, determine the pathophysiology of OCD and related disorders, delineate the mechanism of action for effective anti-obsessional treatments, explore clinical phenomenology in an effort to identify predictors of treatment response, determine the efficacy of various augmentation strategies via double-blind placebo-controlled trials, and promote education about OCD and its treatment.

References

1. Goodman WK, Price LH, Rasmussen SA et al. The Yale–Brown Obsessive Compulsion Scale (Y-BOCS), part I: Development, use, and reliability. Arch Gen Psychiatry 1989; 46: 1006–1011.
2. Goodman WK, Price LH, Rasmussen SA et al. The Yale–Brown Obsessive Compulsion Scale (Y-BOCS), part II: Validity. Arch Gen Psychiatry 1989; 46: 1012–1016.
3. Goodman WK, McDougle CJ, Price LH. Pharmacotherapy of obsessive compulsive disorder. J Clin Psychiatry 1992; 53 (suppl): 29–37.
4. Jenike MA, Hyman SE, Baer L et al. Fluvoxamine for obsessive–compulsive disorder: a double-blind, placebo-controlled trial in 40 patients. Am J Psychiatry 1990; 147: 1209–1215.
5. Pigott TA, L'Heureux FL, Murphy DL. Pharmacologic approaches to treatment-resistant OCD patients. Present at First International Obsessive–Compulsive Disorder Congress, Capri, Italy, 12–13 Mar 1993.
6. Pigott TA, Pato MT, Bernstein SE et al. Controlled comparison of clomipramine and fluoxetine in the treatment of obsessive–compulsive disorder: behavioral and biological results. Arch Gen Psychiatry 1990; 47: 926–932.
7. Grimsley SR, Jann MW. Paroxetine, sertraline, and fluvoxamine: new selective serotonin reuptake inhibitors. Clin Pharmacol 1992; 11: 930–957.
8. Simeon JG, Thatte S, Wiggins D. Treatment of adolescent obsessive–compulsive disorder with a clomipramine-fluoxetine combination. Psychopharmacol Bull 1990; 26: 285–290.
9. Aranow RB, Hudson JI, Pope HG et al. Elevated antidepressant plasma levels after addition of fluoxetine. Am J Psychiatry 1989; 146: 911–913.
10. Hollander E, Liebowitz MR. Augmentation of antiobsessional treatment with fenfluramine. Am J Psychiatry 1988; 145: 1314–1315.
11. Judd FK, Chua P, Lynch C et al. Fenfluramine augmentation of clomipramine treatment of obsessive compulsive disorder. Aust J Psychiatry 1991; 25: 412–414.
12. Hollander E, DeCaria CM, Schneider FR et al Fenfluramine augmentation of serotonin reuptake blockade antiobsessional treatment. J Clin Psychiatry 1990; 51: 119–123.
13. Hewlett WA. The use of benzodiazepines in obsessive compulsive disorder and Tourette's syndrome. Psychiatr Ann 1993: 23: 309–316.
14. Hardy JL. Obsessive compulsive disorder [letter]. Can J Psychiatry 1986; 31: 290.
15. Ketter T, Chun D, Lu F. Alprazolam in the treatment of compulsive symptoms [letter]. J Clin Psychopharmacol 1986; 6: 59–60.
16. Tollefson G. Alprazolam in the treatment of obsessive symptoms. J Clin Psychopharmacol 1985; 5: 39–42.
17. Tesar GE, Jenike MA. Alprazolam as treatment for a case of obsessive–compulsive disorder. Am J Psychiatry 1984; 141: 689–690.
18. Jenner P, Chadwick D, Reynolds EH, Marsden CD. Altered 5-HT metabolism

with clonazepam, diazepam and diphenylhydantoin. J Pharm Pharmacol 1975; 27: 707–710.

19. Hwang EC, Van Woert MH. Antimyoclonic action of clonazepam: The role of serotonin. Eur J Pharmacol 1979; 60: 31–40.

20. Pratt J, Jenner P, Reynolds EH, Marsden CD. Clonazepam induces decreased serotoninergic activity in the mouse brain. Neuropharmacology 1979; 18: 791–799.

21. Wagner HR, Reches A, Yablonskaya E, Fahn S. Clonazepam-induced up-regulation of serotonin₁ and serotonin₂ binding sites in rat frontal cortex. Adv Neurol 1986; 43: 645–651.

22. Bacher NM. Clonazepam treatment of obsessive compulsive disorder [letter]. J Clin Psychiatry 1990; 51: 168–169.

23. Bodkin A, White K. Clonazepam in the treatment of obsessive compulsive disorder. J Clin Psychiatry 1989; 50: 265–266.

24. Hewlett WA, Vinogradov S, Agras WS. Clonazepam treatment of obsessions and compulsions. J Clin Psychiatry 1990; 51: 158–161.

25. Hewlett W, Vinogradov S, Agras W. Clomipramine, clonazepam, and clonidine treatment of obsessive compulsive disorder. J Clin Psychopharmacol 1992; 12: 420–430.

26. Pigott TA, L'Heureux F, Rubenstein CS, Hill JL, Murphy DL. A controlled trial of clonazepam augmentation in OCD patients treated with clomipramine or fluoxetine. American Psychiatry Association Annual Meeting, Washington, DC, 2–7 May 1992.

27. Troung DD, Bressman S, Shale H, Fahn S. Clonazepam, haloperidol, and clonidine in tic disorders. South Med J 1988; 81: 1103–1105.

28. Shapiro E, Shapiro AK, Fulop G et al. Controlled study of haloperidol, pimozide and placebo for the treatment of Gilles de la Tourette's syndrome. Arch Gen Psychiatry 1989; 46: 722–730.

29. Phillips KA. Body dysmorphic disorder: the distress of imagined ugliness. Am J Psychiatry 1991; 148: 1138–1149.

30. Opler LA, Feinberg SS. The role of pimozide in clinical psychiatry: A review. J Clin Psychiatry 1991; 52: 221–233.

31. Stein D, Hollander E. Low-dose pimozide augmentation of serotonin re-uptake blockers in the treatment of trichotillomania. J Clin Psychiatry 1992; 53: 123–126.

32. McDougle CJ, Goodman WK, Price LH et al. Neuroleptic addition in fluvoxamine refractory obsessive compulsive disorder. Am J Psychiatry 1990; 147: 652–654.

33. Hollander E, Mullen L, DeCaria CM et al. Obsessive compulsive disorder depression, and fluoxetine. J Clin Pschiatry 1991; 52: 418–422.

34. Gerner RH. Geriatric depression and treatment with trazodone. Psychopathology 1987; 20 (suppl): 82–91.

35. Jenike MA. Approaches to the patient with treatment-refractory obsessive–compulsive disorder. J Clin Psychiatry 1990; 51 (2, suppl): 15–21.

36. Jenike MA. Management of patients with treatment-resistant obsessive–compulsive disorder. In: Obsessive–Compulsive Disorders (eds Pato MT, Zohar J). APA Press, Washington DC, 1991, pp 135–156.

37. Pigott TA, L'Heureux F, Rubinstein CS, Bernstein SE, Hill JL, Murphy DL. Double blind, placebo-controlled study of trazodone in patients with obsessive compulsive disorder. J Clin Psychopharmacol 1992; 12: 156–162.

38. DeMontigny C, Grunberg F, Mayer A et al. Lithium induces rapid relief of depression in tricyclic antidepressant drug non-responders. Br J Psychiatry 1981; 138: 252–256.

39. Stern TA, Jenike MA. Treatment of obsessive–compulsive disorder with lithium carbonate. Psychosomatics 1983; 24: 671–673.
40. Rasmussen SA. Lithium and tryptophan augmentation in clomipramine-resistant obsessive–compulsive disorder. Am J Psychiatry 1984; 141: 1283–1285.
41. Feder R. Lithium augmentation of clomipramine. J Clin Psychiatry 1988; 49: 458.
42. Golden RN, Morris JE, Sack DA. Combined lithium-tricyclic treatment of obsessive–compulsive disorder. Biol Psychiatry 1988; 23: 181–185.
43. Eisenberg J, Asnis G. Lithium as an adjunct treatment in obsessive–compulsive disorder. Am J Psychiatry 1985; 142: 663.
44. Howland RH. Lithium augmentation of fluoxetine in the treatment of OCD and major depression: A case report. Can J Psychiatry 1991; 36: 154–155.
45. Hermesh H, Aizenberg D, Munitz H. Trazodone treatment in clomipramine-resistant obsessive–compulsive disorder. Clin Neuropharmacology 1990; 13: 322–328.
46. Jenike MA, Baer L, Buttolph L. Buspirone augmentation of fluoxetine in patients with obsessive–compulsive disorder. J Clin Psychiatry 1991; 52: 13–14.
47. McDougle CJ, Price LH, Goodman WK et al. A controlled trial of lithium augmentation in fluovoxamine-refractory obsessive compulsive disorder: lack of efficacy. J Clin Psychopharmacol 1991; 11: 175–184.
48. Pigott TA, Pato MT, L'Heureux F et al. A controlled comparison of adjuvant lithium carbonate or thyroid hormone in clomipramine-treated patients with obsessive compulsive disorder. J Clin Psychopharmacol 1991; 11: 242–248.
49. Jenike MA, Baer L. Buspirone in obsessive–compulsive disorder: An open trial. Am J Psychiatry 1988; 145: 1285–1286.
50. Pato MT, Pigott TA, Hill JL, Grover GN, Bernstein S, Murphy DL. Controlled comparison of buspirone and clomipramine in obsessive–compulsive disorder. Am J Psychiatry 1991; 148: 127–129.
51. Markovitz PJ, Stagno SJ, Calabrese JR. Buspirone augmentation of fluoxetine on obsessive–compulsive disorder. Am J Psychiatry 1990; 147: 798–800.
52. Alessi N, Bos T. Buspirone augmentatiion of fluoxetine in a depressed child with obsessive–compulsive disorder. Am J Psychiatry 1991; 148: 1605–1606.
53. Grady TA, Pigott TA, L'Heureux F, Hill JL, Bernstein SE, Murphy DL. A double-blind study of adjuvant buspirone hydrochloride in fluoxetine treated patients with obsessive compulsive disorder. Am J Psychiatry 1993; 150: 819–821.
54. Pigott TA, L'Heureux F, Hill JL, Bihari K, Bernstein SE, Murphy DL. A double-blind study of adjuvant buspirone hydrochloride in clomipramine-treated patients. J Clin Psychopharmacol 1992; 12: 11–18.
55. Walinder J, Skott A, Carlsson A et al. Potentiation of the antidepressant action of clomipramine by tryptophan. Arch Gen Psychiatry 1976; 33: 1384–1389.
56. Leckman JF, Hardin MT, Riddle MA, Stevenson J, Ort SI, Cohen DJ. Clonidine treatment of Gilles de la Tourette's syndrome. Arch Gen Psychiatry 1991; 48: 324–328.
57. Cohen DJ, Detlor J, Young JG et al. Clonidine ameliorates Gilles de la Tourette syndrome. Arch Gen Psychiatry 1980; 37: 1350–1357.
58. Knesevich JW. Successful treatment of obsessive–compulsive disorder. J Clin Psychopharmacol 1982; 7: 278–279.
59. Lipsedge MS, Prothero W. Clonidine and clomipramine in obsessive–compulsive disorder [letter]. Am J Psychiatry 1987; 144: 965–966.

60. Hollander E, Fay M, Liebowitz MR. Clonidine and clomipramine in obsessive–compulsive disorder. Am J Psychiatry 1988; 145: 388–389.

61. Jenike MA, Surman OS, Cassem NH et al. Monoamine oxidase inhibitors in obsessive–compulsive disorder. J Clin Psychiatry 1983; 44: 131–132.

62. Insel TR, Murphy DL, Cohen RM et al. Obsessive compulsive disorder: A double blind trial of clomipramine and clorgyline. Arch Gen Psychiatry 1983; 40: 605–612.

63. Vallejo J, Olivares, J, Marcos T, Bulbena A, Menchon J. Clomipramine versus phenelzine in obsessive–compulsive disorder: A controlled trial. Br J Psychiatry 1992; 161: 665–670.

64. Satel AL, McDougle CJ. Obsessions and compulsions associated with cocaine abuse [letter]. Am J Psychiatry 1991; 148: 947.

65. Ellinwood EH Jr. Amphetamine psychosis: A multidimensional process. Semin Psychiatry 1969; 1: 208–226.

66. Insel TR, Hamilton JA, Guttmacher LM, Murphy DL. D-Amphetamine in obsessive compulsive disorder. Psychopharmacology 1983; 80: 231–235.

67. Joffe RT, Swinson RP, Levitt AJ. Acute psychostimulant challenge in primary obsessive compulsive disorder. J Clin Psychopharmacol 1991; 11: 237–241.

68. Warneke LB. The use of intravenous chlorimipramine therapy in obsessive compulsive disorder. Can J Psychiatry 1989; 34: 853–859.

69. Fallon BA, Campeas R, Schneier FR et al. Open trial of intravenous clomipramine in five treatment refractory patients with obsessive compulsive disorder. J Neuropsychiatry 1992; 4: 70–75.

70. Baer L. Getting Control. Little Brown, Boston, 1991.

71. Marks IM. Fears, Phobias and Rituals. Oxford University Press, New York, 1987.

72. Salkovskis PM Cognitive techniques to limit non-compliance. First International Obsessive–Compulsive Disorder Congress, Capri, Italy, 12–13 March 1993 [abstr].

73. Marks IM. Resistance to exposure therapy. First International Obsessive–Compulsive Disorder Congress, Capri, Italy, 12–13 March 1993 [abstr].

74. Foa EB. Failure in treating obsessive compulsives. Behav Res Ther 1979; 17: 169–176.

17 CAPSULOTOMY AND CINGULOTOMY AS TREATMENTS FOR MALIGNANT OBSESSIVE COMPULSIVE DISORDER: AN UPDATE

Per Mindus*, Scott L Rauch[†], Håkan Nyman*,
Lee Baer[‡], Gunnar Edman* and Michael A Jenike[‡]

*Department of Psychiatry, Karolinska Hospital, Stockholm, Sweden
†Department of Psychiatry, Harvard Medical School and Massachusetts General Hospital, Charlestown, MA, USA
‡Department of Psychiatry, Harvard Medical School, Boston, MA, USA

Introduction

> The greater the ignorance, the greater the dogmatism
>
> Sir William Osler, Aphorism No. 173

Although the majority of patients with obsessive compulsive disorder (OCD) respond well to behavioral techniques of exposure and response prevention, to pharmacotherapy, or, more commonly, to combinations of the two approaches, a small percentage of OCD patients remain refractory to such treatment and are severely disabled by their symptoms. The term "malignant OCD" has been suggested for this extreme group of patients (1, 2). There is considerable, but uncontrolled, evidence that patients with malignant OCD may respond to neurosurgical intervention (2–8), and such operations are performed, although to a very limited extent, both in the Western world and elsewhere.

Neurosurgical treatment for mental illness, or psychosurgery, may be

Current Insights in Obsessive Compulsive Disorder. Edited by E. Hollander, J. Zohar, D. Marazzati and B. Olivier
© 1994 John Wiley & Sons Ltd

defined as the destruction of apparently normal brain tissue with the objective of alleviating symptoms that have proved refractory to conventional, nonsurgical treatment. "Psychosurgery" is an obvious misnomer, since it is psychiatric patients—not the psyche—that are operated on. More importantly, the term tends to be associated with primitive procedures of the past (e.g. frontal lobotomy), which differ decidedly from today's interventions in a number of important aspects. Contemporary neurosurgical treatment of mental illness has more refined indications, contraindications, targets, and surgical techniques. Consequently, the efficacy and risk profile of today's procedures is far superior than was the case earlier; these operations are, instead, analogous to modern neurosurgery for uncontrollable epileptic seizures, hyperkinesias, or pain conditions. For these reasons, the term psychosurgery should be dropped in favor of "neurosurgery".

None the less, today's restricted, stereotactic operations have had to bear the brunt of criticism more properly aimed at yesterday's extensive, free-hand procedures (9). Although that criticism has been "able to knock down psychosurgery, [it has] not been able to knock it out" (4 p. 531). One independent observer (10 p. xv) notes: "For some of the millions . . . with intractable and disabling mental illness, surgery could be a threat but could also be a benefit that is systematically and unfairly denied them by disinterest, fear, and heavy political opposition", illustrating the complexity of the problem and the ethics involved (9, 11). Another factor that may be contributing is, of course, ignorance. Almost without exception, neurosurgical candidates report having had great difficulties in obtaining information about this last-resort therapy. Although Sir William's aphorism is applicable to all forms of medicine, it would appear to be particularly pertinent in the field of neurosurgery for mental illness.

General guidelines for selecting candidates for neurosurgery

Only few centers have developed modern stereotactic neurosurgry as a treatment for mental illness. In most of these centers, multidisciplinary committees have been established in order to evaluate potential candidates for surgical intervention, because the patients referred for these procedures are complex cases. The difficult clinical judgments to be made regarding candidacy require expertise in general psychiatry, neuropsychiatry, neuropsychology, neurology, and neurosurgery. The following are general selection guidelines: adult patients may be selected who fulfill the current diagnostic criteria for OCD and who have been able to function adequately, or almost adequately, at least for some years before falling ill. Psychotic disorders should be ruled out. The illness must be causing considerable suffering as evidenced by, for example, a current Yale–Brown Obsessive Compulsive Scale (Y-BOCS) score of at least 26 (one inclusion criterion for recent drug trials), and must be causing considerable reduction in the patient's psychosocial functioning as evidenced by, for example, a score of 50 or lower on the General Assessment of Functioning (GAF) scale. The OCD must have been subject to intensive and adequate treatment for a time sufficient to establish its refractory nature. In practice, this means a minimum of 5 years, although the mean duration of illness in most reports exceeds 15 years.

Opinion may vary among experts, or over time, as to the exact criteria used to define treatment-refractory OCD. There is a consensus, however, that patients with OCD should have failed an exhaustive array of alternative treatments before considered for neurosurgical treatment. Questions from the committee about the accuracy of the diagnosis or the adequacy of prior therapies at the time of referral are common. The issue in individual cases is often to determine *when* enough is enough. Given the chronicity and the severity of the disorder in neurosurgical candidates, prolonged expectation may put the patient at increased risk for somatic and psychiatric complications, including suicide. Ultimately, good clinical judgment must be the guiding principle, as always.

Some candidates appear to regard their symptoms as reasonable, not ego-dystonic (which, in the past, has posed a diagnostic problem, since the DSM-III-R require insight into the senseless nature of the OC symptoms in OCD; see Chapter 6). Terms like "obsessional psychosis" (1, 12) or "schizo-obsessive" (13) have indeed been proposed for such cases. After many years of observation it should be clear, however, that a particular candidate for neurosurgery does not suffer from psychotic illness.

There are no systematic data on the response to neurosurgery in the rare cases of OCD who also suffer from schizophrenia.

Indications for neurosurgery in OCD

Although both indications and contraindications may vary slightly between centers they usually include the following:

1. The patient fulfills currrent diagnostic criteria for OCD.
2. The duration of illness exceeds 5 years.
3. The disorder is causing substantial suffering, as evidenced by ratings.
4. The disorder is causing substantial reduction in the patient's psychosocial functioning, as evidenced by ratings.
5. Current, up-to-date treatment options tried systematically for at least 5 years have either been without appreciable effect on the symptoms or had to be discontinued due to intolerable side effects.
6. If a comorbid psychiatric condition is present, this disorder must

also have been thoroughly addressed with appropriate trials of first-line treatments.

7. The prognosis, without neurosurgical intervention, is considered poor.
8. The patient gives informed consent.
9. The patient agrees to participate in the preoperative evaluation program.
10. The patient agrees to participate in the postoperative rehabilitation program.
11. The referring physician is willing to acknowledge responsibility for the postoperative long-term management of the patient.

Contraindications

Again, these may vary between centers, and some are considered only relative contraindications (e.g. upper age limit):

1. Age below 20 or over 65 years.
2. A complicating other, current or lifetime, Axis I diagnosis, for example organic brain syndrome, delusional disorder, or manifest abuse of alcohol, sedative, or illicit drugs. Some authors include somatoform disorders (11). The term complicating is crucial here; for a condition to qualify as complicating, it must substantially complicate function, treatment, or the patient's ability to comply with treatment, or lead to serious adverse events such as overdosage, paradoxical reactions, etc.
3. A complicating current Axis II diagnosis from clusters A (for example, paranoid personality disorder) or B (for example, antisocial, or histrionic personality disorder) is regarded by many experts as a contraindication (although there are no systematic studies published to support this). A current cluster C personality disorder (for example, avoidant or obsessive personality disorder) need not be considered a contraindication because it may, in fact, disappear with successful treatment of the coexistent OCD.
4. The patient has a complicating, current Axis III diagnosis with brain pathology, e.g. atrophy or tumor.

Procedures currently in use

As mentioned earlier only a few centers have developed neurosurgical treatment programs for otherwise intractable OCD. Each center tends to favor one particular type of intervention, the choice of which most often seems to have been determined by local tradition rather than by actual comparison of the relative merits of different methods. There are four procedures in current use: capsulotomy, cingulotomy, subcaudate tracto-tomy, and limbic leukotomy, all of which are stereotactic interventions. This means that a so-called stereotactic frame is mounted on the patient's head and the location of the target area in the patient's brain is then defined neuroradiologically relative to the frame by its coordinates in a three-dimensional space. The system permits high accuracy (± 1 mm) in placing the lesion where intended. As warranted clinically, surgery may be performed under general anesthesia or, more commonly, under local anesthesia with light sedation of the patient. Usually, the lesions proper are produced by means of the radiofrequency-induced heating of the tip of a thermistor electrode introduced into the target area. Normally, the patient will spend the first few postoperative days at the neurosurgical unit and is then transferred to the referring hospital for the postoperative rehabilitation program. In the following sections each procedure is de-scribed briefly.

THERMOCAPSULOTOMY

Developed in Sweden, this procedure has been in use now for three decades in Europe in the treatment of refractory anxiety disorders includ-ing OCD, and it has recently been taken up by neurosurgeons in the USA as well. Two surgical techniques for capsulotomy have been described, the radiofrequency thermolesion, and the radiosurgical, or gamma, capsulotomy techniques.

In the thermocapsulotomy procedure [(14, 15); for reviews, see Sweet et al (5) Meyerson et al (16)], the operation is performed under local anaesthesia and with light sedation of the patient. Only minimal hair shaving is involved, causing no significant postoperative cosmetic prob-lem. The coordinates of the target area in the anterior limb of the internal capsule are determined with CT or, preferably, MRI. Small bilateral burr holes are made just behind the coronary suture, and monopolar elec-trodes with a diameter of 1.5 mm are inserted into the target area. Thermolesions are then produced by the heating of the uninsulated tip of the electrode to approximately 75°C for 75 s, creating a lesion approxi-mately 5 mm wide and 15–18 mm in depth. Figure 17.1 shows the MRIs of the thermolesions in the anterior limb of the internal capsule of a patient treated for malignant OCD.

While the lesions are being produced, the patients do not report any subjective sensations. Postoperative headache is uncommon. As with several other procedures in current use (with the possible exception of cingulotomy), fatigue may be a prominent feature in some but not in all cases during the first week after thermocapsulotomy, and a decrease in initiative and mental drive may be noted during the first 2–3 months. This appears to correlate with circumlesional edema, as determined by

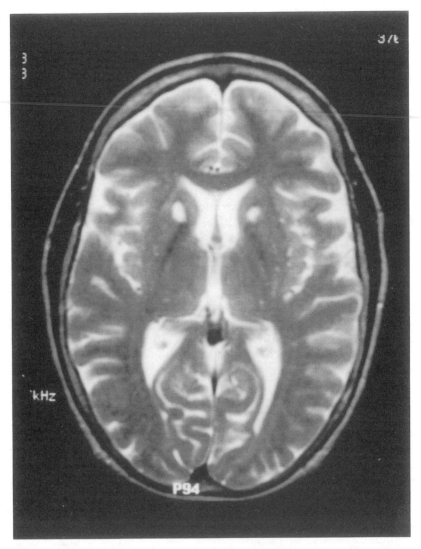

Figure 17.1 Magnetic resonance image demonstrating the thermocapsulotomy lesions in the anterior limb of the internal capsules of a patient with malignant obsessive compulsive disorder

MRI, and disappears simultaneously with its resolution (P Mindus et al, unpublished data); from 3 months, initiative and mental drive have usually returned to preoperative levels.

As is the case with cingulotomy, a second capsulotomy may be performed, if warranted clinically. In a recent, prospective follow up of 22 consecutive OCD patients undergoing thermocapsulotomy, seven patients had a second intervention. Four of the seven patients benefited from the second capsulotomy. Typically, these cases initially responded favorably to the first intervention but relapsed within the first 3 or 4 months. This time course may be related to the time of the resolution of the postoperative circumlesional edema, and may be taken to indicate that the initial lesions were suboptimal with regard to volume, configuration, or site. In a previous small study, we found significant correlations between outcome of capsulotomy and the site/size of the lesions as determined using MRI by two independent evaluators who had no access to the clinical data (17).

GAMMA CAPSULOTOMY

In the radiosurgical, or gamma, capsulotomy procedure, also developed in Sweden (18), the lesions are produced by the crossfiring of approximately 200 narrow beams of 60-cobalt γ irradiation from a stereotactic γ unit, also called the Gamma Knife (though not a knife at all). Craniotomy and shaving are unnecessary. The biological effect of each individual γ beam is negligible. At their point of focus, however, their effects are combined into inducing a radionecrosis (19). The method has been successfully used now for more than 20 years in the treatment of, for example, arteriovenous malformations and fistulae, acoustic neurinomas, craniopharyngeomas, pituitary adenomas, and other forms of deep-seated pathological intracranial processes [for a full acount, see Steiner et al (20)]. No case of radiation-induced malignancy had been observed in the over 20 years during which the Gamma Knife has been in use.

To date, only approximately 40 anxiety patients have undergone gamma capsulotomy, experience of which is considerably less extensive than is the thermocapsulotomy technique. Published results appear comparable, however [(17, 21, 22); see also Mindus (7) and Guo et al (23)]. From a strict neurosurgical viewpoint, gamma capsulotomy can be performed on an outpatient basis. The pros and cons of thermo- and gamma capsulotomy have recently been summarized (24). In one small gamma capsulotomy study, very high radiation doses were, for various reasons, given to multiple targets in the capsule. This considerably increased the risk of undesired side effects such as chronic fatigue, apathy, disinhibition, or other symptoms indicative of involvement of the frontal lobes (23). Today, considerably lower radiation doses are given to smaller target volumes in gamma capsulotomy.

CINGULOTOMY

Cingulotomy is, together with capsulotomy, the most commonly reported neurosurgical procedure in anxiety disorders (4), and has been the neurosurgical approach of choice over the last 20 years in the USA and in Canada for intractable pain and major depression in particular (25, 26), but also in OCD and in non-OCD anxiety disorder [for reviews, see Mindus and Jenike (2) and Chiocca and Martuza (27)]. The procedure is regarded by experts as being relatively benign, having a very low incidence of complications and transient or late side effects, relative to the potential benefit it may afford the patient. The details of the procedure have been described elsewhere (5, 25, 28, 29). In brief, the operation is performed under local anesthesia, and involves only minimal hair shaving just behind the anterior hair line, usually causing no significant postoperative cosmetic problem. Bilateral burr holes, approximately 12 mm in diameter, are made and a magnetic resonance image (MRI) is obtained to help visualize the targets. Electrically insulated thermistor electrodes are introduced stereotactically into the cingulate bundles. The lesions are created by the radiofrequency-induced heating of the tip of the electrode to 80–85°C for 100 s, creating symmetrical lesions in the anterior cingulum bilaterally, approximately 10 mm in diameter and 10 or 20 mm in vertical height. Thermistor electrode-induced lesions in the anterior cingulum of a patient with malignant OCD are shown in Figure 17.2. Postoperative confusion and headache are unusual. It is not unusual, however, for a second intervention to be necessary, in which the lesions are extended. For example, in a retrospective follow up of 33 OCD cases treated with cingulotomy, a mean of 1.9 procedures per case were recorded (30). This is usually done after 6 months, when it is clear that no more benefit may be expected from the operation.

OTHER PROCEDURES

Two other procedures in current use should be mentioned briefly. These are subcaudate tractotomy and limbic leukotomy, both developed in London.

In subcaudate tractotomy the lesions may be created either by using conventional thermistor electrodes or by means of β irradiation from rods, 1×7 mm, made radioactive with 90-yttrium, and inserted stereotactically into the target area beneath the head of the caudate nucleus. The details of the operation have been described elsewhere (31–33). The majority of patients operated on with subcaudate tractotomy have chronic, incapacitating and otherwise intractable affective disorder, but patients with OCD or with non-OCD anxiety disorders have also been operated on (32, 34, 25). To date, over 1200 psychiatric patients are reported to have undergone this procedure in the UK alone (36). Additionally, approximately 20 patients with anxiety disorders have undergone subcaudate tractotomy in Belgium and in The Netherlands. In cases with extensive frontal sinuses,

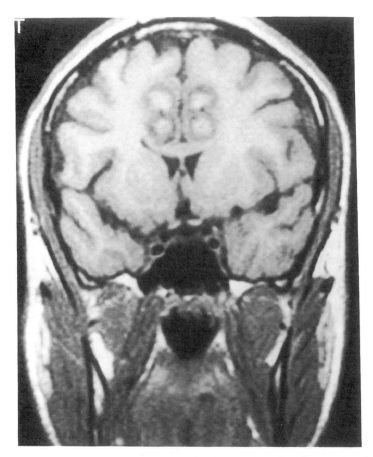

Figure 17.2 Magnetic resonance image demonstrating the thermocingulotomy lesions in the anterior cingulum of a patient with malignant OCD

which pose a technical problem for performing subcaudate tractotomy, capsulotomy is preferred (J Cosyns, personal communication, 1993).

Limbic leukotomy is a multitarget procedure essentially combining subcaudate tractotomy lesions with multiple lesions in the cingulum, with the theoretically interesting and clinically appealing rationale of influencing both the obsessive compulsive component of the illness (by means of the subcaudate lesions) and the anxiety component (believed to be mediated by the cingulum), which would produce better results in OCD than lesions in either site alone [(37, 38); for a review, see Kelly (39)]. The 10 lesions, each approximately 6–10 mm in diameter, are produced by means of radiofrequency-heated electrodes. Side effects include transient postoperative confusion and headache.

Unfortunately, there is no controlled study directly comparing the relative efficacy of subcaudate tractotomy and limbic leukotomy. The comparison of published results in OCD following these two procedures, an indirect approach obviously marred with several methodological shortcomings, does not appear to support the idea of a superior effect of the combined approach, however, since outcome figures are comparable.

Methodological problems

Before discussing the clinical outcome of neurosurgical intervention in malignant OCD, several methodological issues need to be considered. Many earlier reports are only retrospective, and estimates of outcome with documented validity and reliability have not generally been available at the time. The diagnostic practices have changed in the many years during which the studies have been carried out. Only two studies using reference groups for comparison are available. Because the interventions are performed at only a few centers, very few physicians are experienced in the field. Accordingly, it is common that the clinician who was responsible for the selection and the treatment of the patients also performed the assessment of clinical outcome, perhaps after only a short period of observation. The inherent bias problems are obvious.

ESTIMATES OF OUTCOME

In virtually all published reports, a modification of the Pippard Postoperative Rating Scale or an equivalent has been used to monitor clinical outcome [(14, 25); for reviews, see Sweet and Meyerson (5), Mindus (7)] Valenstein (40) noted that in many reports the results "were based on subjective (or poorly defined) criteria" (p. 158), such as the Pippard scale. However, in a recent monograph on the clinical outcome of capsulotomy in patients with OCD and non-OCD anxiety disorders, Mindus (7) found statistically significant correlations between the scores on the modified Pippard scale and those on more recently developed rating scales reported to have high reliabilities and validities. It has been assumed (4, 7) that the many studies that report clinical outcome in the form of Pippard scores, or an equivalent, may yield worthwhile information. The Pippard scale has five points. A score of A indicates that the patient is free of the symptoms that led to surgery. Those with a score of B are much improved, with some symptoms remaining but considerably alleviated, and not requiring additional treatment. The score of C denotes patients who are slightly improved, most symptoms remaining but somewhat relieved; these patients are still in need of medication. Those who are unchanged are given a score of D, and a score of E is assigned to those who are worse after surgery than before it.

RATER BIAS

This is a related, problematic area. Although opinion from the referring physician and from family members are reported to have included in the overall estimate of outcome in most studies, their informants' ratings have not been documented separately. Furthermore, both family members and the referring physician may, of course, be biased (e.g. criticizing or defending the decision to operate on a given patient). Also, there is a lack of published assessments by independent experts. Valenstein (40) reviewed studies reported between 1971 and 1976, and noted that in the vast majority of instances outcome was determined by the neurosurgeons who had themselves been responsible for the operations, or by associated psychiatrists. According to such criteria, 62.8% and 24.3% of 89 OCD patients undergoing cingulotomy reported by three independent groups were assigned to the two best of the outcome categories used in the studies. Ballantine et al (41) compared outcome estimates made by the research team with those made by the patient, the relatives, and the referring physician. Unfortunately, only 84 (55%) of their sample of 154 patients participated in this evaluation, which was not confined to OCD patients. No data were reported on the drop outs, but outcome ratings for the participating 84 patients given by the four groups of evaluators were almost identical. One independent expert prospectively followed 85 patients undergoing cingulotomy for various mental disorders for 5 years (it is unclear how many patients participated in both of the studies mentioned), and reported favorable outcome in "many of the patients, but not all of them" (42). Unfortunately, only four of these patients were diagnosed as suffering from OCD; outcome was reported as "slight" in all of them.

To our knowledge, prospective evaluations by independent experts have not been published for subcaudate tractotomy and limbic leukotomy.

With regard to capsulotomy, the problem of rater bias has been addressed by several independent researchers [for reviews, see Waziri (4) and Sweet and Meyerson (5)]. In studies at Karolinska Hospital (7, 17, 43), the patients' clinical morbidity was rated by one investigator before and at regular intervals after surgery using the Comprehensive Psychopathological Rating Scale (CPRS). This interview-based instrument, which has been translated to a dozen languages, has been shown to be sensitive to symptom changes induced by treatment, and to have high validity and reliability [for a description of the scale, and validity and reliability data, see Åsberg et al (44)]. Rating sessions were recorded on audiotapes, which were used for establishing inter-rater reliabilities between the interviewer and one of two assessors: a psychologist independent from the research team with access to no other clinical data, and a psychiatrist also independent from the team with access to no other clinical data and with no responsibility for the selection and treatment of the patients. The inter-rater reliabilities of the CPRS ratings were statistically highly significant (product moment correlations: 0.87–0.98), as was the concurrent validity between this and several other estimates of outcome. These findings do not, of course, rule out rater bias, but in the absence of controlled data they may give an estimate of the reliability of the scores reported.

POSTSURGERY TREATMENT

Postsurgery treatment is another methodologically weak area, because many reports lack information on ongoing treatment at the time of the postoperative evaluation. Jenike et al (30) retrospectively evaluated 33 OCD patients a mean of 13 years after cingulotomy. Using the Y-BOCS score as the dependent measure, and very conservative criteria, the authors estimated that at least 25–30% of the patients "benefited substantially from the intervention". Several patients attributed their improvement primarily to postsurgery treatments, however. Excluding those subjects, 30–40% of these severely disabled patients believed that they had substantially improved from the cingulotomy alone, and another 10% maintained that the surgery had augmented postsurgery treatments. These operations were often carried out before the common usage of serotonin uptake inhibiting drugs and modern behavior therapy. Thus, it remains unknown as to how many of the cingulotomy patients would have been responders to current anti-OCD treatment.

Some patients with only a limited response to surgery report that treatment modalities that were ineffective before surgery now seem to give them at least some symptom relief (3, 7). This important information requires further study but offers some hope to the patient who has had a poor response to surgery. In such cases, the operation may function as an augmentation strategy, rather than as monotherapy of last resort (see Mindus and Jenike (2)].

Findings from reviews

One official body, the Canadian Psychiatric Association, has advised against the use of "placebo operations", for ethical reasons. Instead, "we . . . have to rely on a more traditional method of evaluation by objectively reviewing the responses of patients who have already received these [nonsurgical] treatments" (45). Obviously, the methodological issues reviewed earlier need to be borne in mind when using this more traditional research approach.

Comparison across different studies is one common method. Despite its limitations, the method can provide an approximation of the outcome after neurosurgical intervention. Several recent reviews have been published (2, 4, 5, 7, 27, 46), with remarkably similar conclusions. For example, Waziri (4) reviewed 12 studies of stereotactic interventions in 253 cases of OCD. An overall 3% of the patients were reported to be worse or dead at follow up. Among the dead was one suicide. Ten percent were reported to be unchanged, 29% markedly improved, and 38% free of symptoms. According to international convention [(14–16); see also Mindus (7)], patients rated as symptom-free and much improved [i.e. patients assigned to the Pippard outcome categories A and B, which is also comparable to a score of 1 or 2 on the modified Clinical Global Improvement (CGI) scale used in other studies] are considered as having a satisfactory response to surgery. An overall figure for satisfactory response to surgery of 67% was reported in the 253 OCD patients. Again, since these were uncontrolled studies, the results may have been influenced by non-surgical factors.

THE RELATIVE EFFICACY OF DIFFERENT PROCEDURES

To obtain an estimate of the relative efficacy of the different procedures, the two best outcome categories (A or B on the Pippard scale, i.e. those with a satisfactory response) may be contrasted with the two worst (D or E, unchanged or worse). It was reported (25) that 18 of 32 or 56% had a satisfactory response to cingulotomy, whereas five of 32 or 16% did not, and that nine of 18 or 50% of the patients were reported to have a satisfactory response to subcaudate tractotomy (32), whereas three of 18 or 17% did not. Following limbic leukotomy, 30 of 49 or 61% were reported (47) as having a satisfactory response, whereas unsatisfactory response was reported in eight of 49 or 16%. Recently, eight studies comprising 165 OCD patients treated with capsulotomy were reviewed (48); capsulotomy was reported to have produced satisfactory responses in 111 (61%) of the patients, compared with 14 (8%) in whom an unsatisfactory response was reported. It would appear that the relative efficacy of the four procedures in producing clinically meaningful symptom reduction is comparable.

Clearly, however, the above method of comparing published results is methodologically inferior to prospective comparative studies. Consequently, the Swedish neurosurgeon–psychiatrist Kullberg (49) compared 13 capsulotomy and 13 cingulotomy patients in a prospective study. She found significantly ($p < 0.05$) better results in the capsulotomy (six of 13 or 46%) than in the cingulotomy group (three of 13 or 23%), but that a transient postoperative "psychorganic syndrome" was "much more marked" after capsulotomy than following cingulotomy. Of interest were the results for two patients undergoing both operations. One was a case of OCD with initially good but later declining effect from capsulotomy; cingulotomy performed a year later led to little further improvement. The other patient suffered from severe non-OCD anxiety disorder. The prompt relief after cingulotomy lasted for only a month, and capsulotomy was performed a year later. The patient again obtained complete relief of symptoms, which was maintained throughout the 2-year follow up. Kullberg reported two more cases with relapse after cingulotomy in whom improvement was subsequently obtained after capsulotomy, the inference being that the OCD patients were usefully improved by capsulotomy but not by cingulotomy. According to Kullberg, anxiety states were affected by both types of operation, but capsulotomy was more efficacious. It should be noted, however, that although the number of patients was equal in both groups, there was an uneven distribution of OCD cases between the two procedures; eight OCD patients underwent capsulotomy, whereas only three OCD patients were treated with cingulotomy.

Kullberg's findings of a superior efficacy of capsulotomy over cingulotomy in OCD is supported by evidence recently provided by Hay et al (50), who noted that patients with cingulotomy lesions extensive enough to involve the anterior limb of the internal capsule did well compared with those whose lesions were more restricted. Waziri (4), in his review of 253 OCD patients undergoing stereotactic intervention, arrived at the conclusion: "The data . . . suggest that internal capsulotomy produces the best outcome, in OCD as in anxiety states". However, as has been pointed out, these data do not permit definitive conclusions as to the relative efficacy and safety of cingulotomy and capsulotomy.

Controlled evidence

NONSURGICAL CONTROLS

Two principal approaches to obtain controlled evidence for an effect of these interventions should be mentioned: the use of nonsurgical controls and the use of sham surgery. For someone to be considered for neurosurgical intervention, his OCD must be of a chronic, incapacitating, and intractable nature. Given the severe morbidity and potential mortality of such a case, finding and using a suitable nonsurgical control case would appear both practically difficult and ethically dubious. As for the use of a waiting list population for comparative purposes, this also poses ethical concerns: is it justifiable to postpone a potentially effective treatment in such severe cases? Two studies using reference groups for comparison are available, however.

Thirteen inpatients who received intensive nonsurgical treatment for OCD were matched and compared prospectively with 24 OCD patients who underwent modified, bimedial leukotomy (51). This intervention is no longer performed, since it carries somewhat greater surgical and mental risk than procedures in current use, but the study provides interesting information. Although the surgery patients were rated as having been more severely ill prior to the treatment than the nonsurgery group, they were shown to have fared significantly better both with regard to obsessions ($p < 0.05$) and anxiety ($p < 0.05$), and they improved in work adjustment to a greater degree than did the controls. Interestingly, both with regard to obsessions and anxiety, maximal improvement occurred within the first 3 months, with little change at subsequent rating sessions. At the 5-year follow up, 50% of the surgery patients were rated as much improved with regard to their target OC symptoms, compared with 23% of the controls, the corresponding figures for anxiety ratings being 89 vs 63% (both intergroup differences being statistically significant; $p < 0.05$). The authors concluded that "modified leukotomy is a useful treatment in highly selected patients with long-standing severe OCD". As these researchers were not themselves involved in the field of neurosurgery, and may therefore be regarded as independent evaluators, their conclusion is all the more compelling.

In another controlled study, two diagnostic groups were compared with regard to their response to subcaudate tractotomy, a procedure in current use. Twenty-four patients with severe OCD were matched for age and sex with 24 patients with severe depressive illness (52). Only two (8%) patients in each diagnostic group reported no improvement at the 3-year follow up, whereas 16 (67%) of the OCD patients were rated as symptom-free or much improved, the corresponding figures for the depressives being 17 (71%). In the OCD group, the number of hospital admissions fell from a mean of seven per year to one per year. Interestingly, OCD patients with a poor response to subcaudate tractotomy had an earlier onset (average 22 years) compared to those who did well (average 33 years), and were considered to be in a generally unsupportive social environment.

SHAM SURGERY CONTROLS

As for sham-controlled studies, there is only a single report (53) in the literature. This involved four psychotic cases, none of whom improved after a sham procedure in which skin incisions and burr holes were made, without the production of cerebral lesions. Considering the ethics, the Canadian Psychiatric Association has, as mentioned earlier, taken a strong stand on these matters: "It is difficult to see how experimental procedures involving the use of 'placebo operations' could be ethically and acceptably undertaken" (45). Although obviously guided by humanitarian consideration, this position may nevertheless prove inhumane, since some clinicians refuse to refer even desolate cases for neurosurgical intervention until double-blind, controlled data have been published to show an effect; as a result, a veritable "Catch 22" dilemma exists.

It must be noted, however, that the above official position was taken with open surgical procedures in mind, which involved craniotomy. As has already been described, no craniotomy is made in Gamma Knife procedures. The lesions are instead made by the crossfiring of the target with thin γ rays from cobalt sources, the radiation being directed to the target through approximately 200 channels or ports in an apparatus that surrounds the patient's head. The ports may be blocked by a technician using tungsten inserts (placebo condition), or left open (active condition). By this mechanism, placebo and active conditions can be administered in a fashion which is blind even to the surgeon. If funding is obtained, such a study will be carried out as a collaborative investigation by researchers from the Karolinska Hospital in Sweden, and from Harvard and Brown universities in the USA.

In the absence of such double-blind, sham controlled data, two recent prospective, independent, nonblind studies will be reviewed here, in which the best available research methodology was used to evaluate the efficacy and safety of capsulotomy and cingulotomy, respectively.

Recent prospective studies

CAPSULOTOMY

One recently completed study comprised all consecutive Swedish speaking OCD patients treated with thermocapsulotomy at the Karolinska Hospital during 1979 to 1990 (P Mindus et al, unpublished data). All patients were selected as outlined in previous sections, and were operated on by the same neurosurgeon using the same technique for the visualization of the targets and the production of the thermolesion as described above. Preoperatively, the patients' diagnoses were established using current diagnostic criteria, and the treatment-refractory nature of their illnesses were carefully documented. The Obsessive–Compulsive Subscale of the CPRS (44) was used as a measure of clinical morbidity. Serial ratings were made by the same rater (PM) before capsulotomy, and after 2, 6, 9, and 12 months, and again after a mean of 8 (range 3–15) years. The patients were also prospectively examined with neuropsychological tests, a personality inventory, and neuroradiological examinations, performed at baseline and at regular intervals after capsulotomy. The preliminary findings of this study are described here.

During the study period 24 patients underwent thermocapsulotomy for otherwise intractable OCD. Two patients were lost to follow up. In the remaining 22 patients, a statistically highly significant symptom reduction was found at the 1-year follow up, compared with baseline ($t = 3.69$, $p < 0.001$, two-tailed). The findings are graphically represented in Figure 17.3. As can be seen, the main changes in scores were already present at the 2-month follow up ($t = 4.03$, $p < 0.002$, two-tailed), with nonsignifi-

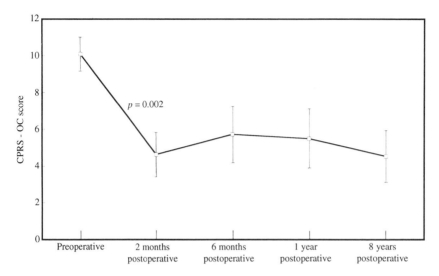

Figure 17.3   Mean change over time in symptoms of 22 consecutive patients with malignant obsessive compulsive disorder treated with thermocapsulotomy as measured by the Obsessive–Compulsive Subscale of the Comprehensive Psychopathological Rating Scale (CPRS-OC). Error bars represent standard deviations; note that the horizontal axis is not a uniform scale

cant changes ($t = 1.08$, $p = 0.291$, two-tailed) at subsequent rating sessions up to the 8-year follow up. Since the mean duration of the patients' illnesses exceeded 15 years, this rapid symptom alleviation following capsulotomy is remarkable. There was no statistically significant correlation ($r = 0.317$) between pre- and 8-year postoperative scores, which might indicate that even the worst conceivable patient has a fair chance of obtaining symptom relief from capsulotomy. There were no statistically significant differences between scores obtained at the 1- and 8-year postoperative examinations ($t = -1.08$, $p = 0.29$, two-tailed), which may be interpreted to mean that relapse is not to be expected beyond the 1-year follow up. Five (23%) of the patients had higher scores at the 8-year follow up compared with baseline, i.e. they were worse on this measure. In terms of the postoperative reduction of their CPRS-OC scale scores compared with baseline, two (9%) patients improved by 1–25%, five (23%) improved by 26–50%, three (13%) improved by 51–75%, and seven (32%) improved by 75–100%. (The relationship between clinical, neuropsychological, and neuroradiological findings will not be reported here.)

The strengths of this study are its prospective, intraindividual design, careful preoperative diagnostic work up and documentation of adequacy of previous nonsurgical treatments, and the independent assessment of OC symptomatology by means of reliable and validated instruments. Its weaknesses include, obviously, the absence of nonsurgical or sham controls.

CINGULOTOMY

In a recent retrospective study of cingulotomy in OCD (30), only six (18%) of the 33 patients had received preoperative trials with clomipramine, the only serotonin transport inhibitor available at the time of the operations. Only three patients had had a trial of behavior therapy, the other cornerstone in current treatment of OCD. Therefore, it was not possible to determine if these patients were refractory to nonsurgical treatment, a major inclusion criterion for surgery. A prospective study by the same researchers (54) was therefore undertaken. All the 18 consecutive patients had their diagnosis confirmed in structured interviews with current diagnostic criteria. The refractory nature of their illness was carefully documented, showing that the patients had failed trials of multiple medications and behavior therapy. Clinical outcome was assessed by the same independent raters before and at 6 month intervals after surgery using modern rating scales such as the Y-BOCS and the modified CGI scale. To classify a patient as a "responder" a conservative criterion used in medication trials was applied, i.e. an improvement of 35% or greater on the Y-BOCS *and* a CGI score of '1' (very much improved) or '2' (much improved).

Of these 18 treatment-refractory patients with malignant OCD who had been ill for over 12 (range 5–37) years, five (28%) were classified as responders according to the above conservative criteria, and another two (11%) patients were "possible responders", according to less stringent criteria. In addition, the patients showed overall improvement in functional status, and few serious adverse events. The mean change over time in OC and in depressive symptomatology following cingulotomy is shown in Figure 17.4.

The strengths of this study are its prospective, intraindividual design, its careful preoperative diagnostic work up and documentation of adequacy of previous nonsurgical treatments, and the independent assessments of OC symptomatology by means of reliable and validated instruments. Its weaknesses include the fact that no effort was made to correlate outcome with lesion characteristics (e.g. site, configuration, and volume) as determined from postoperative MRI scans and, obviously, the absence of controls. A number of factors may account for the discrepancy between outcome figures obtained in this (28%) and in previous reports (56%) (25) from the same site, the most important one probably being the stringent criteria used to define responders in the current study.

The results agree with those of another recently presented prospective, though uncontrolled, study of cingulotomy (55). Twenty-three Chinese

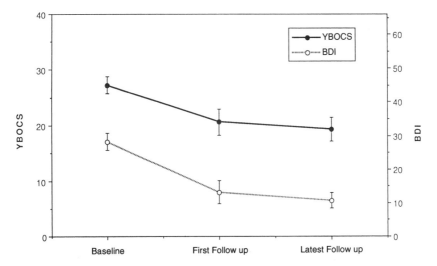

Figure 17.4 Mean change over time in symptoms of 18 consecutive patients with malignant OCD treated with thermocingulotomy as measured by the Yale–Brown Obsessive–Compulsive Scale (YBOCS), and in depression as measured by the Beck Depression Inventory (BDI). Error bars represent standard deviations

OCD subjects refractory to behavioral therapy and clomipramine were assessed before and 3 months, 6 months, and 1 year after surgery. Outcome measures included ratings on Y-BOCS, modified the Maudsley Obsessive Compulsive Inventory (MOCI), and CPRS-OC. Of the 19 patients who had been followed up for 1 year, 42% exhibited a beneficial response (unfortunately, criteria for beneficial response were not given). No severe adverse consequences were noted.

As for the issue of the relative efficacy of cingulotomy and capsulotomy, we compared the number of patients having a reduction of 35% or greater on the dependent measure used in the two studies. Ten of the 22 (45%) capsulotomy cases improved by 35% or more at the 8-year follow up compared with baseline, the corresponding figure for cingulotomy being eight of 18 (44%). It would appear from this indirect comparison that cingulotomy and capsulotomy may be comparably effective in ameliorating obsessive compulsive symptoms in this patient population. This stands in contrast to previous observations, which have suggested that cingulotomy may provide the lesser efficacy.

Risks

SOMATIC RISK

The salutary effects described above have not, of course, been achieved without somatic or mental risk. No death has been reported in conjunction with procedures in current use. Somatic risks include infection, hemorrhages, hemiplegias, epileptic seizures, and weight gain. Although infection and intracerebral hemorrhage cannot always be avoided, their sequelae can, provided that treatment is immediately instituted. In an earlier series, the incidence of hemiplegia following cingulotomy had been estimated at 0.03% (25) when the technique entailed introduction of air into the ventricles to guide electrode positioning. Since the advent of MRI guidance, however, this risk has probably been reduced, and to our knowledge, no such adverse events have occurred. No case of hemiplegia has been reported in relation to capsulotomy, subcaudate tractotomy, or limbic leukotomy. This risk of postoperative epilepsy following these interventions has been estimated to be less than 1% (28, 56). Several authors have reported weight gain in capsulotomized patients (7, 14, 57). It is not known whether this phenomenon is specific for capsulotomy, occurs after other procedures as well (although not reported), or is more common in patients who are on postsurgery drug treatment. This awaits further study. In our experience, patients who are at risk of gaining weight after capsulotomy have had previous weight problems.

The somatic risk of neurosurgical procedures in OCD compares favorably with that of stereotactic interventions of nonpsychiatric illnesses; in one study of 243 consecutive stereotactic interventions for various neurological illnesses, 15 complications were noted, and one death (58).

MENTAL RISKS

Suicide

Ballantine et al (25) discussed the issue of suicide in psychiatric patients who have undergone cingulotomy. Waziri (4), in his review of 253 OCD cases treated neurosurgically, found that 3% of the patients were reported to be worse or dead at follow up. Among the dead was one suicide. Jenike et al (30), in a retrospective study of 33 OCD patients who had undergone cingulotomy, found that, after follow up averaging 13 years, four had died as a result of suicide. According to their medical records, all of these patients had suffered from coexistant, severe depression with prominent suicidal ruminations when they were first evaluated for cingulotomy. It is difficult to draw definite conclusions from the report, as neither the time intervals between cingulotomies and suicides are given, nor the proportion of patients who were suicidal before cingulotomy but did not commit suicide. Furthermore, none of the patients who were not noted to be suicidal preoperatively became suicidal after the operation. It is conceivable, however, that disappointment secondary to failure of this "last resort" treatment may contribute to suicide, at least in predisposed individuals (2). It should be noted that no suicides were reported in the recent prospective cingulotomy study (54).

In our capsulotomy study, described earlier, one patient had committed suicide. This male patient probably did not benefit from capsulotomy. It was not possible to determine his treatment response from the ratings [see also Mindus (7)], since his follow up program was terminated at 6 months, at which time he suffered retinal ablation, considered to be a complication of his severe myopia. Experiencing, in all probability, no benefit from surgery and with his visual acuity severely reduced, the situation was apparently unbearable to him. He committed suicide by hanging. The relative importance of the various factors that were weighing upon his life will never be known, but his death may nevertheless be regarded as a complication not so much of the operation itself but of its probable lack of therapeutic effect in his case. In this cohort of OCD patients who received capsulotomy, he is the only one who has completed suicide during the observation time of up to 15 years.

Personality changes

The same signs and symptoms that are sometimes regarded as "postoperative" side effects may, in fact, also occur in patients who do not undergo surgery. In their prospective, controlled study comparing the efficacy of intensive nonsurgical treatment with that of modified bimedial leukotomy in OCD, Tan et al (51) noted brusqueness and irritability (six patients), apathy, laziness, and general blunting (two patients) among the 13 controls. In other words, symptoms and signs often regarded as postoperative side effects also appeared in the nonsurgery group.

According to anecdotal evidence, negative personality changes following current procedures are rare. Since the interventions may be expected to influence, directly or indirectly, frontal lobe function, and hence personality, more research is needed in this area. For example, personality features in relation to cingulotomy have been studied (42), but to our knowledge the results have not yet been published. With regard to subcaudate tractotomy, tests have been administered, but only at follow up (32). Kelly (47) gave the Leyton Obsessional Inventory (LOI) to 26 OCD patients before and at 20 months after limbic leukotomy and found significant changes in obsessive features in the direction of normality. Unfortunately, the validity of the LOI is not well established.

A widely used personality instrument, the Eysenck Personality Inventory (59), was administered prospectively by two research teams to two cohorts of patients undergoing capsulotomy (14, 21); in none of the 15 cases were negative personality changes observed after capsulotomy. It is well known that impulsiveness is one of the most conspicuous symptoms of frontal lobe dysfunction [for a review, see Stuss and Benson (60)]. For this reason, a method likely to detect negative personality changes following intervention must cover impulsiveness, and related features such as psychopathy, hostility, and aggressiveness. One such instrument is the Karolinska Scales of Personality (KSP), developed by Schalling et al (61). It contains scales measuring traits related to frontal lobe function, and scales reflecting different dimensions of anxiety proneness. A large number of studies have been performed by independent investigators who have shown the KSP to differentiate between diagnostic subgroups, and to correlate significantly with biological markers for vulnerability to certain psychopathological conditions (61). Mindus and Edman (unpublished data) gave the KSP to the 22 OCD patients undergoing thermocapsulotomy described earlier. Before capsulotomy, abnormally high scores (+1 SD to +2 SD) were found in four of the 15 scales, three of which reflect anxiety proneness, and one psychasthenic traits. At the 1-year follow up, the scores remained at the same level on all scales, with two exceptions (indirect aggressiveness, and guilt) with scores changed in the direction of normality. In particular, the scores on KSP scales related to impulsiveness, psychopathy, hostility, and aggressiveness were within the normal range. The findings agree with those reported in mixed groups of OCD and non-OCD anxiety disorder patients obtained using different instruments (14, 43, 62) or with the same instrument (63).

It might be argued that capsulotomy may cause personality changes but that these develop insidiously and become detectable only after many years. In order to elucidate this important issue, the KSP was again administered to the same patients at the 8-year follow up and the results were compared with those at the 1-year follow up. No statistical differences were found, which may be interpreted to mean that personality changes are not likely to occur after capsulotomy.

These observations may permit the conclusion that negative personality changes are not likely to occur after capsulotomy. It must be remembered that this conclusion is based on observations made on groups of capsulotomy patients and do not preclude, of course, that negative changes may occur in individual patients. Particularly, increased lesion volume may increase the risk of adverse personality changes, at least in vulnerable individuals (23).

Cognitive dysfunction

The issue of negative effects upon cognitive functions following modern procedures has been studied by several independent researchers [(28, 32, 33, 38, 42, 64); for reviews, see Sweet et al (5), Mindus (7), Bingley et al (14), Burzaco (15), Kelly (39), Herner (57), and Vasko et al (65)]. Using identical or different psychometric tests pre- and postoperatively the authors found no evidence of reduced intellectual function related to surgery. On the contrary, the patients tended to achieve better test results after operation, a finding for which several explanations have been advanced, including improved concentration ability and freedom from drug effects.

In an independent study of cingulotomy patients, preliminary reports indicated no evidence of lasting neurological, intellectual, personality, or behavioral deficits after surgery (64). In fact, a comparison of pre- and postoperative scores revealed modest gains in the Wechsler IQ scores. The only apparent irreversible decrement identified by these investigators was a decrease in performance on the Taylor Complex Figure Test in patients over the age of 40 years.

As for any cognitive dysfunction after capsulotomy, this question has been addressed by several investigators (14, 21, 62, 65). Using a restricted number of psychometric tests in a total of approximately 200 capsulotomy patients, they found no evidence of reduced intellectual function after capsulotomy. We have pointed out earlier (7) that these findings do not, of course, preclude that dysfunction in systems involving the frontal lobes may follow upon capsulotomy, which may be demonstrated with particular tests. Recent neuropsychological hypotheses concerning the neurobiological basis for OCD focus on frontolimbic circuits (66, 67). Furthermore, although the targets of capsulotomy are not placed within the frontal lobes proper, but in their connections with other parts of the brain, the operation may nevertheless be assumed to influence frontal lobe functioning. For both of these reasons, it would seem appropriate to include tests sensitive to frontal lobe functions. The weaknesses of the earlier studies are, obviously, that the methods used were generally not specific or sensitive enough to reliably demonstrate frontal lobe pathology.

Nyman and Mindus (submitted) recently concluded a study in which an extensive neuropsychological test battery was administered to 17 patients with otherwise intractable OCD ($n = 10$) or non-OCD anxiety disorders undergoing thermo- or gamma capsulotomy, to elucidate whether there is a price, in terms of deteriorated neuropsychological performance, that the patient may have to pay for any symptom alleviation. Ten standardized neuropsychological tests (measuring 41 variables) were used, four of which are described to be particularly sensitive to frontal lobe function. Although extremely disabled by their illnesses at baseline, the patients performed within the normal range on the majority of the tests. Following capsulotomy, neuropsychological performance, as studied with current, up-to-date techniques, remained largely intact or even improved. In five patients, however, the scores on some subtests of two of the four "frontal" tests (the Wisconsin Card Sort and Word Fluency tests) showed perseverations to be significantly more common at follow up. This may indicate a dysfunction in systems involving the frontal lobes in these patients. Unfortunately, no other neuropsychological or clinical factor could be found that distinguished this subgroup from the majority of the patients.

In summary, capsulotomy may give rise to increased perseverative behavior in some patients, the risk of which must, of course, be weighed against the risk of nonintervention in this extremely disabled and sometimes suicidal patient population. Furthermore, it is important to evaluate the surgical candidate's cognitive functions; a case with preoperative abnormal or borderline test scores may conceivably run an elevated risk of postoperative changes, since any adverse effect of surgery may interact with and add to those of persistent illness and to the cumulative impact on the brain of massive earlier treatment efforts (5). With a patient in whom all therapeutic options have been exhausted, the physician has the delicate task of weighing the risk of intervention against the risk of nonintervention. Deferring the decision to operate on a given patient may not spare him complications (7).

What are the mechanisms?

Ideally, a discussion of the putative therapeutic mechanisms of neurosurgery for OCD should rest upon insights into the neurobiology of OCD. Thus far, however, no single pathognomonic structural aberration has been identified. Granted, both structural (CT and MRI) and functional [electoencephalography, positron emission tomography (PET), and single photon emission computerized tomography] abnormal findings have been observed in the brains of OCD patients compared with both other psychiatric patients and normal controls. Interestingly, in responding patients, some of the metabolic changes observed with PET were normalized following both drug and behavior treatment. Particularly, pre- and post-treatment correlation data between the orbital cortex and the caudate nucleus seem to indicate that there is a functional imbalance between these brain regions in OCD, which may become restored with successful treatment, be it with drugs or behavior therapy [for recent reviews, see Jenike (3), Insel and Winslow (67, 68), Baxter et al (69), Baxter (70), and Rauch and Jenike (71)].

This body of evidence indicates that the underlying pathophysiology in OCD may involve multiple brain regions and multiple transmitter systems, and that the pathology of the disorder is indeed heterogeneous, a notion well supported by clinical observation. Consequently, the search for one single pathognomonic abnormality in OCD would appear as futile as the search, in the past, for one single "reason" for schizophrenia (i.e. the "schizococcus").

It is well known that there are extensive interconnections between the frontal lobes, the basal ganglia, and limbic and paralimbic structures. Consequently, neurosurgically induced lesions placed in different brain targets may be expected to exert similar effects in OCD. Indeed, there is evidence to show that this may be the case. For example, intervention in the orbitofrontal area, as in subcaudate tractotomy, or in the orbito-frontal–thalamic tract, as in capsulotomy, or in the midline thalamic nuclei, as in certain forms of thalamotomy (72), have all been associated with improvement in OCD. In other words, although different neurosurgical interventions have different stereotactic targets, they may have the same functional target, i.e. they may be assumed to affect, directly or indirectly, the same brain system(s). Moreover, surgically induced lesions in one brain region may affect other regions, proximal or distal relative to the lesion. For example, it has been shown in man that lesions in the substantia innominata following subcaudate tractotomy cause extensive degeneration in the ventral portion of the internal capsule (73). The fiber tract degeneration could be traced back to the dorsomedial nucleus of the thalamus, which has extensive interconnections with various parts of the limbic system [see Stuss and Benson (60), Modell et al (66), and Nauta (74)].

In recent neurobiological models of OCD, neural circuits involving the basal ganglia, limbic system, and frontal lobes have been implicated in the pathophysiology of the disorder. It is noteworthy that the targets of current neurosurgical intervention in OCD are located within these same structures. With regard to the mechanism underlying the efficacy of capsulotomy, the projections within the implicated circuit, the frontal–striatal–pallidal–thalamic–frontal loop (66), are believed to pass through the anterior limb of the internal capsule, the target of capsulotomy. Furthermore, of the entire neocortex, it is only the frontal lobes that have direct, monosynaptic connections with subcortical regions. These fiber systems have been demonstrated to pass through the internal capsule [(74); see also Malloy (75)]. It has been suggested (29,47) that there may be two important components of the functional neuroanatomy of OCD; the above circuit, which mediates the OC component, and a less specific anxiety component mediated through the Papez circuit including the cingulum bundle, the target of cingulotomy. An alternative theory ascribes a more specific role for anterior cingulate cortex in mediating OC symptoms [see Rauch and Jenike (71)].

Increased metabolic rates in the orbital gyri, and in the caudate, which have been consistently reported findings and assumed to be related to the pathophysiology of OCD, may be decreased or normalized following successful treatment with medication or behavior therapy (70, 76). It may be assumed that similar changes may follow upon successful neurosurgical treatment. The findings of a small study by the Karolinska Hospital give some support for this contention (77). Serial PET examinations of five OCD patients before and at regular intervals after thermocapsulotomy showed significant reductions in absolute values of glucose metabolism at the 1-year follow up as compared with baseline. We speculated that this reduction in regional brain metabolism was somehow related to the reduction in symptoms following capsulotomy. The surgical patients' preoperative values in the orbital gyri were lower, however, than those found in healthy controls, an unexpected finding. This may represent a "burn-out" phenomenon in the surgical patients, who were more severely ill and had longer durations of illness than the patients scanned elsewhere [see Mindus (7)]. One important topic that remains to be studied is whether regional brain metabolism could serve as a marker for unresponsiveness to conventional treatment in OCD or might have prognostic significance with regard to response to neurosurgical intervention.

In summary, the proposed pathophysiological processes that mediate OCD may somehow be counteracted by neurosurgical intervention, the net result being symptom relief.

Future research

There are ethical, clinical and scientific reasons to carry out research in this area. From an ethical point of view, operations that involve the irrevocable destruction of brain tissue must be comprehensively and continuously evaluated with the most sophisticated tehniques available. From clinical and scientific standpoints, it may be argued that in addition to their being potentially life saving in some desperate cases, these procedures could offer a unique opportunity to study brain–behavior relationships in patients suffering from extreme forms of OCD before and after defined interventions in fundamental brain regions.

We hope that the above-described double-blind, sham-controlled study of gamma capsulotomy as treatment for OCD will soon be funded. Should the results indicate significantly superior outcome for patients following active vs sham surgery, then a number of other basic questions may be addressed. For example, prospective comparisons should be made between capsulotomy and cingulotomy, both in OCD and in non-OCD anxiety disorders. The relative merits of thermo and gamma operations should be established, as both types of interventions have their pros and cons. Predictors of prognostic significance should be determined, and characteristics of clinical subgroups with high or low likelihood of responding should be identified. Serial PET and MRI scans should be obtained in order to allow researchers to follow the course of both metabolic and structural lesions in an effort to understand what brain regions are affected and how, both in responding and in non-responding patients. The significance of postoperative rehabilitation and the possible interaction between surgery and postoperative, nonsurgical treatment need to be established.

If such a trial lends support for the beneficial effects of these procedures, then, hopefully, dogmatism will fade, a growing percentage of appropriate candidates will be referred, and at an earlier phase of their illness (the mean duration of illness in most neurosurgery cohorts is 15 years!). In the days of more primitive psychosurgery it would appear that too many were operated on too soon. Today, in contrast, it may well be that too few are operated on too late. In both situations, it is the patients who pay the price.

Summary

A minority of patients suffer from forms of OCD that prove refractory to exhaustive arrays of currently available treatments, and so remain severely disabled. Extensive, but uncontrolled, data indicate that such cases may respond to neurosurgical intervention such as capsulotomy and cingulotomy. We have summarized current inclusion and exclusion criteria for these procedures, as well as surgical techniques, probable outcome, somatic and mental risk, and the putative therapeutic mechanisms. Two recently concluded, uncontrolled, independent, prospective studies of cingulotomy and capsulotomy in chronic, severe, and otherwise intractable, i.e. malignant, OCD have been summarized, showing that a quarter to a half of the patients may improve significantly after intervention. There are ethical, clinical, and scientific reasons for carrying out research in this area. From an ethical point of view, operations that involve the irrevocable destruction of brain tissue need to be comprehensively and continuously evaluated with the most sophisticated techniques available. From clinical and scientific standpoints, it may be argued that in addition to their being potentially life saving in some desperate cases, these procedures could offer a unique opportunity to study brain–behavior relationships in patients suffering from extreme forms of OCD before and after defined interventions in fundamental brain regions.

References

1. Solyom L, DiNicola VF, Phil M, Sookman D, Luching D. Is there an obsessive psychosis? Aetiological and prognostic factors of an atypical form of obsessive–compulsive neurosis. Can J Psychiatry 1985; 30: 372–379.
2. Mindus P, Jenike MA. Neurosurgical treatment of malignant obsessive–compulsive disorder. Psychiatr Clin North Am 1992; 15 (No. 7): 921–938.
3. Jenike MA. Drug treatment of obsessive–compulsive disorder. In: Obsessive–Compulsive Disorders: Theory and Management (eds Jenike MA, Baer L, Minichiello WE). Year Book Medical Publishers, Chicago, 1990, pp 249–282.
4. Waziri R. Psychosurgery for anxiety and obsessive–compulsive disorders. In: Handbook of Anxiety. Treatment of Anxiety (eds Noyes JR, Roth M, Burrows GD). Elsevier Science Publishers, Amsterdam, 1990, pp 519–535.
5. Sweet WH, Meyerson BA. Neurosurgical aspects of primary affective disorders. In: Neurological Surgery (ed Youmans JR). WB Saunders, Philadelphia, 1990, pp 4335–4357.

6. Greist JH. Treatment of obsessive compulsive disorder: psychotherapies, drugs, and other somatic treatment. J Clin Psychiatry 1990; 51: 44–50.
7. Mindus P. Capsulotomy in anxiety disorders. A multidisciplinary study. Doctoral dissertation, Department of Psychiatry and Psychology, Karolinska Institute, Stockholm, 1991.
8. Greist JH. An integrated approach to treatment of obsessive compulsive disorder. J Clin Psychiatry 1992; 53: 38–41.
9. Mindus P. Some thoughts on the anti-psychosurgery attitude in Sweden. In: Modern Concepts in Psychiatric Surgery (eds Hitchcock ER, Ballantine HT Jr, Meyerson BA). Elsevier/North Holland Biomedical Press, Amsterdam, 1979, pp 359–365.
10. Rodgers J Ellison. Psychosurgery. Damaging the Brain to Save the Mind. HarperCollins, New York, 1992.
11. Bouckoms AJ. Ethics of psychosurgery. Acta Neurochirurgia 1988; suppl 44: 173–178.
12. Robinson S, Winnik HZ, Weiss AA. Obsessive psychosis: Justification for a separate clinical entity. Ann Psychiatry 1976; 14: 39–48.
13. Jenike MA, Baer L, Minichiello WO, Schwartz CE, Carey RJ. Concomitant obsessive–compulsive disorder and schizotypal personality disorder. Arch Gen Psychiatry 1986; 43: 296.
14. Bingley T, Leksell L, Meyerson BA, Rylander G. Long term results of stereotactic anterior capsulotomy in chronic obsessive–compulsive neurosis. In: Neurosurgical Treatment in Psychiatry, Pain and Epilepsy (eds Sweet, WH, Obrador, S, Martín-Rodríguez, JG). University Park Press, Baltimore, 1977, pp 287–299.
15. Burzaco J. Stereotactic surgery in the treatment of obsessive–compulsive neurosis. In: Biological Psychiatry (eds Perris C, Struwe G, Jansson B). Elsevier/North Holland Biomedical Press, Amsterdam, 1981, pp 1103–1109.
16. Meyerson BA, Mindus P. Capsulotomy as treatment of anxiety disorders. In: Modern Stereotactic Neurosurgery (ed Lunsford LD). Martinus Nijhoff, Boston, 1988, pp 353–364.
17. Mindus P, Bergström K, Levander SE, Norén G, Hindmarsh T, Thuomas KÅ. Magnetic resonance images related to clinical outcome after psychosurgical intervention in severe anxiety disorder. J Neurol Neurosurg Psychiatry 1987; 50: 1288–1293.
18. Leksell L, Backlund E-O. Stereotactic gamma capsulotomy. In: Modern Concepts in Psychiatric Surgery (eds Hitchcock ER, Ballantine HT Jr, Meyerson BA). Elsevier/ North Holland Biomedical Press, Amsterdam, 1979, pp 213–216.
19. Lindquist C. Hindmarsh T, Kihlström L, Mindus P, Steiner L. MRI and CT studies of radionecrosis development in the normal human brain. In: Radiosurgery. Baseline and Trends (eds Steiner L, Lindquist C, Forster D, Backlund EO). Raven Press, New York, 1992, pp 245–253.
20. Steiner L, Lindquist C, Forster D, Backlund EO (eds). Radiosurgery. Baseline and Trends. Raven Press, New York, 1992.
21. Rylander G. Stereotactic radiosurgery in anxiety and obsessive–compulsive states: psychiatric aspects. In: Modern Concepts in Psychiatric Surgery (eds Hitchcock ER, Ballantine HT Jr, Meyerson BA). Elsevier/North Holland Biomedical Press, Amsterdam, 1979, pp 235–240.
22. Mindus P. Capsulotomy, a psychosurgical intervention considered in cases of anxiety disorders unresponsive to conventional therapy. In: Pharmacological Treatment of Anxiety (eds Strandberg K, Beerman B, Lönnerholm G). Almqvist & Wiksell, Uppsala, 1988, pp 151–167.

23. Guo WY, Lindquist C. Kihlström P, Mindus P. Radionecrosis created in the internal capsule for psychosurgery with the gamma knife. Doctoral dissertation, Department of Neuroradiology, Karolinska Institute, Stockholm, 1993.

24. Mindus P, Meyerson BA. Radiofrequency or radiosurgery capsulotomy in extreme anxiety disorders: What are the pros and cons? In: First Congress of International Stereotactic Radiosurgery Society (ed Lindquist C). Springer-Verlag, Stockholm, 1993, p 177.

25. Ballantine HT Jr, Bouckoms AJ, Thomas EK, Giriunas IE. Treatment of psychiatric illness by stereotactic cingulotomy. Biol Psychiatry 1987; 22: 807–819.

26. Bouckoms AJ. The role of stereotactic cingulotomy in the treatment of intractable depression. In: Advances in Neuropsychiatry and Psychopharmacology 2: Refractory Depression (ed Amsterdam, JA). Raven Press, New York, 1991.

27. Chiocca EA, Martuza RL. Neurosurgical therapy of obsessive–compulsive disorder. In: Obsessive–Compulsive Disorders: Theory and Management (eds Jenike MA, Baer L, Minichiello WE). Year Book Medical Publishers, Chicago, 1990, pp 283–294.

28. Ballantine HT Jr. Neurosurgery for behavioral disorders. In: Neurosurgery (eds Wilkins RH, Rengachary SS). Elsevier/North Holland Biomedical Press, New York, 1985, pp 2527–2537.

29. Martuza RL, Chiocca EA, Jenike MA, Giriunas IE, Ballantine HT Jr. Stereotactic radiofrequency thermal cingulotomy for obsessive compulsive disorder. J Neuropsychiatry 1990; 2: 331–336.

30. Jenike MA, Baer L, Ballantine HT Jr et al. Cingulotomy for refractory obsessive–compulsive disorder. A long term follow-up of 33 patients. Arch Gen Psychiatry 1991; 48: 548–555.

31. Knight CC. Bifrontal stereotaxic tractotomy in the substantia innominata: An experience of 450 cases. In: Psychosurgery (eds Hitchcock E, Laitinen L, Vaernet K). Charles C Thomas, Springfield, Ill, 1972, pp 267–277.

32. Göktepe EO, Young LB, Bridges PK. A further review of the results of stereotactic subcaudate tractotomy. Br J Psychiatry 1975; 126: 270–280.

33. Bartlett JR, Bridges PK. The extended subcaudate tractotomy lesion. In: Neurosurgical Treatment in Psychiatry, Pain and Epilepsy (eds Sweet WH, Obrador S, Martín-Rodríguez JG). University Park Press, Baltimore, 1977, pp 387–398.

34. Lovett LM, Shaw DM. Outcome in bipolar affective disorder after stereotactic tractotomy. Br J Psychiatry 1987; 151: 113–119.

35. Poynton A, Bridges PK, Bartlett JR. Resistant bipolar affective disorder treated by stereotactic subcaudate tractotomy. Br J Psychiatry 1988; 152: 354–358.

36. Malizia A, Bridges PK. Selecting patients for psychosurgery. In: Biological Psychiatry (eds Rascagni G, Brunello N, Fukuda T). Elsevier Science Publishers, Amsterdam, 1991.

37. Richardson A. Stereotactic limbic leucotomy: Surgical technique. Postgrad Med J 1973; 49: 860–864.

38. Mitchell-Heggs N, Kelly D, Richardson A. Stereotactic limbic leucotomy— a follow-up at 16 months. Br J Psychiatry 1976; 128: 226–240.

39. Kelly D. Anxiety and Emotions. Physiological Basis and Treatment. Charles C Thomas, Springfield, Ill, 1980.

40. Valenstein ES. Review of the literature on post-operative evaluation. In: The Psychosurgery Debate (ed Valenstein ES). WH Freeman, San Francisco, 1980, pp 141–163.

41. Ballantine HT Jr, Levy BS, Dagi TF, Giriunas IE. Cingulotomy for psychiatric illness: report of 13 years' experience. In: Neurosurgical Treatment in Psychiatry. Pain and Epilepsy. (eds Sweet WH, Obrador S, Martín-Rodríguez JG). University Park Press, Baltimore, 1977, pp 333–355.

42. Corkin S. A prospective study of cingulotomy. In: The Psychosurgery Debate (ed Valenstein ES). WH Freeman, San Francisco, 1980, pp 164–204.

43. Mindus P, Nyman H, Rosenquist A, Rydin E, Meyerson BA. Aspects of personality in patients with anxiety disorders undergoing capsulotomy. Acta Neurochirurg 1988; suppl 44: 138–144.

44. Åsberg M, Perris C, Schalling D, Sedvall G. The CPRS—development and applications of a psychiatric rating scale. Acta Psychiatr Scand 1978; suppl 271.

45. Earp JD. Position Paper. Psychosurgery. The position of the Canadian Psychiatric Association. Can J Psychiatry 1979; 24: 353–365.

46. Kiloh LG, Smith JS. Psychosurgery. In: Physical Treatments in Psychiatry (eds Kiloh LG, Smith JS, Johnsson GF). Blackwell Scientific, Oxford, 1988, pp 277–333.

47. Kelly D. Physiological changes during operations on the limbic system in man. Conditioned Reflex 1972; 7: 127–138.

48. Mindus P, Meyerson BA. Capsulotomy for intractable anxiety disorders. In: Operative Surgical Techniques (eds Schmidek H, Sweet W). WB Saunders, Philadelphia [in press].

49. Kullberg G. Differences in effect of capsulotomy and cingulotomy. In: Neurosurgical Treatment in Psychiatry, Pain and Epilepsy (eds Sweet WH, Obrador S, Martín-Rodríguez JG). University Park Press, Baltimore, 1977, p 301.

50. Hay P, Sachdev P, Cumming S, Smith JJ, Lee T, Kitchener P, Matheson J. Treatment of obsessive–compulsive disorder by psychosurgery. Acta Psychiatr Scand 1993; 87: 197–207.

51. Tan E, Marks IM, Marset P. Bimedial leucotomy in obsessive–compulsive neurosis: a controlled serial inquiry. Br J Psychiatry 1971; 118: 155–164.

52. Bridges PK, Göktepe EO, Maratos J, Browne A, Young L. A comparative review of patients with obsessional neurosis and with depression treated by psychosurgery. Br J Psychiatry 1973; 123: 663–674.

53. Livingston RE. Cingulate Cortex Isolation for the Treatment of Psychoses and Psychoneuroses. Psychiatric Treatment. Williams & Wilkins, London, 1953.

54. Baer L, Rauch SL, Ballantine HT Jr et al. Cingulotomy for intractable obsessive compulsive disorder: Prospective long-term follow-up of 18 patients [submitted].

55. Mei Q, Yan WW. Cingulotomy for refractory OCD. Sixth Scientific Meeting of the Pacific Rim College of Psychiatrists. Shanghai, 1993, pp 59–60 [abstr].

56. Bingley T, Person A. EEG studies on patients with chronic obsessive–compulsive neurosis before and after psychosurgery (stereotaxic bilateral anterior capsulotomy). Electroencephalogr Clin Neurophysiol 1978; 44: 691–696.

57. Herner T. Treatment of mental disorders with frontal stereotactic thermolesions. A follow-up of 116 cases. Acta Psychiatr Scand 1961; suppl 36.

58. Blaauw G, Braakman R. Pitfalls in diagnostic stereotactic brain surgery. Acta Neurochirurgica 1988; suppl 42: 161–165.

59. Eysenck HJ, Eysenck SBG. Manual of the Eysenck Personality Inventory. University of London Press, London, 1964.

60. Stuss DT, Benson DF. Personality and emotion. In: The Frontal Lobes (eds Stuss DT, Benson DF). Raven Press, New York, 1986, pp 121–138.

61. Schalling DS, Åsberg M, Edman G, Oreland L. Markers for vulnerability to psychopathology: Temperament traits associated with platelet MAO activity. Acta Psychiatr Scand 1987; 76: 172–182.

62. Lopez-Ibor AJJ, Burzaco J. Stereotaxic anterior limb capsulotomy in selected psychiatric patients. In: Psychosurgery (eds Hitchcock E, Laitinen L, Vaernet K). Charles C Thomas, Springfield, Ill, 1972, pp 391–399.

63. Mindus P, Nyman H. Normalization of personality characteristics in patients with incapacitating anxiety disorders after capsulotomy. Acta Psychiatr Scand 1991; 83: 283–291.

64. Corkin S, Twitchell TE, Sullivan EV. Safety and efficacy of cingulotomy for pain and psychiatric disorder. In: Modern Concepts in Psychiatric Surgery (eds Hitchcock ER, Ballantine HT Jr, Meyerson BA). Elsevier/North Holland, Amsterdam, 1979, pp 253–272.

65. Vasko T, Kullberg G. Results of psychological testing of cognitive functions in patients undergoing stereotactic psychiatric surgery. In: Modern Concepts in Psychiatric Surgery (eds Hitchcock ER, Ballantine HT Jr, Meyerson BA). Elsevier/North Holland, Amsterdam, 1979, pp 303–310.

66. Modell JG, Mountz JM, Curtis GC, Greden JF. Neurophysiologic dysfunction in basal ganglia/limbic striatal and thalamocortical circuits as a pathogenetic mechanism of obsessive-compulsive disorder. J Neuropsychiatry 1989; 1: 27–36.

67. Insel TR, Winslow JT. Neurobiology of obsessive–compulsive disorders. Psychiatr Clin North Am 1992; 15 (No. 7): 813–824.

68. Insel TR, Winslow JT. Neurobiology of Obsessive–Compulsive Disorders. In: Obsessive–Compulsive Disorders: Theory and Management (eds Jenike MA, Baer L, Minichiello WE). Year Book Medical Publishers, St. Louis, 1990, pp 116–131.

69. Baxter LR, Schwartz JM, Guze BH, Bergman K, Szuba MP. Neuroimaging in obsessive–compulsive disorders. Seeking the mediating neuroanatomy. In: Obsessive–Compulsive Disorders: Theory and Management. (eds Jenike MA, Baer L, Minichello WE). Year Book Medical Publishers, Chicago, 1990, pp 167–188.

70. Baxter LR. Neuroimaging studies of obsessive-compulsive disorder. Psychiatr Clin North Am 1992; 15 (No. 7): 871–885.

71. Rauch SL, Jenike MA. Neurobiological models of obsessive–compulsive disorder. Psychosomatics 1993; 34: 20–32.

72. Hassler R, Dieckman G. Relief of obsessive–compulsive disorders, phobias and tics by stereotactic coagulation of the rostral intralaminar and medial-thalamic nuclei. In: Surgical Approaches in Psychiatry (eds Laitinen, LV, Livingston KE). University Park Press, Lancaster, 1973, pp 206–212.

73. Corsellis J, Jack AB. Neuropathological observations on yttrium implants and on undercutting in the orbito-frontal areas of the brain. In: Surgical Approaches in Psychiatry (eds Laitinen LV, Livingston KE). University Park Press, Lancaster, 1973, pp 90–95.

74. Nauta HJW. A simplified perspective on the basal ganglia and their relation to the limbic system. In: The Limbic System. Functional Organization and Clinical disorders (eds Doane BK, Livingston KA). Raven Press, New York, 1986, pp 67–77.

75. Malloy P. Frontal lobe dysfunction in OCD. In: The Frontal Lobes Revisited (ed Perecman E). IRBN Press, New York, 1987, pp 207–223.

76. Swedo S, Pietrini P, Leonard HL et al. Cerebral glucose metabolism in childhood onset obsessive–compulsive disorder. Revisualization during pharmacotherapy. Arch Gen Psychiatry 1992; 40: 600–604.

77. Mindus P, Nyman H, Mogard J, Meyerson BA, Ericson K. Frontal lobe and basal ganglia metabolism studied with PET in patients with incapacitating obsessive–compulsive disorder undergoing capsulotomy. Nordic J Psychiatry 1990; 44: 309–312.

18 NEW 5-HT (SEROTONIN) COMPOUNDS

Berend Olivier*† and Jan Mos†

*Department of Psychopharmacology, Faculty of Pharmacy, Utrecht University, Utrecht, The Netherlands
†Department of CNS-Psychopharmacology, Solvay Duphar BV, Weesp, The Netherlands

Introduction

The role of serotonin (5-hydroxy tryptamine, 5-HT) in obsessive compulsive disorder (OCD) is an accepted fact, largely based on the efficacy of the selective serotonin reuptake inhibitors (SSRIs). Although SSRIs are also antidepressant, the antidepressant qualities are not sufficient to be anti-obsessional, because various other antidepressants, such as norepinephrenic uptake inhibitors (imipramine and desipramine), and monoamine oxidase inhibitors are not effective in OCD (1). As in depression, therapeutic effects of SSRIs in OCD only emerge after chronic (4–8 weeks) administration. The relative slowness of this process indicates that adaptational processes in the central nervous system (CNS) may underlie the improvements.

Further evidence that 5-HT is implicated in the etiology of OCD comes from studies with metergoline, a nonspecific 5-HT antagonist and *meta*-chlorophenyl-piperazine (mCPP), a 5-HT_{2C} agonist. Coadministration of metergoline to OCD patients treated with clomipramine (CMI) worsened OC symptoms, whereas administration of metergoline to untreated OCD patients was ineffective (1,2). Clomipramine probably induces changes in the 5-HT activity in the CNS, which can be antagonized by metergoline.

Administration of mCPP, a direct postsynaptic 5-HT_{2C} receptor agonist, may induce anxiety and obsessions (1) in untreated OCD patients but not in patients treated with CMI for 4 months (3). Although other indices of an abnormal functioning of the 5-HT system

Current Insights in Obsessive Compulsive Disorder. Edited by E. Hollander, J. Zohar, D. Marazzati and B. Olivier
© 1994 John Wiley & Sons Ltd

in untreated OCD patients are weak, e.g. 5-hydroxy-indoleacetic acid (5-HIAA) levels in cerebrospinal fluid (CSF) and platelet 5-HT concentrations and uptake sites, the bulk of evidence clearly suggests an abnormal functioning of the 5-HT system in OCD patients. It is unclear, however, how and to what extent the 5-HT system in the CNS contributes to the emergence of OCD.

The 5-HT system contains a limited but well-defined number of serotonergic cells. The cell bodies are mainly located in various raphe nuclei, although groups of 5-HT cells are also located in various other areas in the mid- and hindbrain (4). Serotonergic neurons project both to rostral and to caudal areas in the CNS. In particular, the rostral projections seem relevant for a possible involvement of 5-HT in pathological processes involved in OCD.

The serotonergic system is complicated (see figure 1), and in the last decade an enormous volume of new data has changed the simple concept of the neuron–neurotransmitter–receptor axis dramatically. At present, 10 subfamilies of serotonin receptors are distinguished within the serotonin receptor family (Table 18.1): $5-HT_{1A}$, $5-HT_{1D}$, $5-HT_{1E}$, $5-HT_{1F}$, $5-HT_{2}$, $5-HT_{3}$, $5-HT_{4}$, $5-HT_{5}$, $5-HT_{6}$, and $5-HT_{7}$. The various subfamilies may consist of different subtypes. For example, the subfamily $5-HT_{1D}$ comprises the $5-HT_{1B}$, $5-HT_{1D\alpha}$, and $5-HT_{1D\beta}$ receptors; the $5-HT_{2}$ subfamily comprise the $5-HT_{2A}$ (formerly $5-HT_{2}$), $5-HT_{2B}$, and $5-HT_{2C}$ (formerly $5-HT_{1C}$) receptors.

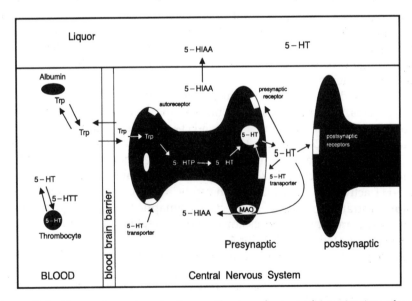

Figure 18.1 The various steps in the synthesis, release and inactivation of serotonin (5-HT)

Table 18.1 The classification of the various serotonin (5-HT) receptors and their second messengers

Super-family	G-protein-coupled									Ion channel
Subfamily	5-HT_{1A}	5-HT_{1D}	5-HT_{1E}	5-HT_{1F}	5-HT_2	5-HT_4	5-HT_5	5-HT_6	5-HT_7	5-HT_3
Receptors	5-HT_{1A}	$5\text{-HT}_{1D\alpha}$ $5\text{-HT}_{1D\beta}$ 5-HT_{1B}	5-HT_{1E}	5-HT_{1F}	5-HT_{2A} 5-HT_{2B} 5-HT_{2C}	5-HT_4	5-HT_5	5-HT_6	5-HT_7	5-HT_3
Second messenger	Decreased cAMP	Decreased cAMP	Decreased cAMP	Decreased cAMP	PI hydrol.*	Increased cAMP	Decreased cAMP	Increased cAMP	Increased cAMP	Gated ion channel

*PI hydrol., phosphoinositol hydrolysis.

The different receptors are neuroanatomically localized at different sites in the CNS (6). For example, 5-HT$_{1A}$ receptors are abundantly present in the hippocampus, septum, neocortex, and raphe nuclei; 5-HT$_{1B/1D}$ receptors in the pallidum and substantia nigra; 5-HT$_{2C}$ receptors in the hypothalamus, pallidum, substantia nigra and, particularly, in the choroid plexus. The main localization of 5-HT$_{2A}$ receptors is in the neocortex, and 5-HT$_3$ receptors are abundant in the substantia gelatinosa. The distribution of 5-HT$_4$ receptors in the CNS is not completely known, although preliminary evidence has shown high binding in the striatum, olfactory tubercle, nucleus accumbens, globus pallidus, and substantia nigra (7). The predominant localizations of 5-HT$_3$ receptors are the cerebral cortex, hippocampus, habenula, olfactory bulb, and cerebellum (8). The localizations of the very recently discovered 5-HT$_6$ and 5-HT$_7$ receptors within the CNS have not yet been determined. Finally, 5-HT$_{1A}$ receptors are localized both pre- and postsynaptically on the cell bodies and dendrites of 5-HT neurons in the raphe nuclei; 5-HT$_{1B}$ and 5-HT$_{1D}$ receptors are localized pre- and postsynaptically, whereas the other 5-HT receptors are presumably postsynaptically localized.

A schematized 5-HT neuron is shown in Figure 18.2, in which, besides the numerous 5-HT receptors, the 5-HT transporter has also been portrayed. The recently cloned 5-HT transporter is localized both at the terminal part of the axon, and at the cell body of the 5-HT cell (9–12).

The 5-HT receptor family belongs to two extended gene superfamilies: the G-protein coupled receptor superfamily and the ligand-gated ion-

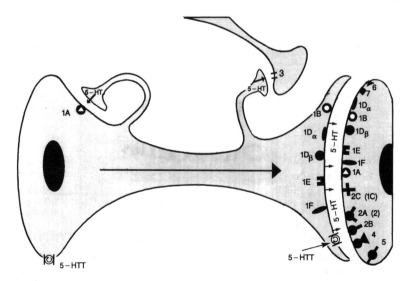

Figure 18.2   The various serotonin (5-HT) receptors and 5-HT transporter (5-HTT) are shown on a hypothetical 5-HT neuron and a postsynaptic neurone

channel superfamily. The $5\text{-}HT_1$, $5\text{-}HT_2$, $5\text{-}HT_4$, $5\text{-}HT_5$, $5\text{-}HT_6$, and $5\text{-}HT_7$ receptors are linked to the modulation of either adenylate cyclase or modulation of phosphoinositol turnover via G-proteins, whereas $5\text{-}HT_3$ receptors modulate an ion channel (Table 18.1). The G-protein coupled receptors display a 7 transmembrane domain, whereas the $5\text{-}HT_3$ receptor consists of five subunits. One of these subunits has been cloned (mouse) and appears to be a protein of 487 amino acids assembled in 4 transmembrane domains. For $5\text{-}HT_3$ receptor, two identical subunits plus three others are necessary to form a functional channel.

It is clear that the 5-HT system is extremely heterogeneous and complex. Unravelling the role of the various 5-HT receptors in brain functioning and pathological processes, including OCD, therefore depends on the development of specific ligands for the respective receptors. In this chapter, we review the available ligands for the various receptors.

$5\text{-}HT_{1A}$ Ligands

In the early 1980s $5\text{-}HT_{1A}$ ligands were found and subsequently numerous others have been synthesized.

Clearly, the front runner as a $5\text{-}HT_{1A}$ ligand is 8-OH-DPAT (see Table 18.2 chemical name), a potent and full $5\text{-}HT_{1A}$ receptor agonist, but it has not been developed for clinical studies. It is the standard tool in pharmacology when studying the $5\text{-}HT_{1A}$ contributions to various physiological and behavioral functions. Since its discovery, various other $5\text{-}HT_{1A}$ receptor agonists have been synthesized. Buspirone (Table 18.2), another $5\text{-}HT_{1A}$ ligand, was not originally developed as a $5\text{-}HT_{1A}$ receptor agonist but was tested in the 1970s as a potential antipsychotic.

In these studies of buspirone, no antipsychotic effects were noted but the compound exerted anxiolytic activity and consequently has been developed for generalized anxiety disorders (GAD). Only later on was the $5\text{-}HT_{1A}$ agonistic character of buspirone detected, and this finding has fuelled the search for other $5\text{-}HT_{1A}$ receptor agonists in order to develop new anxiolytic agents. Ipsapirone, gepirone, and flesinoxan are examples of this approach.

Table 18.2 shows the affinities of various $5\text{-}HT_{1A}$ receptor agonists for a number of 5-HT receptors. Several $5\text{-}HT_{1A}$ receptor antagonists have now been described. First, various nonspecific $5\text{-}HT_{1A}$ antagonists were used, such as propranolol and pindolol (Table 18.2), which are of course primarily β-adrenoceptor antagonists. Then NAN-190 (see Table 18.2) was found and suggested as a $5\text{-}HT_{1A}$ antagonist, but later on it was found that this compound appeared to be a partial agonist which under certain circumstances exerted agonistic properties. More recently, very specific $5\text{-}HT_{1A}$ receptor antagonists have been found, such as WAY100,135 and (S)-UH301. The antagonists WAY100,135 and (S)-UH301 are qualified as

Table 18.2 Affinities (K_i in nM) of 5-HT$_{1A}$ ligands for the various 5-HT receptor sites and other significant binding affinities

Receptor[†]	5-HT							Uptake	Other significant affinities*	Agonist (Ag) or antagonist (Ant)
	1A	1B	1D	2A	2C	3	4			
Serotonin	3.1	3.4	2.8	2500	3.1	4.3	43	930		Ag (by definition)
8-OH-DPAT[‡]	2.8	1800	930	>10 000	7800	2950	>10 000	780		Ag (1A)
Buspirone	15	3000	>10 000	1000	4800	>10 000	>10 000	>10 000	D_2, Σ	Ag (1A)
Ipsapirone	5.5	3500	>10 000	2700	>10 000	>10 000	>10 000	>10 000	D_2, α_1	Ag (1A)
Flesinoxan	1.7	810	160	4500	>10 000	>10 000	>10 000	>10 000	D_2	Ag (1A)
Gepirone	26	8500	>10 000	3800	>10 000	>10 000	>10 000	>10 000	D_2	Ag (1A)
NAN-190	1.3	620	790	220	630	>10 000	>10 000	2100	α_1, D_2, Σ	Ant (1A, α_1)
WAY100,135	10	8900	1000	1800	5300	>10 000	>10 000	>10 000	D_2, α_1	Ant (1A)
(S)-UH301[§]	27	>10 000	>10 000	>10 000	>10 000	>10 000	>10 000	>10 000	Σ	Ant (1A)
(S)-(−)Pindolol	210	400	8700	>10 000	>10 000	>10 000	>10 000	9100	β	Ant (1A, 1B, β)
(±)Propranolol	140	540	>10 000	>10 000	1100	4000	>10 000	1800	β	Ant (1A, 1B, β)

*Significant is defined as a difference of less than a factor of 100 from the highest affinity.
[†]NAN-190, 1-(2-methoxyphenyl)-4-(4-(2-phthalamido)butyl)-piperazine HBr; WAY100,135, N-tert-butyl 3-4-(2-methoxyphenyl)piperazin-1-yl-2-phenylpropranamide dihydrochloride.
[‡]8-OH-DPAT, 8-hydroxy-2(di-n-propylamino)tetralin
[§](S)-UH301, (S)-5-fluoro-8-hydroxy-2-(di-n-propylamino)tetralin

silent antagonists (13) because these compounds have no intrinsic activity. Whereas (S)-UH301 is available as a research tool and will not be developed as a therapeutic, WAY100,135 exerts in some animal paradigms anxiolytic activity (13) and is under development for treatment of anxiety disorders.

Mixed 5-HT$_1$ ligands (5-HT$_{1A,1B,1D}$)

Table 18.3 shows a number of compounds with affinity for a number of 5-HT$_1$ receptors: TFMPP is a 5-HT$_{2C}$ and 5-HT$_{1B}$ agonist; mCPP is primarily a 5-HT$_{2C}$ agonist, but has considerable affinity for the 5-HT$_3$ receptor and is presumably an agonist at that receptor. Compounds such as 5-MeODMT, RU24969 and eltoprazine have mixed activity at various 5-HT$_1$ receptors and at 5-HT$_{2C}$ receptors.

No specific 5-HT$_{1B,1D}$ receptor antagonists are known, although cyanopindolol seems to exert 5-HT$_{1B}$ antagonistic activity.

Sumatriptan, which does not penetrate the brain, is a broad 5-HT$_1$ agonist, with highest potency at the 5-HT$_{1D}$ receptor, its suggested antimigraine mechanism of action.

No clear-cut therapeutic drugs have been developed out of these mixed 5-HT$_1$ agonists, although sumatriptan (migraine) and eltoprazine (aggression) point to the potential possibilities of the 1B/1D receptors.

5-HT$_2$ Ligands

Table 18.4 shows some 5-HT$_2$ ligands. DOI (and other phenylalkylamines like DOB* and DOM†) is a 5-HT$_2$ receptor agonist, with some selectivity for the 5-HT$_{2C}$ receptor over the 5-HT$_{2A}$ receptor. Ritanserine and ketanserine are 5-HT$_2$ receptor antagonists, ritanserine being more selective for the 5-HT$_{2C}$ receptor and ketanserine for the 5-HT$_{2A}$ receptor. Therapeutically, the role of the 5-HT$_{2A}$ and $_{2C}$ receptors in all kinds of psychiatric conditions is not clear. Suggestions of involvement in depression, GAD, and psychosis (14) have been made.

5-HT$_3$ Ligands

Numerous 5-HT$_3$ receptor antagonists have been developed, and Table 18.5 shows only a selected number of them, including ondansetron, granisetron, zacopride, and tropisetron. Quipazine is also a potent 5-HT$_3$ antagonist but also has agonistic activity at the 5-HT$_{2C}$ receptor and inhibits 5-HT reuptake.

---

*DOB, 1(4-bromo-2,5-dimethoxyphenyl)-2-aminopropane
†DOM, 1(4-methyl-2,5-dimethoxyphenyl)-2-aminopropane

Table 18.3 Affinities (K_i in nM) of mixed 5-HT$_1$ ligands for the various 5-HT receptor sites and other significant binding affinities

Receptor[+]	5-HT								Other significant affinities*	Agonist (Ag) or antagonist (Ant)
	1A	1B	1D	2A	2C	3	4	Uptake		
Serotonin	3.1	3.4	2.8	2500	3.1	4.3	43	930		Ag (by definition)
TFMPP	200	49	690	780	13	2100		1100		Ag (2C, 1B)
mCPP	210	79	1100	140	29	6.2		270	α_1, α_2	Ag (1B, 2C)
5-MeODMT	8.5	85	39	2600	20	5600		7		Ag (1A, 1B, 2C, 1D)
RU24969	8.7	5.9	42	1700	48	3800	850	200		Ag (1A, 1B, 2C, 1D)
Eltoprazine	40	52	390	1700	81	25		>10 000	β, α_1	Ag (1A, 1B), Ant (2C)
Cyanopindolol	5.9	17	410	>10 000	>10 000	>10 000	>10 000	>10 000	β	Ant (1A, 1B, β)
Sumatriptan	250	160	68	>10 000	8100	>10 000	>10 000	>10 000		Ag (1A, 1B, 1D)

*Significant is defined as a difference of less than a factor of 100 from the highest affinity.
[+]TFMPP, *Meta*-trifluoromethylphenylpiperazine; mCPP, *meta*-chlorophenyl-piperazine; 5-MeODMT, 5-methoxy-*N*,*N*-dimethyltryptamine; RU24969, 5-methoxy-3-(1,2,3,6-tetrahydropyridin-4-yl)-1*H*-insole succinate.

Table 18.4 Affinities (K_i in nM) of 5-HT$_2$ ligands for the various 5-HT receptor sites and other significant binding affinities

Receptor[+]	5-HT								Other significant affinities*	Agonist (Ag) or antagonist (Ant)
	1A	1B	1D	2A	2C	3	4	Uptake		
Serotonin	3.1	3.4	2.8	2500	3.1	4.3	43	930		Ag (by definition)
DOI	6900	2100	7200	210	6.5	>10 000	3000	>10 000		Ag (2C, 2A)
Ritanserine	830	1700	410	3.2	0.55	7200		1150	D_2, H_2, α_1	Ant (2C, 2A)
Ketanserine	>1000	>10 000	2200	1.7	110	>10 000	2500	>10 000	α_1, D_2	Ant (2A, 2C)

*Significant is defined as a difference of less than a factor of 100 from the highest affinity.
[+]DOI, (±)-1-1(2,5-Dimethoxy-4-iodophenyl-2-aminopropane hydrochloride.

Table 18.5 Affinities (K_i in nM) of 5-HT$_3$ ligands for the various 5-HT receptor sites and other significant binding affinities

Receptor*	1A	1B	1D	2A	2C	3	4	Uptake	Agonist (Ag) or antagonist (Ant)
Serotonin	3.1	3.4	2.8	2500	3.1	4.3	43	930	Ag (by definition)
Ondansetron	> 10000	3700	> 10000	> 10000	5000	1.6		> 10000	Ant (3)
Granisetron	> 10000	> 1000	> 10000	> 10000	> 10000	0.48		> 10000	Ant (3)
Zacopride	> 10000	> 10000	> 10000	3600	2600	0.53	120	> 10000	Ant (3), Ag (4)
Tropisetron	> 10000	> 10000	> 10000	> 10000	> 10000	1.6		690	Ant (3)
Quipazine	2300	620	1800	1100	72	0.19		49	Ant (3), Ag (2C)
2 Methyl-5-HT	1700	810	1800	> 10000	540	36		> 10000	Ag (3)
Phenylbiguanide	> 10000	> 10000	> 10000	> 10000	> 10000	8.7		> 10000	Ag (3)
3,4-diClPB	> 10000	> 10000	> 10000	1100	1100	1.1		830	Ag (3)

*3, 4-diClPB, 3,4-Dichlorophenylbiguanide; NAN-190, 1-(2-methoxyphenyl)-4-(4-(2-phthalamido)butyl)-piperazine HBr.

as tools to study the role of 5-HT$_3$ receptors in the brain. Although 5-HT$_3$ antagonists are therapeutically active as anti-emetics, CNS applications are somewhat troublesome. The 5-HT$_3$ antagonists have been suggested as antipsychotic, anxiolytic and memory-improving, but so far clinical data have been meager and not very convincing.

5-HT$_4$ Ligands

The role of the 5-HT$_4$ receptor in the CNS is almost unknown (15). However, various agonists and antagonists have been found and synthesized, and some potent ligands do now exist, such as SDZ 205,557 (Table 18.6). GR 113808 is, like SDZ 205,557, a potent 5-HT$_4$ antagonist, and numerous other, though less specific, 5-HT$_4$ agonists have been described, such as (S)-zacopride, and SC-53116 (15). It will certainly take time to investigate the possible role of the 5-HT$_4$ receptor in CNS processes and the putative therapeutic role of 5-HT$_4$ ligands.

5-HT Reuptake inhibitors

Numerous 5-HT reuptake inhibitors (SSRIs) exist and are either on the market or in development. All SSRIs have a high affinity for the 5-HT transporter or uptake site (9) and they are also very specific (except chlorimipramine; see Table 18.7).

The SSRIs are clinically proven antidepressant, anti-OCD, and anti-panic agents, and they are presumably also usable as anti-abuse (alcohol), anti-obesity, and antibulimia drugs.

The future

Given the complexity of the serotonergic system, it is as yet impossible to predict whether there are specific 5-HT receptors involved in the pathophysiology of OCD. Although the basal ganglia (16) have been implied in the pathology of OCD, whether 5-HT receptors in the basal ganglia are involved in this process has not been settled. If they are, however, it could be suggested that 5-HT$_{1D}$ receptors are candidates, because they occur in high numbers and density in the basal ganglia (6). Whether, this being the case, 5-HT$_{1D}$ receptor agonists or antagonists are needed is yet unclear, although 5-HT$_{1D}$ agonists seem to be candidates, because SSRIs are indirect 5-HT agonists by enhancing 5-HT neurotransmission. It is known that SSRIs are only (partially) active in OCD after several (4–8) weeks of treatment. Because 5-HT reuptake carriers or transporters (5-HTT) occur both presynaptically in the terminal area and on the 5-HT cell body and dendrites (somatodendritically), the processes underlying

Table 18.6 Affinities (K_i in nM) of 5-HT$_4$ ligands for the various 5-HT receptor sites and other significant binding affinities

Receptor	5-HT							Uptake	Agonist (Ag) or antagonist (Ant)
	1A	1B	1D	2A	2C	3	4		
Serotonin	3.1	3.4	2.8	2.500	3.1	4.3	4.3	930	Ag (by definition)
SDZ 205,557*	> 10 000	> 10 000	> 10 000	> 10 000	> 10 000	280	4.4		Ant (3, 4)
GR 113808†							0.18		Ant
(S)-Zacopride							+		Ag
SC-53116‡							+		Ag

*SDZ 205,557, 2-methoxy-4-amino-5-chlorobenzoic acid 2-(diethylamino)ethylester
†GR 113808, [1-[2-[(methylsulphonyl)amino]ethyl]-4-piperidinyl]methyl 1H-indole-3-carboxylate
‡SC-53116, 4-amino-N-(1-azabicyclo[3.3.0.]oct-4-methyl)-5-chloro-2-methoxybenzamide

Table 18.7 Affinities (K_i in nM) of 5-HT reuptake blockers (SSRIs) for the various 5-HT receptor sites and other significant binding affinities

Receptor	5-HT							Uptake	Other significant affinities*	Agonist (Ag) or antagonist (Ant)
	1A	1B	1D	2A	2C	3	4			
Serotonin	3.1	3.4	2.8	2500	3.1	4.3	43	930		Ag (by definition)
Fluvoamine	> 10 000	> 10 000	> 10 000	1400	> 10 000	> 10 000	> 10 000	5.1		Ant (uptake)
Zimelidine	> 10 000	> 10 000	> 10 000	3600	4900	3200	> 10 000		α_1, Σ	Ant (uptake)
Fluoxetine	> 10 000	> 10 000	> 10 000	2300	830	4200	> 10 000		M$_1$, Σ	Ant (uptake)
Chlorimipramine	> 10 000	> 10 000	> 10 000	74	130	850	> 10 000	2.8	Σ, α_1, D$_2$, musc H$_1$	Ant (uptake)
Sertraline	> 10 000	> 10 000	> 10 000	> 10 000	> 10 000	3600	> 10 000			
Paroxetine	> 10 000	> 10 000	> 10 000	> 10 000	> 10 000	2500	> 10 000			

*Significant is defined as a difference of less than a factor of 100 from the highest affinity.
†Significant binding not yet quantified.

what occurs in the 5-HT system after administration of SSRIs need to be evaluated thoroughly.

Acute administration of SSRIs was always assumed to enhance synaptic levels of 5-HT. Recent microdialysis studies in rats (17, 18) showed, that after acute systemic SSRI administration (clomipramine, fluvoxamine), 5-HT was particularly enhanced in the raphe nuclei whereas no increase or only a limited increase was found at synaptic levels (frontal cortex). The presence of somatodendritic 5-HT$_{1A}$ receptors, which inhibit cell firing and consequently 5-HT release, may explain this finding. Therefore only limited efficacy of the synaptic blockade of the 5-HTT can be expected (Figure 18.3) after acute administration.

After chronic administration, needed to obtain clinically relevant therapeutic effects, the process of 5-HT reuptake blockade is still effectively present. However, the somatodendritic 5-HT$_{1A}$ receptors are desensitized

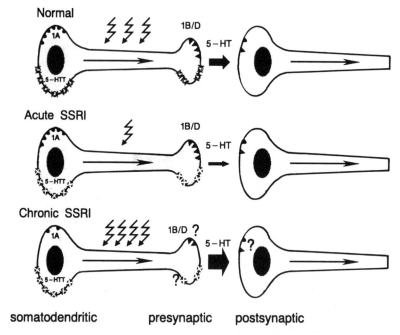

Figure 18.3 The effects of acute and chronic administration of selective serotonin reuptake inhibitors (SSRIs) is schematically illustrated. In the top part, the normal situation of an active, firing 5-HT neuron is shown. Acute administration of an SSRI (middle figure) inhibits the 5-HT transporter (5-HTT) leading to enhanced levels in the synapse and at the somatodendritic level with as a result decreased firing of the neuron. Chronic administration (bottom) leads to desensitization of the somatodendritic 5-HT$_{1A}$ receptor, enhanced firing of the 5-HT neuron, and enhanced 5-HT in the synaptic cleft leading to enhanced 5-HT neurotransmission. This process could be further enhanced by desensitization of the presynaptic 5-HT$_{1B/1D}$ autoreceptors, which normally, when activated, inhibit 5-HT release

and consequently the serotonergic neuron is no longer (or is less) inhibited by the high levels of 5-HT around the cell body. This may lead to a normal or even enhanced 5-HT release, with further enhanced synaptic levels of 5-HT, because the synaptic 5-HT is still blocked. Whether the synaptic 5-HTTs are downregulated is still a matter of dispute, but if they are, such a process might further enhance the 5-HT neurotransmission. The net effect of chronic administration is therefore (strongly) enhanced 5-HT neurotransmission. Postsynaptically, an extensive range of 5-HT receptors is present (1A, 1B/1D, 1E, 1F, 2A, 2C, 3, 4, 5, 6, and 7) and it is very likely that the differential effects of SSRIs (including anti-OCD, antidepressant, antipanic) can be ascribed to the activation of one (or more) of these specific 5-HT receptors by the enhanced 5-HT levels. Therefore, specific ligands for new 5-HT receptors should be tested in OCD patients. The coming decades should further clarify which part of the serotonergic system is involved in the pathophysiology of OCD.

Acknowledgments

We thank Marijke Mulder for technical support.

References

1. Insel TR, Zohar J, Benkelfat C, Murphy DL. Serotonin in obsessions, compulsions, and the control of aggressive impulses. Ann N Y Acad Sci 1990; 600: 574–586.
2. Zohar J, Mueller EA, Insel TR, Zohar-Kadouch RC, Murphey DL. Serotonergic responsivity in obsessive–compulsive disorder: comparison of patients and healthy controls. Arch Gen Psychiatry 1987; 44: 946–951.
3. Zohar J, Insel TR, Zohar-Kadouch RC, Hill JL, Murphy DL. Serotonergic responsivity in obsessive–compulsive disorder: Effects of chronic clomipramine treatment. Arch Gen Psychiatry 1988; 45: 167–172.
4. Török I. Anatomy of the serotonergic system. Ann N Y Acad Sci 1990; 600: 9–35.
5. Humphrey PPA, Hartig P, Hoyer D. A reappraisal of 5-HT receptor classification. In: Serotonin. From Cell Biology to Pharmacology and Therapeutics (Eds Vanhoutte PM, Saxena PR, Paoletti R, Brunnello N, Jackson AS). Kluwer Academic, Dordrecht, 1993, pp 41–47.
6. Palacios JM, Waeber C, Hoyer D, Mengod O. Distribution of serotonin receptors. Ann N Y Acad Sci 1990; 600: 36–52.
7. Grossman CJ, Gale JD, Bunce KT et al. Development of a radioligand binding assay for the 5-HT$_4$ receptor: use of a novel antagonist. Br J Pharmacol 1993; 108: 106.
8. Plassat JL, Boschert U, Amlaiky N, Hen R. The mouse 5-HT$_5$ receptor reveals a remarkable heterogeneity within the 5-HT$_{1D}$ receptor family. EMBO J 1992; 11: 4779–4786.
9. Hoffman B. Molecular biology of serotonin uptake sites. In: Serotonin. From Cell Biology to Pharmacology and Therapeutics (Eds Vanhoutte PM, Saxena PR, Paoletti R, Brunello N, Jackson AS). Kluwer Academic, Dordrecht, 1993, pp 9–19.

10. D'Amato RJ, Largent BL, Snowman AM, Snyder SH. Selective labeling of serotonin uptake sites in rat brain by [³H]-citalopram contrasted to labeling of multiple sites by [³H]-imipramine. J Pharmacol Exp Ther 1987; 242: 364–371.

11. Hrdina PD, Foy B, Hepner A, Summers RJ. Antidepressant binding sites in brain: Auto-radiographic comparison of [³H]-paroxetine and [³H]-imipramine localization and relationship to serotonin transporter. J Pharmacol Exp Ther 1990; 252: 410–418.

12. Chen HT, Clark M, Goldman D. Quantitative autoradiography of [³H]-paroxetine binding sites in rat brain. J Pharmacol Toxicol Methods 1992; 27: 209–216.

13. Fletcher A, Cliffe IA, Dourish CT. Silent 5-HT$_{1A}$ receptor antagonists: utility as research tools and therapeutic agents. Trends Pharmacol Sci 1993; 14: 441–446.

14. van Praag HM. Is serotonin involved in the pathogenesis of schizophrenia? In: Serotonin. From Cell Biology to Pharmacology and Therapeutics (Eds Vanhoutte PM, Saxena PR, Paoletti R, Brunello N, Jackson AS). Kluwer Academic, Dordrecht, 1993, pp 277–288.

15. Clarke DE, Bockaert J. 5-HT$_4$ receptor: current status. In: Serotonin. From Cell Biology to Pharmacology and Therapeutics (Eds Vanhoutte PM, Saxena PR, Paoletti R, Brunello N, Jackson AS). Kluwer Academic, Dordrecht, 1993, pp 107–117.

16. Insel TR. Toward a neuroanatomy of obsessive–compulsive disorder. Arch Gen Psychiatry 1993; 49: 739–744.

17. Bell N, Artigas F. Fluvoxamine increases preferentially extracellular 5-hydroxy tryptamine in the raphe nuclei: an in vivo microdialysis study. Eur J Pharmacol 1992; 229: 101–103.

18. Adell A, Artigas F. Differential effects of clomipramine given locally or systemically on extracellular 5-hydroxytryptamine in raphe nuclei and frontal cortex. An in vivo brain microdialysis study. Naunyn-Schmiedeberg's Arch Pharmacol 1991; 343: 237–244.

INDEX

Compiled by Geoffrey C. Jones